One Town, One Team, One F

A place that we all simply call...Home.

Huddersfield Town

Complied by

John O'Mahoney

All rights reserved. No part of this publication may be reproduced, stored in a retrieval system, or transmitted in any form or by any means, electronic, mechanical, photocopying, recording or otherwise, without the prior written permission of the copyright holder.

© John O'Mahoney

Foreword

This book is something that I had been thinking about writing for some years now. It all started shortly after I had created a social media group 'Those were the days my friend'. One thought I had was that I was very fortunate, as were many other Town fans I'm sure, to have seen Town play in our old football ground at Leeds Road and also in our current home at the John Smith's Stadium. On reaching the Premier League I quickly realised that I had seen Town play in almost every division, except the old First Division, in both our football homes.

I feel that all our historical Town achievements from our old home at Leeds Road, and all our football history taking place in our current home, as Town fans we should be able to remind ourselves of not just where we are now but where we have come from, and how we got to be where we are today as a team, together. Writing this book has given me the chance to reflect on everything so that any Town fan from any era could read all about our marvellous Club under one cover.

See, for me as a Town fan, a football home isn't just any home. It's a place I call home because of the people in it. 'Leeds Road' and 'The John Smith's Stadium' are both home to me because of everyone I have known, past and present, and for all those who have since sadly passed away during these unprecedented times.

Perhaps the biggest compliment I could give every Town fan would be to say that Huddersfield Town Football Club is special to many people in lots of different ways because,

> It's not just a stadium
> It's our home,
> It's not just a kit
> It's our skin,
> We're not eleven
> We're millions,
> We're not a ground
> We're family,
> It's not just 90 mins
> It's a lifetime,
> It's not just a passion
> It's an emotion,
> It's not just a game
> It's our life.

This is my very first genuine attempt as an author. So, I sincerely hope that everyone who reads this book gets as much enjoyment from it as I have writing it.

John O'Mahoney

Acknowledgements

Much of the historical and statistical information contained in this book has been researched and sought out by the author John O'Mahoney. Any errors that may have occurred are inadvertent. The author of this book apologies for any unintentional errors or omissions which should be notified to the publisher.

Other written/photographic/digital contributions, integrated into this book, have been kindly supplied with their full permission and consent by: -

- George Chilvers   - Artist
- Roger Pashby   - Huddersfield Town collector
- Peter May   - Huddersfield Town Fan
- Ian Robins   - Huddersfield Town player (1978-1982)
- Lynne Barrett   - Huddersfield Town Fan
- Phil Starbuck   - Huddersfield Town player (1991-1994)
- Raymond Chappell   - Huddersfield Town Leeds Road Groundsman

All photographs/digital images/artwork used in this book are listed accordingly below:-

Cover design Digital image– Personal photograph of John O'Mahoney's (Leeds Road 'Cowshed')

Digital image **a1** -Taken on personal mobile phone of John O'Mahoney's (Huddersfield)
Digital image **a2** -Taken on personal mobile phone of John O'Mahoney's (Huddersfield)
Digital image **a3** -Personal old photograph of John O'Mahoney's (Fartown)
Digital image **a4** -Artwork kindly supplied by George Chilvers
Digital image **a5** -Personal old photograph of John O'Mahoney's (Bradley Mills –Banking)
Digital image **a6** -Personal old photograph of John O'Mahoney's (Bradley Mills –Banking)
Digital image **a7** -Taken on personal mobile phone of John O'Mahoney's at John Smiths Stadium
Digital image **a8** -Photograph kindly supplied by Roger Pashby
Digital image **a9** -Artwork digitally created by John O'Mahoney
Digital image **a10**-Artwork digitally created by John O'Mahoney
Digital image **a11**-Photograph kindly supplied by Roger Pashby
Digital image **a12**-Artwork kindly supplied by George Chilvers
Digital image **a13**-Artwork kindly supplied by George Chilvers
Digital image **a14**-Taken on personal mobile phone of John O'Mahoney's (John Smiths Stadium)
Digital image **a15**-Photograph kindly supplied by Peter May (Town fan)
Digital image **a16**-Photograph kindly supplied by Peter May (Town fan)
Digital image **a17**-Personal old photograph of John O'Mahoney's (Leeds road – Cowshed)
Digital image **a18**-Personal old photograph of John O'Mahoney's (Leeds Road – Cowshed)
Digital image **a19**-Photograph kindly supplied by Roger Pashby
Digital image **a20**-Photograph kindly supplied by Roger Pashby
Digital image **a21**-Personal old photograph of John O'Mahoney's (Leeds Road – Boys Enclosure)
Digital image **a22**-Taken on personal mobile phone of John O'Mahoney's (John Smiths Stadium)
Digital image **a23**-Personal old photograph of John O'Mahoney's (Leeds Road – Rugby posts)
Digital image **a24**-Personal old photograph of John O'Mahoney's (Leeds Road – East Terrace)
Digital image **a25**-Personal old photograph of John O'Mahoney's (Leeds Road – East Terrace)
Digital image **a26**-Personal old photograph of John O'Mahoney's (McAlpine – Kilner Bank Stand)
Digital image **a27**-Personal old photograph of John O'Mahoney's (McAlpine – Riverside Stand)
Digital image **a28**-Personal old photograph of John O'Mahoney's (McAlpine – Both Stands 1993)
Digital image **a29**-Artwork kindly supplied by George Chilvers

Digital image **a30**-Taken on personal mobile phone of John O'Mahoney's (John Smith's Stadium)
Digital image **a31**-Photograph kindly supplied by Roger Pashby
Digital image **a32**-Artwork kindly supplied by of George Chilvers
Digital image **a33**-Photograph kindly supplied by Peter May (Town fan)
Digital image **a34**-Personal old photograph of John O'Mahoney's (open end/old scoreboard 1993)
Digital image **a35**-Personal old photograph of John O'Mahoney's (Floodlights – Cowshed)
Digital image **a36**-Personal old photograph of John O'Mahoney's (Floodlights – Open end)
Digital image **a37**-Digital enhanced artwork of Jimmy McGill's fan club in 1969
Digital image **a38**-Digital enhanced artwork of a newspaper report from 1968
Digital image **a39**-Personal old photograph of John O'Mahoney's (East Terrace/Cowshed)
Digital image **a40**-Digital enhanced artwork of an old press cutting (David Tagg 1969)
Digital image **a41**-Digital enhanced artwork of an old press cutting (David Tagg 1969-Leeds Road)
Digital image **a42**-Personal old photograph of John O'Mahoney's (Cowshed blue and white wall)
Digital image **a43**-Digital enhanced artwork of an old press cutting (Cowshed moat/Bill Brook)
Digital image **a44**-Personal old photograph of John O'Mahoney's Leeds Road/ McAlpine 1995)
Digital image **a45**-Personal old photograph of John O'Mahoney's (Signed photo of Ian Robin's)
Digital image **a46**-Digital enhanced image of John O'Mahoney's (Ian Robins 2018)
Digital image **a47**-Artwork kindly supplied by George Chilvers
Digital image **a48**-Photograph kindly supplied by Lynne Barrett (Town fan)
Digital image **a49**-Photograph kindly supplied by Lynne Barrett (Town fan)
Digital image **a50**-Taken on personal mobile phone of John O'Mahoney's (Phil Starbuck 2018)
Digital image **a51**-Personal old photograph of John O'Mahoney's (Town shop at our old home 1995)
Digital image **a52**-Taken on personal mobile phone of John O'Mahoney's (Raymond Chappell 2018)
Digital image **a53**-Personal old photograph of John O'Mahoney's (Bradley Mills Demolition sign)
Digital image **a54**-Personal old photograph of John O'Mahoney's (Bradley Mills Demolition 1995)
Digital image **a55**-Personal old photograph of John O'Mahoney's (Our old home and new Stadium)
Digital image **a56**-Personal old photograph of John O'Mahoney's (Our old home during demolition)
Digital image **a57**-Personal old photograph of John O'Mahoney's (Leeds Road Retail Park)
Digital image **a58**-Personal old photograph of John O'Mahoney's (Alfred McAlpine Stadium)
Digital image **a59**-Personal old photograph of John O'Mahoney's (North Stand view)
Digital image **a60**-Personal old photograph of John O'Mahoney's (South Stand construction)

Special Acknowledgement

A special acknowledgement must go to my loyal loving wife, Sue, who has not only afforded me the time and luxury to write this book. She has also given me her loving support, over the last 31 years, for which I am eternally thankful for.

Bibliography

Huddersfield Town - 75 Years On (George Binns)
Leeds Road - Home of My Dreams (Ian Thomas)
Huddersfield Town - 99 Years and Counting (Alan Hodgson, Gwen and Ian Thomas, (Ret'd) Flt Lt John Ward)
Huddersfield Town - 100 Years All That's worth Knowing (George Binns, Gwen and Ian Thomas, Alan Hodgson)
Huddersfield Town match-day programmes
The Huddersfield Examiner

CHAPTERS

Grassroots football 1

In the beginning 2

Town's 'Babes to Teens' years 3

Town's 'Roaring Twenties'..4

Town's 'Depression'..5

Town's 'War Years' 6

Town's 'Fight in the Fifties' 7

Town's 'Swinging Sixties' 8

Town's 'Me Decade' 9

Town's 'Greed Decade'...10

Town's 'Football's coming home Decade'...11

Town's 'Noughties Decade'..12

Town's 'Ten's Decade'..13

'The Final Word'..14

Grassroots football - Chapter 1

Going back through the sands of time, and retracing our football history, right back to the very humble grassroots of Huddersfield Town. One man's name more than any other can be traced to the very first thought of even having Association Football in Huddersfield.

This part of West Yorkshire had always been a Rugby League stronghold given that the sport was founded in our Town in 1895. After a meeting in the George Hotel in Huddersfield, it was agreed that a breakaway of the northern clubs from the Rugby Football Union was to take place.

So, at a public meeting on Wednesday 7th February 1906 at the Imperial Hotel in Huddersfield, to even consider the feasibility of having a football club in the Town the name of David Dickinson, a local Schoolmaster and member of the District FA is at the very beginning of Town's football roots. He was the driving force at a public meeting about forming a company to run a First-Class Association Football Club which was also attended by Dr. Whitehead, A.B. Hirst, N. Robinson, C.E.W. Halle, H.A. Nelson, F.W. Reedor, J.H. Blackwell, Sergeant-Major Topps, Mrs J. Hall, F. Bates, L.H. Gill, and G. Milner.
During the public meeting, various discussions took place, which also mentioned having Rugby and Association Football in Huddersfield. David Dickinson stated in the meeting that "I do not wish, nor do I ever wish, to kill one sport for another". J.H. Blackwell explained that "The estimated capital needed to bring about Association Football to Huddersfield could be as high as £5,000". Which in the modern world of football, with all its riches of the Premier League and the high fees paid for players along with their wages and agents fees, £5,000 was small change. In 1906 though it was a huge amount of money to the working townsfolk of Huddersfield and its District. The all-important question was then asked, "Had any thought been given about a ground". David Dickinson replied with "It's been suggested the 'showground' on Leeds Road could be secured". It was noted that with the proposed ground the branch tram line already existed which could accommodate any traffic to and from the ground. It was then proposed to form a new committee to consider the idea. The President of the new committee was none other than David Dickinson who along with officials of the Huddersfield and District Football Association was elected along with influential local gentlemen.

On Friday 8th March 1907 the 'Huddersfield Town Association Football Ground Company Ltd' was formed for the purpose of purchasing land to be used for important matches. In this same year 1907, negotiations between the 'Huddersfield Town Association Football Ground Company Ltd' and the Northern Union (Rugby League) for full ground sharing at the Fartown Rugby Ground proved unsuccessful. Had the Northern Union rescinded their ruling of 1905, to ban the playing of Association Football from taking place on any Northern Union Club Ground, things may have been very much different for Huddersfield Town and our old home at Leeds Road.

In late 1907 negotiations between the 'Ground Company' and Ramsden Estate to purchase the ground along Leeds Road, having previously been used by the Technical College, had started. By Saturday 18th January 1908 the Technical College old ground, at Leeds Road, had been purchased. Money was spent on getting the ground into a good condition along with the erection of a fence topped with barbed wire. It was further documented by the Ground Company that money was readily available for a stand. When the ground was in proper working order and maybe another stand added, then it would be the time to turn the existing private company into a public one.

Events moved on at such a pace that the proposed football club was admitted into the North Eastern League even before they were formed and given a proper footballing name. On Friday 19th June 1908 in a meeting at the Albert Hotel in Huddersfield, between the Ground Company and 'others', a decision was made to form a limited company to bring about the professional game to Huddersfield.

A provisional committee was set up to sort out plans in order to make it happen. Just a week later on Friday 26th June 1908, at the same venue as the week before, the plans of the provisional committee was heard, and unanimous approval of the ideas led to the amalgamation of the Ground Company with a new limited company. 'The Huddersfield Town Association Football Club Limited' was registered as a limited company and by 15th August 1908 with shareholders now firmly in place the Leeds Road Ground was let on rental for the very first time, shortly after, to the newly formed club.

15th August 1908 was the actual birth date of Huddersfield Town Association Football Club Limited

Town's first ever football game at Leeds Road involved a practise match on Wednesday 19th August 1908. The gate money of two guineas, just over £2, was collected and kindly donated to the Huddersfield Royal Infirmary. A second practise match took place a week later and the day's takings were kindly donated to the Wigan Colliery Disaster Fund.

It was decided by the provisional committee that they should be Directors with an Honorary Secretary of the Company and a Player-Manager who would also act as Secretary.

The first Directors of Huddersfield Town Association Football Club were:

John Hilton Crowther (Chairman)
Amos Brook Hirst (Vice-Chairman)
James Cotton (Manufacturer)
William Lawson Hardcastle (Proprietor - Albert Hotel Huddersfield)
Gilbert Jenkins (Woollen salesman)
Llywelyn Bath Jones (School Master)
David Dickinson (School Master)
F. Ibbotson (Billiard Professional)

Bankers:

The Lancashire and Yorkshire Bank Limited – Market Place Huddersfield

Solicitors:

Ward and Hirst – Market Place Huddersfield

Auditor:

T. Herbert Kaye (Accountant) - New Street Huddersfield

Hon. Secretary and Registered Office:

J.H.R Appleyard – 5 Willow Lane East Huddersfield

Historical Huddersfield photos

Digital image **a1** (left) – Photograph of John O'Mahoney's of the Albert Hotel Huddersfield where meetings were held in 1908 and where 'The Huddersfield Town Association Football Club Limited' company was first formed. The Albert Hotel built in 1879 at a cost of £3,000 was designed by Edward Hughes who also designed the Ramsden Building on Queensgate. (Taken on John O'Mahoney's mobile phone at the Albert Hotel in Huddersfield).

Digital image **a2** (left) – Photograph of John O'Mahoney's of the historical blue plaque (left) celebrating the birth of Rugby League located at the old Fartown ground in Huddersfield in 2015 to commemorate Huddersfield playing Wakefield on 14th September 1895. (Taken on John O'Mahoney's mobile phone at the site of the old Fartown ground).

Digital image **a3** (below) – Photograph of John O'Mahoney's of the old Fartown Rugby Ground as it last looked on 30th August 1992. For their first rugby game at Leeds Road a turn-out of 2,907 watched the Second Division match against Featherstone Rovers. Huddersfield Rugby took a share in the new Alfred McAlpine Stadium, now known as the John Smith's Stadium, with their first game against Barrow on 21st August 1994.

In the beginning – Chapter 2

Life in the North Eastern League was far from ideal from a Leeds Road point of view. The pitch, for many of the Leeds Road faithful, was totally alien in that it was actually parallel to Leeds Road with the touchline being where the old 'Cowshed' used to stand.

Other revenue was gained by allowing tipping to be done on the banking along the touchline, which ran opposite the 'Cowshed', at the old Bradley Mills end. A tramcar had been purchased from the London and North West Cricket Club and was for some time used as a dressing room and also as a ticket office with the accommodation and seating very basic. This was further illustrated by the fact that Town's registered office was at 5 Willow Lane East, the private residence of the appointed Honorary Secretary Mr. J.H.R. Appleyard.

A small roofless stand along the Leeds Road touchline was also built during October 1908. Dressing rooms, besides the tramcar mentioned, alternated between 'tented' accommodation and a local hotel (before permanent dressing rooms were completed in November 1908). These were situated where the Main Stand used to be with the 'home' dressing room facing the pitch and the 'visitors' dressing room at the back. Bathing was all done in one room which joined onto both dressing rooms. Due to the absence of turnstiles, gates had to have a ticket seller and a 'checker' with both paid the handsome total of 2/- (10p) each for their services.

Huddersfield Town's first ever football match at Leeds Road was a friendly on Wednesday 2nd September 1908 against Bradford Park Avenue. The match was played 30 minutes each way due to the gloomy evening and a lack of lighting (No Denis Law floodlights just yet). I'm glad to say that Huddersfield Town won the match 2-1 in front of a 1,060 crowd who paid a sum total of £20 to watch the match. The match referee was Joe Dyson of the Huddersfield Referees Society as Town played in white shirts and black shorts.

Even at this early stage of football in Huddersfield in 1908 steps were taken that are still fondly remembered by anyone whoever stood or sat in our old home at Leeds Road. For that Archibald Leitch's services were sought, and implemented by 1910, given that he had a considerable reputation as an architect.

He was born in Glasgow in 1865 and moved into stadium design when he was commissioned to build Ibrox Park, the new home ground of his boyhood heroes Rangers in 1899. His stadiums were initially considered functional rather than aesthetically elegant and were clearly influenced by his early work on industrial buildings. Typically, his stands had two tiers with criss-crossed steel balustrades at the front of the upper tier and were covered by a series of pitched roofs, built so that their ends faced onto the playing field. The central roof span was larger and incorporated a distinctive pediment. In his initial report to Town, Archibald Leitch recommended amongst other things that our playing area be turned at right angles as this would give increased protection from inclement weather for the spectators. It was a valid point given the wind that used to blow down and around our old home at Leeds Road.

Archibald Keir Leitch – Architect (left)
Digital image **a4** (left) - Kind permission granted by artist George Chilvers 'Colourised by George' to replicate and display his artwork.

On 5th September 1908 Huddersfield Town A.F.C took to the field to play their first ever football match away to South Shields in a North Eastern League fixture. Sadly, Huddersfield Town lost the match 2-0 while wearing salmon pink shirts. The Town team that day, on 5th September 1908, consisted of the following players;

Goalkeeper – William Crinson after four appearances in the First Division with Sheffield Wednesday 'Bill' signed for Huddersfield Town for the entire 1908 season before leaving in 1909 for Brighton and Hove Albion of the Southern League.

Defenders – Richard Ray, Robert L. Trenam, John Morris, Frederick Walker (who played 24 games and later managed Huddersfield Town from 1908 until 1910).

Midfield – William Hooton, J. Shackleton, Harry Wallace, Sam McAllister

Forwards – C. Flowitt, Richard Morris (spent the entire 1908 season with Huddersfield Town before retiring from football completely in 1909).

Trainer – Andy Rudge

Some match reports which Town played in the North Eastern league was reported as;

10th October 1908 Carlisle United 0 – Huddersfield Town 1

Town enjoyed the scenic railway journey on the Settle to Carlisle route in order to keep a Saturday afternoon date with the United team. It was a happy first ever visit to the Cumbrian outpost- who also played in the North Eastern League despite their geographical situation. The home team was down to nine players at one stage, during the second half, because of injuries but was back to full strength before full-time. Edward Didymus making his debut on the right wing for Town played a part in providing his ex-Portsmouth colleague W.S. Cookson with the opportunity from which the centre-forward scored the only goal of the game during the first period.

17th October 1908 Huddersfield Town 1 – Sunderland Reserves 5

Town took on the mighty Sunderland Reserves side and for the first time in their six league matches so far was soundly beaten and outclassed. It was a sharp reminder of how far they had to rise before aspirations of League Football were to be fulfilled. Sunderland shot into a three-goal lead, but Richard Morris pulled one back for Town before the interval. At the time Sunderland were of course one of the giants of Edwardian football and had finished third in the First Division that season.

24th October 1908 North Shields Adelaide 1 – Huddersfield Town 2

Once again Town had a long journey – this time to the North East Coast to play North Shields. When John Morris failed a late fitness test there was panic as our travelling Town party contained only ten fit players and the Trainer Andy Rudge. Thankfully Rudge, registered as a player still, turned out for one of only two appearances he ever made in our Town team. The deputy half-back put in a courageous display as our team lifted themselves after conceding an early goal to score twice.

31st October 1908 Huddersfield Town 2 – Shildon Colliery 3

The last Saturday of this month saw Shildon Colliery visit our old home at Leeds Road. Town after leading 1-0 at half-time then saw Houldsworth score his second goal of the match to become the first Town player to have ever scored two goals in a North Eastern League match, sadly we lost 3-2.

Temporary tented changing rooms were erected at our ground and were used during the season. With an ageing senior team and players of only average ability the first ever season in the North Eastern League with a final league placing of 16th it was one of;

Played 34 games; won 10, lost 20, drew 4, goals for 47, goals against 78, Points 24

It's worth pointing out that in this season Huddersfield Town was only a part-time club which was evident in the fact that football training was done on a Tuesday and Thursday night. Also given the ground improvements and ongoing works, which was done to Leeds Road in this year, no mention can be found of any kind of grassed football pitch at all even before Raymond Chappell (Town's last ever groundsman at Leeds Road) could shout those immortal words of "Oi-Get off my pitch".
Even stranger in this year was the fact that Town was in a quite unique situation in that they weren't the sole hirers of the ground from the 'Ground Company' yet all the while Town owned the dressing rooms on the site which were then rented out to the Huddersfield and District FA and West Yorkshire FA for football that was also played at the ground. Stranger still was that Huddersfield Town's 'first' ever nickname was 'The Scarlet Runners' after it came from a press report about their red football kit.

On Saturday, April 17th 1909 Arthur Moore was sent to represent Huddersfield Town at a meeting in Birmingham. The meeting with other ambitious non-league clubs from all over the country was to discuss the possibility of setting up a *Third Division* of the Football League. Thankfully the meeting came to nothing and Huddersfield Town carried on with their ambition to become a Football League member. As the season ended in 1908-09 there was a financial loss showing of £1,150 for the eight months previously, with the largest home gate being £25 pounds. Members of the Crowther family, now on the Board of Directors, erased Town's financial loss.
By the end of their first season, even though they finished a lowly 16th out of a division of 18 teams in the North Eastern League, plans were still ongoing to make Huddersfield Town a Football League member. Steps were taken for Town to secure admission into the Midland League for the following 1909-10 season. It was decided that they would, in the coming season, play in blue jerseys with white shorts.

John Hilton Crowther – was born in September 1879 in Marsden, West Yorkshire. He was one of four sons to Joseph Crowther a wealthy mill owner, who owned the Milnsbridge Woollen Mill in Huddersfield. Hilton Crowther came forward to provide the financial backing and held a strong desire to succeed at bringing about Association Football to our town. Other members of the Crowther family notably David Stoner Crowther also became involved at the time. John Hilton Crowther went from hero to villain in the eyes of Town fans in the years thereafter, but not before the story of Huddersfield Town Association Football Club was eleven years old. Sadly, John and David's father, Joseph Crowther died from a fatal road accident in Slaithwaite in June 1905. After his father's death David Stoner Crowther completed the process of buying up the rest of the mills in the area; Elm Ing Mill, Spring Mill(rebuilt in 1912) and finally Burdett Mill in 1931.

By the start of the 1909-10 season with John Hilton Crowther as Town's major financial backer, along with other members of his family, and with all their debts wiped out Huddersfield Town A.F.C set about making Leeds Road more of a home. They installed turnstiles with specific instructions to raise the fencing (something that even in 1994 in our last ever days in our old home couldn't stop us Town fans from *shall we just say* 'watching the match'). Better lighting facilities (not the Denis Law floodlights just yet) and working telephones were installed. After the Press and Directors boxes had been enclosed some thought was then given to the state of the ground. Jack Taylor, a Town player, was paid 6/- (30p) per week for rolling the field after every match.

On October 23rd 1909, against Nottingham Forest, Huddersfield Town had its first ever football mascot (long before our current mascots of Terry and Tilly the Terriers was even 'born'). A teddy bear decked in the then colours of Huddersfield Town was acquired by the Board of Directors. Town co-incidentally won the match 4-2.

The Town team of 1909-10 season comprised mainly of the following players;

Fred Walter (defender and Town captain)	William Hooton (half-back)
James Roberts (full-back)	John Thomas North (defender)
David Ewing (full-back)	Ernest Kenworthy (forward)
Jack Samuel Foster (forward)	Arthur Doggart (goalkeeper)
Alonzo Drake (forward)	Thomas Felstead (goalkeeper)
Joseph 'Joe' William Jee (forward)	Charles Stephenson (half-back)
G. Rowley (defender)	William Thomas (forward)

It seems that Jack Foster was one of Town's great unsung heroes, having signed from Southampton in 1909, he played one season in the Midland League. During this time he became Town's leading goal scorer, with 27 goals in 42 league and cup games. His four goals in an FA Cup game at Heckmondwike on September 18th 1909 have never been beaten in any year since. Jack left Town for a while only to return after his playing days were over and became Assistant Trainer, Chief Scout and Assistant Manager. In pre-war days it is claimed that Jack discovered and brought into the game more footballers, who eventually played for their country, than any other person connected with the game. Alf Young, Harry Raw, Billy Smith, Sam Wadsworth, Ned Barkas and Hugh Turner are numbered amongst the great Town players he discovered. After 28 years unbroken service Jack left Town in October 1937 and became Chief Scout for Portsmouth. (Sadly, Jack Samuel Foster passed away due to bronchitis in February 1946 aged 68).

Joseph William Jee – 'Joe' was an outside-left and one of only a select few to have played both league and non-league football for Town. Having signed from Brighton for a transfer fee of £25 in August 1909 he missed only one game during our first Football League campaign of 1910-11. He was on the books until October 1919 when his £50 transfer fee to non-league Nelson was set by the Football League. Joe was also awarded £150 in lieu of a benefit.

It is interesting to note that in the third qualifying round of the FA Cup against South Kirkby Colliery a report submitted to the FA about the game described the match as a 'rough-house from both sides'. Fred Walter the Town captain was transported to the local Infirmary in an unconscious state and a South Kirkby Colliery player had his leg broken while trying to kick a Town player. Towards the end of April 1910, Hilton Crowther, now Chairman of Huddersfield Town wrote to all the Football League Clubs looking for their support at the forthcoming A.G.M in Town's application for membership and admission to the Second Division. Such was the way in which Hilton Crowther had carried out his plans and studies that even on the day of the decision, 13th June 1910, it was still a close-run thing for Town. The outcome of the voting that day was as follows:

Birmingham…………………… **30** votes
Huddersfield Town………… **26** votes
Grimsby Town………………….17 votes
Darlington………………………. 7 votes
Chesterfield……………………. 6 votes
Hartlepools United……………. 1 vote
Rochdale……………………….. 1 vote

The top two named clubs became Football League members of the Second Division as of September 1910. This meant that Huddersfield Town Association Football Club after only two seasons in football existence had made it into the Football League at the first time of asking.

Digital image **a5** (below) - John O'Mahoney's photograph of our old home at Leeds Road (taken during our football season of 1994-95 just after Town had moved to the Alfred McAlpine Stadium).

Digital image **a6** (below) - John O'Mahoney's photograph of our old home at Leeds Road being demolished in 1995.

It was from this very banking, but with the landscape and our old home looking completely different in 1979, that at the tender age of twelve my friends and I saw our football ground for the very first time. I often wondered, from 1910 until our last home match in 1994, how many thousands of townsfolk had actually stood on this very same banking watching Town play over the years.

At the end of the season 1909-10 in the Midland League with a final league placing of 5th it was one of;

Played 42 games; won 22, lost 14, drew 6, goals for 92, goals against 77, Points 50

Huddersfield Town's history from 1900

Eleven years after the inauguration of the Huddersfield and District Football Association in 1897 Huddersfield Town Association Football Club Limited entered the North Eastern League in 1908.

1908-09 16th in North Eastern League   FA Cup did not apply

1909-10 5th in Midland League   FA Cup fourth round

Town's 'Babes to Teens' years – Chapter 3

Football League rules at the time in 1910 didn't allow for any competitive football to be played before September, so Town started their very first professional football season in the Second Division with a Midland League reserve match at Leeds Road on Thursday 1st September 1910 against Doncaster Rovers.

Digital image **a7** (left) – Taken on personal mobile phone of John O'Mahoney's at the John Smith's Stadium. This was the first gate money taken at our newly constructed Leeds Road ground containing a penny and two half-pennies. After being mounted onto a plaque it was presented to Mrs Eva Crowther, wife of Town Chairman, Hilton Crowther. The plaque itself in its entirety was presented to our Club by a Mr Robert Field of Solihull. This can still be found in our current home in the John Smith's Stadium (along with other priceless Town memorabilia).

Digital image **a8** (left)– Courtesy of Roger Pashby, The Huddersfield Town Collection, with kind permission to replicate his original photograph from our 1910 -11 season.

Town were on their way and aptly nicknamed the 'Colnesiders' (one assumes the name came about due to the fact that the River Colne flowed past the Bradley Mills end of our old home at Leeds Road). On 3rd September 1910 Town played their first ever Second Division league match away against Bradford Park Avenue decked out in their new white shirts with a blue 'yoke' (around the neck) and white shorts. The match was played out in front of a 16,000 crowd and Town came back with the two points* from a 1-0 win thanks to a goal from Harry Hamilton. The Town team that day was made up of the following players; Sandy Mutch, Archie Taylor, Charlie Morris, Simon Beaton, Ellis Hall, Willie Bartlett, George Blackburn, John Wood, Harry Hamilton, Sandy McCubbin and Joe Jee.

Two points* was the maximum for a league win until it was proposed to the Football League by Jimmy Hill that it should be changed to three points (Three points for a win was first introduced into English football in 1981).

Second Division Burnley was the first ever Football League visitors to our old home at Leeds Road on September 10th 1910. The game played in front of a 9,000 crowd saw Town defeated 1-0, but not before the game had its moments, as Sandy Mutch in the Town goal, blinded by the sun, was unable to stop Burnley from scoring. One assumes that the construction of the ground wasn't complete yet, and as such, the actual pitch was more exposed to the September sunlight than in later years'. Which may explain further that during the same game Sandy Mutch was injured when he collided with a post trying to make a save and was unable to continue for several minutes. Again was this a factor of the September sunlight. Interesting to note in the Burnley match was Town's new mascot, a goat named 'Billy', which was decked out in blue and white. Meanwhile, a Yorkshire newspaper reported that Town had signed ex-Newcastle full-back Albert Earnest Richard Pudan as Team Manager. 'Dick' Pudan was Manager from 1910 until 1912. On 24th September 1910 against Leeds City (who were later disbanded due to irregular payments) Leeds Road celebrated the opening of part of their new West Stand (Main Stand).

At the end of Town's first ever season as a Football League member in 1910-11 it was one of 13th in the 2nd Division;

Played 38 games; won 13, lost 17, drew 8, goals for 57, goals against 58, Points 34

During the close season of 1910-11 our ground was drained and re-turfed and the West Stand (Main Stand) completed. The stand officially opened on 2nd September 1911 for the first game against, Town's South Yorkshire rivals, Barnsley. The pre-match ceremony was presided over by the Football League President, John McKenna with the Town dignities performed by Mr. J.H. Kaye. Attention to detail had not just been confined to the Main Stand, it has to be said, Leeds Road had been considerably extended and improvements made on the other three sides of the ground.
One new player had joined our team this season and became a player who should never be forgotten for one historical reason or another.

Fredrick Edwin Bullock – 'Fred' was a left-back that played for Town from 1910 until 1922 during this time he was also team captain. He was married to Maude, and they had one son. Having served as a Corporal in the First Football Battalion, the 17th Middlesex, during the First World War Fred received a bullet wound to the right shoulder during the Battle of the Somme in 1916, in the region of Delville Wood and Guillemont. He was also injured in the left knee after an accident in 1918 and left the Army in March 1920. After the war he returned to Town and supported the fundraising to save our club (after certain plans emerged in our 1919-20 season).
In 1919 Fred helped Town to win promotion from the Second Division and was also captain when they lost 1-0 to Aston Villa in the FA Cup Final in 1920. Having had to retire from football in 1921 the £753 pounds that was raised for his benefit game, when Town played Manchester City on 6th November 1920, was used by Fred to become Landlord of the Slubbers Arms pub in Huddersfield. Tragedy struck in November 1922 when his wife, Maude, came downstairs to find Fred, who was only 36 years old at the time, collapsed on the floor. Next to him was a beer bottle which Maude had used to store ammonia in. When Maude spoke to him, he managed to say "Ammonia, a great mistake, a great mistake". Fred died of heart failure due to ammonia poisoning as an inquest heard that he had suffered with nerve troubles. As author of this book, maybe Fred Bullock had not truly survived the war. Given that it were later estimated that 500 of its 600 members of the Football Battalion had sadly died by the early 1930s, those that escaped bombs and bullets had fallen to the lingering effects of gas inhalation or other injuries or had suffered from depression. Town's former Manager Herbert Chapman, even though he had left our Club by the time of Fred Bullock's death, still attended at his funeral along with the rest of our Town squad.

As the season came to a close it was painfully obvious that there was a genuine possibility that Town may have to appear at the next League A.G.M. in the unhappy role of applicants for re-election something unthinkable after only two seasons in the Football League. The standard of football which had been played by Town had a detrimental effect on the attendance figures for this season which should they have had to re-apply it could have had a major impact on their application. Thankfully the threat never became a reality as Gainsborough Trinity failed re-election and Huddersfield Town ultimately survived.

It was noted that the support for the Club wasn't forthcoming especially after the Town Board had spent vast sums on extending and improving our old home at Leeds Road. On days when the Rugby League side was in action, at Fartown, there was no doubt football took second place. An overall crowd average of around 5,000 was not good enough to sustain a Football League club on a sound financial footing and there were serious doubts about the future of our football club in 1911. By the end of the season there were significant changes and things to consider for the future of Huddersfield Town Association Football Club.

At the end of the season 1911-12 with a final league placing of 17th it was one of;

Played 38 games; won 13, lost 19, drew 6, goals for 50, goals against 64, Points 32

On 15th April 1912 Dick Pudan, then Huddersfield Town's Secretary-Manager, felt the need to recommend to Town's shareholders that the Club should be wound up. Eight days later after the shocking news had been digested a meeting was held at Leeds Road to discuss the situation in full. So on 8th May 1912, a creditors meeting was called and held in the Station Street offices of Ramsden, Sykes and Ramsden with Mr T.H. Kaye appointed as Liquidator. On 20th July 1912 a motion to reconstruct the company was approved and carried. Arthur Fairclough was appointed Secretary-Manager on 28th August 1912 as a new Board of Directors, headed by William Hardcastle, was put in place.

On 2nd September 1912 Huddersfield Town Association Football Club was formally registered as a private company with a capital of ten thousand pounds in £1 shares to take over assets of a 'company with a similar title in liquidation'. The initial changes that had taken place off the field, in the pre-season, had to have some major impact with the football activity on the field of play in 1912. Given that by the end of the season Town had finished in their highest ever league position of fifth in the Second Division.

One sad story that my research led me to, while writing this part of the book, was that of Dentist Ron Brebner who kept goal during Town's 1911-12 season. He later joined Leicester Fosse and tragically died due to a result of his internal injuries which was sustained, while playing his 18th game for the old Fosse club, on Boxing Day 1913. Having collided with a player during the match against Lincoln City Brebner was carried off the pitch as complications set in. (Sadly, after a lengthy spell in hospital Ron Brebner passed away in November 1914 aged just 33).

At the end of the season 1912-13 with a final league placing of 5th it was one of;

Played 38 games; won 17, lost 12, drew 9, goals for 66, goals against 40, Points 43

In time for the start of the 1913-14 season Huddersfield Town adopted the colours that became famous throughout the footballing world blue and white vertical striped shirts and white shorts. It was also the year in which Town Directors gave permission for 'Pathe's Animated Gazette' to take films during the football season.

Town's 1913-14 season should always be remembered for the very fact that a certain William Henry Smith came for a trial against Bury reserves and the Club was sufficiently impressed to invite him back again for a further trial.

William's reply, precise and to the point, stated that he was not willing to accept a weekly wage of less than 50/- (£2.50) and for that reason he would not be attending for a further trial. The response from Huddersfield Town was to urge him to reconsider his position and to do as they suggested. Somewhere along the lines there must have been further 'negotiations' because on 14th October 1913 William Henry Smith signed at the tender age of eighteen for £2 10s (£2.50). This was the catalyst of Huddersfield Town's most legendary player.

William Henry Smith – was known simply by Town fans as 'Billy' Smith from Tantobie Durham. He is still, even in today's modern footballing world, the current holder of our Club's record appearances with 574 peacetime and cup games to his credit from over two decades of football from 1913 until May 1934. During a First Division match on 6th April 1920 he had a fight with a Stoke City player and as such both players were sent off which caused Smith to miss the 1920 FA Cup Final against Aston Villa. He scored a total of 126 goals for Town including the penalty which brought the FA Cup home to Leeds Road in 1922. In the second half of the FA Cup Final against Preston North End in 1922 Smith after being brought down on the edge of the penalty area the referee pointed to the spot. Billy stepped up to take the penalty himself while the Preston keeper (Mitchell) jumped around on the goal-line in an attempt to distract him. Clem Stephenson just whispered to Smith "Never mind the dancing devil, just shove it in the net". Smith duly obliged and the cup was on its way to Town.

After a league rule change by the FA in the close season, on October 11th 1924 in a 4-0 home win over Arsenal at Leeds Road, Billy Smith became the first player ever in English League history to score direct from a corner-kick. With his sweet right foot he swerved the ball into the goal, like a boomerang, at the near post past the goalkeeper.

Smith was a key member of Herbert Chapman's famous team and in 1926 received his first England cap and was one of five Town players who played in the 'Wembley Wizards' 5-1 defeat of England. He, Bob Kelly, Roy Goodall and Tom Wilson played for England, while Alex Jackson played for Scotland. Alex Jackson scored a hat-trick, while Kelly scored a consolation goal for England. On 11th November 1933 Billy received his fourth benefit from the President of the Football League. He also had a stint as Player-Manager at Rochdale before he retired from football completely. (Sadly, William Henry Smith passed away due to cancer, in 1951, after having his left leg amputated due to a mistreated football injury).

By the time the 1914-15 football season had started, conflict which became known as 'The Great War' sickened and devastated Europe. As the season drew to a close, due to the onset of war and with most of the country working long hours, with the production of materials for war, no one was paying much attention to any football match taking place.

Amongst the four and a half million men lost by the allies in WWI was two Town players Larrett Roebuck from Rotherham and Sidney James from Sheffield. Two fine and upstanding young men whom a bright future in the game of football had been forecast had been sadly lost to war along with; Henry Cyril Crozier, Leigh Richmond Roose, Ernest George Kenworthy, Charles Edward Randall and John Edward Didymus. Other brave soldiers who had fought in a war and wore our Town colours were; John Gilbert Cock, James Isaac Whelpton, Thomas Wilson, Craig Benjamin, Tom Carter and Francis Chivers. While those brave souls sadly lost in WWII were; Robert Henry Gordon, Francis Cornelius Chivers, Thomas Carter, Ralph Shields and Alexander Skinner Jackson.

For everyone who has bravely fought in any battle for our Country, I'd like to take this opportunity as author of this book to say, we are indebted to your bravery and for your unselfishness to serve King and Queen. For that we Town fans will never forget, and why I am so proud to be a Terrier, as we all remember the fallen and salute the brave still amongst us.

Digital image **a9** (left) - John O'Mahoney's personal artwork and tribute which was also used on 'Those were the days my friend'- Showing respect for Remembrance Day from our old home at Leeds Road.

Digital image **a10** (left) - John O'Mahoney's personal artwork and tribute which was also used on 'Those were the days my friend'- Showing respect for Remembrance Day from the John Smith's Stadium.

Because of the outbreak of war from 1915 until 1919, no Football League games was played, but in the Central League in 1915 Huddersfield Town in only their second year of membership became Central League Champions. Sadly given the war years, it was given little or no significance, one could only imagine the atmosphere in the dressing rooms after the players returned from the war. Though football can do little to ease the pain of war far better days were in store for Town but not before great adversity was to strike first in 1919. Our reserve team in 1915 contained some truly great names; in goal Alex 'Sandy' Mutch, left-back Fred Bullock, Charlie Slade as number 8 and outside-left none other than Billy Smith who went onto to become a truly legendary figure at Town during the 1920s.

Digital image **a11** (left)– Courtesy of Roger Pashby, The Huddersfield Town Collection, with kind permission to replicate his original photograph from our 1914-15 season – Central League Medals.

Since Town had achieved Football League status in 1910 attendances had been extremely poor and up to the suspension of football in 1915 our home games had rarely exceeded crowds of 5,000. It wasn't helped by our poor form in five years of endeavour the best league position had been fifth in the Second Division in their 1912-13 season. During this same period Town had never advanced beyond the second round of the FA Cup. Coupled with the presence of the well-established and well-supported Huddersfield Northern Rugby Union Club, while Town played to a near-empty ground which had been redeveloped to house thousands of spectators, could not have been encouraging for players, management or the Board of Directors.

During the outbreak of war, with no League Football played at Leeds Road, Town's revenue was extremely low if not altogether zero. It was recognised that since the birth of Huddersfield Town they had not been operating at break-even figures let alone on a viable basis. In order to help Town financially family members of the Crowther family, who were on the Town board, agreed to continue to supply credit facilities to enable our beloved club to continue its existence.

On 30th August 1919, with the Football League resuming, the story of Town's very real crisis now starts. Ambrose Langley, firmly in place as Manager, should always be remembered for his great achievements in the face of such a huge financial crisis and real-life adversity.

Ambrose Langley – was a full-back in his playing days who started out his football career with his local side Horncastle then moved to Grimsby Town in 1889. Then having joined First Division Sheffield Wednesday in 1893 he won an FA Cup winners medal in 1896. They also won the Second Division title in 1900 and the Football League title in 1903 and 1904 while he was at the club despite suffering a rib injury (which finished his playing career off in the topflight). He was appointed as Player-Manager of Hull City in 1905 and in his first season in charge City finished fifth in the Second Division. In 1908-09 he led them to fourth place, in 1909-10 they finished third and only just missed out on promotion to the topflight on goal average. He resigned from Hull City at the end of their 1912-13 season and was appointed Town Manager in December 1919. Five new players had joined Town's playing side with three that should never be forgotten at Town for one reason or another.

Samuel James Taylor – 'Sammy' was an inside-forward and in his first season with Town in 1919 he scored 35 league goals in just 42 league appearances. This made Taylor the top goalscorer in the Second Division and the record holder for the highest number of league goals scored in one season by a Town player until equalled by George Brown and finally beaten by Jordan Rhodes in April 2012. Sammy played for Town until 1921 when he signed for Sheffield Wednesday. (Sadly, Samuel James Taylor passed away in 1973 aged 80).

Jack Swann – was a central striker who played for Town until 1922 and also appeared in the 1920 FA Cup Final for Town against Aston Villa. Interestingly when Jack was 89 years young he attended at the Centenary 1972 FA Cup Final at Wembley (Leeds v Arsenal) as a V.I.P given that he was the oldest surviving footballer from an FA Cup Final. (Sadly, Jack Swann passed away in 1990 aged 96).

Thomas Wilson – played as a centre-back for Town from 1919 until 1932. He was one of only a few players who, over the next 12 seasons, was a virtual ever-present with Huddersfield. He helped Town to promotion to the First Division in 1920 and then captained the side to become the first 'Thrice Champions' of the Football League as well as victory in the FA Cup in 1922. In his time at Huddersfield, they also reached the FA Cup final in 1920, 1928 and 1930 and went on to make one England appearance in the 5-1 defeat by Scotland on 31st March 1928. After 448 league appearances in our mighty blue and white shirt Thomas left in 1932. Having retired from professional football he returned to Huddersfield Town briefly as Assistant Trainer. (Sadly, Thomas Wilson passed away in 1948 aged 51).

From the start of the new season Town won four home games and lost three games away from Leeds Road. Jack Cock meanwhile had scored six goals in the first seven games and Jim Baker had scored three goals while Sammy Taylor at this point of the season had only scored one goal. Having played four home games since the start of the new season Town saw a low crowd turnout at Leeds Road. The home match against Bury on Tuesday 9th September 1919 attracted a crowd of just 4,000. In October after two more home games had attracted an average Leeds Road crowd of just 5,000 things got much more serious for Town, and financially the worst it could possibly get until their 2002-03 season.

John Gilbert Cock – 'Jack' joined Town just before the war and became our first ever full England international just four days before he was sensationally transferred to Chelsea on Wednesday 29th October 1919. It was left to our Town Manager, Ambrose Langley, to state that "The transfer of Jack Cock had taken place only because the player himself wished to return to London". The following month even worse news broke into the footballing world regarding Huddersfield Town Association Football Club.

After the home match against Fulham on Saturday 1st November 1919, which had attracted a lowly Leeds Road crowd of just 3,000 fans and raised just a paltry £49 pounds in gate receipts. Just five days later a devastating bombshell landed, on Thursday 6th November 1919, 'In all probability the last ever league game had been played at Leeds Road'. As the terrible news broke the Football League Management Committee also met on the same day to discuss the possible transfer of our entire beloved football club, lock, stock and barrel, to Leeds to take the place of the recently disbanded Leeds City. Locally in the town it was felt that the Fulham gate receipt was the last straw in terms of the Club being heavily subsidised. Such was the belief that on Saturday 8th November 1919 the local newspaper's headline read" TOWN CLUB DEAD" as the article continued "The Huddersfield Town Association Football Club so far as this town is concerned, is to all intents and purposes, extinct". Something which they were once again very near to becoming in their 2002-03 season.

Within days of the awful news a handful of Town fans, after a Central League match, held a prolonged demonstration on the pitch in front of the Director's box. They demanded an explanation from the Club and the Town Board agreed to hold a public meeting at Leeds Road. A crowd of 3,000 Town fans attended at the ground to protest at the proposed transfer of our club. Actively encouraged by the support the Town Board sent a counter request to the Football League. Just as such an announcement would be sickening to our present-day supporters, so it must have been to the Town fanatics of 1919. Meanwhile, at Leeds Road it was evident that the time had come when Town faced the task of supporting themselves financially, without the vital subsidy of the Crowther Family, Town had simply reached the point of no return. Such was the football support in the town and district that local citizens, along with Amos Brook Hirst, banded together in a show of civic pride and enthusiasm and met with Hilton Crowther. Eventually a resolution was passed that the Town Directors were asked not to be party to the transference of the Club until the Huddersfield public had the opportunity to try to save the Club. It's at this point in time that the name of Dick Parker is first mentioned a man whose services to Huddersfield Town in the years to come was to be of massive proportions. By July 1920 he became a Club Director and remained so for fifty-four years uninterrupted service, at that time a Football League record. Amos Brook Hirst having returned to serve the Club he helped to form, along with his firm of Solicitors, was appointed to act on behalf of Huddersfield Town and was successful in postponing the appointment of the Receiver thereby ensuring vital breathing space for all. The task of raising the necessary funds to save the Club then started.

Given that a sum total of £30,000 was needed before Saturday 6th December 1919. £25,000 for the Crowther brothers and the remaining £5,000 was required to continue the Club going forward. Collections were made everywhere and everyone contributed what they could afford. Unbelievable it may seem, but just before Christmas 1919 a public announcement was made that our own Mr Arthur Fairclough, Town Secretary, had accepted the post of 'Receiver' if an application was successful. Needless to say that Arthur Fairclough was asked immediately to resign his post from the Club.

The Town team of 1919-20 season, on the field of play, was performing amazingly well considering the internal goings-on within the Club. Highlighted none more so than by the very fact that on Christmas Day 1919, Town boosted by a 26,000-home crowd, ran out 7-1 winners against Rotherham United and by the end of the year stood third in the Second Division (one point behind second place Birmingham City). At the start of 1920 a news headline appeared in the local paper which simply said, "TOWN STILL ALIVE" and with that Town's cup run to the 1920 FA Cup Final commenced.

On 16th January 1920, at the George Hotel in Huddersfield, Amos Brook Hirst attended a meeting with the Football League Management Committee to persuade them to defer a winding up order on Huddersfield Town. Amazingly they agreed and Town's Second Division match against table topping Tottenham Hotspur achieved a record 27,000 attendance for Leeds Road. Such was the effect on the townsfolk and district of Huddersfield that by the time that Town were due to face Liverpool in the FA Cup fourth round at Leeds Road on 6th March 1920 it was anticipated that a 40,000 crowd would be present. In fact, it was the highest home attendance of the season given that a crowd of 47,527 were present to see Town win 2-1. Then having beaten Bristol City 2-1 in the Semi-Final of the cup they were up against Aston Villa in the Final. Thousands of Town fans had travelled down to London by train overnight and were present in the Stamford Bridge crowd of 50,018. Unfortunately Town's lucky charm, a lamp borrowed from a local panto production of 'Aladdin', failed to work despite being rubbed by each player prior to kick-off. It was the first time that Town had appeared with the Huddersfield coat of arms as a club badge on our FA Cup Final blue and white shirts. Sadly, after extra time had been played, Town lost 1-0 against 'The Villa'. The game itself was historical for two reasons, not only was it the first ever FA Cup Final to require extra-time to be played it was also the birth of our Town Club song *'Smile Awhile'*. (which was based on an original song called *'Till We Meet Again'*).

> There's a team that is dear to its followers,
> Its colours are bright blue and white,
> 'Tis a team of renown,
> The pride of the town,
> And the football is their delight.
>
> All the while upon the field of play,
> Thousands loudly cheer them on their way.
>
> Often you will hear them say,
> Who can beat the Town today,
> Then the crowd will cheer so merrily.
> Every goal will be a memory,
> So Town play up and bring the Cup,
> Back to Huddersfield.

While researching the original author of the song it seems that a Mr. Chappell of Longwood in this season 1919-20 should be credited with the actual words for 'Smile Awhile'.

By the end of the 1919-20 season after overcoming a financial crisis and real adversity Town proudly recorded the following, second in the Second Division-**Promoted** as runners-up;

Played 42 games; won 28, lost 6, drew 8, goals for 97, goals against 38, Points 64

Billy Smith had been suspended for the Cup Final due to having been sent off against Stoke City on 5th April 1920. If that wasn't bad enough, on April 20th 1920 a telegram arrived at Leeds Road to say that Smith had been suspended from League Football for a total of two months.

Digital image **a12** (left) - kind permission granted by artist George Chilvers 'Colourised by George' to replicate and display his artwork.

(left) - Action from the actual 1919-20 F.A Cup Final at Stamford Bridge between Town and Aston Villa. The referee for this match was Mr J.T. Howcroft and the two linesmen was Mr H. Ayling and Mr A. Scholey.

From this season onwards Town was nicknamed 'Babes' due to being The original 'Babes' of the Football League when after promotion to the First Division they then won the Championship in only their fourth season (and the fifth and sixth).

10 years of Huddersfield Town's history from 1910

1910-11 13th in Division 2   FA Cup 4th round

1911-12 17th in Division 2   FA Cup 1st round

1912-13 5th in Division 2   FA Cup 2nd round

1913 -14 13th in Division 2   FA Cup 2nd round

1914-15 8th in Division 2   FA Cup 1st round
Central League Champions

No league football played 1915-1919 due to World War I

1915-16 3rd in Midland Section Competition 3rd in Subsidiary Competition (Northern Division)

1916-17 4th in Midland Section Competition 6th in Subsidiary Competition (Northern Division)

1918-19 8th in Midland Section Competition 7th in Subsidiary Competition (Northern Division)

1919-20 **2nd in Division 2 (promoted)**   FA Cup Finalist

Town's 'Roaring Twenties' – Chapter 4

It soon became apparent, that Town having been promoted to the First Division, the football demands were somewhat greater than what they had been used to at Leeds Road. Something which was also recognised in Town's 1970-71 First Division season and their Premier League season in 2017-18. A final league position of 17th in the First Division in 1920-21 was far from comfortable while one statistic stood out in this season. No Town player scored double figures (Jack Swann was the highest goalscorer in this season with just eight goals) something which was also evident in Town's 1971-72 season and also in both Premier League seasons 2017-18 and 2018-19.

For the start of the 1920-21 season improvements were made to our old home at Leeds Road. The playing area was redone, the Paddock asphalted, the terracing increased to accommodate up to 24,000 Town fans, while the Main Stand and Offices was repainted. Two major events took place during the season which had huge historical importance for everyone at Huddersfield Town. Firstly, Herbert Chapman was brought in as Town Secretary in December 1920 and then became Manager on 31st March 1921, having replaced Ambrose Langley. Four wins out of the last seven games of this season saw Town survive relegation from the First Division thankfully and secondly Herbert Chapman convinced the Town Board to spend money on a player, by the name of Clem Stephenson, from Aston Villa.

Herbert Chapman finished his playing career with Northampton Town in 1909. He then made his coaching debut with Northampton Town and quickly made his mark in lower league football. In an era where most coaches focused on physical training ahead of tactics, Chapman proved to be an astute strategist. In 1912, he joined Leeds City where his team's brand of well-organised attacking football drew large numbers of spectators. Leeds were aiming for promotion in the 1914-15 season, but their campaign derailed because of the outbreak of war. As a result, Chapman, away from football, focused his energy on managing a munitions factory to help the war efforts. In December 1918 he resigned from the post at Leeds City before taking up a job as Superintendent in an oil factory. Almost a year after he left the post, Leeds came back to haunt him with the Club found guilty of financial irregularities, three of its Directors, Chapman and his Assistant were all banned from football for life. The following year brought more bad news for him as he received his pink slip from his factory job. Chapman out of work, and with a family of four to feed, received some respite when Town offered him a route back into football. They actively campaigned to overturn his ban as it was rightly argued that he was away from Leeds for significant periods during the war. With the ban scrapped in February 1921 Herbert Chapman was officially appointed as an Assistant to Ambrose Langley (It was to be a temporary position) and took over as Manager in March 1921.

Huddersfield Town began to gain a good name beyond England in the 1920s as Chapman took our Town team on post-season tours at the invitation of European clubs. An insight into the great man himself was largely evident in his footballing thoughts and logical thinking on the game. His idea was to make Town play quick rapid and direct football without the need to play a close-passing game. He wanted the best possible football, but it had to have a 'kick' in it. His one golden rule was never to be satisfied. He believed that no matter how good the team may be, the thought was always to improve it. Others believed that a winning team got together by luck, it wasn't Chapman's in my opinion as author, It seems to me, he watched his team like a hawk hunted its prey and his logical thinking is as relevant today as it were at the time.

Sadly, on 11th May 1925, a sporting headline had devastating consequences for everyone at Town.

Arsenal had advertised for a Manager and had already spoken to Herbert Chapman about taking their job. They followed this up with an irresistible offer of an annual salary of £2,000 pounds which was unheard of in those days. The Town Board had tried to persuade Herbert to stay and even offered to match his salary but the attraction of London, where his two teenage boys had better career prospects, proved too much an opportunity to turn down. One could even surmise that the great depression had hit the North much harder than it had done in the South, which in turn affected the income of Northern clubs. Herbert had felt the pinch himself after a bad business venture had wiped out his savings so the chance to double his salary with a move to London was quite possibly an answer to his prayers. So on 10th June 1925 he resigned his position at Town to take up the offer of Arsenal Manager. Sadly, In the early hours of 6th January 1934 Herbert Chapman, who having suffered from pneumonia, passed away at his family home in Hendon as the death of the world's finest Manager shocked the footballing world. Over two thousand people lined the route to the church on the day of his funeral.

Herbert Chapman's legacy in football is legendary, even to this day, having been the pioneer to name but a few; floodlighting matches, using rubber studs on boots and numbering players' shirts. He also introduced the tactics board and proposed a 'West Europe' competition (20 years before the European Cup was first played out). The 1930 Cup Final was another first at Wembley when the teams walked out side by side in honour of Chapman. He had also taken a gramophone player that day and started the trend of playing music in the dressing room before a match.

Clem Stephenson had played for Herbert Chapman at Leeds City as a guest during the war. An inside-forward, he was known for his vision and passing, with reports describing him as an 'expert schemer'. He was 32 years old when Town signed him and considered past his peak, but Chapman was still determined to secure his services. "You have talented mostly young players they now need a general to lead them," were his wise words to our Town Board. Clem went onto to play for Town from 1921 until 1929 and played a total of 248 league games during which time he scored 42 goals. He retired while at Town and became Manager, taking over from Jack Chaplin in 1929 until 1942. He is still to this day the longest serving Town Manager. (Sadly, Clem Stephenson passed away in 1961 aged 71).

Besides the signing of Stephenson, Town's squad already had a number of other quality players.

Samuel John Wadsworth – 'Sammy' was a defender Town signed in the summer of 1920. He was a war veteran that was deemed surplus to requirements at Blackburn after returning from fighting in Europe. Wadsworth became one of the best in his position and a mainstay for England's national team so much so that he was captain of England for the last four of his nine caps. Sammy went on to play for Town from 1920 until 1930 and played a total of 281 league games during which time he scored four goals. (Sadly, Samuel John Wadsworth passed away in 1961 aged 64).

Herbert Chapman's most famous legacy, the W-M formation was still not perfected yet. But thanks to the defensive skills of Tom Wilson, Chapman was able to utilise a deep-lying centre-half who broke down opposition attacks.

William Watson – 'Billy' had made his Town debut before the war but had only registered a handful of appearances. The left-half remained a one-man club from 1912 until he retired in 1927 after 292 league games. He was a major lynchpin in Chapman's formidable team. (Sadly, William Watson passed away in 1962 aged approximately 68-69).

At the end of the season 1920-21 with a final league placing of 17th it was one of;

Played 42 games; won 15, lost 18, drew 9, goals for 42, goals against 49, Points 39

Chapman's first full season as Manager in 1921 started off badly as they only won twice in the first eight games. By October Town had put together a six-match winning streak, but they were not able to maintain it and ended the season on the same points as the previous season. However, in the FA Cup it was a different story altogether as Town reached their second FA Cup Final in just three years. It was only the third occasion that a final (since 1872) had been contested as 'The War of the Roses'.

On 29th April 1922 down at Stamford Bridge Town started the match as favourites against Preston North End. The match was decided by a penalty midway through the second half when Billy Smith was fouled in the box. The referee, Mr John W.D. Fowler, a local Schoolmaster pointed to the spot ignoring protests from all the Preston players that the foul had occurred outside the penalty area. Smith scored the decisive penalty to bring the FA Cup home to Huddersfield Town for the very first time. Barely three years after almost going bankrupt Town had won the greatest prize in football. On returning from London with the cup they were greeted by a huge crowd which according to a local newspaper report, at the time, described it as the biggest public gathering in Town's history. Huddersfield Town also won the Football Association Charity Shield having beaten Liverpool at Old Trafford. Having consolidated his position, Chapman then turned his sights towards the league and the up-and-coming season.

Digital image **a13** (left) - Kind permission granted by artist George Chilvers 'Colourised by George' to replicate and display his artwork.

Back row (L to R) D. Parker, H. Dodson, W. Dawson, J. Barlow, A.B. Hirst, J. Rayner, N. Robinson

Middle row (L to R) J.W. Wood, C. Slade, A. Mutch, T. Wilson, W. Watson, S.J. Wadsworth

Front row (L to R) H. Chapman, G. Richardson, F. Mann, E. Islip, C. Stephenson, W. Smith, J. Chaplin

At the end of the season 1921-22 with a final league placing of 14th it was one of;

Played 42 games; won 15, lost 18, drew 9, goals for 53, goals against 54, Points 39

For Town's 1922-23 season it was acknowledged that they had great defenders but needed a more capable goalkeeper to improve on their recent record of conceding 54 goals from the previous season. Town signed *Edward Hallows Taylor* from Oldham, to improve the quality of goalkeeping. Just four months after he signed 'Ted' had made his international debut for England. (Sadly, Edward Hallows Taylor passed away in July 1956 aged 69).

Wing-half *David Morton Steele* having signed for Town from Bristol Rovers played a total of 186 league games, during which time he scored one goal, before he left in 1929 only to return as Town Manager in 1943 then left again in 1947. He made a final return later in life as a Town Scout. (Sadly, David Steele passed away in May 1964 aged 69).

Another key transfer in this year was the signing of Tottenham's centre-forward *Charlie Wilson*. He'd caught Chapman's eye having scored 13 goals in 26 matches. Sadly injury forced him to retire, in 1925, but not before he had played 99 league matches and scored a total of 57 goals. (Sadly Charles Wilson passed away in May 1971 aged 76).

Town started the 1922 season and by November was 13th in the First Division. Having won eight out of their last twelve league matches of the season they finished seven points behind Champions Liverpool. The defence had vastly improved and conceded just 32 goals the second-best record in the division. At the other end Wilson was top goalscorer with 16 goals while Chapman had taken Town's strong foundations and built a talented squad on top of it. His team was already filled with experienced, battle-hardened footballers, and soon featured two youngsters who went on to become club legends.

At the end of the season 1922-23 with a final league placing of 3rd it was one of;

Played 42 games; won 21, lost 10, drew 11, goals for 60, goals against 32, Points 53

George 'Bomber' Brown was barely 18 when he signed straight from his local colliery team in 1921. He was a powerful and prolific striker who amazed fans with his dribbling skills and scored a total of 159 goals in 229 games, to this day it's still a club record that's never been beaten. George was used sparingly in his first two seasons, but by 1923 had become a first team regular. In August 1929 Town were persuaded to sell him to Aston Villa. (Sadly, George Brown passed away in June 1948 aged 44).

The other youngster, *Fredrick Roy Goodall*, also made his debut this season and became one of the best defenders in the league, he was noted for his superb leadership skills. Roy stayed at Town for 12 years and played 403 league games during which time he scored 19 league goals. He earned 25 England caps and would have been captain for England at the first ever World Cup had they taken a team. Roy went on to be associated with Town as a player, Trainer and Scout for over forty years. (Sadly, Fredrick Roy Goodall passed away in January 1982 aged 79).

On 1st March 1924 Town played Cardiff City at Leeds Road. An 18,000 Leeds Road crowd saw George Brown score twice as Town won 2-0. With the final match of the season, Cardiff City was on 56 points and had to travel to Birmingham City and Town, who were on 55 points, was at home against Nottingham Forest. Town needed to win and Cardiff to lose in order to win the league by a clear margin. 'The Bluebirds' had a goal average of 1.794 better than Town's average of 1.727. Both matches kicked off at the same time and soon Town were 2-0 up thanks to two goals from George Cook. In Birmingham the first half ended 0-0. In the second half Cardiff won a penalty in the dying minutes, Len Davis, their leading goalscorer stepped up to take it and missed. Meanwhile, at Leeds Road, George Brown popped up with Town's third goal and at the final whistle they were crowned *'Champions of England'* by a goal average of 0.024 goals.

At the end of the season 1923-24 as worthy *'CHAMPIONS'* it was one of;

Played 42 games; won 23, lost 8, drew 11, goals for 60, goals against 33, Points 57 goal ratio – 1.818
Cardiff City Points 57 goal ratio – 1.794

For the start of the 1924-25 season back at our *'CHAMPIONS'* home at Leeds Road there were further improvements. The scoreboard had been enlarged so that it could be seen from any part of the ground. The heating at the ground had been changed, from coke to gas, providing a cleaner system. On the field of play there was the introduction of the Huddersfield Infirmary and Victoria Nurses Charity Cup. Which, in the time before the 'welfare state' it was a valuable source of income for the Hospital Charity. Town began the season as favourites having retained their league winning squad which was further strengthened by the fleet-footed *Joey Williams*. They started the new campaign having not lost a match in their first ten games.

Unfortunately an injury to Town's first-choice goalkeeper Ted Taylor, who'd broken his leg, meant our reserve goalkeeper Leonard Boot had to deputise, and he struggled to compete at league level. Town lost four out of their next five matches, so Chapman reacted by buying *William Mercer* from Hull City. 'Bill' had played for Town in their 1910-11 season and once again donned Town's colours from 1924 until 1928 when having played 79 games he signed for Blackpool. (Sadly, William Mercer passed away in 1965 aged approximately 67).

With Mercer providing much needed confidence between the posts, Town's famed defence was able to keep thirteen clean sheets for the rest of the season. The following six months saw Huddersfield Town become unconquerable and in the process lost only one game. Charlie Wilson and George Brown had formed a deadly partnership and had jointly scored forty-four goals. Town retained the title of **'Champions of England'** this time by two clear points from West Bromwich Albion.

At the end of the season 1924-25 as worthy **'CHAMPIONS'** it was one of;

Played 42 games; won 21, lost 5, drew 16, goals for 69, goals against 28, Points 58

It's worth noting that Town had only conceded 28 goals all season, but Chapman still looked to improve on our team's overall performance. In preparation for a change in the laws of football Herbert Chapman signed a young Scottish international winger from Aberdeen by the name of Alex Jackson.

The laws of the football game was changed to increase the number of goals scored, to make the game more appealing, in the hope of increasing the numbers on the terraces. The FA decided that for a player to be onside there had to be two instead of three opponents nearer to their own goal-line.

Alexander Skinner Jackson – signed just before Chapman's departure to Arsenal in 1925 after Town beat Bolton, Everton, Aston Villa, Sunderland and Liverpool to the winger's signature. Herbert Chapman had travelled up to Renton and got the blessing of the player's father to sign for Town. With the footballing business completed both men went to the only pub in the town to seal the contract with a nice glass of scotch. The problem was that the whole village had heard about Chapman being there, and were keen to meet the famous man, so they all ventured to the pub to catch a glimpse for themselves. Herbert, generous as always, made a sweeping gesture with his hand and invited everyone into the pub from the village for a drink. Unbeknown to Chapman though, in accordance to an old Scottish custom, everyone in the pub ordered a whiskey and a pint of beer.
Alex Jackson helped Town retain our league title and runners-up spot over the next two years. He also led Town to two FA Cup Finals and scored in the 1928 FA Cup Final against Blackburn Rovers in a 3–1 defeat. In 1930, he was once again on a losing side, this time against Herbert Chapman's Arsenal as Town lost 2-0. Chelsea, newly promoted to the topflight as runners-up in the Second Division, got out their cheque book and embarked upon a massive spending spree. Three days of tough negotiations took place before a deal was agreed with Alex keen to move to London.
Jackson in no time at all had taken over as the Landlord of a pub in Covent Garden, he also had an interest in the Queen's Hotel in Leicester Square, and had a weekly column syndicated in local newspapers across the whole country. He was given special privileges at Chelsea as their *'Wandering Winger'* scored more goals than many forwards and was well-known in the footballing world in which his name alone attracted huge crowds.

All that attention brought problems for Jackson though and he soon went from darling to villain.

One of Chelsea's final matches of the season was away at Manchester City. In the team hotel on the night before the match Jackson ordered a round of drinks for the entire team to be sent to his room. The following day he played and scored in a 1-1 draw but the Directors when they got wind of his transgression suspended Jackson, transfer-listed him, and told him he'd never play for the Club ever again.

The Club never reported the reason for their decision and refused to reveal any details on one of the greatest footballers of his time, as Jackson's contract expired Chelsea hung on to his registration. Without their blessing Jackson couldn't play league football for anyone anywhere but non-league clubs weren't covered.

So in September 1932 the greatest player in the world signed for Ashton National in the Cheshire League. They paid him, £15 per week, nearly double the wages of any other player in the country. Due to the huge financial drain on Ashton National Alex left after just one season to sign for Margate in the Kent League, who paid him £10 per week. In September 1933 Alex Jackson got married and went on a motoring honeymoon to Paris.

Chelsea were still demanding £4,000 for Jackson's registration that no league club was willing to pay, so he stayed in France and played for Nice and Le Touquet before he gave up on football altogether at the age of 28. Jackson's career with the Scottish national team is perhaps what he is best remembered for as he won his first cap at the age of 19. He was one of the Wembley Wizard's, and scored a hat-trick, as Scotland beat England 5–1 at Wembley. He also scored the winner against England just two years earlier. His international career was later hindered by the ban on Anglo-Scots who had played for English clubs, as a result of a dispute between the Scottish FA and the FA he finished with 17 caps and eight goals. At the end of WWII after he had first served with the Eighth Army in North Africa, and then with the Pioneer Corps, Alex extended his stay in Africa and was assigned to the Suez Zone. Sadly, in November 1946 Alex Jackson while driving a truck near his army base lost control and the vehicle overturned. He suffered serious head injuries and was pronounced dead before he even reached the hospital. (Sadly, the greatest player in the world or Major A.S. Jackson as he was then known by is one of 1,205 soldiers buried in Fayid War cemetery Egypt).

Cecil Potter, previously Manager of Derby County, became Town's next Manager after Herbert Chapman had left for Arsenal. Without Chapman in charge Town carried on regardless as George Brown scored 35 league goals, in just 41 games. He was well-supported with both Alex Jackson who scored 16 league goals and George Cook who scored 14 league goals. Hard to believe, but on 24th October 1925 at home against Newcastle United at Leeds Road, Town lost 1-0 which brought to an end an unbeaten run of 27 matches which had lasted since 17th January of the previous season. Mick Buxton and John Haselden oversaw our Town team of 1982-83 go the entire season unbeaten at Leeds Road (It's the only time that Town remained unbeaten at Leeds Road in a season). The 1925 record was beaten in 2011, at the Galpharm Stadium, by Lee Clark's record-breaking 43-match unbeaten run.

Given the fact that Town were First Division Champions the state of our pitch obviously left a lot to be desired back then. The muddy state of Town's pitch in mid-winter was at that time worse than most. This was noted in a description of a Sunderland match on Boxing Day 1925. 'The playing area which was completely bare of any grass due to the use of the many braziers needed to thaw the ice on the pitch. Around the pitch were piles of muddy straw with ice and standing water in the middle of the pitch with boggy areas filled out with straw'. Amazingly Town won their record-breaking **'THRICE CHAMPIONS'** title in style having lost only twenty-one league games in the last three years.

At the end of the season 1925-26 as worthy *'Thrice Champions'* it was one of;

Played 42 games; won 23, lost 8, drew 11, goals for 92, goals against 60, Points 57

So, an unfashionable team from a small West Yorkshire woollen mill town had managed a feat, which all previous footballing giants of the English League of their time had been denied. Preston, Sunderland, Aston Villa, Sheffield Wednesday and Liverpool had all taken the title twice BUT none had managed the hat-trick like Huddersfield Town. It's only ever been equalled in later years by Arsenal, Liverpool and Manchester United but never beaten. It was suggested by some in the footballing world that the Championship Trophy should have been kept by Town as a memento. However, it was decided that a special trophy was to be made to commemorate our amazing feat. It used to reside in the Town Boardroom in our old home at Leeds Road but can now be found in more recent times in our John Smith's Stadium.

Digital image **a14** (left) - Taken on personal mobile phone of John O'Mahoney's at the John Smith's Stadium of Town's 'Special Trophy'

a15 (left)

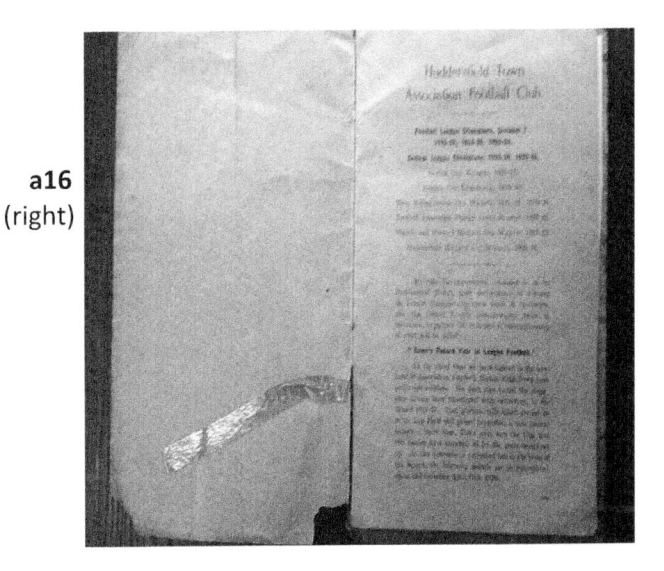

a16 (right)

Digital images **a15** (above left) and **a16** (above right) kindly supplied with his full permission by Peter May (Huddersfield Town fan) from his own personal collection of Huddersfield memorabilia. A genuine Huddersfield Town Association Football Club souvenir from our 1925-26 season to commemorate Town's historical '**Thrice Champions**' achievement.

Having had the best three years of football ever seen in our old home at Leeds Road the 1926-27 season was one full of sheer optimism and great expectations. Sadly all good things, as they say, have to come to an end. Firstly Cecil Potter resigned in August 1926 due to health reasons, and so it was that Town ended up as First Division runners-up to Newcastle United by five points. It was especially hard to take given that in the final seven league games of the season Town only won once. A 1-0 home victory against Newcastle United on Easter Tuesday, in front of a home record crowd of 44,636, against the very team that replaced Town as First Division Champions.

By mid-February 1927 after fourteen years of faithful service to Huddersfield Town, during which time he had been through the many trials and triumphs with the Club, Billy Watson played his last ever game as our first choice left-half (for virtually all of this Town career). After hanging up his boots Billy joined Town's backroom staff and continued his association with our club.
Ted Taylor our Town goalkeeper also left during the season to sign for Everton as Hugh Turner and Billy Mercer challenged each other for the number one shirt. Hugh was given the nod for the number one shirt for the rest of the season and went onto hold Town's consecutive appearance record for over sixty years. With injuries to Clem Stephenson, Alex Jackson and Billy Smith in the final seven matches it wasn't surprising that Town didn't manage to create an even more unique piece of footballing history by winning the title for an unrivalled record-breaking fourth time. By the end of the season George Brown had equalled Sammy Taylor's all-time goalscoring record of 35 league goals in a season and was chosen to represent England at the same time Town signed *Robert Kelly* from Sunderland. This completed an all-international front-line for Town, which many footballing experts perceived as the best club forward line in the world. Four English internationals; Billy Smith, George Brown, Clem Stephenson and 'Bob' Kelly, plus Scottish international Alex Jackson completed Town's formidable line-up.

At the end of the season 1926-27 as runners up it was one of;

Played 42 games; won 17, lost 8, drew 17, goals for 76, goals against 60, Points 51

One thing that I have thought about since starting to write this book, is what and where would Town have been in the world of football had there been a European Cup Competition in the 'Thrice Champions' years and during all the glory years. Instead of 1955 had the competition started 30 years earlier in 1925 Town may well have also had their name on a European Trophy to go along with all their domestic successes in England. Anyone reading this section of the book may well think the author is insane but having thoroughly researched and looked into this part of our history I can safely say that during this period Huddersfield Town was **THE** most successful football club in the world.

The 1927-28 season was even more agonising for Town fans given that at one point they looked like favourites to complete the first 20th Century league and FA Cup double. Town was a free-scoring team with an impressive forward line beating Cardiff City 8-2, Sheffield United 7-1 and Sheffield Wednesday 5-0 in the Football League and Tottenham 6-1 in the FA Cup sixth round.
By early February 1928 Town having played Everton in a top of the table clash at Leeds Road was watched by 51,284 fans. (A record league crowd for Leeds Road which stood for over thirty years). In the same month Town was watched by 55,200 fans at Leeds Road as cup fever hit our townsfolk as they beat Middlesbrough 4-0 in the fifth round of the FA Cup. By the time they played Tottenham at home in the following round on 3rd March 1928 Town was a well-oiled machine on the front line, so much so that after just 19 minutes on the clock they were 5-0 up, as goals cascaded in at the open end. Brown scored the first four goals while Smith scored the other. Just before half-time Smith scored another and made it 6-0. In the second half Town conceded a goal, but still won the game 6-1.

Before international call-ups signalled the cancellation of any league match Town had to play Bury away without five internationals that day; Roy Goodall, Tom Wilson, Bob Kelly, Billy Smith and Alex Jackson never mind anyone else who were also injured from our first team that day. Town won 3-2 on 31st March 1928 against Bury with a vastly changed and inexperienced line-up against a team that finally finished fifth in the First Division.

There is no doubt that the three semi final matches against Sheffield United which was played on 24th March, 26th March and 2nd April 1928 which left six league matches still to be played all within the last fortnight of the season, contributed to Town's failure at the last hurdle. This was further compounded by losing the FA Cup Final to Blackburn Rovers at Wembley.

After just 60 seconds from kick-off from a throw-in, just in front of the Royal Box, Syd Puddefoot and George Thornewell worked the ball up field for Blackburn. A pass found Roscamp with just Town defender Sam Barkas to beat before he descended onto our goal. Roscamp chipped the ball over Barkas head and ran around him. He then hit the ball hard as Mercer our keeper rose to catch it Roscamp was on him, and bundled Mercer ball and all over the line, a goal was given by the ref Mr. T.G. Bryan. Town never really recovered from this injustice and after 22 minutes conceded another goal to make it 2-0 to Rovers. In the second half Alex Jackson pulled a goal back with a low shot which Rovers keeper Jock Crawford could only deflect onto a post from which it bounced into the net. Five minutes from the end Roscamp scored his second, and Rovers third goal, to make the final score 3-1.
This was then followed by two further defeats for Town, at Leeds Road, against Burnley and Sheffield United. The end of season showing meant that Town finished as double runners-up in the First Division.

At the end of the season 1927-28 as runners up it was one of;

Played 42 games; won 22, lost 13, drew 7, goals for 91, goals against 68, Points 51

By the start of the 1928-29 season it was evident that Town's greatest generation of players was ageing and weren't adequately replaced in time meaning that they soon lost their way and dropped down the division. The forward line remained largely unchanged and there were problems that developed on both the wing-half positions, at right-half eight players appeared in this position and five at left-half. Town were ultimately forced to settle for their lowest final league position in the table for many years as a poor run of results in the second half of the season didn't help their cause.
Thankfully this season was another when Huddersfield had a good cup run which resulted in an FA Cup Semi-Final match at Anfield, against Bolton Wanderers, unfortunately it ended in a 3-1 defeat for Town. Given the problems on the field of play for Town with their ageing team the only ever-presents in the league this year were Roy Goodall and Hugh Turner.

Two great footballing legends that were part of Town's triumphs since the war played their last game for the Club. Two years earlier Billy Watson had played his last game for Town and now with the retirement of David Steele only Thomas Wilson remained from our defence which had been the backbone of our side for so many years. Of greater significance was the loss of the skills and organising ability on the field from Clem Stephenson. The contributions he made in the previous ten seasons was immeasurable, thankfully it wasn't long before he was back serving as Manager until 1939.

At the end of the season 1928-29 with a final league placing of 16th it was one of;

Played 42 games; won 14, lost 17, drew 11, goals for 70, goals against 61, Points 39

Town's ground at Leeds Road during the 1920s remained largely unchanged except for the construction of the North Stand in 1929. The structure provided covered accommodation over the open terracing for about 7,500 Town fans as a 'Belfast-Truss' style lattice-work roof was installed. It was popular on farms at the time and over the many years became commonly known to Town fans as simply our 'Cowshed'. The endearing construction of our 'Cowshed' with its wooden barrel-shaped roof endured the years and survived fire, storm and falling floodlight pylons.

I don't know about any other Town fan, but for me as author, I can still remember the very first time I walked into our old home at Leeds Road in August 1979, via the 'Cowshed' turnstiles. I walked up towards the first set of concrete steps which, still to this day, causes the hairs on the back of my arms to stand up on end remembering my first time in our old home. Not only that, but I can still clearly visualise myself right on the very last step as a 12-year-old as I looked out to the open end at Bradley Mills, and all around our old home, for the very first time ever. It's hard as an author to put into precise words what home means for everyone else, but for me, it felt like I belonged there, like I had waited my whole life to be somewhere and to be part of something, this for me was it, my home. Over the years it was a place where I grew from a child into a man, where great friendships were made and where we all saw many triumphs, despair and our Town history being made.

a17 (left)   **a18** (right)

Digital image **a17** (above left) – John O'Mahoney's photograph of our old home at Leeds Road of the 'Cowshed' turnstiles. Also, a trip down memory lane if you ever need one again of the dirt track between our 'Cowshed' and the houses on Leeds Road (Photo taken around springtime of 1995)

Digital image **a18** (above right) – John O'Mahoney's photograph of our old home at Leeds Road from our East Terrace of our 'Cowshed' and its 'Belfast-Truss' style lattice-work roof (Photo taken towards end of our 1993-94 season)

For the final season of the 1920s, Town's 1929-30 season not only brought about the start of a new era but also a sense of realisation that they were unlikely to make any positive steps towards regaining the First Division title anytime soon. On the FA Cup front Town mounted a serious challenge and once again appeared at Wembley in their fourth FA Cup Final. Following the lowly league placing in the First Division the previous season Jack Chaplin stepped down as Manager and became Assistant to the recently retired Town legend Clem Stephenson. The season produced mixed results which varied from a 4-1 win over eventual First Division Champions Sheffield Wednesday in February 1930 to a massive 7-1 defeat to Bolton Wanderers on New Year's Day 1930.

The biggest win, psychologically, was in the Semi-Final of the FA Cup as Town faced Sheffield Wednesday for the third time this season. Honours were even with the away game at Sheffield Wednesday on 19th October 1929 won 3-1 by Wednesday, and our home game which was won 4-1 by Town on 22nd February 1930. Alex Jackson our *'flying winger'* had scored seven goals in the previous five FA Cup matches (Bury in the third round went to a replay). Town went into the Semi-Final match at Manchester United's Old Trafford ground with high hopes for a win. Given the deadly finishing abilities of our flying winger they ran out 2-1 winners thanks to his two goals. The genius of Alex and his value to our Town team was clear to see given the fact that out of the eleven goals scored, at this stage of the FA Cup, Jackson had scored nine of them.

The FA Cup Final on 26th April 1930 at Wembley Stadium which was witnessed by a crowd of over 92,000 fans is remembered for many different and varied reasons. Firstly, Alex Jackson recorded a 78' gramophone record in which he forecast the outcome of the match. Such was the interest that it sold in its thousands and copies of it still exist even today. (One such copy was recently donated to Huddersfield Town Football Club and can now be found in the John Smith's Stadium). Secondly, this was the first Cup Final in which both teams entered the pitch side by side, in honour of Herbert Chapman. Thirdly, the German propaganda machine, the *'Graf Zeppelin'* passed over Wembley Stadium at the start of the second half. (It was the largest Airship ever built and was round 776 feet in length). Finally, after first being broadcast on BBC Radio in 1928, the 1930 Cup Final was the first for which a fee was paid for the television rights. Sadly, Town lost the 1930 FA Cup Final to Arsenal 2-0. Herbert Chapman had devised a cunning plan to thwart our prolific free-scoring Alex Jackson. Arsenal, having cancelled out Town's attack, after just 16 minutes were 1-0 up. Roy Goodall was injured in the second half and finished the match with his head in bandages. By the 88th minute it was all but over, as Arsenal went 2-0 up, after Town had given them a second half battering as they tried to break down 'The Gunners' defence.

Sammy Wadsworth left the Club during the season as Town captured the signing of wing-half Austen Campbell from Blackburn Rovers. Austen earned England international honours while at Town as two other players also made their first team debut in this year *Alfred Young* and *Reginald Mountford*. 'Alf' had played as understudy to Thomas Wilson, for some time, and began to make occasional first team appearances. With Dave Mangnall as our main striker, although short his Town career was, it was obvious Town had found a ready-made replacement for George Brown who had left at the end of the previous season.

At the end of the season 1929-30 with a final league placing of 10th it was one of;

Played 42 games; won 17, lost 16, drew 9, goals for 63, goals against 69, Points 43

Herbert Chapman's Town team was without doubt the first great dynasty in English football. His insistence to 'organise victory' ensured Town's consistency from 1921 to 1928. It needs to be remembered though that this was an era where footballers had a wage cap, and it was significantly easier for clubs to hold onto their best players, making the league more competitive.

As the 1920s draws to a close it is perhaps a fitting moment to talk about Town's mascots in this era. There were various mascots throughout this period of Town's history. At one time in 1922 they had a stuffed donkey but in a joke which went wrong someone set fire to the poor animal, at the home of Burnley international Tommy Boyle. After a visit to the theatre to see 'Aladdin' some players were presented with a 'magic lamp' which they kept in the changing room and gave a quick rub just before going out onto the field of play. It worked for a while but gradually lost its magic and was then dispensed with.

The most interesting mascot was that of John William Richards aka 'Jack' Richards an amateur entertainer. The Charlie Chaplin imitator lived in the Colne Valley area, Marsden, if local folklore history is correct. He became Town's mascot from 1927 until war broke out, during which time, he barely missed a match at Leeds Road. The first time he went onto the pitch he was chased off by the local constabulary but soon became the 'official' mascot and attended the 1928 and 1930 FA Cup Final. At Leeds Road John often performed with the Club's black cat (which was kept in order to deter mice and rats). A black cat appeared for many years at Leeds Road and one even had an unusual escape in the great fire that occurred in the Boys Enclosure in 1950.

An even crazier story goes that when Richards appeared at Wembley in the 1927-28 season, he led the Town team out to face Blackburn Rovers, then ran onto the pitch firing a starting pistol. One can only imagine the look on everyone's face, even back then, when guns were a less emotive issue the anxiety and embarrassment it must have caused off the field must have been enormous.

Another great story, which was reported locally, was in the FA Cup sixth round match on Saturday 27th February 1932 at our old home at Leeds Road. 67,037 was in attendance, including Richards, while thousands more stood on the nearby banking to watch the match. Arsenal scored after only two minutes as Town tried to fight back but were ultimately knocked out of the cup. At the end of the game Richards and the huge crowd dispersed never to be seen in such huge numbers again. The many townsfolk then piled into local hostelries and drinking houses where a local reporter is recorded as seeing a rather drunk 'Charlie Chaplin' mascot, aka Richards, staggering home to Marsden just before midnight.

10 years of Huddersfield Town's history from 1920

1920-21 17th in Division 1	FA Cup third round
1921-22 14th in Division 1	**FA Cup Winners**
	FA Charity Shield Winners
1922-23 3rd in Division 1	**Norfolk and Norwich Hospital Cup Winners**
	FA Cup third round
1923-24 Champions Division 1	Central League runners-up
	Huddersfield Hospital Cup Winners
	FA Cup third round
1924-25 Champions Division 1	**Central League Champions**
	FA Cup first round
1925-26 Champions Division 1	**Central League Champions**
	FA Cup fourth round
1926-27 2nd in Division 1 (**runners-up**)	FA Cup third round
1927-28 2nd in Division 1 (**runners-up**)	**FA Cup Finalist**
1928-29 16th in Division 1	FA Cup semi-finalist
1929-30 10th in Division 1	**FA Cup Finalist**
	West Riding Senior Cup Winners

Town's 'Depression' - Chapter 5

Having had such amazing football success in the 1920s Town struggled in the 1930s to recapture anything remotely like that of our previous decade. In fact just like the country did as a whole, in footballing terms, Town sank into a mild football depression. (If not winning a title or a cup can indeed be called a depression).

Clem Stephenson led Town through this decade as our eighth Manager and in doing so became the longest serving. His league and cup exploits were fraught with irony given that Herbert Chapman who actually signed Clem to play at Town in the first place was the very man who stood, for much of this early part of the new decade, in Clem's way of gaining any kind of silverware. Clem led Town to second place in the First Division in their 1933-34 season, having lost the title to Arsenal by just three points, the very year that Herbert Chapman sadly passed away. Clem and Town reached two FA Cup Finals but sadly lost both, the first to a Herbert Chapman led Arsenal and the other to Preston North End in an exact reversal of the 1922 Final. Clem and Town also lost an FA Cup Semi-Final to Portsmouth the following year (Town have never reached an FA Cup Semi-Final since 1939 but have reached a Football League Cup Semi-Final in their 1967-68 season, ironically against none other than Arsenal).

Town's 1930-31 season was one of mixed fortunes with Alex Jackson signing for Chelsea during the season and Town beaten in the FA Cup, at the early stage of the third round, by our old West Yorkshire adversaries Leeds United. Joe Robson, who had signed from Grimsby Town in September 1930, and Dave Mangnall led our front line as Town finished fifth in the First Division. Joe was leading goalscorer in this season with eighteen goals in twenty-four appearances while Dave Mangnall scored nine goals in twelve appearances.

Town won 6-0 away against Manchester United in September with Alex Jackson and Bob Kelly both having scored hat-tricks that day. For Alex though this was his last ever game for Town in a blue and white shirt, having agreed the week after to transfer to Chelsea. Town then lost 6-1 away to Aston Villa in October and lost 5-3 away to Blackburn Rovers in November before Town recorded a record-breaking 10-1 win at Leeds Road over Blackpool on 13th December 1930. Every forward in the Town team that day scored, as Robson scored a hat-trick, and McLean scored four goals. The other three goals were each scored by Bob Kelly, Jimmy Smailes and Harry Davies. Town led 3-0 at half-time with a further seven goals scored in the second half with only one goal conceded in Blackpool's reply. George McLean meanwhile had just recently signed from Bradford Park Avenue and was at Town for four years as an inside-forward.

Given the state of our Leeds Road pitch, in our glory years in winter, one could only assume that the pitch at our old home on that fateful record-breaking day in December 1930 was like a quagmire and played in failing light by the end of the match. By the end of February, at Leeds Road this time, Town once again lost 6-1 against Aston Villa.

One saving grace in this season was that Town won the Central League Championship for the fourth time. In the process they scored almost 120 goals including a 7-1 defeat of Blackpool reserves (just a week after Town's first team had won 10-1). Dave Mangnall was the shooting star in the Central League for Town having scored over forty goals in just thirty appearances. Sadly though, it was also the last occasion in which Huddersfield Town won the Central League competition.

At the end of the season 1930-1931 with a final league placing of 5th it was one of;

Played 42 games; won 18, lost 12, drew 12, goals for 81, goals against 65, Points 48

The 1931-32 season saw Town once again, like they do and have done so for so many countless years since, lose form as the season reached its closing stages. Why this happens one may only make a guess or give an assumption from our terraces. They finished the season in fourth place while one player above everybody else shone through.

David Mangnall – 'Dave' was a central striker who signed for Town from Leeds United and scored a Club record of 42 goals in just 39 appearances in all competitions. With 33 league goals combined with his nine goals in the FA Cup, Mangnall's total of 42 goals to this day, gives him the individual record of most goals scored in one season that has never been equalled or beaten in our entire history. In Town's 2011-12 season Jordan Rhodes was the top goalscorer in England with 36 league goals breaking our Club record for the most league goals scored in a season (Jordan scored a total of 40 goals in all competitions that season but failed to equal or beat Mangnall's record of 42 goals). Perhaps if injury had not cut short his Town playing career in their 1932-33 season then his strike rate may have been even higher. He also scored forty goals in just thirty central league appearances to help Town win the Central League Championship in their 1930-31 season. In 1934 Mangnall joined Birmingham City after failing to overcome his injuries at Town. (Sadly, David Mangnall passed away in April 1962 aged 56).

One match Mangnall didn't score in was in an historical sixth round FA Cup match. On 27th February 1932 Herbert Chapman's Arsenal team played Town at Leeds Road in front of an official record-breaking crowd of 67,037. The crowd was so vast in its numbers that at times during the game they had to be forced back, by the police and others, in order that corner kicks could be taken. The East Terrace was so tightly packed that folks were unable to move and many fainted as some were crushed against the barriers. About one hundred casualties was passed over the heads of Town fans down the terracing to the pitch perimeter and removed to the player's gymnasium. Large numbers of fans were allowed over the rails and sat on the cinder track while hundreds more were moved in front of the paddock. Besides the 67,037 official paying fans it's rumoured that at least 5,000 non-paying fans stormed an exit gate at the back of the East Terrace. Thousands more fans, after finding the gates locked, made their way to watch the match from the nearby hillside. Rare and unique footage of this match can be found recorded on Cine by British Movietone News who had the sole rights having paid the princely sum of £10 for the privilege to film this game. Unfortunately after only two minutes Town were 1-0 down to Arsenal and that was sadly the final score. The result meant Town had lost a proud unbeaten record in the FA Cup stretching back to 1913 which stood at 26 unbeaten home cup ties with 25 won while the other ended in a draw.

Hugh Turner our goalkeeper, sustained an injury at Goodison Park in a league match on 19th March 1932 and so ended a club record of 181 consecutive appearances which had stretched back almost four seasons. A record which stood for over fifty years until surpassed by Malcolm Brown in Town's 1981-82 season. Alf Young had started to make his mark as centre-half in this season after taking the impressive Thomas Wilson's place in the team, and it wasn't long before his name was mentioned for the England team.

On 7th May 1932, Town's final match of the season was away against Aston Villa, It was also Bob Kelly's final Town appearance. His £6,500 transfer from Burnley to Sunderland had broken the British football transfer record in 1925. Bob went on to play a total of 186 league games during which time he scored 39 league goals and also appeared for the England team while still with Town. (Sadly, Robert Kelly passed away in September 1969 aged 75).

At the end of the season 1931-32 with a final league placing of 4th it was one of;

Played 42 games; won 19, lost 13, drew 10, goals for 80, goals against 63, Points 48

A rare photograph (below) dated 29th May 1932 shows our Town team on tour in Denmark. The photo was taken before they played their final game against local side Aalborg Byhold. Town won the match 7-1 with goals from McLean (3), Mangnall, Kelly, Bott and Mountford.

Digital image left **a19** – Courtesy of Roger Pashby, The Huddersfield Town Collection, with kind permission to replicate his original photograph.

For most of the 1932-33 season Town struggled, to score goals, due to an injury to Dave Mangnall that kept him out of the starting line-up for all but three matches of this season. No less than six different players tried to fill the gap for the number nine shirt. As a replacement for Bob Kelly Town signed, what they considered to be an established international player from Leicester City, Ernie Hine. His stay at Town lasted from the start of the season until they played and lost to Blackpool in the FA Cup fourth round in January 1933. This surmounted to a total of 25 games with a return of just four goals. While Town had problems up front, thankfully they didn't have the same problems with their half-back line. In fact with Alf Young and Austen Campbell now well established there was another name to add to the list Ken Willingham a right-half who quickly established himself in the first team.

Charles Kenneth Willingham – 'Ken' was a member of the ground staff at Leeds Road before he signed professionally for Town in 1930. He spent most of his football career at Town and figured in the 1938 FA Cup Final team line-up (which co-incidentally was the first FA Cup Final to be broadcast live on British Television). Ken won international honours with England while still at Town. After WWII in 1947, after a seventeen-year career with Town, Ken signed for Sunderland. (Sadly, Charles Kenneth Willingham passed away in 1975 aged 62).

Another unique record was set that sadly resonates with all Town fans from our 1978-79 season*. The record that was set in 1933 was for the lowest ever recorded attendance for a First Division League match. Just 2,218 fans turned up at Leeds Road for the Sheffield United match that took place on Wednesday afternoon on 1st February. Meanwhile, our old home at Leeds Road had a slight change to it given that a Boys Enclosure had now been erected in the North-West Corner (between the Main Stand and our 'Cowshed').

At the end of the season 1932-33 with a final league placing of 6th it was one of;

Played 42 games; won 18, lost 13, drew 11, goals for 66, goals against 53, Points 47

*After four seasons battling in the Fourth Division Monday 30th April 1979 is now etched into Town's history as the day that only 1,624 Town fans bravely fought the severe weather conditions and attended a Football League match at Leeds Road against Torquay United. It was a re-arranged match which was originally scheduled to have been played on Saturday 30th December 1978. Officially it's now the lowest ever recorded attendance for a Football League match played at Leeds Road.

For the 1933-34 season, given Town's previous glorious history in the First Division, they were regarded as one of the strongest teams in the division. So having finished second as runners-up to Arsenal, by three points, with Town seven points clear of Tottenham in third place it was deemed by many as a better season altogether. In fact, it was the highest league placing Huddersfield Town had in this decade.

Five Town players; Wilf Bott (13 goals), Charlie Luke (17 goals), Dave Mangnall (10 goals), George McLean (18 goals) and Jack Smith (15 goals) all scored ten goals or more during the season and helped Town become the top goalscorers in the division with a total of 90 goals. Dave Mangnall left mid-season after he had scored 10 goals in 16 games to move to Birmingham and his replacement Jack Smith made an immediate impact with 15 goals. For George McLean this was his last season with Town. Both Mangnall and McLean left our club due to a succession of football related injuries.

Our back line was impressive this season, but the forward line had to have a few changes. Wilf Bott signed previously from Doncaster Rovers took over from the ageing legendary Billy Smith. Wilf Bott and Charlie Luke both had the speed on the left wing that helped Town's front line as Smith reverted back to where he had first played on the right wing in the 1914-15 season.

In the fourth round of the FA Cup Huddersfield Town were knocked out by Third Division Northampton Town. A true David and Goliath moment for them as 28,423 fans saw Northampton win 2-0 at Leeds Road. Far from being outplayed in the cup, Northampton Town was reported as worthy winners.

Had they not lost either of their home or away games to Arsenal this season then it may well have been possible that Town might have won the First Division title once again. Only a 1-0 Leeds Road defeat on 25th November 1933, and a 3-1 away defeat at Highbury on 7th April 1934, stopped them from being champions once again as Arsenal went on to claim their second successive title.

A special moment occurred, on 10th February 1934 at Sheffield United's ground, for the legendary Billy Smith when he scored his final two goals in his last ever appearance in a Town shirt. The match was watched by a crowd of 19,988 who all saw Town beat 'The Blades' 4 -1. A Town career which had begun 20 years earlier in which he was highly regarded by his fellow professionals and the Football League. So much so that during the season, the President of the Football League, John McKenna paid a visit to our old home at Leeds Road and made a presentation to Billy Smith. He was awarded the League's Long Service Medal on 11th November 1933. Quite apt and very fitting for a real club servant who played a total of 574 games that leaves him unchallenged as the record holder for the highest total of Town appearances.
Billy Smith had his moments in football though, with one such occasion in early April 1920, when Town played an Easter fixture at Stoke. Billy having brawled with a Stoke City player it ended up with both players getting sent off and the ensuing football ban cost Smith to miss the 1920 FA Cup Final. Such was the quality and depth of feeling in our Town side for Billy that Ernie Islip, who had replaced him, offered his finalist medal as consolation. Billy kindly refused to accept Ernie's generous offer.

At the end of the season 1933-34 with a final league placing of 2nd (runners up) it was one of;

Played 42 games; won 23, lost 9, drew 10, goals for 90, goals against 61, Points 56

The time had come for change for Town in their 1934-35 season as Clem signed a number of players who made their first team debut. Many fans thought that they were finally going to claim back their First Division title from Arsenal and prevent them from becoming the second 'Thrice Champions'.

John Thomas Ball – was a forward signed from Manchester United. He played five games and scored one goal before he departed from Town, for some unknown reason, just one month later. (Sadly, John Thomas Ball passed away in 1976 aged 68).

Alfred Peter Lythgoe – 'Alf' was signed from Stockport County as a forward and fared better than John Ball. Alf went on to play for Town for four years until 1938 during which time he scored 46 goals in just 79 appearances. (Sadly, Alfred Peter Lythgoe passed away in 1967 aged 60).

George Russell Anderson – was a forward signed from Bury. He played 14 games, during which time he scored four goals, before he signed for Mansfield Town at the end of the season. (Sadly, George Russell Anderson passed away in 1974 aged 70).

James Robert Richardson – 'Jimmy' was another forward who transferred to Town in October 1934 from Newcastle United. He made 125 appearances, during which time he scored 32 goals, before he transferred back to Newcastle United in October 1938. (Sadly, James Robert Richardson passed away in 1964 aged 53).

Albert Malam – was a midfielder signed from Chesterfield but had left by the end of the season due to a serious leg injury. (Sadly, Albert Malam passed away in 1992 aged 79).

John Renton 'Jock' Wightman – was a wing-half signed from Bradford Park Avenue. Having made 67 appearances he then signed for Blackburn Rovers in 1937. (Sadly, John Renton Wightman passed away in 1964 aged 51).

Thomas Lang – 'Tommy' was a forward signed from Newcastle United. After just 26 games for Town he signed for Manchester United in 1935.

William Edward Hayes – 'Bill' came to Leeds Road as a right-back just before the start of the 1932-33 season and was with Town until the 1949-50 season. During the war years he played for Cork and made his First Division first team debut against Derby County at Leeds Road in August 1934. It wasn't until the 1937-38 season that he became Town's regular right-back. By October 1937 he had gained his first international cap playing for Ireland against England at Windsor Park, Belfast. Bill was a fearless tackler and could hit a ball as hard as the best and was Town's penalty expert for a time. By February 1950 he had signed for Burnley. (Sadly, William Edward Hayes passed away in 1987 aged 71).

Robert Taylor Hesford – 'Bob' made his debut as our goalkeeper in this season and went onto play for Town from 1933 until 1948. He made a total of 220 appearances both before and after WWII. (Sadly Robert Taylor Hesford passed away in June 1982 aged 66).

Town started the season of 1934 with only one win after the first eight matches. Injury problems played a major role in this season along with team performances that were inconsistent given the new personnel. A 5-0 defeat away to Portsmouth and an 8-0 home win against Liverpool at Leeds Road in November set the tone for the rest of the season. In the FA Cup Town lost a third round replay 3-2 against Portsmouth at Leeds Road. It was the third defeat at Leeds Road in the FA Cup in the last four years. By the end of the season Arsenal had become only the second team in history, after Town, to have won the First Division three times in a row.

At the end of the season 1934-35 with a final league placing of 16th it was one of;

Played 42 games; won 14, lost 18, drew 10, goals for 76, goals against 71, Points 38

By the start of the 1935-36 season having spent the previous year rebuilding the playing side Town found themselves in a better position to start the season with one signing of note.

Leonard George Butt – 'Len' was signed from Macclesfield as an inside-forward on the opening day of the season. He made 70 appearances, during which time he scored 11 goals, before he left in 1937 having signed for Blackburn Rovers. (Sadly, Leonard George Butt passed away in 1994 aged 83).

The season was a marked improvement in that for the first nine games of the season Town were unbeaten until early October when they lost against Middlesbrough. Their lowest league standing was a lowly fourth position. Once again an injury to a key player, Alf Lythgoe in the final three months of the season, hampered any chance of a higher league placing. Even with an injury Alf was still Town's leading goalscorer with 15 goals. It didn't help Town's cause when Charlie Luke transferred to Sheffield Wednesday during the season and nine players appeared in the wing-forward position at various times of the season. Town lost 1-0 away, in the fourth round of the FA Cup, to Tottenham Hotspur.

At the end of the season 1935-36 with a final league placing of 3rd it was one of;

Played 42 games; won 18, lost 12, drew 12, goals for 59, goals against 56, Points 48

Town's 1936-37 season was as remarkable, as it was historical, in that they played all season and failed to win a single away match. In fact the true extent of their run went from 1st February 1936 until 25th September 1937 a total of 32 matches. So, given that dismal run it's hardly surprising Town struggled to finish in the top half of the First Division.
In October *Albert Pat Beasley* a left-winger signed from Arsenal. He spent three seasons with Town during which time he played 108 league games. He won his one and only England cap In 1939 against Scotland, while still a Town player, before WWII had started and later signed for Fulham. (Sadly, Albert Beasley passed away in 1986 aged 72).

Just before Christmas *William MacFadyen* signed for Town from Motherwell. 'Willie' played 54 games during which time he scored 19 goals before he left just before the start of WWII. (Sadly, William MacFadyen passed away in January 1971 aged 66).

Town's away form was so poor that by the time they had played newly promoted Brentford in the FA Cup third round in January 1937 it came as no surprise that they lost the game. The real shock for Town fans though was the heavy 5-0 defeat, at that time, a record cup reversal. In March, just before deadline day, Town signed Robert Barclay and Edmond Boot, both from Sheffield United for a combined fee.

Robert Barclay – 'Bobby' was a forward who featured for Town at Wembley in their 1938 FA Cup Final. After WWII had ended in 1946 he was released by Town having scored 19 league goals from 74 league appearances. He returned to Town in 1947 as Assistant Trainer to Jack Martin. (Sadly, Bobby Barclay passed away in 1969 aged 62).

Edmund Boot – 'Eddie' was a left-half who made his first-team debut against Portsmouth at Leeds Road. He was captain in Town's post-war period and played 305 league games before he retired after the Fulham match in April 1952. He then assisted at Town and was appointed as Player-Coach before he went on to become Chief Coach before finally becoming Manager after Bill Shankly had left. (Sadly, Edmund Boot passed away in 1999 aged approximately 84).

At the end of the season 1936-37 with a final league placing of 15th it was one of;

Played 42 games; won 12, lost 15, drew 15, goals for 62, goals against 64, Points 39

In a season when Town first won promotion to the First Division and also appeared in a FA Cup Final in 1919, their 1937-38 season was a season that similarly confounded the footballing world. Given that Town faced a nerve-racking fight to retain their First Division status while they also appeared in an FA Cup Final for the fifth time since the war. (It was also the last time that Town got to an FA Cup Final while at Leeds Road).

In the FA Cup, Town beat Hull City 3-1 at home and was then drawn against Notts County in the fourth round at Leeds Road. Having won 1-0, Town were then faced with Liverpool away in the following round. A 1-0 win in front of a crowd of 57,682 saw Town go through to the sixth round. Then having drawn York City away, 28,123 witnessed a 0-0 draw. The replay just four days later was watched by 58,066 fans who all saw Town beat York City 2-1 at Leeds Road. Over at Ewood Park, in the Semi-Final Town faced Sunderland who were not just recent First Division champions but also the current holders of the FA Cup. In front of 47,904 fans Town beat Sunderland 3-1. For the first time ever the FA Cup Final was played at Wembley Stadium. It was settled by a dubious penalty given for a foul by Alf Young in extra time. Preston North End scored the spot-kick and ultimately won the FA Cup.

Just 48 hours after the FA Cup Final, Town beat Stoke City 3-0 which meant that for the final match of the season to preserve their status in the First Division they had to win against Manchester City at Leeds Road. Of all the sides at the foot of the table, Town and Manchester City were the only teams to play each other. Thankfully a Bobby Barclay goal gave them both points and thereby condemned Manchester City to relegation. The decline of City in this season was more spectacular than our own demise in the 1970s, given that just twelve months before Manchester City had been crowned Champions of the First Division.

Digital image left **a20** – Courtesy of Roger Pashby, The Huddersfield Town Collection, with kind permission to replicate his original photograph from our 1937-38 season.

The photograph was taken in the grounds of Town's 1938 FA Cup Final Hotel on the eve of the match. From left to right they are; Pat Beasley, Jimmy Isaac, Bobby Barclay, Edwin Watson, George Wienand, Bill Hayes, Alf Young, Eddie Boot, Benny Craig, Reg Mountford, Jack Chaplin (trainer), Ken Willingham, Bob Hesford, Town Director, Clem Stephenson (Manager), Town Director.

Albert James William Price – 'Billy' was a centre forward who started his professional football career with Town on Easter Monday in 1938. His career was sadly halted by the start of WWII but Billy continued to play for Town in local regional football during the war. Against Crewe on 23rd October 1943 a young Jimmy Glazzard scored Town's first goal while Billy scored another seven goals to make the final score line 8-0. This gave him the unofficial record of the highest goalscorer in a single senior game for Town at Leeds Road. After the war had ended he signed for Reading in 1947. (Sadly, Albert James William Price passed away in 1995 aged approximately 78).

At the end of the season 1937-38 with a final league placing of 15th it was one of;

Played 42 games; won 17, lost 20, drew 5, goals for 55, goals against 68, Points 39

By the summer of 1938 the perimeter track around our old pitch at Leeds Road was raised up and trolley buses had replaced trams for any Town fan who travelled to our old home at Leeds Road.

Just like in previous seasons the 1938-39 season saw some players play for the very last time. For one particular player, 'Harry' Baird a forward who signed in September, it was his first and last ever season with Town. (Sadly Henry C. Baird passed away in May 1973 aged 59).

Town started the season badly while the FA Cup third round against Nottingham Forest at Leeds Road ended goalless. Thankfully they won the replay 3-0 and were faced with our old adversaries, Leeds United away, in the next round. Billy Price claimed a hat-trick to seal a memorable 4-2 win for Town. He followed this up with two more goals in a 3-0 win against Walsall in the next round. The sixth round at Leeds Road against Blackburn Rovers ended in a 1-1 draw before Town beat them 2-1 at their place. The Semi-Final against Portsmouth at Highbury started well for Town as they went into 1-0 lead before 'Pompey' ran out 2-1 winners. By the end of the season the likes of Bobby Barclay, Pat Beasley, Reg Mountford, Ken Willingham and Alf Young had sadly pulled on our club colours for the last time.

At the end of the season 1938-39 with a final league placing of 19th it was one of;

Played 42 games; won 12, lost 19, drew 11, goals for 58, goals against 64, Points 35

By the end of August 1939 it became obvious that the war with Germany, and their allies, couldn't be avoided. As the opening league matches had started with the threat of an outbreak of war, the season carried on until 2nd September 1939 when Prime Minister Neville Chamberlain made his announcement to the country on 3rd September 1939 that we were at war. World War Two had sadly started. In 1914 there was no cancellation of any fixture and the season carried on until the end. This time there was an immediate cancellation of all football league fixtures. Town resumed football on a limited regional basis after being placed in the North Eastern League. As a point of historical interest and one worthy of a special mention after World War Two had ended only Billy Price remained of the eleven who appeared for Town against Brentford in 1939. He had scored in the last ever game played by Town before the war and also scored their first goal, post-war, when he equalised in an FA Cup match on 5th January 1946 against Sheffield United.

10 years of Huddersfield Town's history from 1930

1930-31 5th in Division 1 — FA Cup 3rd round
Central League Champions

1931-32 4th in Division 1 — FA Cup 6th round

1932-33 6th in Division 1 — FA Cup 4th round

1933-34 2nd in Division 1 — FA Cup 4th round

1934-35 16th in Division 1 — FA Cup 3rd round

1935-36 3rd in Division 1 — FA Cup 4th round

1936-37 15th in Division 1 — FA Cup 3rd round

1937-38 15th in Division 1 — **FA Cup Finalist**

1938-39 19th in Division 1 — FA Cup semi-finalist

1939-40 17th in Division 1 (Abandoned) 1st in North East Division

No league football played 1939-1946 due to World War II

Town's 'War Years' – Chapter 6

During the war years of 1939 to 1946 various local war-time football competitions kept football in existence in our old home at Leeds Road. Sadly, Robert Henry Gordon a Leading Aircraftman with Nine Squadron, RAF Volunteer Reserve tragically became the first casualty of World War Two for Huddersfield Town. He tragically died on September 18th 1940 from wounds received while serving with the Royal Air Force. He had only joined Town four years previously, from Shankhouse Northumberland, and on the numerous occasions he appeared with the first team Robert showed himself to be a player of unusual accomplishments.

Given the vastly different era, just 74 years later, in 2020 and in extremely different circumstances to WWII the (Covid-19) pandemic wasn't something that could easily be seen, if at all, but it still nonetheless brought the world to a halt and with-it untold deaths, misery and devastating consequences for everyone. The world as we knew it had changed, and with the changes it brought, while we attempted to safeguard ourselves and protect the NHS by staying home all major sporting events, including football, was banned at the height of the pandemic. Given the unprecedented times we were in no-one could say or predict when, or if football normality as we once knew it would resume, much less what changes had to be made to allow any sporting activity to take place which involved any form of social gathering.

In 1946 as football started to resume with some form of normality, David Steele now newly installed as Town Manager, had a major rebuilding job on his hands given that Eddie Boot, Bill Hayes, Bob Hesford and Billy Price were the only first team players who had reported back at Leeds Road after the war. It meant building a squad almost from scratch (Similar to the job Jacko had to do in our 2003-04 season) in rebuilding the team Town had 32 players appear in their mighty blue and white shirt. Three of the players who appeared this season went on to become legends. The first was a real master-stroke signing as Town captured the signature of one Peter Doherty.

Peter Dermot Doherty – was an inside-left who was one of the top players of his time, having won a league title with Manchester City and having played and scored in an FA Cup Final for Derby County, he signed for Town in December 1946. During his time at our Club he made 87 appearances and scored 36 goals in all competitions. Apparently in October 1947 in a league game against Liverpool at Leeds Road, as was the standard practise at the time, the referee left the match ball on the centre-spot at half time. When Town and Liverpool came back out onto the pitch for the second half Doherty waited in the centre circle for a pass from the kick-off when a whistle sounded. As Town kicked off Peter set off on a run through the Liverpool defence but was stopped by the referee who had only just emerged from the tunnel and had blown his own whistle to halt the game. (Sadly, Peter Dermot Doherty passed away in 1990 aged 76. There is now a blue plaque to mark his actual birthplace in Magherafelt County Londonderry and was inducted into the English Football Hall of Fame in 2002).

Two others who wrote themselves into our club's history in this season and became Town legends were Vic Metcalfe and Jimmy Glazzard.

Victor Metcalfe – 'Vic' was a winger who came to Town from Ravensthorpe Boys Club as an amateur in 1940. He played for Town in the Wartime League and after his service as a wireless operator in the RAF he signed professional forms with Town in December 1945. He was known for his pace and shooting power and for a long time was Town's regular penalty-taker. Along with Metcalfe, Town set a league record in 1952-53 season when their entire defence of Jack Wheeler, Ron Staniforth, Laurie Kelly, Bill McGarry, Don McEvoy and Len Quested played every league match.

Against strong opposition Vic Metcalfe won two caps for England against Portugal and Argentina in May 1951. In both matches his fellow Town player Harold Hassell played at inside-left. After 459 games during which Vic had scored 90 goals for Town he retired from professional football. (Sadly Victor Metcalfe passed away in 2003 aged 81).

Jim Glazzard – 'Jimmy' was a striker with the finest header of a ball any player has ever had on our old pitch at Leeds Road. He spent most of his playing career with Town after starting out as an amateur for Altofts Colliery in Normanton and had been on the books with Bolton. Due to the outbreak of war Jimmy, unable to sign for Bolton professionally, signed for Town as an amateur in October 1943. He played his first game for Town in the Wartime League, after WWII had ended, he resumed his playing career in 1946 and scored Town's first league goal of the 1946-47 season. He soon settled as centre-forward and his most memorable achievement in our old home at Leeds Road was in the 8-2 win over Everton in April 1953. 30,721 fans saw Jimmy score four headed goals from just four crosses from Vic Metcalfe. Glazzard was Town's top goalscorer on six different occasions and joint top goalscorer in the First Division with 29 goals in 1954. He then won the golden boot in 1955 as top goalscorer in the First Division with 32 goals.

Jimmy had his injury setbacks, which included three operations on his right knee for cartilage trouble. By 1st September 1956 after 13 years with Town, during which time he had made 321 appearances and scored 154 goals, he signed for Everton. Glazzard retired from professional football in the summer of 1957 aged 34 but continued to live in Huddersfield and ran a successful grocery business on Browning Road.

With Nat Lofthouse firmly placed as England centre-forward and with other competition from the likes of 'Jackie' Milburn, 'Stan' Mortensen and 'Ronnie' Allen it's no surprise that Glazzard's only England honour was a 'B' reserve international against West Germany in March 1954. In any other era and at any other time Glazzard and Metcalfe would, and should, have won more international honours. (Sadly, in later years Jim Glazzard suffered from Alzheimer's disease and passed away in 1995 aged 72).

The one and only 'full' international match that was played at Leeds Road was on Wednesday 27th November 1946 when England beat Holland 8-2. Leeds Road was held in high regard at the time by the Football Association given that some Semi-Finals had already been staged there. In 1955, it was designated as the Cup Final Replay venue had Manchester City and Newcastle not been able to settle the issue at Wembley. Some Dutch officials were upset at the choice of the chosen venue for the international match and their worst fears were not dispelled when the afternoon arrived. Huddersfield, on a wet, dismal, foggy November day, long before any 'clean-air' act produced its mini-miracle, was a foreboding place indeed as 32,000 fans made their way down to Leeds Road and watched on as England ran riot.

At the end of January until the middle of March 1947 due to five-foot snow drifts on the terracing in our old home at Leeds Road. Town played three league matches away from home along with two team trips one to Holland and one up to Greenock Morton. Those seemingly pointless trips may well have indeed given the Town squad a much-needed boost in order to avoid relegation. On 10th May 1947 against our old adversaries Leeds United a Peter Doherty penalty at Leeds Road won the match and secured both points that saved Town from relegation for another season. David Steele offered his resignation as Manager to our Town Board as the season ended, and it was duly accepted.

At the end of the season 1946-47 with a final league placing of 20th it was one of;

Played 42 games; won 13, lost 22, drew 7, goals for 53, goals against 79, Points 33

Clem Stephenson's brother George became Town's new Manager for the start of the 1947-48 season, but sadly even with a new manager safely installed they didn't fare any better in the league while George Hepplewhite made his presence known.

George Hepplewhite – was a no-nonsense centre-half who played for Town from 1946 until 1951 and made a total of 156 league appearances during which he scored three league goals. (Sadly, George Hepplewhite passed away in 1989 aged approximately 70).

In the league, last season's finish had to be improved upon in order to ensure that Town wouldn't suffer the humiliation of relegation. They made a good start with three wins in their first six matches including a 5-1 win against Grimsby Town in September. The following month, Town beat Bolton Wanderers 5-1 away. At one point, in early March 1948, they sat next to bottom in the table. Thankfully by the end of the season they had managed to pull themselves up from the depths of the league.

Having had some football success in reaching previous FA Cup finals in both the 1920s and 1930s not to mention actually winning the cup in their 1921-22 season. This season should be remembered for the precise opposite. In the FA Cup third round on 10th January 1948 away to Colchester United in front of 17,000 fans Town were catastrophically defeated 1-0 by a non-league side that played their football in the Southern League. To this day, in FA Cup history, it is still one of the most high-profile giant-killings. Having looked at the Town team on the day we played Colchester United I am still puzzled as author of this book as to how our players, who took to the field, actually lost.

Goalkeeper
Bob Hesford
Defence
Eddie Boot, Jeff Barker, Bill Hayes, George Hepplewhite, Les Smith
Midfield
Albert Bateman, Vic Metcalfe, Conway Smith
Forward
Peter Doherty, Jimmy Glazzard, Alf Whittingham

Sadly in February 1948, during a league match against Sunderland at Roker Park keeper Bob Hesford suffered a broken ankle and was forced to retire after a football career with Town that began in May 1933. He had given sixteen years to Town through the war period and made 220 league and cup appearances. As understudy to Hugh Turner Bob became Town's regular keeper in the 1936-37 season and played in the 1938 FA Cup Final at Wembley and was considered by many to be a worthy successor to our first-rate goalkeepers such as Sandy Mutch, Ted Taylor and Hugh Turner. Although he did not win an England cap he did play representative football, including an FA side that met an all-British team, and was on standby duty for a Continental tour in 1939.

The following year in 1940 he served his country in a different capacity when he joined the Duke of Wellington's Regiment and had three and a half years with the famous Chindits in the Far East. He was demobilised in 1946 with the rank of captain and continued his professional football career with Town. After breaking his ankle and forced to retire he became a teacher at Stile Common Junior School in 1950. (Sadly, Robert Taylor Hesford passed away in 1982 aged 66).

At the end of the season 1947-48 with a final league placing of 19th it was one of;

Played 42 games; won 12, lost 18, drew 12, goals for 51, goals against 60, Points 36

The 1948-49 season is regarded by local townsfolk as the original 'Great Escape'. Having had season after season battling relegation after WWII this season was the closest Huddersfield Town actually got to being relegated to the Second Division. By the end of April 1949 Town sat bottom of the First Division with just two games left as the bottom four in the division were separated by just three points. Sheffield United lost their game in hand 3-2 against Manchester United in mid-week, as Town played Wolverhampton Wanderers at Leeds Road just 24 hours after the Sheffield result. The fact that Wolves had actually just returned from their Wembley FA Cup Final match against Leicester City the previous Saturday having won the cup only added to the pressure Town faced against them. With two goals from Arnold Rodgers and one each from Jonny McKenna and Karl Aage Hansen Town beat Wolves 4-0.

The result gave Town a much-needed boost for their final home match of the season against none other than Manchester City. The final home match at Leeds Road against City was watched by 27,507 fans. The City fans had turned out in their large numbers to see Frank Swift's final appearance as goalkeeper. Huddersfield Town had no other choice but to win the match, no matter what, to survive. It didn't help that elsewhere at half-time Middlesbrough and Preston were both winning and Sheffield United like Town were both drawing their matches.

In the second half, with the pressure mounting on our players, they won a corner. From Jonny McKenna's cross into the City penalty area Frank Swift went up to clear the ball, but it fell behind him into a crowd of players. Somehow the ball ended up in the back of the City net as the ref indicated a goal. Records state that Arnold Rodgers scored the vital goal but given the fact Town had actually scored what did it really matter. For the final ten minutes players and fans alike at Leeds Road waited nervously for the final whistle.

At the end of the match no Town fan dared leave the ground without knowing the results from the other matches that had taken place. Bearing in mind that in this season there was no transistor radios or mobile phones about to provide an instant football update. The announcement that came through the speakers at Leeds Road was 'Ladies and Gentlemen, I have good news for you Sheffield United have drawn their game with Newcastle United and Town therefore remain in the First Division'. Huddersfield Town had survived relegation, and in doing so had sent Preston North End and Sheffield United down to the Second Division.

By the end of the season a certain Harold Hassell had started his Town career off having played three league matches and scored one goal.

Harold Hassell – was a forward who started his Town career off in 1948, and by the following season had played a further eleven games and scored four goals. By the 1950-51 season he had firmly established himself in the first team having played 40 games and scored 18 goals. His natural footballing abilities didn't go unnoticed, and by the end of his first full season in football he was picked to play for England where he continued his left-sided Town partnership with Vic Metcalfe. Harold scored on his England debut against Scotland and went on to win a total of five England caps. As well as international honours Hassell also had a personal honour at club level to cherish against Preston in 1951 after standing in for our regular goalkeeper Jack Wheeler, he saved a penalty from one of football's all-time greats Sir Tom Finney.

By 1952, after Town were relegated for the first time ever, Harold was sold to Bolton Wanderers. His football career was sadly over by 1955 due to a serious knee injury he sustained at Bolton on New Year's Day, in a 5-2 defeat against Chelsea. (Sadly, Harold Hassell passed away in 2015 aged 85).

At the end of the season 1948-49 with a final league placing of 20th it was one of;

Played 42 games; won 12, lost 20, drew 10, goals for 40, goals against 69, Points 34

In July 1949 our old home at Leeds Road was visited by Royalty as Princess Elizabeth and the Duke were met by thousands of school children lining up to greet them.

The 1949-50 season began with only one win from the first ten matches played. It was a season when relegation was considered a distinct possibility. Coupled with a devastating fire that affected our old home at Leeds Road this year is remembered for the wrong reasons. A 7-1 defeat away to Wolves in late September, along with a 6-0 defeat in early November was two devastating results for Town. In the FA Cup third round, away against Sunderland, it ended in a shocking 6-0 defeat.

At 3.45 pm on 3rd April 1950 a fire was seen in the Boys Enclosure which was located, in the north-west corner of Town's ground, between the Main Stand and our old 'Cowshed'. With the strong wind it didn't take long for the Main Stand wooden seating and roof to catch fire. The whole roof of the Main Stand had virtually collapsed while water from the nearby River Colne was used to put out the now blazing fire. Two home matches against Derby County and Newcastle United which were scheduled to take place at Easter was quickly transferred to Leeds United's Elland Road ground. Ironically the game against Newcastle United, while the match was underway at Elland Road, a fire had started in their Main Stand which thankfully was quickly brought under control.

Digital image **a21** (left) – John O'Mahoney's photograph of our old home at Leeds Road from the Main Stand looking towards our old 'Cowshed'. The Boys Enclosure stood between the Main Stand and our old 'Cowshed'.

Photograph taken on 9th August 1993 – during the close season.

Through the many successes Huddersfield Town have historically achieved from 1910, from when they were first voted into the Football League in our old home at Leeds Road, right through to our present home at the John Smith's Stadium in our Premier League days, Town became a household name. Their name was used on various items ranging from a Grimsby Trawler, a range of bottled beers and even a steam locomotive which all bore the name 'Huddersfield Town'. The locomotive was a B17 class called 'Sandringham' a further 22 locomotives bore the team colours of other football clubs and was decorated down the side of them. The Engine 2853 'Huddersfield Town' was first built as B17/4 in April 1936 and then rebuilt as B17/6 in May 1954, both of which were used on the Great Eastern Line. Sadly, by January 1960 the locomotive was cut up and its nameplate given to Huddersfield Town and hung for 34 years in the foyer of our old home, at Leeds Road. It can now be found over the doorway of the Director's Boardroom at the John Smith's Stadium.

Digital image **a22** (left) – Taken on personal mobile phone of John O'Mahoney's at the John Smiths Stadium of the old engine 2853 'Huddersfield Town' nameplate.

In July 2014, at Huddersfield Railway Station, Town had a second train named after our famous Club. This time it was a class 66 diesel engine, which was first built in 2005, and run by GB Railfreight carrying the number 66738 with the name 'Huddersfield Town' on the side. The current diesel engine carries the blue and yellow livery of GB Railfreight and can be found at the depot on Roberts Road in Doncaster.

At the end of the season 1949-50 with a final league placing of 15th it was one of;

Played 42 games; won 14, lost 19, drew 9, goals for 52, goals against 73, Points 37

In 1949 the Northern Intermediate League was first established for 'under 19 years of age' players up to then Town had run a third team in the Yorkshire League. Since WWII the N.I.L had been the nursery for some Town players who went on to reach the heights of international football.
Both the Central and Northern Intermediate League teams were an integral part of Town's football structure at Leeds Road. After a number of years most clubs, including Town, was forced to produce young 'homegrown' players given that they weren't able to match any transfer fee paid by the now wealthier football clubs. In 1975 when Ian Greaves became Town Manager he set about forming a youth policy. Sadly, Town's youth team system was scrapped in the mid-70s so when Mick Buxton became Manager it was clearly evident that the Club did not have any money to buy players. This meant Mick had to try to attract young potential players while he competed against the richer clubs in football. Given by this time Town was a struggling Fourth Division team it took a number of years before the likes of Mark Lillis, Ian Measham, Julian Winter and Liam Robinson made their first team debut.
With finances now in the modern game, at such ridiculously high levels, it's even more critical Town have re-categorised themselves from a Category two system under the Elite Player Performance Plan to a Category four system. This means they can focus on the higher academy age groups which Town fans have seen in recent years the progression of Tommy Smith and Philip Billing. Both of whom had joined Town at a very young age and have since gone on to have a professional playing career elsewhere. More recently Town fans are now witnessing the progression of Lewis O'Brien's football career.

10 years of Huddersfield Town's history from 1940

No league football played 1939-1946 due to World War II

1940-41 11th in North Regional League

1942-42 11th in North Regional League 1st competition 6th in North Regional League 2nd competition

1942-43 5th in North Regional League 1st competition 8th in North Regional League 2nd competition

1943-44 6th in North Regional League 1st competition 32nd in North Regional League 2nd competition

1944-45 1st in North Regional League 1st competition 13th in North Regional League 2nd competition

1945-46 15th in North Regional League   FA Cup 3rd round

1946-47 20th in Division 1   FA Cup 3rd round

1947-48 19th in Division 1   FA Cup 3rd round

1948-49 20th in Division 1   FA Cup 4th round

1949-50 15th in Division 1   FA Cup 3rd round

Town's 'Fight In The Fifties' – Chapter 7

Having struggled to maintain their First Division status since the end of WWII in 1946 this new decade started as badly as the last one had ended. Town's league form in their 1950-51 season was to say the very least up and down as they won five out of their first seven league matches and were top of the First Division by the end of August. As is always the case though with a good start for Town they couldn't maintain it and by September had suffered three devastating away defeats. The first against Newcastle United in front of 34,031 fans at St James Park ended in a heavy 6-0 defeat. A week later, surprisingly, Town gained a credible 0-0 draw against them in front of 30,343 at Leeds Road. Three days later against Arsenal at Highbury in front of 54,200 fans they lost 6-2 with our goals coming from Vic Metcalfe and Albert Nightingale.

By far the worst result in this year was the 8-0 battering that Middlesbrough handed out to Town away at Ayesome Park at the end of September. It was the highest league defeat until that fateful day on Saturday 7th November 1987 when Town lost 10-1 against Manchester City at Maine Road.

During the season as our defence struggled they signed two of their best defenders, Laurie Kelly and Bill McGarry, while Don McEvoy was switched from centre-forward to centre-back. The defence now seemed like it was good enough to keep them in the First Division this season.

Laurence Kelly – 'Laurie' was a defender signed from Wolverhampton Wanderers who ended up covering the left-back position. He went onto make this position his own over the next six years and was a member of our defence that was ever-present in their 1952-53 season. In all he made 239 appearances, during which time he scored 2 goals, and also helped Town reach the quarter-final of the FA Cup. In Town's 1956–57 season it was the Club's policy to reduce the average age of the team and as such Kelly lost his place to the up-and-coming Ray Wilson. At the end of the season he left to play and manage at non-league club Nuneaton Borough, but had resigned his post by December 1958. (Sadly, Laurence Kelly passed away in 1972 aged 47).

William Harry McGarry – 'Bill' was a defender signed from Port Vale in March 1951 and went on to be one of George Stephenson's most inspired signings. In his first full season he was an ever-present in defence as Town suffered relegation for the very first time. He continued his ever-present record during the 1952-53 season and was joined by six other ever-present Town players. The following season still having not missed a game, since his signing three seasons earlier, McGarry's run in the side continued, and he remained Town's ever-present captain. England international honours followed in 1954 while he was still at Town and earned two caps in the 1954 World Cup Finals in Switzerland, he won his last two caps the year after. Only an injury in late March 1955, after 168 consecutive appearances, halted his Town career momentarily while he recovered from a broken cheekbone. After ten years solid service during which he made 381 appearances and had scored 26 goals Bill signed for Bournemouth in 1961 as their Player-Manager. (Sadly, after a long battle against illness, William Harry McGarry passed away in March 2005 aged 77).

Donald William McEvoy – 'Don' was initially a centre-forward when he signed for Town in 1947. Due to Jeff Taylor displacing him in the starting line-up Don was given a run-out as a centre-half. It was such a success that he replaced the ageing George Hepplewhite, until 1954 when he signed for Sheffield Wednesday. (Sadly, Donald William McEvoy passed away in October 2004 aged 75).

Not surprisingly with all the changes in the defensive line-up this season Town only won two league matches between December 1950 and mid-March 1951. Even with Harold Hassell up front and winning international honours alongside the ever-faithful Jimmy Glazzard they struggled to win games as Hassell finished as leading goalscorer with 18 goals. In the FA Cup Town recovered some of their pride by getting through to the fifth round, against Wolverhampton Wanderers, before they lost 2-0 away in front of a 52,708 Molineux crowd. In February 1951 Huddersfield Town signed young Ronald Simpson.

Ronald Simpson – 'Ron' began his football career with Town after he received his £10 signing on fee his terms were £7 during the playing season and £5 in the closed season. In 1952 Ron signed to go into the army, so fans had to wait until 1953 before he actually made his first team debut. Then in 1958 after 118 games Ron signed for Sheffield United. (Sadly, Ronald Simpson passed away in November 2010 aged 76).

By the middle of March, Town were near to the bottom of the First Division and only a five-match unbeaten run from the end of the month, in which they won four games and drew the other, enabled them to gain enough points to survive another season. It was during this unbeaten run that on 7th April 1951 at Leeds Road in front of Town's highest ever record league gate of 52,479 they beat Blackpool 2-1. As author of this book a few reasons I can surmise why it became the highest league attendance was that Blackpool were hoping for the Championship, and also the up-and-coming England v Scotland match was a week away with Town's newest international Harold Hassell about to make his England debut. Three of Hassell's international colleagues were also due to play for Blackpool; Sir Stanley Matthews, Stanley Mortensen and Bill Perry, while Allan Brown was a Scottish international forward. Additionally, it may well have been that Blackpool were also FA Cup Finalists as well as the fact they were undefeated in the league since Boxing Day 1950.

The last match of the season on 28th April 1951 was away at Old Trafford against Manchester United, given the fact Town was on a run of five unbeaten games, no one had a clue that by the end of the game a heavy 6-0 defeat was their fate in front of 25,560 fans.

At the end of the season 1950-51 with a final league placing of 19th it was one of;

Played 42 games; won 15, lost 21, drew 6, goals for 64, goals against 92, Points 36

For the very first time since 1910 when they became a Football League member, and after winning promotion from the Second Division, 1952 was the year that they were sadly relegated from the First Division. Since the war it had been hard on Huddersfield Town without them being able to reproduce anything like their glorious past, and so the fourth longest membership of the First Division was finally broken.
With George Stephenson still as Manager they started the season well enough with a 2-2 draw against Arsenal at Highbury. The next match at Leeds Road saw Manchester City get battered 5-1 with goals from Bill McGarry, Albert Nightingale (2), Harold Hassell and Jeff Taylor. The next half dozen matches, both home and away, for some unexplained reason ended in defeat leaving Town almost bottom of the First Division by the middle of September.
The visit of Wolverhampton Wanderers to Leeds Road on Saturday 29th September 1951 is now etched into Leeds Road history whether Town fans like it or not. 32,496 fans saw Huddersfield Town get battered 7-1 against Wolves that day. During the time of the Wolves defeat it were rumoured that dressing room unrest focused on Town's latest England international Harold Hassell. In the weeks that followed, with no change to how the season was going, Harold Hassell signed for Bolton Wanderers while both Willie Davie from Luton and Len Quested from Fulham signed for Town.

Wilfred Leonard Quested – 'Len' was a defender who signed from Fulham in November 1951. He converted to a wing-half and joined Bill McGarry and Don McEvoy in a half-back line and also earned himself a tour of South Africa with the English FA in 1957. After 236 games for Town, during which time he scored nine goals, Len emigrated to Australia. (Sadly, Wilfred Leonard Quested passed away in August 2012 in Queensland, Australia aged 87).

Albert Nightingale – was a forward who signed from Sheffield United in March 1948 in exchange for Graham Bailey, George Hutchinson and a nominal fee. After 127 appearances, during which time he scored 21 goals, Albert signed for Blackburn Rovers in 1951. (Sadly, Albert Nightingale passed away in February 2006 aged 82).

William Clarke Davie – 'Willie' was a forward who signed from Luton Town in December 1951. He made 118 appearances during which time he scored 16 goals. Willie stayed with Huddersfield Town until July 1957 when our new incoming Manager, none other than Bill Shankly, transferred him to Walsall. (Sadly, William Clarke Davie passed away in 1996 aged approximately 71).

By the end of December 1951, Huddersfield Town were rock bottom of the First Division. They stayed there until early April 1952 when a 2-0 home win over Preston North End lifted them up a place momentarily. George Stephenson had tendered his resignation shortly after they had beaten Manchester United 3-2 at Leeds Road. United were at the time attempting to win the First Division, but while there was an improvement in our league standing there weren't in our all-round performances. The next away game against Sunderland proved that, as Town was heavily beaten 7-1 in front of 34,640 fans at Roker Park. Miraculously they went undefeated for the next three league games giving fans some slight hope that they could perhaps avoid relegation. Having played their last match of the season down at Craven Cottage against Fulham a crowd of 21,295 fans watched Huddersfield Town not only lose 1-0, but ultimately relegated for the first time in their history.

At the end of the season 1951-52 with a final league placing of 21st (**relegated**) it was one of;

Played 42 games; won 10, lost 24, drew 8, goals for 49, goals against 82, Points 28

Digital image **a23** (left) – John O'Mahoney's photograph of our old home at Leeds Road from Kilner Bank (taken during our football/rugby season of 1993-94).

Although Leeds Road is always to be fondly remembered for our historical footballing past. It was also once the venue for the Rugby League Championship Final. When Wigan defeated Bradford Northern 13-6 on 10th May 1952 it was the first time ever a Rugby League match had taken place on Town's ground in their entire 44-year history. It would be another four decades before the next rugby match was to be played at Leeds Road. On 30th August 1992 Fartown, having been forced out of their ground with no fanfare or formal curtain call, moved into Leeds Road on a ground sharing basis.

Andrew Beattie having gratefully accepted the position of Manager, set about ensuring promotion back to the First Division at the first time of asking. Huddersfield Town gained promotion back to the First Division in 1953 and sustained their status until they were relegated in 1956. Beattie offered to resign that August, only to be persuaded to carry on as Town appointed Bill Shankly to assist him. The two were former teammates at Preston North End and had ironically faced Town in the 1938 FA Cup Final. As both Beattie and Shankly struggled to get Town promoted back to the First Division, Andy Beattie resigned his position which left Shankly in sole charge. (Sadly, Andrew Beattie passed away in September 1983 aged 70).

During the summer months of the 1952-53 season, Beattie made three crucial signings. First he signed Ron Staniforth, then he signed utility player Tommy Cavanagh from Stockport County, while inside-forward Jimmy Watson was signed from Motherwell to beef up Town's attack. Just three months after the arrival of Staniforth, a youngster from Langworth Boys Club in Mansfield also came to Leeds Road. From the very start his potential was clear to see by all who watched him, and just two years later he established himself in Town's side. This was the start of an illustrious football career for Ramon Wilson.

Ronald Staniforth – 'Ron' was a defender signed from Stockport County. He was a part of Town's defence that played every game in their 1952-53 season and played in the England side which famously lost 7-1 to Hungary. By July 1955 Ron Staniforth after 118 appearances, along with Roy Shiner, moved to Sheffield Wednesday in an exchange deal that brought Tony Conwell and Jackie Marriott to Town. (Sadly, Ronald Staniforth passed away in October 1988 aged 64).

Thomas Henry Cavanagh – 'Tommy' was a forward who signed from Stockport County. After 93 league games he signed for Doncaster Rovers in 1956. (In 2002 Thomas Henry Cavanagh was diagnosed with Alzheimer's disease and sadly passed away in March 2007 aged 78).

James Watson – 'Jimmy' was a forward who signed from Motherwell and made 140 league appearances during which time he scored 29 league goals. He also earned two Scottish caps between 1947 and 1953. By 1957 Jimmy had signed for Dunfermline Athletic (Sadly, James Watson passed away in April 1996 aged 72).

Town started the season of 1952-53 in great fashion, unbeaten in the first ten games, and was top of the Second Division by the end of September. By the end of November, they were in second place and for the remainder of the season chased Sheffield United down for the title. In the FA Cup they were eliminated in the fourth round by Blackpool. The match at Blackpool was played in a howling gale and with just seven minutes to go Garrett, the Blackpool full-back, took a massive kick at the ball while stood in Blackpool's half. Aided by the gale the ball flew towards the Town goal and with our keeper, Jack Wheeler, unable to keep the thunderous ball out it hit the back of the net with such force it nearly burst through it. That was enough to earn Blackpool a 1-0 victory.

What stood out in this season, apart from Vic Metcalfe and our ever-present defence in the league, was the fact we had two legends in Jimmy Glazzard up front and Vic Metcalfe at outside-left who between them both scored 46 league goals. For the final league game of the season Town took to the field against Plymouth Argyle. With promotion already assured, in front of 19,624 fans at Leeds Road they all saw Roy Shiner score a hat-trick in a 4-0 win. Shiner had only played due to an injury to Glazzard and was the only match that Jimmy had missed out of the entire season.

Roy Albert James Shiner – was a forward who started his football career with Town. He made his debut in a 2-1 defeat on Christmas Day 1950 against Wolverhampton Wanderers in front of a crowd of 24,952 at Leeds Road. Roy made a total of 21 league appearances, during which time he scored 6 goals, before he signed for Sheffield Wednesday along with Ron Staniforth. (Sadly, Roy Shiner passed away in 1988 aged approximately 64).

In the spring of 1953, the Huddersfield Hospitals Broadcasts Association was formed and provided match day commentary from our old home at Leeds Road to local hospitals. Their first live broadcast was a 1-0 Town win, thanks to a goal from Roy Shiner, over Leicester City. In 1963 a fire broke out in the boiler room which damaged the electrical wiring as well as the loudspeaker system and apparatus used to broadcast to the hospitals.

A total of only 15 players appeared for Town in all 42 league games. Given the settled team it is perhaps a reason why they only conceded 33 goals all season and ultimately had the best goal average in the entire division.

At the end of the season 1952-53 with a final league placing of 2nd **(promoted)** it was one of;

Played 42 games; won 24, lost 8, drew 10, goals for 84, goals against 33, Points 58

The start of Town's First Division 1953-54 season saw them go unbeaten in their first four matches. By the end of August they topped the division with a side that was relatively unchanged from the previous season. Midfielder Gerry Burrell was signed from Dundee while local born Kenneth Taylor made his first team debut this season.

Gerald Burrell – 'Gerry' was a midfielder who was signed in 1953 from Dundee and played for Town for three seasons. He made 59 league appearances, during which time he scored nine league goals before he left for Chesterfield in 1956. (Sadly, Gerald Burrell passed away in October 2014 aged 90).

Kenneth Taylor – 'Ken' was a defender who started his playing career with Town in 1953 and made 269 appearances and scored 14 goals. One particular match where Ken made his mark was in the 1956-57 season when pushed up as a forward he scored four goals against West Ham United. Then just three seasons later, in an FA Cup match, he was once again pushed forward to help Town earn a 1-1 draw before they won the replay 5-1. During his football career with Town in the summer of 1957 he earned his first cricket cap for Yorkshire. Ken had retired from football completely by 1967 and his retirement from cricket followed a year later. In later life he taught art in Norfolk before retiring completely.

Injuries in the 1953-54 season did not help the battle for the First Division title. Kelly, McEvoy, Davie, Watson and Quested were all at some point absent due to injury. The injury to Len Quested was by far the worst injury, and he was absent from the first team for virtually half a season. His injury, a broken leg came in an FA Cup third round match at West Ham United which Town lost 4-0. Thankfully the front partnership of Metcalfe and Glazzard continued where they had left off from last season and by the end of the season Glazzard had scored 29 goals while Metcalfe had scored 12 goals. Given that Town were playing football at the highest level again it wasn't surprising that McGarry, Staniforth, Watson and Quested was selected for various international matches. Andy Beattie was subject to an offer himself from the Scottish FA, that if Scotland qualified for the World Cup he was primed to take charge of the national side.

Town finished the season in third position having never been out of the top six all season. Some say that Vic Metcalfe having missed the last seven games of the season was a reason why Town failed to win the title for the first time in 28 years. Nonetheless, this was still the best finish to a season since World War Two. To date it's still the highest league position they have finished in the Football League, at either our old home at Leeds Road or at our John Smith's Stadium, since the war.

At the end of the season 1953-54 with a final league placing of 3rd it was one of;

Played 42 games; won 20, lost 11, drew 11, goals for 78, goals against 61, Points 51

For the 1954-55 season Town started off badly having lost their first three matches and found themselves bottom of the league towards the end of August. By December, they were up to fourth in the league but then a 15-match win-less run from December 11th 1954 until 12th April 1955 saw them drop right down the league.
Ken Taylor was a shining light in this season as he became a first team regular at centre-half as both Don McEvoy and Ron Staniforth had moved onto Sheffield Wednesday by the end of the season. For Ron Staniforth this season was particularly hard to take, given that he had been capped twice for England earlier in the season. During an FA Cup sixth round match at our old home at Leeds Road, and in the replay against Newcastle United away, Ron got the run around by a young Bobby Mitchell which ultimately saw his last ever appearance in a Town shirt.
The FA Cup match against Newcastle at our old home at Leeds Road was an all-ticket affair and was a near 55,000-capacity crowd sell-out. This was also the last time our old home at Leeds Road was filled to that level which involved Town in any football capacity.
Jimmy Glazzard meanwhile became the leading goalscorer for the First Division with 32 goals this season, 26 in the league and six in the FA Cup. This season was also sadly the last time that any Town player topped the charts for the First Division.

At the end of the season 1954-55 with a final league placing of 12th it was one of;

Played 42 games; won 14, lost 15, drew 13, goals for 63, goals against 68, Points 41

By the summer of 1955 with both McEvoy and Staniforth now transferred to Sheffield Wednesday our Directors decided to use some of the transfer money to change the appearance of our old home at Leeds Road. Money was spent on covering the East Terrace to allow fans to be able to stand in moderate comfort to watch future FA Cup Final replays and Semi-Finals. Unfortunately, they did not transpire instead they were left with an improved East Terrace that, until our last days in 1994, went untouched from our 1955 season.

Digital image **a24** – (left) Personal old photograph of John O'Mahoney's of our old home at Leeds Road showing the East Terrace. Original photo taken in our 1993-94 season.

Digital image **a25** – (left) Personal old photograph of John O'Mahoney's of our old home at Leeds Road showing the East Terrace roof framework. Original photograph taken in 1995.

Digital image **a26** – (left) Personal old photograph of John O'Mahoney's of the then McAlpine Stadium showing the Kilner Bank Stand being constructed. Original photograph taken in 1993.

Digital image **a27** – (left) Personal old photograph of John O'Mahoney's of the then McAlpine Stadium showing the Riverside Stand during construction. Original photograph taken in 1993.

Digital image **a28** – (left) Personal old photograph of John O'Mahoney's of the then McAlpine Stadium showing both the Riverside Stand and Kilner Bank Stand being constructed.
Original photograph taken in 1993.

For the 1955-56 season while they had improved their ground with the covering of the East Terrace it was evident that, not for the first time, they had failed to improve an ageing side by not recruiting younger players at an earlier stage. The first match of the season saw Town mark the occasion with a moments silence for the passing of Sir Amos Brook Hirst. As Dave Hickson's Town career began Glazzard by the end of the season had finished his and signed for Everton.

David Hickson – 'Dave' was a forward who signed for Town in 1955 from Aston Villa. The folklore tales of Hickson are that he was an aggressive player who had a shot like cannonball, which earned him the nickname 'cannonball kid'. He signed for Everton in 1957 from Town and retired from playing football in 1963. (Sadly, David Hickson passed away in July 1983 aged 83).

The changes that were made on the playing side for the 1955-56 season also included the first appearance of a certain full-back Ramon Wilson. To all Town fans he was simply 'Ray' Wilson who went on to become not just a legend at Town but also a World Cup winner in 1966 with England. A young John Coddington also made his first team debut in this season.

John William Coddington – was a centre-half who started his football career with Town in 1953 and made his first team debut in 1955 and carried out his National Service before signing as a full-time professional with Town in 1958. He made 332 league appearances during which time he scored 17 goals. He signed for Blackburn Rovers in 1967 and had retired from playing professional football altogether by 1971.

Ramon Wilson – 'Ray' is arguably the most successful and best-known player to have ever pulled on a Town shirt. As part of England's World Cup winning team he is immortalised as a member of the only Three Lions team to ever lift the greatest prize in football. Ray actually started his Town career as a left-half in our 1955-56 season. By the following season under Shankly's guidance he became a first team regular, as Town's left-back, gaining confidence and strength in his new role in our first team. He went onto win the first of his 63 caps for England in 1960 and won 30 caps while still at Town, and to this day he is still our most capped England player. By June 1964 Ray Wilson had signed for Everton for £25,000 pounds plus their player Mick Meagan.

Ray's last England appearance while at Town was against Argentina and still remains to this day the last player to be capped for England while on the books of Huddersfield Town. In 2000 after his historical achievement in 1966, along with others from the England team he was awarded an M.B.E. Sadly, Ray Wilson was diagnosed with Alzheimer's disease in 2004. In 2008, Wilson was inducted into the English Football Hall of Fame by a select committee of ex-footballers. (Sadly, in May 2018 Ramon Wilson passed away after suffering from Alzheimer's disease for 14 years aged 83).

a29 (below left)   **a30** (below right)

Digital image **a29 (**above left) – Kind permission granted by artist George Chilvers 'Colourised by George Chilvers' to replicate and display his fine artwork of 'Ray' Wilson in his Town shirt.
Digital image **a30** (above right) – Taken on personal mobile phone of John O'Mahoney's of Ray Wilson's autographed training boots, which was similarly worn during Town's 1962-63 season, and can be found at the John Smiths Stadium.

In November 1955, a certain Bill Shankly resigned his position as Workington Manager and took up the post of Assistant Manager here at Huddersfield Town, in order to work with his old friend Andy Beattie. Workington operated on a shoestring and Shankly had to do much of the administration work himself, which included answering the telephone and dealing with the mail by using an old typewriter to answer letters. In addition, he had the risky job of going to the bank each week to collect the payroll. One of his main problems was sharing the ground with the local Rugby League club which concerned Shankly in regard to the state of the pitch after every rugby match had finished. The situation led to numerous arguments with the Club's Board, which included some Rugby League men, whose interest in football took second place to rugby. Ultimately Shankly decided to leave Workington.

By Christmas of 1955, Town were bottom of the First Division and stayed there until the middle of February 1956, by which time, from mid-February until April they surprisingly put up a real battle and climbed up to 20th in the table. Town needed to win their last four games of the season in order to have any chance of survival. On 28th April 1956, with the last match of the season against Bolton Wanderers, Glazzard scored his 142nd goal for Town equalling George Brown's record league aggregate figures. Dave Hickson scored the other two Town goals that day in a 3-1 win, but it wasn't enough to stop them being relegated to the Second Division on goal average. Sadly, this was also the last match Jimmy Glazzard ever played for Town, and it was to be another fourteen seasons before Leeds Road saw First Division football again.

At the end of the season 1955-56 with a final league placing of 21st **(relegated)** it was one of;

Played 42 games; won 14, lost 21, drew 7, goals for 54, goals against 83, Points 35

Following relegation Town's 1956-57 season was memorable for quite a few reasons with some fondly thought of, and to this day still spoken about, amongst sections of our fans.

Andy Beattie's attempt to get Town back into the First Division, at the first time of asking, started well with a 3-2 away win over Liverpool at Anfield in front of a crowd of 49,344. For the next two months they moved slowly up and down the league table without hitting any real consistent form. By early November, with Town tenth in the league, Andy Beattie resigned his position and was replaced by Bill Shankly.

William Shankly – 'Bill' resigned his position at Workington in November 1955 to take up the post at Town of Assistant Manager. His initial role was as Reserve Team Coach and Shankly soon found himself in charge of several promising youngsters who graduated into the first team after they were relegated. One of those was Kevin McHale who had previously been given his first team debut at the tender young age of 16 years and 329 days old. On 5th November 1956, Shankly succeeded Beattie as Manager and by Christmas Eve had given a first team league debut to none other than Denis Law, who at the tender age of 16 years and 303 days old broke the record set by John Kevin McHale earlier in the year. Another real prospect in Shankly's team this year was left-back Ray Wilson who went on to become our most capped international player.

In November 1959, Shankly received an approach for his services from Liverpool and decided to think about the offer as he realised the great potential at Liverpool, who like Town, were in the Second Division at that time. Rumours began and were fuelled by Liverpool's visit to our old home at Leeds Road on 28 November 1959. Although Town won the game 1–0, Shankly accepted the Liverpool offer and resigned his position as Manager at a Board meeting on 1st December 1959. On the morning of 26 September 1981, Bill Shankly was admitted to Broadgreen Hospital following a heart attack. (Sadly, William Shankly passed away in September 1981 aged 68).

John Kevin McHale – was an outside-right and a very gifted youngster who made an impressive first team debut, against Leicester City, and actually scored Town's second goal in a 2-2 draw. He went on to become a true Town legend and made his partnership debut with Denis Law on Christmas Eve 1956, Kevin was virtually an ever-present in our team for the rest of the season. Town fans who witnessed their debut partnership against Notts County realised that they had seen something amazing. It was the third round FA Cup second replay against Sheffield United which was played at Maine Road, Manchester, with both McHale and Law turning in amazing performances, that no doubt first alerted the Manchester City scouts to Law's natural ability. McHale meanwhile went onto play 375 games for Town during which time he scored a total of 68 goals.

By 1968, Tom Johnston having transferred McHale to Crewe Alexander, then helped 'The Railwaymen' gain promotion to the Third Division before he retired from League Football in 1972. McHale is one of the most enduring figures of our football history at Leeds Road given that our fans affinity with McHale was not just down to his consistency, or his awe-inspiring relationship with Law. They had seen him grow and develop into a true terrace favourite.

Denis law - was described by Bill Shankly as 'The greatest footballer there had ever been'. Given his very young age and his physical size Denis was used sparingly in Town's 1956-57 season. The talk about Law had started in 1955 when he first played in a junior match at our old home at Leeds Road against Doncaster Rovers. For our young forward Brian Payne, it was a great match in that he actually scored ten goals that day. John Coddington also weighed in with a hat-trick, but for anyone who was present that day the talk and performance anyone spoke about was that of a tiny young boy. They were the very first fans in our old home at Leeds Road to have witnessed the emergence of a true football genius. Denis Law scored the other goal in the 14-0 win against Doncaster Rovers which lay claim that this was the highest win by any team at our old home at Leeds Road. Law was given his Leeds Road FA Cup debut in a fourth round match against non-league Peterborough United in January 1957. The crowd that day was over 48,500 with a third of the crowd coming from Peterborough. The whole country had got wind of the tie and was expecting some sort of giant killing act. Pathe News and the television cameras (for the very first time at Leeds Road) was present to witness a young lad whose Town shirt looked like it was actually drowning him take to the field and score the first of what was to become an all-time career record for the competition. Town won the cup match 3-1 with their other two goals coming from Dave Hickson and Ron Simpson. Sadly, Town lost 2-1 at Leeds Road in the FA Cup fifth round to Burnley.

After four years with Town in which he had played 91 games and scored 19 goals, Denis Law signed for Manchester City in 1960 for a transfer fee of £55,000, which set a new British record. Just as Denis had illuminated our Leeds Road pitch, he would do so long after he had left, as our Board bought Town's first ever floodlights with part of the transfer money. Law is still the only Scottish player to have ever won the Ballon d'Or award. Then having retired at the start of the 1974–75 season, in November 2005, Denis Law was at the bedside of his former United teammate George Best when he sadly died of multiple organ failure. In February 2010, Denis Law was named as patron of the UK based charity Football Aid, taking over from the late Sir Bobby Robson. In 2012, a statue to Law, commissioned by the Denis Law Legacy Trust, was unveiled at the entrance to Aberdeen Sports Village.

Denis was appointed Commander of the Order of the British Empire (CBE) in the 2016 New Year Honours for services to football and charity. In 2017, he received the Freedom of the City of Aberdeen. Not bad for a kid from Aberdeen that went barefoot until he was twelve years old. (Sadly, Denis Law is currently suffering with his health in 2021 due to the onset of Alzheimer's Disease).

Leslie Massie – 'Les' was a forward who started his Town career in 1956. He made 363 appearances during which time he scored 108 goals before signing for Darlington. He is still the fifth highest goalscorer after George Brown, Jimmy Glazzard, Billy Smith and Andy Booth. (Sadly, Leslie Massie passed away in November 2020 aged 85).

This season was one in which they spent it re-organising and changing the Club. It also marked the end of an era with the departure of Beattie and started a period in history where First Division football didn't appear again until the end of the 1969-70 season.

At the end of the season 1956-57 with a final league placing of 12th it was one of;

Played 42 games; won 18, lost 18, drew 6, goals for 68, goals against 74, Points 42

The 1957-58 season was sadly the last year Vic Metcalfe played for Town. It was the decision of the Town Board to do something about reducing the average age of the playing side. Ray Wilson meanwhile firmly established himself at left-back and over the following years went onto the world stage and became a true Town legend. This season was Shankly's first as Town Manager.
Town sat fourth in the Second Division in early September but by 21st December 1957 was down to eleventh in the league. Against Charlton Athletic at the Valley, in front of 12,535 fans, Town was involved in a league game which to this day still ranks as one of the most bizarre and most unusual score lines ever recorded. Charlton had been reduced to ten men for most of the match, and at one point trailed 5-1 to Town, the game then turned on its head in the last 27 minutes as they went on to win 7-6 having been inspired by Charlton's five-goal winger Johnny Summers. To this day it remains the only match in professional football where a visiting team scored six goals and still lost the game.

On 4th January 1958 Huddersfield Town played Charlton Athletic for the third time this season, this time it was in the FA Cup third round at Leeds Road and a certain Denis Law scored, but it wasn't enough to win the game as they drew 2-2 in front of a crowd of 20,223. In the replay four days later down at the Valley they lost 1-0 in front of a crowd of 26,637. The season finished with Huddersfield Town twelve points behind second placed Blackburn Rovers.

At the end of the season 1957-58 with a final league placing of 9th it was one of;

Played 42 games; won 14, lost 12, drew 16, goals for 63, goals against 66, Points 44

Digital image a31 (left) Courtesy of Roger Pashby, The Huddersfield Town Collection, with kind permission to replicate his original image.
The Town team on that fateful day Town lost 7-6 was;

Goalkeeper
Sandy Kennon

Defenders
Ray Wilson   Tony Conwell
Bill McGarry, Jack Conner, Ken Taylor

Forwards
Ron Simpson   Bob Ledger
Les Massie, Alex Bain,
Denis Law

a32 (left)

Digital image **a32** (above) Kind permission by artist George Chilvers 'Colourised by George Chilvers' to replicate and display his fine artwork of Charlton v Huddersfield Town at the Valley.

The 1958-59 season saw Huddersfield Town go from eighth in the league in August to a lowly position by the New Year of 1959. At one point relegation was thought about more than promotion. Ray Wood signed for Town from Manchester United just before Christmas 1958 as Derek Hawksworth signed in a player-exchange that saw Ron Simpson move to Sheffield United. Derek scored eleven goals this season while Stan Howard played up front as a striker and scored eight goals.

Raymond Ernest Wood – 'Ray' was a goalkeeper at Manchester United and was an England international by the time he had put pen to paper for Town in 1958. During the 1957 FA Cup Final against Aston Villa he was the victim of what was then a perfectly legal shoulder charge. In the sixth minute of the game Wood successfully claimed a cross however, Villa outside-left, Peter McParland clattered into him and broke Wood's jaw due to him ducking to avoid the challenge. Given that the game was played in an era before substitutes Jackie Blanchflower was forced to play in goal following the incident. Ray eventually came back on after treatment to play as a forward as United lost the game 2–1. His compensation was a Football League First Division title medal to add to the first medal he had gained a year earlier. He was among the survivors of the Munich air disaster on 6th February 1958 and suffered minor injuries but saw untold horrors. Having played just one first-team game after that tragic event he was later sold to Town where he spent seven seasons and played 207 first-team games before he left in 1965 to play in the Canadian Professional Soccer League. By 1968 Ray had retired from professional football altogether. (Sadly, Raymond Ernest Wood passed away in July 2002 aged 71).

Derek Marshall Hawksworth – was a winger who signed for Town in 1947 but never figured in the first team. Having re-signed from Sheffield United in 1958 he played 59 games during which time he scored 14 goals for Huddersfield Town before he signed for Lincoln City in 1959. (Sadly, Derek Marshall Hawksworth passed away in March 2021 aged 93).

Stanley Howard – was a striker who started his football career with Town in 1957. He played 64 games during which time he scored 13 goals. Having signed for Bradford City in 1960 he carried on playing professional football until 1965. (Sadly, Stanley Howard passed away in 2004 aged 70).

In the third round of the FA Cup Huddersfield Town lost 1-0 to Ipswich Town.

At the end of the season 1958-59 with a final league placing of 14th it was one of;

Played 42 games; won 16, lost 18, drew 8, goals for 62, goals against 55, Points 40

The 1959-60 season should be remembered for many reasons none more so than the fact Denis Law made his final appearance in this season and Bill Shankly managed Huddersfield Town for the final time. They started the season well having won five games from their first seven matches and by the middle of September were second in the league. In October, they played Portsmouth in a league game at Leeds Road in front of a crowd of 15,452 who all witnessed an extraordinary game. 'Pompey' scored three goals in quick succession and after only 15 minutes Huddersfield Town were 3-0 down. By half-time they had fought back to 3-2, but it took well into the second half before they managed to make the score 3-3. Just ten minutes remained, and they actually went ahead for the first time in the match as Kevin McHale scored the fourth goal. In the final ten minutes they scored another two goals, from Ken Taylor and Les Massie, which made the final score 6-3. To this day it is still the highest scoring match in which Huddersfield Town have ever played against Portsmouth.

In November 1959, with problems on the field for the forward line, Shankly discussed buying a Scottish international forward with the Board of Directors. They refused to finance the move and on 1st December 1959 Shankly announced his intention to leave Huddersfield Town and take over as Manager at Liverpool. Ex-Town player Eddie Boot agreed to take over, as Caretaker Manager, with his first match in charge they beat Bristol City 6-1. A few weeks later against West Ham United in an FA Cup match at Leeds Road they managed a 1-1 draw thanks to a Denis Law goal.

The replay a week later at Upton Park saw Town win 5-1. Some say it was because of the fact we played Jack Conner as a forward, others say it was from a tactical genius in that Eddie Boot made a footballing decision in the footwear they played in that day. He actually sent out the players in their training pumps and black and white socks. Whatever the reason, with the now inspired Denis Law they ran riot against them. Unfortunately they lost 1-0 in the next round of the FA Cup against Luton Town at Leeds Road.

By March 1960 Denis Law was on his way to Manchester City having just broken the British transfer record when they agreed a deal to buy a young 20-year-old Scottish lad who went on to conquer the footballing world. Given that since the Second World War Huddersfield Town had struggled financially to recover their First Division status and had seen their attendances drop in ten years from an average of just over 27,000 in 1950 to just over 14,000 in 1960. It was impossible to refuse the record offer from Manchester City. Town gave John Christopher Balderstone, a Huddersfield born 19-year-old from Paddock, Denis Law's position and boots to fill. As by way of some small offering of comfort the news was disclosed that Huddersfield Town, with part of the proceeds of the sale of Law, was to install floodlights for the start of the new season.

John Christopher Balderstone – 'Chris' was a midfielder who started his football career with Town in 1958 and played 131 games during which time he scored 25 goals. Having signed for Carlisle United in 1965 he was one of the last sportsmen to combine English Professional Football and Cricket. His cricketing career began in 1961 when he first appeared for Yorkshire while still a Town player. (Sadly, John Christopher Balderstone passed away suddenly at his home in Carlisle in March 2000 having suffered from a form of cancer aged 59).

Eddie Boot agreed to become Town Manager for the start of the new decade in football.

At the end of the season 1959-60 with a final league placing of 6th it was one of;

Played 42 games; won 19, lost 14, drew 9, goals for 73, goals against 52, Points 47

During the 1950s Huddersfield Town was the first ever football club in England to install an electric scoreboard. It was donated to Town by the Dutch football club P.S.V Eindhoven. Sadly, it was burnt down by an act of arson and was replaced with the one Town fans all knew and loved until our last ever days in our old home at Leeds Road in 1994.

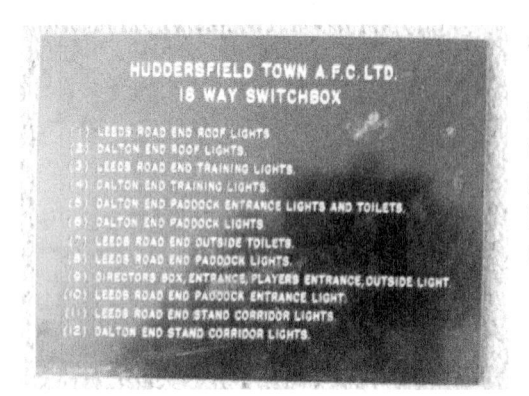

a33 (left)

Digital image **a33** kindly supplied by Peter May (Huddersfield Town fan) from his own personal collection of Huddersfield memorabilia. A genuine 18-way switch box/fuse box sign from Leeds Road which was bought by Peter at Town's official auction of Leeds Road memorabilia.

a34 (left)
Digital image **a34** - Personal old photograph of John O'Mahoney's showing the open end with our old scoreboard.
Original photo taken from the Main Stand in the close season of August 1993.

10 years of Huddersfield Town's history from 1950

1950-51 19th in Division 1 — FA Cup fifth round

1951-52 21st in Division 1 **(Relegated)** — FA Cup third round

1952-33 **2nd in Division 2 (Promoted)** — FA Cup fourth round

1953-54 3rd in Division 1 — FA Cup third round

1954-55 12th in Division 1 — FA Cup sixth round

1955-56 21st in Division 1 **(Relegated)** — FA Cup third round

1956-57 12th in Division 2 — FA Cup fifth round

1957-58 9th in Division 2 — FA Cup third round

1958-59 14th in Division 2 — FA Cup third round

1959-60 6th in Division 2 — FA Cup fourth round

Town's 'Swinging Sixties' - Chapter 8

The 1960-61 season was an historical one, for the Football League, given that it marked the first league and cup double 'domestic double' in the twentieth century won by Tottenham Hotspur. It was also the year when a new cup was to be played in British football, the Football League Cup. It wasn't well-received by some in football, given that many thought that the season was already overloaded, without an extra cup to be played for.

Following Denis Law's record-breaking transfer, to Manchester City, Town's strike force was seriously short of quality. Despite the purchase of Derek Stokes from our near-neighbours Bradford City and the arrival of James Ridley Kerray from Dunfermline.

Derek Stokes – was a striker signed from Bradford City in 1960 who scored on his home debut against Luton Town at Leeds Road in a 1-1 draw. He made 170 appearances, during which time he scored 69 goals, before he left at the end of the 1965-66 season. He had been our top goalscorer for four out of the five seasons he was a Town player. In the 1962-63 season he earned four England U23 caps and scored two goals before leaving for Bradford City in 1966.

James Ridley Kerray – 'Jim' was a striker signed from Dunfermline in 1960. He made 60 appearances for Town during which time he scored 13 goals. In February 1962 he was used in a player-exchange when Len White arrived from Newcastle United. By the start of the 1970 season Jim had retired from professional football altogether.

By October 1960 Town were faced with Aston Villa away in the second round of the newly formed League Cup. In front of 17,057 fans they lost 4-1 to 'The Villa' as John Milner scored our first ever League Cup goal. Town's average home attendance, at Leeds Road, was becoming something of a real concern at Boardroom level with the league match against Brighton in particular watched by just over 5,000 fans.

Patrick Saward – 'Pat' was signed as a defender to try to stop the number of goals Town had shipped in from their poor defensive play. From Boxing Day until the end of the season they kept only four clean sheets in the league. Saward played for Town until 1963 and appeared in 59 league games and scored one goal before he retired from professional football. (Sadly, Pat Saward passed away from Alzheimer's disease in September 2002 aged 74).

With Les Massie and Derek Stokes up front their combined 31 league goals helped Town to survive relegation by just two points. It also helped that they won 4-0, against Bristol Rovers at Leeds Road in their last league match of the season, thanks to two goals from Derek Stokes and one goal each from Mick O'Grady and Les Massie.

This season is probably best remembered for our exploits in the FA Cup third round. Town, bottom of Division Two at the time were given virtually no chance by anyone of beating the current holders, and Division One leaders at the time, Wolverhampton Wanderers. Somehow they managed to hang onto a 1-1 draw thanks to a goal scored by Derek Stokes. The replay on 11th January 1961 at Leeds Road was the first match in which they used the newly erected 'Denis Law' lights. A crowd of 46,155 saw them beat Wolves 2-1 with goals from Derek Stokes and Mick O'Grady. In an FA Cup fourth round replay Town sadly lost 1-0 to Barnsley.

At the end of the season 1960-61 with a final league placing of 20th it was one of;

Played 42 games; won 13, lost 20, drew 9, goals for 62, goals against 71, Points 35

Digital image **a35** (left) – John O'Mahoney's photograph of our old home at Leeds Road of the 'Cowshed' Floodlights.
Original photograph taken during our 1993-94 season.

Digital image **a36** (left) – John O'Mahoney's photograph of our old home at Leeds Road of the open-end floodlights.
Original photograph taken during our 1993-94 season.

The floodlights in the two digital images **a35** and **a36** was the second set of lights Town had installed at Leeds Road. The reason for the second set was that two of the original floodlight pylons had blown over during a gale in February 1962. The two pylons that came down were the ones located between the 'Cowshed' and the Main Stand and the open end and the East Terrace. The original floodlights were forty-four metres high and had cost around £23,000 to install.

In 1957 Jimmy Hill became Chairman of the Professional Footballers' Association (PFA) and campaigned to have the Football League's maximum wage scrapped. By January 1961, after threats from its members about striking, he had succeeded when his Fulham teammate Johnny Hayes became the first £100 a week player.

In Town's 1920s heydays all league clubs were able to compete financially in regard to paying relatively the same wages for all football players. So the need for a player to leave one club for another for monetary reasons was relatively low. By the 1970-71 season, after returning to the First Division, within 12 months of promotion Huddersfield Town saw how the financial side of football had affected things at Leeds Road. Over the years, and the many decades since, they have struggled to compete with other clubs and concentrated on astute meagre buying and also relied on producing their own players from their own ranks. The Bosman ruling of 1995, which gave a player the freedom to move without a transfer fee when their contract was up, only further strengthened a player's position.

The days of heavy transfer money dealing, in order to buy players, were over until they achieved promotion to the Premier League in 2017. Once in the Premier League and with its untold riches, to be able to compete on a level playing field with the rest of the league, Huddersfield Town had to increase the cost of their transfers and wages dramatically.

So the policy of buying astutely and relying on their youth had to change but even with their newfound riches, to attract and retain players, was still an almost impossible task for Huddersfield Town.

In today's modern world the balance of power has truly shifted towards the players. Pay levels within the higher reaches of the English game mean that certain individuals earn more in a week than any iconic player, from our World Cup winning team and their generation, have made in a lifetime. In fairness to a club like ours at Town, attracting and retaining players becomes harder and harder each passing season due to the riches that other clubs can afford to pay in comparison to Town. Sadly for a lot of Football League clubs now, in my opinion as author of this book, they are considered nothing more than a rich club's nursery with the cream of their talent persuaded to join the Premier League for vast financial gains. Most clubs simply can't afford to compete with them due to the lack of revenue they create annually.

By the time Town reached the Premier League in 2017 the issue of wages was a major factor in our ability to even consider signing a player. Perhaps in the not-too-distant future there may be a time when there is a happy medium for all parties concerned. Which will give every player, supporter and club the same level playing field because without the players there is no game, but it has to be said, that without football fans, where would the professional game be. Stuck in the middle are all the Football League clubs who are trying to achieve football success, and more importantly survival, balanced against financial restrictions imposed on them within the financial fair play ruling. While trying to attract a calibre of player that not only excites the supporter on the terrace but also adds real value to their club.

After thankfully just missing out on relegation, to the Third Division, Eddie Boot took his first full season in charge to try to raise Town up to the top half of the Second Division. They made a promising start with four wins from their first six games, including a 5–1 win against Plymouth Argyle and a 4–3 win against Luton Town. Derek Stokes had a great start to the season with nine goals from the first nine league games which included a hat-trick in a 4–2 win against Walsall. An indifferent spell in October and November saw Town lose ground in the league. During that time they played in the Football League Cup and won the first round replay at home against Carlisle United 3-0 after a 1-1 away draw in the first game. The League Cup second round saw Town knocked out of the cup having lost 3-2, against their old adversaries, Leeds United at Elland Road. In the FA Cup they won their third round home tie against Rotherham United 4-3 but sadly lost 2-1 to Aston Villa away in the fourth round. By the middle of January 1962 Town were below halfway in the league. In the following weeks Eddie Boot decided to strengthen our front-line with a player exchange. Leonard Roy White was a player signed from Newcastle United, in early February, who was previously known by Town fans from the 1954-55 season. Len had scored a last-minute equaliser for United in an FA Cup sixth round tie at Leeds Road and ultimately helped them win the replay.

Leonard Roy White – 'Len' was a forward who signed for Town and helped to prevent them from slipping into the Third Division. The following season he continued where he had left off and scored 13 league goals in 41 appearances which made him Town's second highest goalscorer of the season. By the time he left, after four seasons with Huddersfield Town, he had gone from being the villain in 1955 to hero in 1965 thanks to his consistent goalscoring which enabled Town to retain their Second Division status. (Sadly, Leonard Roy White passed away in June 1994 aged 64).

At the end of the season 1961-62 with a final league placing of 7th it was one of;

Played 42 games; won 16, lost 14, drew 12, goals for 67, goals against 59, Points 44

The Town team of 1962-63 season with two full England internationals, one U23 England international, one Republic of Ireland international and one ex-England international, must rank as one of the strongest international squads Town had in the sixties. An impressive start to the season saw them go unbeaten in their first 13 league games of the season, which saw them go top of the Second Division. Town's run was finally ended by a 3-2 home defeat against Southampton in October, as Michael O'Grady was called up for England and became Town's second England international in this month.

Michael O'Grady – 'Mick' was a midfielder who started his football career with Town in 1959. He played 174 games and scored 28 goals before he signed for Leeds United in 1965. Having earned two caps and scored three goals for England from 1962 until 1969 he had sadly retired from playing football completely by 1975 due to the effects of his injuries.

In September Town lost 3-1 away to Bradford Park Avenue in the Football League Cup second round and by December the worst winter for a hundred years had set in. It created a huge backlog of 300 FA Cup and league fixtures and caused an extension to the season until the end of May. It was early March 1963 before football resumed and once it did Town won 2-1 to Chelsea away at Stamford Bridge. Just two days later they were faced with having to play Manchester United away in the FA Cup third round, which had been postponed five times before, Town lost 5-0 in front of a crowd of 47,703 at Old Trafford. Due to the postponement of games they played six games in March but another nine games were still to be played in April. Even with the games that had already taken place there were another five games still to be played in May. The final match of the season against Cardiff City on 18th May resulted in a 3-0 defeat for Town this meant that they finished sixth just four points off Chelsea who took the second promotion spot for the First Division. The only ever-present Town player in this season was Peter Dinsdale.

At the end of the season 1962-63 with a final league placing of 6th it was one of;

Played 42 games; won 17, lost 11, drew 14, goals for 63, goals against 50, Points 48

For the 1963-64 season Town signed Kevin Lewis from Shankly's Liverpool for £20,000 pounds and teamed him up with both Len White and Derek Stokes. All three scored a total of 36 league goals for Town in this season.

Kevin Lewis – was a winger signed from Liverpool who having played 52 games, during which time he scored 15 goals, left in 1965 and signed for Wigan Athletic in the Cheshire League.

Many Town fans who thought that last season's performance was the springboard for possible promotion, in this year, were sadly disappointed. By Christmas relegation, more than promotion, was a real concern amongst everyone on our terraces. A young Bob McNab made his debut and figured in two league games this season.

Robert McNab – 'Bob' was born in Huddersfield and started his football career with Town at left-back. He made 76 appearances before Arsenal Manager Bertie Mee signed him for £55,000 pounds in October 1966 (a record fee back then for a full-back). While at Arsenal he went on to play for England at international level on four different occasions. In 1984, he brought his football playing days to an end in Washington USA.

In the Football League Cup, for the very first time, Town progressed through to the third round but were faced with two replays before they finally beat Plymouth Argyle 2-1 at Villa Park, Birmingham. Faced with Third Division Workington away in the following round Town surprisingly lost 1-0.

Town were once again faced with Plymouth Argyle, but this time it was in the FA Cup third round. In front of a Home Park crowd of 13,883 they all witnessed Kevin McHale score to earn Town a 1-0 win. For the following round they were drawn against First Division Chelsea at Stamford Bridge and thanks to goals from Kevin McHale and Len White they won 2-1. At Leeds Road in the fifth round in front of a bumper crowd of 39,326 they sadly lost 3-0 to Burnley.

The last match of the season, against Scunthorpe United, caused some real concern in our Boardroom given that just 5,158 fans had turned out to see them play at Leeds Road.

At the end of the season 1963-64 with a final league placing of 12th it was one of;

Played 42 games; won 15, lost 17, drew 10, goals for 57, goals against 64, Points 40

The close season of 1964-65 was the year when fans first saw how the effects of scrapping the maximum wage affected a football club. Ray Wilson, who by now had firmly established himself in the full England side, was a player that everyone on our terraces and Eddie Boot as Manager would have preferred to have kept in our Town team. Various clubs had been queuing up to sign Ray for quite some time. Even Sir Matt Busby as far back as 1955 when Town first played Manchester United, with a young Wilson in our side at left-back, had wanted to sign him. Given his obvious footballing skills it had already been noted by Busby back then. Town were interested in a player-plus-cash deal and looked at their winger, Albert Scanlon as a possible exchange, whether he was prepared to move or not was another story. As it were the move by United for Ray failed. Sadly an offer that was too good for our club, and Ray, meant he left for Everton in exchange for a transfer fee of £25,000 plus their player, Mick Meagan.

For the start of the 1964-65 season Town had a new Chairman in charge, Roger B. Kaye. His first job by the beginning of September in this year was to choose a new Manager, with Eddie Boot leaving the job, after they had suffered a 2-1 Leeds Road home defeat. Eddie Boot's reaction to the defeat was to say to the waiting reporters 'That's enough'. Thomas Deans Johnston was appointed Manager at the end of October 1964.

Thomas Deans Johnston – 'Tom' as he was commonly known to Town fans by, became Manager in October 1964 and stayed until 1968. By the time he left he had signed some prolific players during his four years in charge. He also left Huddersfield Town in clear profit with his business dealings during his tenure. By 1975 Tom was back in charge again as General Manager, after Ian Greaves had left. In February 1977 Johnston went on to win a Manager of the Month award but by the end of August 1978 had resigned. In doing so it allowed First Team Coach Mick Buxton to be his natural successor. (Sadly, Thomas Deans Johnston passed away in November 1994 aged 75).

The players who were signed in this season certainly added some much-needed experience to our Town side, firstly with Mick Meagan, then Jimmy Nicholson, then with Tony Leighton and finally Johnny Quigley.

Michael Kevin Meagan – 'Mick' was a defender signed from Everton in a part-ex deal for Ray Wilson and cash. He stayed with Town until 1968 and made 132 appearances during which time he scored one goal in a 3-1 home win against Coventry City in the 1966-67 season. By 1968 he had signed for Halifax Town and had retired from football completely by the end of that season.

James Joseph Nicholson – 'Jimmy' was a midfielder signed from Manchester United in 1964. He went on to become a legend as Town captain and made 310 appearances during which time he scored 28 goals.

His debut was a memorable one, against Ipswich Town at Portman Road on Boxing Day 1964, given that he managed to score for 'the Town' not Huddersfield Town but Ipswich Town. His goal was an absolute brilliant own goal from a diving header on a snowbound pitch as Ray Wood, our goalkeeper, screamed at Jimmy to leave the ball to him. By the time Nicholson had left in 1973 having signed for Bury he had steered Town to First Division promotion and was an ever-present in the promotion side that year along with several others. He also became our most capped player internationally with 41 caps in an 11-year Northern Ireland international career.

Antony Leighton – 'Tony' was a striker signed from Barnsley in 1964. He made 97 appearances in a Town shirt, during which time he scored 44 goals, before he signed for Bradford City in 1968. He had retired from professional football altogether by 1970. (Sadly, Antony Leighton passed away at the very young age of 38 due to motor neurone disease in April 1978).

John Quigley – 'Johnny' was a midfielder signed from Nottingham Forest in February 1965. He made 71 appearances in a Town shirt, during which time he scored six goals, before he left in October 1966 for Bristol City. By 1968 he had moved onto Mansfield Town where he helped them defeat West Ham United in the 1968-69 FA Cup fifth round. He retired from professional football altogether in 1970. (Sadly, John Quigley passed away in November 2004 aged 69).

Stephen Smith – 'Steve' was a midfielder who started his football career with Town having joined in 1961 straight from school with his obvious talents already noted by Eddie Boot. He made his first team debut in September 1964 against Newcastle United in place of Kevin McHale and went on to make a total of six appearances in our 1964-65 season. He played the final three games of the season on the right-hand side of midfield.
With Kevin McHale's form it wasn't easy for Smith to get a game in his preferred position so over the following season he played on the left or right of midfield and also as a striker. Steve earned a unique honour in that he became the first ever substitute for Town in a game against Preston North End on September 18th 1965 at Leeds Road. It took him until our 1968-69 season, under Ian Greaves, before Smith firmly established himself in the first team and was part of our promotion winning team the following season when they made a return to the First Division. Steve made a total of 381 appearances in a Town shirt from 1964 until 1981. His last appearance was against Workington in the FA Cup first round in 1981.
Steve has the unique distinction of being the only person born in Huddersfield to have gone on to be named as Huddersfield Town Manager. During his time at Town, which lasted for over 25 years, he had two spells as a player 1964 to 1977 and as a non-contract player from 1979 to 1987. His time also included a ten-month spell as Manager as well as positions as; Reserve Team Coach, Youth Team Coach, Chief Scout and more recently in 2012 was Head of Town's academy recruitment. (Sadly, in 2013 Steve was diagnosed with Alzheimer's disease).

In the Football League Cup second round Town lost 3-2 against our old adversaries Leeds United at Elland Road. Meanwhile, in the FA Cup they beat Doncaster Rovers 1-0 at their place in the third round thanks to a goal from Les Massie. The following FA Cup round saw them travel down to Wales only to come away with a 1-0 defeat against Swansea City. By the end of January with them bottom of the Second Division league pride was all that Town had left to fight for and didn't they just fight, until the end of the season they only suffered three league defeats in 18 games.

At the end of the season 1964-65 with a final league placing of 8th it was one of;

Played 42 games; won 17, lost 15, drew 10, goals for 53, goals against 51, Points 44

Tom Johnston's first full season in charge as Manager saw them win their first three matches and draw the next as Allan Gilliver scored seven goals in the first four games. Towards the end of August both Gilliver and Massie each claimed a hat-trick in a 6-0 win over Middlesbrough at Leeds Road.

Allan Henry Gilliver – was a forward who started his playing career with Town in 1962. He played 53 games, during which time he scored 22 goals, before he signed for Blackburn Rovers in 1966. His transfer was, at the time and to this day, quite controversial which rocked the whole of British Football. In his last season with Town in 1965 he played with a painful back problem and spent more time in the treatment room then he did on the training pitch. Allan still managed to score 18 goals in 27 games which then prompted a bid from Blackburn Rovers.

He made five appearances at the start of the following season for Rovers before his injury became too much with his last appearance strangely enough against Town. After the match Allan was unable to play again during the season and Blackburn made an official complaint to the Football League about his transfer. It became the subject of a two-hour tribunal at the Victoria Hotel in Sheffield and Huddersfield Town were eventually ordered to pay back £18,000 of the £30,000 transfer fee they had received. They were found not guilty of misrepresenting Gilliver's illness, but the tribunal decided that they had erred in not making such evidence available to Blackburn during the negotiations which deprived them of the opportunity to assess a player's fitness. Allan Gilliver meanwhile had to undergo an operation to have a disc removed from his back before he tried to resume his playing career the season after. He retired from professional football in 1979 while at Bradford City. (Sadly, Allan Gilliver was diagnosed with dementia in the early part of 2010s which is thought to be connected with his career in football).

In the Football League Cup second round Town beat Bury 2-0 away but sadly lost 1-0 to Preston North End at Leeds Road in the following round. In the FA Cup they beat Hartlepools United at home in the third round and then faced Plymouth Argyle away in the following round. Having won 2-0 they were then faced with Sheffield Wednesday in the fifth round at Leeds Road. Sadly, Town lost 2-1 in front of a home crowd of 49,514.

By the end of March Town were still top of the division and in line for promotion. Sadly, in the final run-in to the season from the beginning of April, until the last match of the season against Coventry City, they won only two of their remaining eight games and eventually missed out on promotion by just three points.

At the end of the season 1965-66 with a final league placing of 4th it was one of;

Played 42 games; won 19, lost 10, drew 13, goals for 62, goals against 36, Points 51

The Town Supporters Club in September 1965 put out a message to all Town fans that the Club wanted to hear from composers and writers (or anyone who could help) and offered a £5 prize for the winner who could supply words and music for a new 'Town' song. They felt that 'Smile Awhile' was for the past. By 6th November 1965 for the Town v Bury match it was announced that the winner of the competition for a new Town theme song was Mr Stuart Atkins from Flockton, near Wakefield.

> They're the boys from Huddersfield, you know,
> And of them we feel real proud;
> And when they all take the field,
> We know they will entertain the crowd
> With their kind of soccer majesty
> That is fit to beat the band;
> We are sure that you will all agree
> They're the best team in the land.
> Goals, goals, goals, goals, goals,
> For the boys in blue and white.
>
> When they go a-wandering,
> For their matches far away,
> And when those two points they home-ward bring
> It is sure to make our day.
> And the next home game we all go down to Leeds Road with delight.
> They're the pride and joy of our Town,
> They're the boys in blue and white.
> Goals, goals, goals, goals, goals,
> For the boys in blue and white.

(A master tape of the music was made and heard over the public address system at Leeds Road).

The Board of Directors announced that in November 1965 following the purchase of premises that adjoined the Town Ground, preparations towards the formation of a club had been made. 'The Terrace Side Club' as it was hoped to be called was to be controlled by the Directors, the Manager and the Secretary of Huddersfield Town A.F.C Ltd, with the power to co-opt. Facilities were to be available for the new Club's own members activities and also for Huddersfield Town Supporters and Junior supporters meetings and functions. While the Club was to use a portion of the premises as an indoor gymnasium for training in bad weather. Other facilities envisaged was licensed bars, refreshment and tearooms, supporter's room, ladies' room, cloakrooms and usual amenities. A Steward and Stewardess was to supervise the club and alterations was to be put into place once the premises was vacated in the New Year of 1966.

Special notices were given out this season that asked for all young supporters who wished to move from a position behind one goal to a position behind the other goal, they did so along the East Terrace and not to invade the running track and playing area. The police were advised to take strong action against anyone who was found on the track or playing area. (The movement of fans from our old 'Cowshed' to the East Terrace and vice versa was something that happened at every home game until the Taylor Report was commissioned).

By the mid-sixties it was almost impossible for Town to hold onto any player that went on to achieve any type of international honour. First Ray Wilson, then it wasn't long after that Mike O'Grady had made the short journey down the M62 to join Leeds United. Derek Stokes had returned to Bradford City and Chris Balderstone who was considered one of our best long ball players at the time was allowed to join Carlisle United. On the positive side though, Town was now producing quality full-backs. Ray Wilson, Chris Cattlin, Derek Parkin and Geoff Hutt had all cost our club nothing, but in turn, some broke transfer records when they moved to other clubs.

Christopher John Cattlin – 'Chris' was a full-back who started his football career with Town in 1964. He pulled on our mighty blue and white shirt on 70 different occasions during which time he scored two goals (one in the league in 1966 and one in the FA Cup in 1967). By 1968 Chris had signed for Coventry City.

Derek Parkin – was a full-back who started his football career with Town in 1964. His Football League debut was on 7th November 1964 against Bury at the tender age of 16 years and 10 months old. He pulled on our mighty blue and white shirt on 70 different occasions and scored one goal for Town in our 1966 season. In February 1968 he became, at the time, the most expensive full-back in British football when he joined Wolverhampton Wanderers for £80,000. In over 14 years' service at Molineux he made over 500 appearances for them and received a testimonial match in 1979. He also appeared in two Wembley Cup Finals and collected a winner's medal each time as Wolves won the League Cup in both 1974 and 1980. He also earned a Second Division championship medal in 1977 before he finally retired from professional football altogether in 1983. Derek Parkin was one of the first inductees into Wolverhampton's Hall of Fame.

Geoffrey Hutt – 'Geoff' was a full-back who started his football career as a 16-year-old trainee with Town in 1965. He made his first senior appearance in their 1968-69 season and by the following season was an ever-present in our 'Champions' promotion winning team. He was committed to the cause and stayed loyal to Town, even when after just two seasons in the First Division they were relegated, and in the subsequent years thereafter with a further relegation. As author of this book I believe he chose to stick with Town, in our worst ever period in post-war history, through loyalty. Geoff Hutt had a chance to go to Everton, as they were interested in signing him, instead he chose to stay at Town until 1975. Then having first gone out on loan to Dutch side Haarlem he signed permanently for Blackburn Rovers in 1976.

Denis Atkins – was a full-back that started his football career with Town in 1955 and had made 194 league appearances by the time he left in the summer of 1967. He had retired from professional football altogether by 1971. (Sadly, Denis Atkins passed away in September 2016 aged 78).

For the 1966-67 season an attempt was made by Tom Johnston to improve on the league position from the previous season. Various players were added to the team during the close season and more were also added who were given their first team debut. For some strange reason known only to Johnston, and his liking of Rangers Football Club, Town played all their home matches in a single colour blue shirt with a white round collar. That was until common sense prevailed when they reverted back to blue and white by our promotion winning season of 1969-70, after a local newspaper poll was conducted.

Trevor John Cherry – was a defender that went on to become a true football legend. Having started out at Huddersfield YMCA he continued his football career at Town in 1963 and had signed professional forms by 1965. He made his first team debut at the young age of 17 in our 1966-67 season. By the following year Trevor had started to make his mark in the first team with a total of 30 appearances and scored a goal in the Football League Cup. By now he was fast becoming a truly classy defender who was able to play anywhere across our back line. The following season he was an ever-present and was firmly established as a first team player. In Town's 1969-70 season he helped them to win promotion to the First Division after our club had spent 14 years in the Second Division. After time spent served as Town captain, due to an injury to Nicholson in October 1971, Trevor signed for Leeds United. (Sadly, Trevor John Cherry passed away suddenly in April 2020 aged 72).

Colin Dobson – was an inside-forward who signed for Town in August 1966 from Sheffield Wednesday. He built a hugely successful partnership in our team with Frank Worthington and claimed nine goals in 33 appearances as Town achieved promotion as worthy 'Champions'. However, he only appeared in eight games in Town's 1970–71 campaign and claimed just one goal. Having gone out on loan from Leeds Road he played four Third Division games for Pat Saward's Brighton & Hove Albion team before he signed permanently for them shortly afterwards in 1972.

Roy Ellam – was a centre-half signed from Bradford City in 1966. He made 206 league appearances and scored eight goals before he transferred across to Leeds United in 1972. He played 11 league games for them before he returned for the 1974-75 season. Back at Town for a second spell, he made a further 21 appearances and scored two goals before he left to play football in America. Roy Ellam is the only player to have played every league game from our promotion winning season in 1969-70 until his transfer and Town's relegation in 1972.

Peter Dinsdale – was a defender who started his football career with Town in 1956. He made 239 appearances and scored ten goals before he signed for Vancouver Royals in 1967. There he was subject to one of the earliest football loan transfers when he played on loan with Bradford Park Avenue and made nine appearances. On his return to England in 1970, under his former Town teammate Pat Saward, he became Assistant Manager at Brighton until 1972 and later emigrated back to Canada. (Sadly, Peter Dinsdale passed away in June 2004 aged 65).

Michael Stephen Hellawell – 'Mike' was a winger who had twice played for the England team in 1962 and had won a League Cup Final medal in 1963 with Birmingham City before he joined Town in 1966. He made a total of 54 appearances and scored one goal before he signed for Peterborough United in 1968 and had retired from professional football altogether by 1969.

Brian Donald Clark – was a striker signed from Bristol City in October 1966 in exchange for John Quigley but failed to settle in our Town team and was unable to adjust to life in Yorkshire. So after 34 appearances in two years by 1968 he had signed for Cardiff City. He is probably more famous for having scored the only goal in a 1–0 victory for Cardiff City against Real Madrid in the first leg of the European Cup Winners Cup Quarter-Final in 1971. (Sadly, Brian Donald Clark passed away in August 2010 from Lewy Body Dementia aged 67).

George David Shaw – was a striker who started his football career at Town in 1966 after leaving Rawthorpe High School. He is the grandson of the late David Steele, our former player and manager. As part of a player-exchange for Les Chapman at Oldham Athletic Shaw moved across the Pennines to join the Lancashire club but was forced to retire from football in 1978.

Robert Hoy – 'Bobby' was a midfielder who started his football career with Town in 1966. He made 140 league appearances and scored 18 goals before he left in 1975 and had retired from playing football completely by 1981.

Frank Stewart Worthington – was a forward who started his football career with Town in 1966 and went on to become a true legend in football. He made two appearances and was named as a sub in his first season as a professional. By the following season Town's new attacking line-up of Jimmy Lawson, Steve Smith and Frank Worthington was supported in midfield with two outstanding players in Jimmy Nicholson and Jimmy McGill. Worthington was an ever-present in Town's promotion year of 1969-70. His style of play was that of an easy-going player, who more often than not, did not wear any shin pads. His socks were to be found round his ankles while he effortlessly glided round a pitch, almost ghosting at times, into a goalscoring position.

After a total of 192 appearances, during which time he had scored 48 goals, and having previously failed with a chance to sign for Shankly's Liverpool. Frank by the end of the 1971-72 season had been sold to Leicester City for £80,000. (Sadly, Frank Stewart Worthington passed away in March 2021).

Town's start to the season was mixed with around as many league wins as they had losses. In the Football League Cup they lost 2-1 away at Lincoln City in the second round. The mid-part of the season saw them go on an impressive run of only two defeats in 18 league games between November and mid-March. During which time Town lost 2-1 to Chelsea in the third round of the FA Cup, which was watched by a Leeds Road crowd of 36,494 fans.

By 14th January 1967, for the first time ever, a television gantry had been erected in the roof of the East Terrace which was used by ABC television for the filming of the Town v Bolton Wanderers match. Due to the location of the gantry any filming which was done, when the sun set over the Main Stand, was ruined. The gantry was eventually moved over to the Main Stand because of this problem. The rise up the league table was helped by the goals of Colin Dobson and Tony Leighton, who scored 35 league goals between them as Town finished nine points behind second placed Bolton Wanderers. For John Coddington this was his final season after a career which had started in 1953. For Les Massie this sadly was also his last season in a blue and white shirt. Les Massie is one of only five players who have scored a hundred league goals or more for Town:-

George Brown 142 league goals (159 total goals scored 1921-1929)
Jimmy Glazzard 142 league goals (154 total goals scored 1946-1556)
Andy Booth 133 league goals (150 total goals scored 1991-1996 & 2001-2009)
Billy Smith 114 league goals (126 total goals scored 1913-1934)
Les Massie 100 league goals (108 total goals scored 1956-1966)

At the end of the season 1966-67 with a final league placing of 6th it was one of;

Played 42 games; won 20, lost 13, drew 9, goals for 58, goals against 46, Points 49

The 1967-68 season saw our league form as anything but consistent as Johnston began his third full season in charge as Manager. Following a pretty impressive previous season many fans hoped that Town were now on course for promotion back to the First Division. After winning their first two league games against Bristol City and Millwall, Town failed to win any of their next seven games in the league. Their league form never seemed to truly recover at all this season.

Paul Edward Aimson – began his football career as a centre-half for his first club Manchester City before been utilised as a striker. Having transferred from Bradford City to Town along with Alec Smith in exchange for Tony Leighton and Denis Atkins along with £20,000. Paul Aimson scored 13 league goals in 34 games before he moved to York City in 1969. Injury cut short his football career, and he retired from playing in 1974 after a second operation on a problematic knee. Paul was actually given his last rites as complications from the surgery arose, thankfully he survived. (Sadly, Paul Aimson passed away after suffering a heart attack in January 2008 aged 64).

Joseph Montgomery Harper – 'Joe' was 20 years old and actually a winger when Town signed him from Morton for £35,000 in 1967. After 26 league appearances, during which time he scored four goals, he left the season after to go back to Morton in a £15,000 deal.

Town once again had no luck with new signings and injuries, as Raymond Mielczarek found out. 'Ray' was a defender who signed from Wrexham in September 1967 and after just 25 league games suffered a snapped cruciate ligament injury.

By January 1971 he had signed for Rotherham United but due to a reoccurrence of his cruciate ligament injury he was forced to retire completely from football. (Sadly, Raymond Mielczarek passed away in October 2013 aged 67).

Tom Johnston in September 1967 made a shrewd signing from Arsenal namely a young James Morrison McGill. After trying unsuccessfully to dislodge Frank McLintlock from the Arsenal team, after just 12 appearances, 'Jimmy' McGill signed for Town.

James Morrison McGill – 'Jimmy' or 'Chopper', as he was affectionately known by, signed for Town as a midfielder from Arsenal. His style of play was noted as that of a tough tackling Scottish midfielder who took no prisoners on the pitch. 'Chopper' was a strong and brave player who never dodged a tackle, nor shirked away when he needed to win the ball, in his life. Some say that he would have tackled a shire horse if he had to. He was seen as the enforcer on the pitch and was an ever-present in our promotion year of 1969-70. By October 1971 'Chopper' had been transferred to Hull City for £55,000. Having researched many things in order to be able to write this book I stumbled across an advert for Jimmy McGill's own fan club in 1969.

Digital image **a37** (left)
Digital enhanced image of Jimmy McGill's fan club dated 4th March 1969.

I have to say as the author of this book, and as someone who through marriage and distant relations of his, I knew 'Chopper' to be a real family man who would do anything and everything for his family. Jimmy unfortunately suffered with his health in later life due in part to having cortisone injections while he was at Arsenal. (Sadly, James Morrison McGill passed away on 25th March 2015 in a Leeds hospital shortly after being admitted aged 68. I know his family still miss him very much, and I also know one of his grandchildren certainly inherited Jimmy's footballing genes).

Town's Football League Cup campaign during this season is currently still the best in our entire history. Following a 1-0 home win in the second round against Wolverhampton Wanderers in front of a crowd of 11,850 they were faced with an away match at Norwich City in the next round. Thanks to a Nicholson goal they won the game 1-0 then played West Ham United in the fourth round and won 2-0 at Leeds Road. Fulham were the next opponents in the next round, after a 1-1 draw, Town won the replay 2-1 and were faced with First Division Arsenal in the Semi-Final of the competition.
Following a narrow 3-2 defeat at Highbury in the first leg some fans thought that a trip to Wembley for our first ever Football League Cup Final wasn't out of the question. Tony Leighton gave Town an early lead in the second leg at Leeds Road but 'The Gunners' scored three further goals, to secure their final berth, as Town lost 6-3 on aggregate. Having researched this period of Town's history I came across an interesting news clipping which I feel I must add to this Football League Cup campaign. This shows that the 27,312 that was in attendance, on February 6th 1968 for our second leg Semi-Final at Leeds Road was predominately made up of just Town fans.

Digital image **38** (left) –Sporting news in 1968 that appeared locally in a newspaper which has since been digitally enhanced by John O'Mahoney.

In the FA Cup, just ten days after the League Cup Semi-Final first leg defeat, there was a third round shock as Town faced Tranmere Rovers away at their ground. 20,038 fans saw Tranmere beat Huddersfield Town 2-1.

One bright note in this season was the fact that Town went onto win the West Riding Senior Cup on Monday 6th May 1968 In front of a crowd of just over 2,750 at Bradford Park Avenue. They all saw Town bring home the cup back to Leeds Road for the eighth time with all four goals, in a 4-1 win, scored by Paul Aimson.

At the end of the season 1967-68 with a final league placing of 14th it was one of;

Played 42 games; won 13, lost 17, drew 12, goals for 46, goals against 61, Points 38

By 31st May 1968 Tom Johnston was replaced as Manager by Ian Greaves. Ian was an ex-Manchester United player who was in their 1958 FA Cup Final team. In a somewhat rather unexplained phenomenon, Ian was injured and out of the United team by the time the Munich air disaster had occurred on 6th February 1958. After the tragic disaster Ian Greaves was the first player to occupy the left-back position after the death of United's captain, Roger Byrne, at Munich.

When Ian took over as Town Manager he gave the following personnel various roles within our club.

Henry Cockburn – was an ex-Manchester United player who was given the job as Senior Coach. Ian had worked with Henry previously and felt that Henry would be a tremendous asset to Huddersfield Town as Chief Coach and Trainer. (Sadly, Henry Cockburn passed away in February 2002 aged 82).

Roy McLaren – was an ex-Sheffield Wednesday goalkeeper who had retired from the professional game due to a back injury. He was given the job as Town's new Assistant Coach after leaving Grimsby Town. Having joined Town in his second coaching appointment Ian's thoughts were that he felt that Roy was well qualified for the job.

Roy Lambert – was an ex-Rotherham United player who had retired from the game due to a knee injury. He had worked with Town's youngsters since the previous season and was given the dual role of Youth Team Coach with that of Scout by Ian Greaves.

Robin Wray – was a Local Education P.E Teacher and Coach who had been engaged part-time in 1967 at Town. Ian felt that he could provide an important link with the Local Education Authority in a full-time role in 1968. He led our youth team to the FA Cup Youth Final in 1974. By the late 1980s he had left Town to join Sheffield Wednesday only to return again in 1998 to work alongside Gerry Murphy in our Academy. Robin went onto coach players such as Jon Stead, Jon Worthington, Andy Holdsworth, Alex Smithies and Shane Killock before he finally retired in the summer of 2002 after 35 years of youth coaching.

Brian Hustler – was a chartered physiotherapist who also became Town's Welfare Officer. His duties included, the wellbeing and welfare of Town's players, their diets, weights and rehabilitation, aside from his customary responsibility of treating injured players.

A part-time role of Chief Scout was given to Jack Jackson who had previously carried out the same work for Blackpool F.C. After laying what foundations were needed by Ian Greaves to set up his backroom staff, in order that Town was able to compete with other league clubs and what was based on the First Division at the time, he set about trying to achieve the near impossible task of promotion back to the First Division. Ian's thinking at the time was that when they achieved their ambition Town and his backroom staff would be more than ready for it.

In his first season in charge, at the start of the 1968-69 season, Ian signed Terry Poole at the age of 18 from Manchester United and Jimmy Lawson from Middlesbrough.

Terence Poole – 'Terry' was a goalkeeper Town signed from Manchester United. He made his first team debut in a 4-0 defeat at Maine Road on Wednesday 11th September 1968. Terry became our regular first choice keeper and was part of an unchanged defence during the 1969-70 promotion winning season. Bad luck and injuries kept his career at Town down to just 231 appearances when his consistent brilliant displays should have earned him more reward. His ambition to be a top-flight keeper in the First Division was realised with Town, but disaster struck him in the New Year of January 1971. In an FA Cup third round replay at Birmingham City Terry had his leg broken in a tackle with Bob Latchford and missed the rest of the season. He was absent for the following season and had to watch from the touchlines as Town lost their First Division status by the end of the 1971-72 season.

By November 1972 he had resumed his football career but sadly by this time Town were back in the Second Division. In another twist of bad luck he suffered another broken leg, this time, against Preston North End in January 1973. By the following season he had returned to first team football and by January 1976, after being nominated for the P.F.A Fourth Division team, he had signed for Ian Greaves who was Manager at Bolton Wanderers at the time.

James Peter Lawson – 'Jimmy' normally played as a striker, but Town played him in an advanced midfield role when he signed from Middlesbrough in 1968. Having played for Town until 1976 he then took over as Player-Manager at Halifax Town.

After the first three games of the 1968-69 season Town had drawn one and lost the other two matches which wasn't an ideal start to the new season for either Town or our new manager. The first win of the season came against Derby County on 24th August when 10,442 fans saw Town win 2-0 at Leeds Road. At the beginning of September they were faced with Manchester City at home in the second round of the League Cup and managed to secure a 0-0 draw.

Days later faced with Birmingham City in the league no-one in the 25,001 crowd that day could have anticipated, that having lost the same game last season 6-1, Town would suffer another heavy battering as the game ended in a 5-1 defeat. Just four days after that they lost the City League Cup replay 4-0.

By the beginning of December Town fans had for the first time ever their own 'Talk of THE TOWN' shop. It was located behind the Leeds Road goal at the 'Cowshed' end. By Christmas 1968 Town were up to eighth in the Second Division and things looked like they were slowly improving in the league. Faced with Bury away in the FA Cup in January 1969 they won 2-1. The fourth round saw Town faced with West Ham United and in front of a Leeds Road crowd of 31,842 they all saw 'The Hammers' win 2-0.

At the start of February Town played Millwall away in the league and was beaten 5-1 with all six goals scored by the home side. Thankfully by the beginning of April they had recovered their league form and finished the season unbeaten in their last five matches. With the average playing age down to just 22, they were not just one of the youngest in the Second Division, Ian Greaves had also set about trying to make Town one of the fittest. As part of his plans the dressing rooms and the gym in our old home at Leeds Road was refurbished in order to set them up on a more professional level.

A poll was undertaken, by Huddersfield readers in a local newspaper, in which they were asked if they preferred Town in (a)Town's present all-blue strip (b) The club's traditional blue and white stripes or (c) A newly designed strip. Of the 300 'votes' received more than 250 indicated a desire, for a return to Town's old colours, of our mighty blue and white shirt.

All other interested parties, including our players, were consulted before the Football League was notified that they were making a return to our famous blue and white shirt. Just in time, for our Diamond Jubilee year in the Football League, for the 1969-70 season. (what a season it was to celebrate).

At the end of the season 1968-69 with a final league placing of 6th it was one of;

Played 42 games; won 17, lost 13, drew 12, goals for 53, goals against 46, Points 46

In this decade there were a lot of changes that took place both on and off the field at our old home at Leeds Road. It was also the last time anyone saw our vast terraces packed to its rafters with 50,000-plus crowds. Nonetheless, no matter what, this decade should always be fondly remembered for the many local playing talents that Huddersfield Town managed to unearth.

By the 1963-64 season Town's support had grown outside the local Huddersfield district as the 'Huddersfield Town Supporters Association' continued to flourish it had branches in Ravensthorpe, Mirfield, Cleckheaton, Thornhill, Cleckheaton, Hightown, Pudsey, Elland and Brighouse. By the time Town had gained promotion in 1970 further branches had been set up over in Saddleworth and in some Mossley Districts. Many Town fans were instrumental in raising funds for our Club as away day trips was organised from 286 Leeds Road, next to our 'Town Cafe', in later years 286 Leeds Road was home to our Town shop before it moved to the side of our old 'Cowshed'.

For the forthcoming 1969-70 season Town decided to close three sides of the ground for Central League matches because of dwindling gates. Only the West Stand (Main Stand) and Paddock (Main Stand) were opened to limit supporters to one area of the ground.

The 1969-70 season aside from being our Diamond Jubilee in the Football League is fondly remembered as the year in which Town, after a fourteen-year wait, was finally promoted back to the First Division. Not only promoted, but as clear **'Champions'**, with the style and grace of that of a First Division team. The groundwork having been completed by Ian Greaves, the season before, reaped some fabulous rewards in this year. One important appointment this season, which even today we should all be thankful for, was that of Bill Brook as Promotions Manager. It was Bill who first suggested a new nickname for Town **'THE TERRIERS'**. Our new nickname was announced at the end of September 1969 at our home game against Bolton Wanderers. The 'model' that was used for the promotion of our nickname was Skippy a six-year-old Yorkshire Terrier who was owned by Colin Fisher of Honley. By the 1974 season, after a Board meeting, Town were no longer calling themselves 'Terriers'. In more recent times in 2017 in our very first season in the Premier League David Wagner, our then Head Coach, stated to the listening media "It's not the size of the dog in the fight it's the size of the fight in the dog" truly apt words indeed that referenced our 1970 'terrier spirit'.

A further idea of Bill Brooks was that of the 'Terrier Pool' whereby people effectively won cash prizes in return for injecting our Club with some much-needed cash. (More recently in our John Smith's home it's now called 'Golden Gamble') In our old home at Leeds Road aside from our admission prices having gone up there were also improved refreshment facilities with five new tea-bars sited all around the ground.

Digital image **a39** (left) – John O'Mahoney's photograph of our old home at Leeds Road of the East Terrace/ 'Cowshed' refreshment bar. (Behind the floodlight pylon-taken August 1993).

As author of this book I have fond memories of the refreshment bars from my own Leeds Road days having spent most of my teenage youth flitting between our 'Cowshed' and East Terrace at half-time as Town played towards or away from our 'Cowshed'. The best things for me, if you ignored the smell of urine from round the back of the refreshment bar, was a half-time Holland meat and potato pie and a cup of Oxo.

Town started their 1969-70 season with three wins and a draw in their first four games and were third in the Second Division towards the end of August. Away to Carlisle United in the Football League Cup second round Town was defeated 2-0. By September 1969 they had signed Leslie Chapman from Oldham in exchange for George Shaw.

Leslie Chapman – more commonly known as 'Les' or sometimes as 'Chappy' actually started his football career in our Town boys before leaving and coming back to sign as a midfielder in September 1969. Town fans from this era still fondly remember Chappy for the goal he scored against Arsenal at Leeds Road on 16th January 1971. 30,450 fans saw Bob Wilson unable to get anywhere near the ball after it had left the foot of Chappy as he bent his shot, from about two yards outside the penalty box to the left-hand side of the Arsenal goal, at the open-end. By 1974 Les had returned to Oldham Athletic and in later life became our Youth Coach from 1996 to 1997.

On December 13th 1969 for the Blackpool away game, for the first time ever, Town had an iconic red terrier badge on their red and black striped away shirt. Peter May, a Town supporter for many years, kindly gave his best recollection of the Blackpool away match in which it were reckoned 2,500 Town fans had made the trip that fateful day to the seaside coast.

"Having gone to the away match at Bloomfield Road with my Dad's mate we all waited for the Town bus to arrive. When it did Frank Worthington actually sorted out some free complimentary tickets for us all to watch the match, sadly Town lost 2-0. By the end of the game, outside the ground, all the Town fans that had arrived by train were battling on their way back to the train station after being attacked by the Blackpool fans. For all the other Town fans that had arrived by Hanson Coaches they were all getting stoned by a Blackpool mob. The coach drivers were actually advised to park their coaches up, and wait under a nearby bridge, while the local police dispersed the home crowd".

The highest Leeds Road crowd of the season saw Town beat Sheffield United 2-0 on Boxing Day as 30,907 fans watched Steve Smith score both our goals. Having lost 3-1 away at Aldershot in an FA Cup third round replay Ian Greaves was then named Manager of the Month for January. At the end of March Town having travelled up to the North-East, on an emotional night, earned a vital point in a 1-1 draw against Middlesbrough.

It was a night to celebrate as they earned themselves promotion in front of a crowd of 27,519. Promotion as **'Champions'** was achieved in the very next league game, away at Blackburn Rovers. 15,125 fans saw Town win 2-0 at Ewood Park, on that memorable day, thanks to Frank Worthington scoring twice.

For the final match of the season, which Town won 3-1 at home against Watford, the 'Cowshed' was in full voice as they all sang 'Nicholson's king of Huddersfield' as a crowd of 29,000 fans went wild. This was followed up with a celebration of our players doing a lap of honour around the track-side which gave them a chance to parade the Second Division Trophy to all our fans. Town had only used 15 players for the whole season and seven of them had played every league match; Terry Poole, Dennis Clarke, Geoff Hutt, Roy Ellam, Jimmy Nicholson, Jimmy McGill and Frank Worthington. Our defence was outstanding given that they had only conceded ten goals all season at our old home at Leeds Road. With just as much importance as the tenacity of Jimmy McGill's tackling at inside-left was Frank Worthington's goals for the season, both of which, were a major factor in games that they won throughout the season. This was the first major trophy Huddersfield Town had won since winning the First Division title for the third time way back in 1926.

Club Secretary Tony Galvin ended his career with Huddersfield Town on a high when he retired at the end of April to be succeeded by our Promotion Officer, Bill Brook. George Binns had earlier arrived as Assistant Secretary.

At the end of the season 1969-70 with a final league placing of **'Champions'** it was one of;

Played 42 games; won 24, lost 6, drew 12, goals for 68, goals against 37, Points 60

In this amazing season, as author of this book, I felt compelled to include this heart-warming story of Huddersfield Town who are not just any old football club they are indeed a true family club. One in which we are all 'One Town, One Team, One Family'. In 1969 David Tagg was a 19-year-old devoted Town fan who had sadly suffered with muscular dystrophy for the last eight years and was bed-ridden. He had longed to watch our mighty Town in action at Leeds Road ever since he had been admitted into Mill Hill Hospital.

When our great club heard about David's plight, they decided something just had to be done. The slight problem was to get David to Leeds Road, to watch a game live, Town had to bring his bed also. So they set about organising and arranging for the removal of David and his bed in the back of a van. David Tagg proudly attended our home game against Blackpool on 13th September 1969 and saw Town beat 'The Seasiders' 2-0 thanks to two goals from Colin Dobson.

Digital enhanced images below show David been placed in the back of a transport van (**a40**) and taken to our old home at Leeds Road to be positioned between the Main Stand and the Open End at Bradley Mills (**a41**).

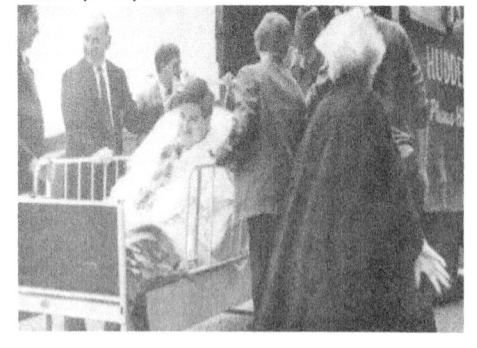

a40 (above left)   **a41** (above right)

10 years of Huddersfield Town's history from 1960

1960-61 20th in Division 2   FA Cup fourth round
                                                    Football League Cup second round

1961-62 7th in Division 2   FA Cup fourth round
                                                    Football League Cup second round

1962-63 6th in Division 2   FA Cup third round
                                                    Football League Cup second round

1963-64 12th in Division 2   FA Cup fifth round
                                                     Football League Cup third round

1964-65 8th in Division 2   FA Cup fourth round
                                                    Football League Cup second round

1965-66 4th in Division 2   FA Cup fifth round
                                                     Football League Cup third round

1966-67 6th in Division 2   FA Cup third round
                                                    Football League Cup second round

1967-68 14th in Division 2   FA Cup third round
                                                 Football League Cup **semi-finalist**
                                                West Riding Senior Cup Winners

1968-69 6th in Division 2   FA Cup fourth round
                                                    Football League Cup second round

1969-70 **'Champions' Division 2**   FA Cup third round
                                                    Football League Cup second round

Town's 'Me Decade' - Chapter 9

For the start of this new decade Town found themselves back in the First Division, but as the story unfolds in the 1970s it also took us down to the depths of football's basement to a place where they had never ever been before.

During the close season the popular cosy 'Paddock' in the West Stand was demolished to make way for 2,000 additional seats in our Main Stand. Huddersfield Town also extended office accommodation and improved the catering facilities. In 1972 there was the construction of a new television gantry which went unchanged for the rest of our days in our old home at Leeds Road. The cost of all these ground improvements was in the region of £50,000. There was a caravan parked in the main car park, opposite our main entrance, which overtime became known as our 'ticket caravan'.

Our 'Cowshed' was given a coat of paint on the back wall which became iconic to every Town fan, thereafter, this season. It was painted blue and white striped by local youngsters and was supposed to be reserved for Town fans only. This remained the colours of our 'Cowshed' until the final day at Leeds Road on 30th April 1994.

Digital image **a42** (left) – John O'Mahoney's photograph of our old home at Leeds Road of our old 'Cowshed'. The iconic blue and white back wall was all that remained when this photo was taken in 1995 after we moved home to the McAlpine Stadium. (It's my opinion as the author of this book, that with the demolition of this truly iconic landmark it should have had a part of it preserved and moved into our new home).

Town had some young fresh faces in our team this season with David Lawson taking over from Terry Poole in goal whilst Brian Mahoney and Mike Barry made their Town debut. Terry Dolan also figured but only as a named sub in Town's FA Cup run. Alan Jones also made his mark in this season playing in defence. Sadly, though Colin Dobson had played his last ever Town game by February 1971.

David Lawson – was a goalkeeper signed from Bradford Park Avenue in 1970. He played 51 league matches before he signed for Everton in 1972 for £80,000 and became the costliest goalkeeper in Britain at the time. He finally retired from professional football in 1981.

Brian Mahoney – was a striker who started his football career with Town in 1970. He played 20 league games for the Club, during which time he scored three goals, before he signed for Barnsley in 1972. He had finished with professional football completely by 1975.

Michael James Barry – 'Mike' was a midfielder who started his football career with Town in 1970. He pulled on our shirt on 23 different occasions, as player and as a sub, before he left in 1973 having signed for Carlisle United. By 1985 he had retired from football completely.

Terence Peter Dolan – 'Terry' was a midfielder signed from Bradford Park Avenue in 1970 when they dropped out of the Football League. He won the Hargreaves Memorial Trophy in our 1974-75 season and by August 1976 had moved to Bradford City for £10,000. After he retired from professional football altogether in 1981 Terry returned to work for Town in later years as our Reserve Team Coach, under Peter Jackson, but had left by the year 2000.

Alan Jones – started his professional football career with Town in 1970 and made 30 league appearances before he left in 1973.

The first two games of the new season, in the First Division, brought two emphatic home wins over Blackpool and Southampton. Steve Smith led our goalscoring charts with three goals as Town topped the Division. (Something which Town repeated in our Premier League days in 2017, after three games, having gone top of the Premier League on goal difference from Man City). The next two games resulted in two away defeats against Liverpool and Arsenal. The first against Liverpool, in front of an Anfield crowd of 52,628, was a 4-0 defeat with Les Chapman having to be substituted off in the last twenty minutes due to a nasty knock he had received. He was out of action for two weeks after having stitches to a wound on his anklebone. To cap it off the Town coach broke down on the way home and all our players were stuck on the East Lancashire Road while hordes of unsuspecting fans drove past them and gave them the horn.
The match against Arsenal was watched by 34,848 and saw 'The Gunners' win 1-0 as Jimmy Lawson took the place of the injured Les Chapman. Faced with Nottingham Forest in the League Cup second round Town drew 0-0 but lost the replay 2-0 just seven days later. The next home league match at Leeds Road against Crystal Palace ended in a 2-0 defeat and as the final whistle went Town had two more injured players in Dennis Clarke and Trevor Cherry. (Trevor Cherry needed a knee operation).

Lady luck still didn't shine down on Town, given that Ray Mielczarek had his nose broken in a reserve match during the week, and Geoff Hutt at the end of a 3-1 league defeat to Wolves at Molineux had a dislocated nose and suffered concussion. The goal against Wolves was Colin Dobson's 50th in our colours as they sat 18th in the First Division just four points off bottom of the league and eight points away from the top of the division. In the reserves a young Brian Greenhalgh and David Smith, eleven goals in nine games, were scoring for fun and the 'Terrierette's' now made their appearance at all our home games on the Leeds Road pitch.

By the start of October, Town having struggled to score goals on a regular basis were near the bottom of the First Division. It was clearly evident that Worthington, alone up front, needed a strike partner who was able to assist with the physical side of the First Division.

Bill Brook meanwhile was busy bringing Brazilian tactics to our old home at Leeds Road, but it had nothing at all to do with Pele. It was all to do with increasing spectator safety, Town had a moat built behind our 'Cowshed' goal, to separate the players from fans. Unlike South American grounds, where the moat preserved the peace and protected the players from fanatical fans, for Town it was a safety zone for all fans who packed into our 'Cowshed'. The idea was that it acted like an escape area for fans who spilt forward if a sudden rush developed. It also acted as a deterrent to prevent our younger fans from running onto the pitch given the height of the wall in front of the moat. The first home match of the season against Blackpool saw the effect of the moat, after a huge crowd of fans had surged forward, after the third goal in the final minutes of the game. Thankfully most fans ducked under the barriers and moved forward into the moat safely.

Digital enhanced image **a43** (left)
Bill Brook inspects our new Cowshed moat in 1970.

On 10th October 1970 at Leeds Road against Ipswich Town in front of a crowd of 17,944 Town won 1-0, this was only the third league win of the season, thereby ending a run of eleven games without a win. It took until 14th November, nearly a month later, for them to record another league win. Over at Turf Moor 18,112 fans saw Town beat Burnley 3-2 with our goals scored by a double from Bobby Hoy and one from Jimmy Lawson. Ian Greaves aptly described Jimmy's goal at the time by saying "He beat three pie-sellers, four Directors, and a full-back before shaking hands with the tea-lady".

The Burnley game saw Brian Arthur Greenhalgh make his First Division debut for Town wearing our number eight shirt.

Brian Arthur Greenhalgh – was a striker signed from Leicester City for £15,000 pounds in August 1969 and made just 17 appearances, during which time he scored two goals, before he left in 1971 having signed for Cambridge United.

On 2nd January 1971 against Birmingham City in the FA Cup third round our goalkeeper Terry Poole was hospitalised with a broken leg as Town drew 1-1 in front of a crowd of 26,486 at St. Andrews. Three days later in front of a Leeds Road crowd of 26,558 Town won the replay 2-0. The fourth round FA Cup match against Stoke City took two replays before Town sadly lost 1-0 at Old Trafford. Over 100,000 fans from both Stoke and Town had witnessed three epic cup battles which had taken place.
The last two league games of the season saw Town travel down to London to face Tottenham Hotspur and West Ham United. Having managed a 1-1 draw against Tottenham, Town then beat West Ham 1-0. Town's most notable performance this season was the home win over Arsenal in January. When thanks to the goal of the month from Les Chapman and a Frank Worthington penalty Town beat 'The Gunners' 2-1. Huddersfield Town won the West Riding Senior Cup Trophy at Leeds Road with a 1-0 win over Halifax Town, courtesy of a Frank Worthington header.

At the end of the season 1970-71 with a final league placing of 15th it was one of;

Played 42 games; won 11, lost 17, drew 14, goals for 40, goals against 49, Points 36

In May 1971, for the first time ever in Town's 63-year history, they took part in an Anglo-Italian Interleague Clubs Competition against Sampdoria and Bologna. The winners received a gold medal and the players of the losing teams all received silver medals. Town played both Sampdoria and Bologna at Leeds Road and finished with two wins against Sampdoria (home and away) and two defeats against Bologna (home and away).

Our 1971-72 season, in my opinion as author of this book, was when the start of our football decline truly began. It did not end until they hit a level so low that at one point re-election to the Football League was considered a real possibility at Leeds Road. The balance of being able to perform at the highest level, while competing to sign any player, proved impossible this season.

Town started the season having been added to a footballing venture The Texaco Cup. It was a competition sponsored by Texaco Oil Company in which Football League teams in England, Scotland and Ireland, who were not involved in European competitions, were invited to take part. Derby County, Coventry City, Manchester City, Newcastle United and Stoke City were the other English teams that were invited. From Scotland, it was Airdrieonians, Dundee United, Falkirk, Heart of Midlothian, Morton and Motherwell. From Ireland, it was Ballymena United, Coleraine, Shamrock Rovers and Waterford.

The first league match of the new season saw Town draw 2-2 against Leicester City. The following two games saw them lose 1-0 to Arsenal and 4-1 to Tottenham. By now Town were 20th in the First Division with just one point on the board and by the end of month had suffered four league defeats out of their first six games.

The start of September brought a much needed 2-1 league win against Southampton. Sadly, in the Football League Cup second round against Bolton Wanderers they suffered a 2-0 defeat in front of just 10,131 fans at Leeds Road. The next two home games saw Town win 1-0, on both occasions, against West Bromwich Albion in the league and against Morton in the Texaco Cup. The Morton game was watched by a Leeds Road crowd of 5,769 fans. Our league form then suffered as they lost 1-0 away to Stoke City. Thankfully they recovered enough for their next league game to beat Leeds United 2-1 which was watched by a Leeds Road crowd of 26,340. They rounded off September having won 2-1 away at Morton in the Texaco Cup. The first league match in October saw them win 2-1 away at Nottingham Forest but then for the remainder of the month every game thereafter ended in defeat. Town lost 2-1 to Airdrieonians in The Texaco Cup in front of a Leeds Road crowd of 5,462. If that wasn't bad enough they then lost their reserve goalkeeper Gary Pierce to injury with a cracked bone in his hand, which occurred during training.

In November Town lost to Airdrieonians away and was knocked out of the Texaco Cup. While in the league they suffered six further defeats and won only two games. By the end of the month for many of the Leeds Road faithful they had only seen three league wins all season, and this sadly was all they saw this season. Down to 19th in the league by the end of December, Town started the New Year with two consecutive draws in the league and were then faced with Burnley in the FA Cup third round. Thanks to a Dennis Clarke goal Town beat them 1-0 and went through to the fourth round where they beat Fulham 3-0 at Leeds Road. West Ham United were our next opponents in the fifth round, and in front of 27,080 fans at Leeds Road they all saw Town beat United 4-2.

Faced with Birmingham City in the FA Cup sixth round in March Town was badly beaten 3-1. The match itself was memorable for all the wrong reasons given that our goalkeeper David Lawson had a collision with Bob Latchford, which left our keeper unconscious and had to have an x-ray on a damaged shoulder.

In March Brian Mahoney left and signed for Barnsley, while Hugh Curran the Wolves centre-forward failed on a medical technicality in a projected transfer to Town. Ian Turner a goalkeeper, who had been signed by Ian Greaves in 1970 signed for Grimsby Town in 1972 having never made a first team appearance for Huddersfield Town.

The story of Ian Turner is rather unique given that he only went in goal, after starting out as a defender, to help his local team South Bank Middlesbrough against Town reserves. Turner was spotted by Ian Greaves during the reserve game, who promptly signed him on the spot. Having transferred to Grimsby Town Ian Turner played under Lawrie McMenemy, and by 1974 had signed for McMenemy at Southampton. Ian played in the 1976 FA Cup Final at Wembley against Manchester United and helped Southampton to win the FA Cup with some outstanding saves.

By the end of March Roy Lambert our Chief Scout had recruited ten young footballers. (Some made a real name for themselves in later years). Richard Taylor from Farnley Tyas, Francis Firth from Dewsbury, David Nichol from Bradford, Martin Fowler from York, Alan Simpson from Barnsley, Bob Newton from Mansfield, Martin Muhl from Morley, Kenny Ward from Heyton, Peter Hart from Mexborough and Bob Mountain from Wombwell. David Nichol had already played for England Schoolboys against France and, just before joining our apprentice ranks, he was selected and played in two more England Schoolboy Internationals that took place in Holland.

Sadly, at the start of April Ian Greaves informed Billy Legg that his football career with Huddersfield Town was over after he had failed to recover from a car accident in 1969. In the treatment room at Town was; Colin Dobson with a broken leg, Jimmy Nicholson with fluid on the knee after having a knee operation, Terry Poole with a broken leg and David Lawson with a shoulder injury. On a more positive note, Nellie Thomson, our laundress had seen our new signing installed at our old home at Leeds Road. (A brand new washing machine for our mighty blue and white kits).

Given the injuries to both Poole and Lawson, for the rest of the season, Gary Pierce was Town's only injury-free goalkeeper. Pierce had only just signed from non-league football the previous season, so it was a huge leap to First Division football in a season when Ian and the backroom staff had worked wonders in setting up and attracting young promising players. Our first team squad was sadly not strengthened with any real quality signings.

The last match of the season, and ultimately our last ever game in the old First Division, was away down at Crystal Palace. Having drawn nil-nil against 'The Eagles', and after the result from Nottingham Forest had filtered through, the final insult for Huddersfield Town was that they finished bottom of the First Division on goal difference. Relegation to the Second Division after just two solitary seasons in the top tier of football also ironically mirrored our recent Premier League days when once again, after just two seasons, Huddersfield Town was relegated in 2019.

At the end of the season 1971-72 with a final league placing of 22nd (**Relegated**) it was one of;

Played 42 games; won 6, lost 23, drew 13, goals for 27, goals against 59, Points 25

This season is historically recorded as the worst ever in the First Division For Huddersfield Town given that only scored a miserable 27 league goals and won six First Division games all season.

Still to this day some fans can't comprehend how a team just two years before were playing football in a style and calibre of an established First Division team yet ended up relegated in such a poor manner. Quite a few fans was unhappy about the fact that by the end of the season in 1972, while still in the First Division, the biggest outlay which involved Town was the transfer of Jimmy McGill out of our club to Hull City. The realism for many Town fans had set in as they knew the odds were stacked against Town doing what they did in 1953, when they managed to regain their First Division status back at the first attempt. During the close season of 1972 Town fans saw Trevor Cherry and Roy Ellam both depart for Leeds United while Frank Worthington went on his way to Leicester City. David Lawson having signed for Everton was the fourth Town player who had left, including McGill, it meant a total of five top players had exited Leeds Road, thereby removing the heart of a truly excellent young Town team that just two years before had been runaway Second Division Champions. During this period in time Leicester City full-back David Nish signed for Derby County for £225,000, and broke the British transfer record, while Cherry and Ellam signed for Leeds United for a combined fee of just £130,000. Town meanwhile spent just £105,000 when they signed Sheffield Wednesday's John Graham Pugh and Alan Edwin Gowling from Manchester United.

John Graham Pugh – was a midfielder who signed from Sheffield Wednesday in 1972. His signature was actually captured for Huddersfield Town in a lay-by on the M6. He played 80 league games, during which time he scored one goal, before he signed for Chester in 1975. He was briefly our highest record signing until Town signed Alan Gowling just two weeks later.

Alan Edwin Gowling – was a Manchester United forward who signed for Town in 1972 for a record-breaking transfer fee of £65,000. He had been in good company as a junior at United having played alongside legendary figures such as Bobby Charlton, George Best and our former Town player Denis Law. Alan was an England U23 player when he signed for Town in the Second Division. He made 139 appearances in a Town shirt and was our leading goalscorer season after season until he left for Newcastle United in 1975.

The two new summer signings took their place in our team alongside younger players; Alan Jones, Terry Dolan, David Lyon and Gary Pierce. Christopher Charles Wood was a young goalkeeper from Penistone who played for Town and made seven league appearances before he left in 1975, after being loaned out to Barnsley and Doncaster Rovers previously.
Dennis Clarke sadly was side-lined at the start of the season due to an ankle injury he suffered during training which required an operation. Mick Fairclough meanwhile had suffered a sprained wrist in a pre-season friendly against Dunfermline. Town's youth team of 1972 contained the additional young players; Chris Wood, Robert Newton, John Dungworth, Freddy Rose, Brian Marshall, Brian Young, Paul Smith, Graham Aslett, Paul Garner, Grahame McGifford, Stephen Spriggs and Paul Holmes. Terry Gray had joined Town as an 18-year-old on professional terms and Lloyd Maitland had joined on apprentice forms as a 15-year-old.

The opening league game against Blackpool ended in a 1-0 win for Town at Leeds Road. Their next league win came at the end of the month when they travelled down to Portsmouth. Thanks to two goals from Alan Gowling they beat 'Pompey' 2-1, which helped Town to go eighth in the Second Division. Gary Pierce was our keeper for the League Cup second round tie down at Tottenham when Town lost 2-1.

Gary Pierce – played football as a centre-forward prior to starting his footballing career in 1970 at non-league Mossley. He signed for Town for £2,250 during the 1971-72 season and made 24 appearances before he signed for Wolves in a £45,000 transfer in 1973. He was second-choice to Phil Parkes at Wolves but an injury to Parkes in 1974 meant Gary Pierce played in their FA Cup Final against Manchester City. Having made some outstanding saves he helped Wolves to beat City 2-1.

By the middle of September Chris Wood was joined in Town's first team squad by two other junior players; Grahame McGifford and John Dungworth. Grahame McGifford was selected along with Wood, Freddie Rose, John Dungworth and Paul Garner to go for England Youth International trials. Gary Pierce by the middle of September had sustained a shoulder injury, against Fulham, and was out of first team action. Town were mid-table in the Second Division by the start of October and our leading goalscorers were Alan Gowling with five goals and Dave Smith with four goals. John Dungworth made his first team debut away to Middlesbrough and marked the occasion by scoring Town's only goal in a 2-1 defeat. John Saunders had recently signed from Mansfield Town and was 21-years-old at the time he made his debut wearing the number six shirt.

Sadly, immediately after the Middlesbrough game, Mrs Emily McSweeney tragically passed away. Emily was part of Town's 'welcoming committee' at many of our away games for when the Town team coach turned up and was also an active member of our Town Supporters Association Committee for many years.

By November our old home at Leeds Road had a new floodlight scheme in place to replace our now ageing old lights. Our second set of lights had sadly deteriorated over the years since they were first installed. The installation of the new floodlights was completed by December 1972.

Meanwhile Gary Pierce had been sent off at Swindon Town for the first time in his playing career. Thankfully by the end of November Terry Poole had made his comeback from a two-year injury and played in the league game at Millwall. His return to first team football at the Den saw Town beaten 1-0. On a brighter note Sir Alf Ramsey was reported to have been at the Den to watch Millwall's keeper but came away suitably impressed with our own Terry Poole.

By early December Town had managed a 0-0 draw against Preston North End at Leeds Road which was watched by a crowd of only 6,900. The next two away games were postponed due to a flu epidemic at the Club which resulted in Town dropping to 17th place in the Second Division. On 23rd December Town faced Hull City at Leeds Road and one player in their team who didn't need much introduction was ex-player Jimmy McGill. Wearing their number seven shirt 'Chopper' helped 'The Tigers' to beat Town 3-1 while a young 17-year-old Paul Garner made his first team debut in place of the injured Geoff Hutt, who was out with a shoulder injury.

The FA Cup third round tie against Carlisle United ended in a 2-2 draw, thanks to Mick Fairclough having scored both our goals. Sadly, the replay back at Leeds Road saw Town lose 1-0. Town's Chairman Frank Drabble surprisingly resigned his position in February 1972 which left Stanley Kinder to succeed him, after being a member of the Board since 1964. In 1963, he had been awarded an O.B.E for his work in the export field and owned the 500-acre Whitley Hall Estate near Huddersfield where he bred both dairy and beef cattle together along with raising arable crops.

Sadly, without a home or away win since the middle of November Town were down to 20th in the Second Division by the time Phil Summerill had signed as a striker. Jimmy Nicholson meanwhile had agreed to come off the transfer list and Paul Holmes had signed professional forms as a striker for Town. On 3rd March 1973 Phil Summerill scored his first goal for Town in a 1-1 draw against Nottingham Forest in front of a 7,473 Leeds Road crowd.

By the middle of the month Town fans were saddened with the news that Mr Ardley had passed away. He had lived in Crosland Moor and was a long-standing member of our Supporter's Club who had also served on the Committee. He was well-known to our Leeds Road faithful as a Stand Steward with many years loyal service and support to our beloved Huddersfield Town.

Sadly, the Juniors lost their Northern Intermediate League Cup Semi-Final against Sunderland while Ian Greaves watched on from the Main Stand. Suitably impressed with Dick Taylor in goal Ian promoted him to reserve keeper. Meanwhile, Dennis Clarke having suffered with an injury at the start of the season was once again out injured with a gash to his ankle.

In April Brian Marshall, a central defender, was another of our young prospects who made his first team debut this season. Having signed as a full-time professional just before Christmas he made his first team debut alongside John Saunders against Preston North End away. With Geoff Hutt and Steve Smith both out injured Town lined up against Portsmouth at Leeds Road for the last match of the season. Nothing less than a win against 'Pompey' was needed due to the fact that Town sat next to bottom in the league table. Town fans were asked to dig deep and think back to the day when in 1906 some local citizens sat round a table at the Imperial Hotel and decided it was time for League Football in Huddersfield. Having won the game 2-0 thanks to Mick Fairclough and Phil Summerill the final humiliation for Town came after the Cardiff City result. Huddersfield Town had been relegated on goal difference with Cardiff City extracting their ultimate revenge for the 1923-24 season. Only this time it was in reverse leaving Town in a division they had never played in before, until now.

At the end of the season 1972-73 with a final league placing of 21st (**relegated**) it was one of;

Played 42 games; won 8, lost 17, drew 17, goals for 36, goals against 56, Points 33

The worst aspect of this season was our average attendance, since our promotion season, had been drastically declining. Over 23,000 in 1970-71 season, just under 16,000 in 1971-72 season and now in this season 1972-73 it was just over 8,000. The days of 1919, when Town was unable to support ourselves financially, were slowing coming back to haunt us all at Leeds Road.

For the very first time in our entire football history Town started the 1973-74 season in Division Three. The first league match in this division, away to Watford, resulted in a 1-1 draw as Alan Gowling left the pitch early due to an injury he sustained when the ball struck him in the face. Mick Fairclough meanwhile had to go to hospital after the match due to a gash to his leg. The first ever Third Division match at Leeds Road was against Cambridge United on Saturday 1st September 1973. Just 5,559 fans turned up and saw Town beat them 2-1. By the end of August they were out of the League Cup at the first time of asking having lost 1-0 to York City in the first round.

The Bournemouth match, at the end of September, was an historical occasion given that it was the first ever visit of the South Coast club to our old home at Leeds Road. The match ended in a 1-1 draw with our goal coming from Gowling. Jimmy Nicholson thankfully was now back after his leg injury but by the middle of September Mick Fairclough had to undergo a cartilage operation. Other positive news in this month was that three of our teenagers were selected to attend the final England Youth International trials at Lilleshall; full-back Paul Garner, goalkeeper Dick Taylor and centre-half Peter Hart. Geoff Hutt was also back in first team action after an operation on a shoulder injury. Against the league leaders, Bristol Rovers, Town lost their unbeaten home record 2-1 to 'The Pirates' in front of a Leeds Road crowd of 9,532.

With the floodlight ban throughout football Huddersfield Town were faced with playing league football in just the daylight hours once again. The crisis had started in October 1973 when the war in the Middle East quadrupled oil prices as Arab countries reduced supplies to the West. With the price of coal rising and stocks dwindling, Britain's miners rejected a pay increase and voted to ballot for a national strike. On November 12th miners and electricity workers began an overtime ban. On November 13th the day before our nation celebrated the wedding of Princess Anne and Captain Mark Phillips, Prime Minister Edward Heath declared a state of emergency. The use of electricity for floodlighting, advertising and for the heating of shops, offices and restaurants was banned. Britons had to get used to living under candlelight as power cuts became a feature of everyday life. For many it was like wartime Britain again but without the bombs. Sporting fixtures had to be rearranged to get around the floodlight ban. Midweek football matches were switched from evenings to afternoons.

The Football Authorities asked the Government for permission to play matches on a Sunday and on January 6, 1974, the first ever Sunday FA Cup matches were played. The Sunday Observance Act prohibited the charging of admission for entertainments, so clubs got around this by making admission free, but only allowed fans in if they had paid for a programme.

The first match in November saw Town lose 5-2 away to Southend United. Watched by a crowd of 7,255 at Roots Hall Terry Gray made his first team debut as a 19-year-old full-back while Martin Fowler was given a late run out as sub. Dick Taylor made his first team debut as a 16-year-old in the Brighton match at Leeds Road which ended in a 2-2 draw. At the end of the month Town were faced with Wigan Athletic in the FA Cup first round at Leeds Road and won 2-0 thanks to two goals from Bob Newton.

For the Southport match, at Haig Avenue, Town struggled with the severe weather conditions on a frozen pitch as neither team were able to keep their feet. If our players had been able to safely take one foot off the pitch in order to shoot, such was the dangerous playing conditions, then Town may well have taken both points. As it were 2,109 fans endured the cold and saw a 0-0 draw.

An appeal was put out by Town for a 400-volt generator to use at our old home at Leeds Road, in order to beat the floodlight ban, given that if the scheduled second round FA Cup match away against Fourth Division Chester had gone to a replay Town would have had to kick off at 1.15pm without a generator. Surprisingly, before the match had even started at Chester some of our fans had already been accompanied out of the ground by local police. So they didn't get to witness Town lose 3-2 and ultimately knocked out of the cup.

Town started the New Year with a 2-2 draw, away at Cambridge United, thanks to goals from Bobby Hoy and Les Chapman. This was then followed up with a 1-0 defeat away at Aldershot and a 2-1 home defeat to Watford. Towards the end of the month Town sat seventh in the Third Division but trailed eleven points behind divisional leaders Bristol Rovers. By the end of February Francis Firth had made a first team appearance, late on against Rochdale as a sub, and helped to create three of our five goals that day. His full team debut came the following Saturday against Halifax Town at their place. He then went onto help our youth team to beat Manchester United to reach the Semi-Final of the Youth Cup. Both Francis Firth and Bob Mountain scored against United as 1,000 Town fans turned up that Wednesday afternoon to watch them in action. Given that children were meant to be at school and Wednesday was a working day for all those who were on a three-day working week the attendance that day was extraordinary. Over 2,000 fans then saw our young team beat West Bromwich Albion 1-0 in the next round with Town's goal coming from a Franny Firth corner via Bob Mountain's head. The second leg watched by nearly 5,000 fans at Leeds Road saw our young side manage a 1-1 draw. So, for the first time ever in their entire football history Huddersfield Town had a team in an FA Youth Cup Final. Most of the team were simply outstanding this season while Paul Garner, having earned various England Youth caps, looked like he was going to have a truly promising football career.

Paul Garner – was a left-back that started his football career with Town. He made 96 league appearances, during which time he scored two league goals, before he signed for Sheffield United in 1975. Sadly, due to an injury in 1989 he was forced to retire from professional football.

Peter Osborne Hart – was a defender who made his first team debut against Southend on March 30th 1974 in front of a crowd of just 4,453. He is still to this day Town's youngest ever debutant to pull on a blue and white shirt at the tender age of just 16 years and 229 days old which beat Billy Legg's record set in 1965 by 39 days. He was captain of our youth team when they reached the FA Cup Youth Final and was also captain of the first team when they were crowned 'Champions' of the Fourth Division in our 1979-80 season. By the summer of 1980 Peter Hart had signed for Walsall and continued playing for 'The Saddlers' until he retired from professional football in 1990.

At the end of the season 1973-74 with a final league placing of 10th it was one of;

Played 42 games; won 17, lost 16, drew 13, goals for 56, goals against 55, Points 47

The FA Youth Cup Final first leg, against Tottenham Hotspur on Saturday 11th May 1974, finished 1-1 down at their place. The second leg at Leeds Road on 14th May was an evening kick-off and was watched by a crowd of 15,300. It was the biggest crowd anyone had seen at Leeds Road for more than two years. The match went into extra-time and with only five minutes left Roger Gibbins scored Tottenham's winning goal to make it 2-1 on aggregate. By the end of the season Ian Greaves had tended his resignation as Manager, and it was duly accepted by our Town Board. Within months came the decision to unravel years of Ian's hard work in which he, and his backroom staff, had meticulously spent developing our youth policy.

Sadly in 1974 Dick Parker Town's longest-serving Director, and probably that of the entire Football League, passed away just three weeks short of his 90th birthday. In 1919 when they needed a prominent figure to step up, and take on the financial woes of Town, Dick Parker came forward. He headed proceedings so that they were able to overcome the amalgamation with Leeds United. With Parker's enthusiasm, they were able to step out of the shadow of Rugby League and not only held their own as they went onto win promotion, league honours and Cup glory. Having taken his rightful place on our Town board, Dick Parker was instrumental in bringing Herbert Chapman to Leeds Road. With both Chapman and Parker firmly in place at Leeds Road, they went on a journey which to this day is still quite rightly highly respected as the best and most historical period in our entire Town history. His loyal service at our club should never be forgotten given that it lasted for over half a century. It covered every aspect of our club from collecting money in the street in 1920 in raising much-needed valuable funds to that of Chairman. Up to 1972 Dick Parker still attended most home matches and sat in on meetings with the Town Board.

As author, I must add a rather funny story about Dick Parker and Herbert Chapman that I came across while doing some research. Both Parker and Chapman were on a scouting mission together looking at a young player in the lower leagues of football. The striker they both looked at won the admiration of Dick Parker but not that of Herbert Chapman who stated that the youngster lacked the necessary skills. Chapman's decision was final and Town didn't sign the player. The ground they attended at belonged to Tranmere Rovers and the young player under review was none other than Dixie Dean, later of Everton and England, who in the 1927-28 season established the all-time record for the number of goals scored by a player in a single season.

Robert Young Collins was installed as Town Manager before the start of the 1974-75 season, it was his first managerial appointment. As a football club Huddersfield Town was not in debt at this stage, but some were concerned that what little money our club had was quickly running out. Town Chairman Stanley Kinder planned for sufficient money to be made available for the running costs and for some transfer expenditure during the season, but it was stated that if they didn't win promotion from the Third Division then their expected losses was approximately £110,000. (excluding any profit or loss on transfers). To help our club and also to be able to engage with Town supporters the creation of a Supporters Club Room along with a Vice-Presidents Club was discussed by our Town Board.

Robert Young Collins – 'Bobby' was installed as Manager in early July 1974. He was in charge of Town for a total of 23 games in which they won 7 drew 4 and lost 12 games. Towards the end of December 1974 he was replaced with Tom Johnston as General Manager. By mid-season the following year, due to some unrest over team control, Bobby resigned leaving Tom Johnston to take over once again as Manager. (Sadly, Robert Young Collins passed away in January 2014 aged 82).

In early August there was a well-deserved testimonial for our long-serving player Steve Smith. To mark his first ten years with Town in professional football, a game was held against Leeds United. Just three days later Town won 1-0 In the West Riding Cup Final against Bradford City.

The first league match of the new season ended in a 2-1 defeat at Leeds Road against Peterborough United. Town were then faced with playing York City away in the League Cup first round. Thankfully they won 2-0 thanks to goals from John Saunders and Phil Summerill. By the beginning of September, after a 1-0 defeat away at the Valley against Charlton Athletic, Town were next to bottom in the Third Division. Our Football League Cup second round match, at Leeds Road, against Brian Clough's Leeds United team on Tuesday 10th September 1974 ended in a 1-1 draw. It was the last game that Brian Clough ever managed at their club.

Two days later on 12th September, after just 44 days in the job, Brian Clough was sensationally sacked. Billy McGinley made his first team debut in the first United Cup match as the tie went to two replays before Leeds finally won 2-1.

William David McGinley – 'Billy' was a forward signed from Leeds United in 1974. He made 13 appearances for Town, during which time he scored two goals, before he left in 1975. Having signed for Bradford City at the age of 23 he had left the professional ranks of the Football League altogether by 1978.

Two new players, Brian O'Neill and Ally McLeod were signed by Town from Southampton in October. Brian signed permanently while Ally having signed on loan played four games before he returned to Southampton. Brian made his first team debut against Brighton at Leeds Road, and was also made captain that day, as he led Town to a 1-0 victory.

Brian O'Neil – was a midfielder signed from Southampton in 1974. He made 60 league appearances before he left professional football altogether in 1976.

Towards the end of October Town had moved up to 21st in the Third Division on 11 points, four points away from the bottom, and eight points away from the top of the league. By November our FA Youth Cup Final Team of 1974 had played an England Youth International side at our old home at Leeds Road. In front of just over 4,000 fans our junior side had earned a credible 2-2 draw thanks to Bob Mountain and David Nichols having scored for Town. Dick Taylor was in goal for England that day, having previously played in our Central League team at the tender age of 15, it was an incredible achievement at a young age for him to be picked for England.
Lloyd Maitland made his first team debut as Town put together an unbeaten run of six matches. The FA Cup first round match against Grimsby Town saw Dick Taylor make his first senior league appearance in goal as 5,940 fans saw Town defeated 1-0. By this time Huddersfield Town were second from bottom in the Third Division on 15 points, just two points off rock bottom.

Town signed Colin Garwood from Oldham Athletic in December. He made 22 league appearances and scored eight goals before he signed for Colchester United in 1975. Meanwhile, during the festive month of December Tom Johnston was unveiled as Town's new General Manager.

By the beginning of February Huddersfield Town was in dire straits at the bottom of the Third Division on 19 points, while Blackburn Rovers led the division with a massive 35 points. Town had already lost keeper Terry Poole to another injury in the Preston game, by the end of January. With that in mind Tom Johnston went on record to say that he had tried unsuccessfully for 14 players to come in on loan. On medical advice Michael Hickman had been turned down at Town but was later signed by Blackburn Rovers. On a more positive note our young team once again excelled by getting through to the FA Youth Cup fifth round after they had beaten Leeds United at their place. By the end of February Rod Belfitt a forward, added his name to the growing list of players who had made their first team debut in this season when he appeared in a 1-0 defeat at Watford. Barry Endean made his first team league debut wearing our number ten shirt at Peterborough United in March and scored the only goal in a 2-1 defeat.

Our young Town team managed to reach the Semi-Final of the FA Youth Cup and faced Ipswich Town at Leeds Road in an evening kick-off on Tuesday 25th March. Meanwhile, Alan Sweeney made his first team debut for Town against Plymouth Argyle.

Barry Endean – was a forward signed from Blackburn Rovers in exchange for Bobby Hoy. Having made 12 appearances for Town he then signed for Hartlepool United in 1976.

Alan Sweeney – was a full-back who started his football career with Town in 1972. He pulled on our shirt on 71 different occasions before he left in 1978.

Town's 1974-75 season was a season in which the way they played, along with constant team changes and alterations to our team, didn't help or support a team aiming to recover any self-respect, pride or even look like being promoted, in fact It was the opposite. Unbelievably a total of 33 players for this season wore our blue and white shirt which was a record number of players used until our 1996-97 season. Eight new names were added to our first team squad in this season to go with Roy Ellam who had made a return to Leeds Road. The added worry for the Board of Directors was that our attendances was still going down. Ultimately it meant our revenue was also in dire straits as Town was relegated to the Fourth Division for the first time in their football history.

At the end of the season 1974-75 with a final league placing of 24th (**Relegated**) it was one of;

Played 46 games; won 11, lost 25, drew 10, goals for 47, goals against 76, Points 32

There were some new faces in our first team squad during this season. Defender Steve Baines eventually replaced John Saunders and robust player Bobby Campbell was signed from Aston Villa. On loan midfielder William Coulson played three games, while some of our juniors made a first team appearance. Town's shirt colours this season was a royal blue shirt with a white collar and two white stripes down each sleeve, while our shorts and socks were all white.

Stephen John Baines – 'Steve' signed as a defender from Nottingham Forest in 1975. He made 113 league appearances, during which time he scored ten goals, before he signed for Bradford City in 1978. On retiring from playing professional football he went onto become a Football League Referee in 1995. He spent eight years as a referee before he retired from football.

John George Saunders – was a defender who signed from Mansfield Town in 1972. He made 121 appearances for Town before signing for Barnsley in March 1976. (Sadly, John George Saunders passed away in January 1998 aged 47).

Robert McFaul Campbell – 'Bobby' was a striker signed from Aston Villa in May 1975. He made 33 appearances and scored ten goals for Town before he signed for Sheffield United in 1977. By the following year Bobby was back at Town and made a further seven appearances before signing for Halifax Town. In later life he became a Steward at Oakes Working Men's Club. (Sadly, in November 2016 Robert McFaul Campbell tragically took his own life aged 60).

William John Coulson – 'Billy' was a midfielder signed on loan from Southend United in November 1975. He made his first team debut against Darlington on 15th November 1975 at Leeds Road and made a total of three appearances in our Town colours.

Wayne Goldthorpe – was a striker who started his football career at Town. He pulled on our colours on 28 different occasions, during which time he scored seven goals, before he left for Hartlepool United in 1978. Due to illness he was forced to retire from professional football altogether in 1980.

Arnold Sidebottom – 'Arnie' signed as a defender from Manchester United in 1975. He pulled on our Town colours on 66 different occasions, during which time he scored six goals, before he signed for Halifax Town in 1978.

Michael Butler – 'Mick' was a striker signed from Barnsley in March 1976. He pulled on our first team shirt on 87 different occasions during which time he scored 25 goals. In Town's 1977-78 season he was leading goalscorer with 19 goals, but by the start of the following season he had signed for AFC Bournemouth.

The first ever Fourth Division League match at Leeds Road on 16th August 1975 ended in a 1-1 draw against Northampton Town. Terry Gray scored Town's goal that day which was watched by a lowly Leeds Road crowd of just 3,595. Keith Longbottom was by now Town Chairman, and after our team had finished a short pre-season tour of Scotland, he was hopeful that over the last four years they had put a stop to the dramatic slide down the Football League. His intentions was to give some pride back to every Huddersfield Town fan. In the League Cup first round at Leeds Road Town beat Barnsley 2-1 thanks to goals from Terry Gray and Terry Dolan. Away at Oakwell in the second leg they drew with Barnsley 1-1 to go through to the next round. Sadly, Town lost 2-1 away to Derby County in the second round.

By the beginning of September, Town were top of the Fourth Division on six points by goal difference from Tranmere Rovers. The league match against Lincoln City match on Saturday 13th September 1975 saw a presentation of a new 'Town' flag. The Town Supporters Club presented a flag to our Club, which had a brand-new design bearing the recently introduced Town crest. It had been introduced two seasons ago following a competition by Town to find the best design. The flag already had some history to it in that it was used at Wembley in the 1972 FA Cup Final celebrations to mark the centenary of the birth of the Football Association Challenge Cup. Previous winners from each club were invited to take part in the celebration parade inside the stadium before the match. The flag which was presented to our Club was exactly the same as the one used in the Wembley celebrations. It was the only time that the flag had been on public display and prior to the Lincoln match it was presented to our Chairman Keith Longbottom. Meanwhile, Bob Newton made his first appearance of the season as a sub against Lincoln City in a 1-0 defeat at Leeds Road.

Robert Newton – 'Bob' started his football career as a striker with at Town in 1973 and played a part in the FA Youth Cup Final in 1974. He was named as the most valuable player in a World Youth Competition at the age of 17. Sadly, due to injury his league appearances at Town was limited to just 37 occasions before he signed for Hartlepool United in 1977.

Ray Kennan was installed as Town's new Commercial Manager. Bill Brook, who was previously the Commercial Manager was by now a Town Director. Lloyd Maitland while wearing our number seven shirt against Workington scored Town's first goal in a 2-0 win at their place. Martin Fowler also made his first appearance of the season wearing our number four shirt in a 2-1 home win over Newport County. Chris Simpkin meanwhile made his first team debut wearing our number five shirt in the 2-0 defeat away at Reading. At this point in the season Town sat ninth in the Fourth Division on 15 points while Tranmere Rovers topped the division with 20 points.

Lloyd Curtis Maitland – started his football career with Town as a midfielder in 1974 and pulled on our first team shirt on 46 different occasions during which time he scored two goals. He also played a part in our FA Youth Cup Final in 1974 but by 1977 had signed for Darlington.

Martin Fowler – was a midfielder who started his football career with Town in 1973. He also played a part in our FA Youth Cup Final in 1974 and pulled on our first team Town shirt on 79 different occasions before signing for Blackburn Rovers in 1978.

Christopher John Simpkin – 'Chris' was a defender signed from Scunthorpe United in 1975. He made 29 appearances for Town before he went out on loan. Having signed for Hartlepool United in 1976 he left professional football altogether just two seasons later.

For Town's away match at Doncaster Rovers on 4th November 1975 there were more than just mischief and fireworks going off that night. Besides having lost the match 4-1 our Supporters' Club coaches had almost every window put through. By the beginning of December Town were sixth in the Fourth Division on 23 points while Tranmere Rovers still topped the table with 31 points. Having previously beaten Walsall 1-0 at their place in the FA Cup first round Town was faced with Port Vale in the next round. Thanks to goals from Rod Belfitt and Stephen Baines they beat the 'Valiants' 2-1.

The Boxing Day clash at Leeds Road against top of the table Tranmere Rovers attracted the best league crowd of the season so far. A crowd of 6,672 all witnessed Town win 1-0 thanks to a goal scored by Rod Belfitt. Having reached the last 16 in the FA Youth Challenge Cup Competition Huddersfield Town was drawn at home to play Q.P.R. Meanwhile, Tom Johnston was confirmed as Town's General Manager.

Grahame McGifford made his first start of the season wearing our number three shirt in a 2-0 win against Cambridge United at Leeds Road. Town's FA Cup fourth round match on 24th January saw them line-up against Bolton Wanderers, who was now managed by Ian Greaves. Watched by the best crowd seen at Leeds road for several years, 27,894 football fans sadly saw Bolton win 1-0.

Grahame Leslie McGifford – was a right-back who started his football career with Town after coming on as a sub in their 1972-73 season. He also played a part in our FA Youth Cup Final in 1974 and pulled on a first team shirt on 45 different occasions. By 1976 Grahame had signed for Hull City and by the summer of 1978 had finished playing professional football altogether.

The 3-0 defeat away at Tranmere Rovers on 17th April 1976 ultimately cost Town promotion. The match itself was deemed highly controversial given that, from three Tranmere attacks, three penalties were awarded to the home side. For that, the match referee was never again received with much hospitality by Town fans on his many visits to Leeds Road. It didn't help Town either that our two main strikers in this season Terry Gray and Bobby Campbell were both out of action with broken legs for the last dozen or so games. For Geoff Hutt and Jimmy Lawson this was their last ever season, six years after previously helping to take our club into the First Division, they had both sadly finished their Town careers.

At the end of the season 1975-76 with a final league placing of 5th it was one of;

Played 46 games; won 21, lost 11, drew 14, goals for 56, goals against 41, Points 56

Given our performances last season it appeared that there was some optimism amongst some fans at Leeds Road that our 1976-77 season was going to be a year when a promotion bid was successful. Having signed Kevin Johnson from Hartlepool United to strengthen our midfield things looked promising for the start of the season. Other up and coming players who made their first team debut in this season were; Paul Cooper, Paul Garland, Terry Armstrong and Peter Howey. Meanwhile, Martin Fowler had by now become an established member of our first team.

Kevin Peter Johnson – was signed as a midfielder from Hartlepool United in 1976 and was top goalscorer for Town with 13 goals. He pulled on our Town colours on 87 different occasions, during which time he scored 23 goals, before he signed for Halifax Town in 1978.

Paul Terence Cooper – was a defender who started his football career with Town in 1976. He made two appearances before he left in 1977. By the following season he had left professional football altogether. (Sadly, Paul Terence Cooper passed away in March 2020 aged 62).

Paul Gartland – was a defender who started his football career with Town and made three appearances in 1976. He made five further appearance before he left professional football altogether in 1979.

Terence Armstrong – 'Terry' was a midfielder who started his football career with Town in 1976. Having pulled on our Town colours on 40 different occasions, during which time he scored two goals, he signed for Port Vale in 1980 and by 1985 had left professional football altogether.

Peter Howey – was a midfielder who started his football career with Town in 1976 and pulled on our Town colours on 28 different occasions. By 1979 he had signed for Newport County.

Other players who through the course of the season made their first team debut after signing for Town were; Neil Hague, Peter Oliver, Jim McCaffery and Terry Eccles.

Neil Hague – was signed as a defender in 1976 from Bournemouth and made 30 appearances, during which time he scored two league goals, before he signed for Darlington in 1977.

Peter Francis Raeside Oliver – was signed as a defender in 1976 from York City. He made 47 appearances and scored one league goal before he left in 1977 and never played professional league football again.

James McCaffery – 'Jim' was signed as a midfielder in 1976 from Mansfield Town he pulled on our Town shirt on 35 different occasions before he signed for Portsmouth in 1978.

Terence Stuart Eccles – 'Terry' was signed as a striker in January 1977 from Mansfield Town along with Jim McCaffery. He pulled on our Town shirt on 49 different occasions, during which time he scored ten goals, before signing for Greek side Ethnikos Piraeus in 1978.

Town started the season with a first round Football League Cup tie at Leeds Road against Hartlepool. Having won the first leg 2-0 in front of a crowd of 3,603 the second leg away saw Town beat them 2-1 on the night. The second round tie against Northampton away saw Town beat them 1-0. Then faced with Chelsea away in the third round, and watched by 19,860 fans, Town sadly lost 2-0. By the end of September, Town were ninth in the Fourth Division with Franny Firth our leading goalscorer with two goals. The first round FA Cup match at Leeds Road, against Mansfield Town, was watched by a crowd of 9,025 who all witnessed a 0-0 draw. The replay just two days later, at their place, saw Mansfield beat Town 2-1. In November Jim Branagan signed on a month's trial basis and by December had signed professional forms as cover for the centre-back spot.

Two Town fans became members of the '92 club' after visiting all 92 league clubs. Mr Joe Haywood of Tingley and Mr Keith Walker of Mirfield were believed to be the only two members of the club that had visited all 92 grounds supporting Town.

James Patrick Stephen Branagan – 'Jim' was signed as a full-back by Town in 1977 after he had returned from South Africa. He pulled on a Town shirt on 39 different occasions before he signed for Blackburn Rovers in 1979.

From the middle of January until almost the middle of March 1977 Town went on an eight-match unbeaten run which took them up to fourth in the league. Terry Poole had requested a transfer, to join ex-manager Ian Greaves at Bolton Wanderers, so Dick Taylor took over in goal but a cruel hand of fate affected his Town career. On 27th March 1977 Taylor hobbled off with a back injury during a match with Colchester United at Leeds Road. The injury ultimately ended his football career in tragic fashion as Alan Starling, recently signed from Northampton Town, played in goal for the rest of the season.

Alan William Starling – signed for Town in March 1977 and became a legend in his own right as our keeper. He pulled on our Town colours on 126 different occasions before he left in 1980. During his time with Town he was often seen during games leaning against a goalpost while smoking a crafty cigarette that he had managed to persuade a willing fan to part with. His most memorable Town moment was reserved for the away game against Scunthorpe United when after our travelling contingent of Town fans had started singing the usual chant of 'Starling, Starling show us your ****' Alan duly obliged, and in the process, was fined by Humberside Police. In December 1979 after a training ground injury Alan was finally forced to retire from football in October 1980.

Tom Johnston had won the Manager of the Month Award for February but by April had taken a step back from management as John Haselden took over. From almost the middle of April until the end of the season Town went nine games without a league win which saw them finish ninth in the Fourth Division. Steve Smith after many years of loyal service was released by our Club at the end of this season, but it wasn't the last that Town fans had heard from him.

At the end of the season 1976-77 with a final league placing of 9th it was one of;

Played 46 games; won 19, lost 15, drew 12, goals for 60, goals against 49, Points 50

Along with Cambridge United. Peterborough United and Sheffield Wednesday, Town played in a pre-season Shipp Cup Tournament. One name which appeared on Town's team sheet on Saturday 30th July 1977, for the very first time ever, was that of Malcolm Brown who went on to become a true legend in every sense of the word.

Malcolm Brown – was a right-back who was affectionately known by all as 'Mally' Brown. He was signed by Tom Johnston from Bury on 18th May 1977. He not only played consecutively for a record 259 matches for our club but was named as our player of the year in 1980 as well as being named in the Professional Football Association Fourth Division team 1979-80. Mally was named in the Professional Football Association Third Division team for three consecutive seasons in 1980-81, 1981-82 and 1982-83. Sadly he left Town in 1983 and signed for Newcastle United in a £100,000 deal. Injury cruelly robbed him of not just his playing career at United, but also potentially in my opinion as author of this book an international career with England. After he had recovered from injury in 1995 he returned to Town but by 1989 had signed for Rochdale. He went on to be named in the P.F.A Fourth Division team while at Stockport County in 1991. Then after returning to Rochdale, Malcolm Brown retired from professional football in 1992.

In the Shipp Cup Town had created another unique part of football history when they became the first team ever to have won all three matches. It started with a 1-0 against Cambridge United in front of a Leeds Road crowd of just 1,338, this was followed up with a 5-1 home win over Peterborough United. The final match against Sheffield Wednesday at Hillsborough saw Town beat them 2-0 in front of a 3,840 crowd. Town had won the Shipp Cup at their very first attempt and was presented with the trophy prior to the home match against Swansea City on 20th August 1978, on the very day that Mally Brown made his Football League debut for Town and helped them to a 0-0 draw.

Thankfully for the start of this season Huddersfield Town had gone back to our traditional blue and white shirts. Phil Sandercock having recently signed for the Club wore our mighty blue and white shirt along with some of our young apprentices this season; Brett Mellor, Mark Lillis, Michael Reid, Everton Facey, David Heptinstall and Daryl Brook.

Phillip John Sandercock – 'Phil' was signed as a defender from Torquay United in June 1977. Having made 89 appearances for Town he signed for Northampton in 1979.

Our League Cup first round first leg match at home against Carlisle United ended in a 1-1 draw. The second leg at their place having also ended in a draw meant the tie had to be replayed. Town finally beat Carlisle United 2-1 at Leeds Road and earned a second round tie against First Division Coventry City. The tie watched by a crowd of 8,577 at Leeds Road saw Town knocked out of the League Cup, having lost 2-0 to the 'Sky Blues'.

Just two league matches had been played this season, and they were already third from bottom in the Fourth Division on one point. On a more positive note, on 13th August 1977 Town signed Dave Cowling who went on to become a true legend, in every way possible.
Then having travelled down to take on Northampton at their place on Tuesday 27th September, in front of a crowd of just 3,942, Town lost the match 3-1 which left them next to bottom in the Fourth Division. If that wasn't bad enough the day after a local newspaper ran the headline 'Town next to bottom in night of shame'. Two days later on 29th September Tom Johnston had once again taken charge as Manager. Then on 1st October, in front of a Leeds Road crowd of 4,592, Town won 4-1 against Doncaster Rovers to record their first league win of the season.

Ian Holmes signed for Town on 25th October 1977 from York City and four days later scored on his debut, in a 3-1 home defeat to Grimsby. The match itself was marred with crowd trouble as both Town and Grimsby fans fought on our terraces during the game. Bob Mountford was our other new signing in this month.

Ian Michael Holmes – was a midfielder signed from York City in 1977. He played 65 league games and scored 21 goals before he left professional football altogether, after being given a free transfer in 1980.

Robert William Mountford – 'Bob' was signed as a forward in October 1977 from Rochdale for £10,000. Having struggled with injuries he pulled on our shirt on 14 different occasions, during which time he scored four goals, before he signed for Halifax Town in 1978.

On 25th October Town staged a gala family event at our old home at Leeds Road with the proceeds donated to the "Queen's Silver Jubilee Appeal Fund" for young people.

Thankfully by the beginning of November Town was up to 15th in the league on 15 points while Watford led the division with 26 points.

At the very first hurdle in the FA Cup first round at Barnsley, on 26th November, Town lost 1-0 in front of a crowd of 9,579. On December 13th our newly appointed First Team Coach Mick Buxton had joined from Southend United. Little did anyone know at our club just how important this appointment was to be in the coming years at Leeds Road. Town Coach, Walter Joyce, by this time, had left and joined Ian Greaves at Bolton Wanderers. Steve Baines meanwhile earned an unlikely record for him and for Town at the start of the New Year. His 40-yard power drive in the fifth minute of our Bank Holiday fixture at Brentford put Town into an early lead. It was enough to earn our first point of the year and give Steve his accolade of scoring the first Football League goal in 1978.

A benefit match was held on Monday 23rd January for Tony Leighton who was in poor health due to suffering with Multiple Sclerosis. Just under 10,000 fans paid tribute to Tony and his family and helped raise £7,400. (Sadly, Anthony Leighton passed away due to MS on 4th April 1978 aged just 38).

In March 1978 Town signed David Sutton on a month's loan from Plymouth Argyle, before they made his transfer permanent. Sutty made his first team debut on 11th March 1978 against Darlington with just 4,481 fans watching on as Town beat 'The Quakers' 2-1 at Leeds Road.

David William Sutton – 'Sutty' was a central defender that was signed from Plymouth Argyle who became a legend in his own right. He went on to form an amazing defensive partnership with Keith Hanvey as the rock to our defence. Having helped Town to achieve two promotions in just four years Sutty then signed for Bolton Wanderers in 1985 for £12,000, before retiring from professional football in 1989.

The main concern at Town was the fact that it was the lowest ever finish to a season since they had entered the Football League in 1910. On the financial side the average attendance figure was down to a measly 4,508 per match. So it was no real surprise to Town fans that both Mick Butler and Kevin Johnson were moved on at the end of the season.

At the end of the season 1977-78 with a final league placing of 11th it was one of;

Played 46 games; won 15, lost 16, drew 15, goals for 63, goals against 55, Points 45

Following on from the previous disappointment of last season, and given our early poor form this season Tom Johnston had resigned as Manager by the end of August after three friendlies, three league games and both home and away legs of the first round of the Football League Cup had all been played this season without so much as a Town win. Mick Buxton given the role of Caretaker Manager, with John Haselden as his Assistant, set about transforming our great Club from top to bottom. First team players who made their Town debut thanks to Mick and John were; Chris Topping, Peter Fletcher, Keith Hanvey and Ian Robins. Mark Lillis, Dave Cowling and Paul Bielby stepped up from our reserves while Frank McGrellis arrived on a month's loan from Coventry City.

Christopher Topping – 'Chris' was a central defender Tom Johnston signed from York City for £20,000 in 1977. Having taken up the role of central defender at Town he sadly, in a league game against Grimsby Town, tore his cartilage in 1979. After surgery Chris found Sutty and Hanvey were in formidable form, so much so, that he was often utilised as our 'twelfth' man and became someone fans knew to be dependable and reliable from our subs bench. In 1981, he signed for Scarborough and by the following year had left professional football altogether.

Peter Fletcher – 'Pete' was a striker who had started his football career at Manchester United in 1973 and after a handful of appearances he was used as part of a transfer deal that took Stuart Pearson to United from Hull City. Then after two seasons with the 'Tigers' Fletcher moved onto Stockport County. In 1978, he signed for Town on a free transfer and his first game was a pre-season friendly against Bury on July 29th 1978. He made 31 league appearances and scored 12 league goals in his first year at Town. Sadly, by the end of our 'Champions' promotion winning Fourth Division season Pete struggled with injury problems and the league game against Lincoln City in April 1982 was his last ever game in a Town shirt. After 115 appearances during which time he had scored 45 goals Peter Fletcher retired from football as a true legend after earning himself the tag of 'super-sub'.

Keith Hanvey – was a central defender that Tom Johnston signed from Grimsby Town in July 1978 for a fee believed to be around £15,000. Having just signed Chris Topping, from York City, Keith ended up playing on the left-hand side of our midfield under Johnston. Thankfully when Buxton took over he immediately put Hanvey back in his preferred defensive position. With Sutty winning every header in the air, and Keith reading the game and organising our back line on the pitch, along with Chris Topping as back-up it was the perfect set-up all round. In 1984 after 235 appearances during which time he had scored 15 goals Keith signed permanently for Rochdale. By the following year he had retired from professional football altogether, but it wasn't the end of Keith at Town. In his new role as Commercial Executive it was Keith who actually tried to persuade our Chairman Keith Longbottom and our Town Board that our old home at Leeds Road was in dire need of replacing given its age and condition. When the idea of a new ground was turned down at Boardroom level Keith left to work for Bradford City. Thankfully though, just six months later, Graham Leslie, our new Chairman got in touch with Keith to discuss the proposal of a new stadium. Keith, now loyal to Bradford City, gave his ideas and plans for a new stadium to Graham Leslie. In doing so Paul Fletcher was then tasked as our new Commercial Manager, to drive the plans into becoming a reality. Keith Hanvey was not only a football legend but is also to be remembered by Town fans, as someone who had an idea and vision to give Town a second home, long after he had hung up his football boots.

Digital enhanced image **a44** (above) – Personal photograph of John O'Mahoney's of both the Alfred McAlpine Stadium and our old home at Leeds Road (photographed together possibly for the last time).

Ian Robins – 'Robbo' was a striker who became a true legend in every sense of the word. Buxton had signed him from Bury in September 1978 for £20,000, and he wore our Town colours for the very first time at Leeds Road on 26th September as a sub against Grimsby Town. He made a total of 38 appearances in his first season with Town and was leading goalscorer with 16 league goals.

At the end of our 'Champions' promotion winning Fourth Division season in 1979-80 Ian was once again our leading goalscorer with a total of 25 league goals and two Football League Cup goals. Ian, along with Mally Brown, was named in the 1979-80 Football League Fourth Division PFA Team of the Year. The following year in our first season back in the Third Division Robbo scored 15 goals. After a total of 186 appearances, during which time he scored 67 goals, Ian Robins retired from professional football altogether in 1982 because of heart-breaking circumstances.

As author of this book I will never forget our 1979-80 season given that every player who played that season became a legend in my eyes, but none more so than Robbo. His two goals against Hartlepool United, in our final match of the season at Leeds Road, is still to this day one of the best games I have ever had the good grace to see. Seeing Robbo, my Town idol, score our 100th and 101st goals at the 'Cowshed' end in a record-breaking season in front of 16,807 fans at Leeds Road was amazing. It was like it was carnival time given how Robbo celebrated with everyone in front of our 'Cowshed'. That day still lives on in my memories, and I'm sure in everyone else's who was there that day also, even if Town didn't play well on the day we were still crowned worthy '**Champions**'.

Digital enhanced image **a45** (left)

Digital enhanced image **a46** (left)

Photographs **a45** and **a46** are personal photographs of John O'Mahoney's, with **a45** personally signed by Ian Robins, of our 101st goal at Leeds Road. The original photograph **a46** was taken in 2019 and is one I still treasure very dearly to this very day.

Mark Anthony Lillis – Tom Johnston started his Town career off when he gave him his first professional contract in football. Mick Buxton then gave Lillis his first team debut on 14th October 1978 in an away game at Newport County. During the 1978-79 season Mark made 11 league appearances, one FA Cup appearance and was sub on five different occasions. The 1979-80 season saw him make one sub appearance, ironically, against Newport County at our old home on 8th September 1979. By the following year Lillis had started to establish himself in our first team and his style of play was soon rewarded by Buxton with the captain's armband and was named as Town's player of the year in 1981. By the end of the 1982-83 season he had led Town to a second promotion in just four years and was leading goalscorer with 20 goals. Some say he was spurred on due to an unconventional sponsorship deal with a local butcher, given that every goal he scored he was rewarded with a steak. I would say as author of this book that after he had scored nine goals in just four games, with four goals coming in one particular match against Cardiff City, he was certainly 'steaked' out by the end of the season.

Mark wore his number seven shirt with pride and with a passion that epitomised him amongst our fans as a true legend in every way. He not only played as a striker but also played in every other position in the team that included playing in goal when Andy Rankin was badly injured during a cup match against Shrewsbury Town. He also stood in for our injured keeper Brian Cox after he had scored in the same game.

Mark sadly signed for Manchester City in 1985 for £132,500 after having his transfer fee set by a tribunal. After retiring from playing football he came back to our club as Youth Team Coach but had left by 1996, having taken on the role of Assistant Manager at Scunthorpe United. In December 2011 he was back as our Academy Manager and just two months later was appointed Caretaker Manager after Lee Clark had left. In January 2013 Mark took over from the departing Simon Grayson as Caretaker Manager for five games. Following the departure of Mark Robins, in August 2014, Lillis once again stepped in as Caretaker Manager for a third time. After Chris Powell had left our club, once again, Lillis stepped up as Caretaker Manager. By 2017 Mark Lillis had left our club but was someone who through hard-work and commitment personified the Buxton way of giving his all to Town in every way possible. He had everything Town supporters wished for on our terraces in terms of ability, leadership and true dedication.

David Roy Cowling – 'Dave' was a left-winger who had been signed by Tom Johnston in August 1977 from Mansfield Town. It was Buxton that handed him his first team debut on 16th September 1978 away at Barnsley. He wore our number five shirt that day due to Paul Bielby having the number eleven shirt out on the wing. Dave went on to become a true legend who should always be remembered for scoring the winning goal against Leeds United in the Milk Cup third round. Even more importantly he scored the winning goal against Newport County at Leeds Road that helped Town clinch promotion to the Second Division in our 1982-83 season.

As author of this book I am pained to write this section, but I feel I must because the reason why is still beyond me even to this present day. Certain sections on our home terraces picked out Cowling to be a player they loved to hate. By early April 1980 the abuse was so bad for him that at half-time, against Halifax Town, Buxton subbed him off the pitch to save him from any further abuse. In the Walsall match-day programme on 12th April 1980 Buxton addressed his programme notes to that section of fans, while on the terraces Town fans were often seen arguing amongst ourselves about the constant abuse he received. As a 12-year-old lad at the time, who frequented our 'Cowshed', I was confused as to why we would even do that to anyone wearing a Town shirt. Thankfully Cowling outlived the abuse and continued with his Town career while being linked with moves to Manchester United, Leeds United and Nottingham Forest on more than one occasion. After a Town career which lasted for ten years he went initially on loan to Scunthorpe United, then had a brief spell at Reading, before he finally signed permanently at Scunthorpe United in 1988.

Paul Anthony Bielby – was a left-winger who started his football career at Manchester United in 1973 he then signed for Hartlepool United in 1975 and was later signed by Town. After retiring from football in the New Year Honours list in 2008 Paul was appointed a Member of the Order of the British Empire for his services to young people.

Town were third from bottom of the Fourth Division when Mick Buxton took up the reins as Caretaker Manager. By the time he had been given the job full-time, in December 1978, Town were 16th in the league and out of the FA Cup after a 2-1 away defeat to Doncaster Rovers in the first round. The start of the New year in 1979 with both Mick and John at the helm saw Town's league position slowly improve. Three young players who made their first team debut this season were; Daryl Brook, Keith Ripley and Tommy Smith.

Daryl Brook – was a striker who started his football career with Town along with his brother Nicky in our youth ranks. They both turned professional at the start of the 1978-79 season and by the end of the season after just one appearance Daryl was unfortunate to have his leg broken and never played for Town again. By 1980 he had moved into non-league football.

Keith Anthony Ripley – was a full-back Tom Johnston signed from non-league Gainsborough Trinity in 1978. He made his first team debut in a friendly at Altrincham wearing our number eleven shirt. His first team debut at Leeds Road was as sub in a League Cup first round second leg match against Preston North End, where he scored his first goal in a 2-2 draw. By the end of the season having made two league appearances and been sub on six different occasion he signed for Doncaster Rovers and had left professional football altogether by 1980.

Thomas Edgar Smith – 'Tommy' was a striker that signed from Sheffield United in 1978. As author of this book I can personally remember watching him in a reserve match and saw first-hand just how fast he could run with a ball. He had amazing speed and coupled with good ball control I thought he would go on to carve out a great football career with Town. Sadly, after just two sub appearances in 1978 and one league cup appearance in 1979 he signed for non-league Emley.

Once again, the worry at Town was the fact that only one game played at our old home this season had topped the 6,000 mark. That was the Barnsley league match in which 'The Tykes', aiming for promotion, had brought nearly 5,000 visiting fans to Leeds Road in a crowd of 9,382.

At the end of the season 1978-79 with a final league placing of 9th it was one of;

Played 46 games; won 18, lost 17, drew 11, goals for 57, goals against 53, Points 47

The 1979-80 season was the first full season that Mick Buxton and John Haselden was in charge. For the start of this memorable season Town signed Micky Laverick from Southend United in exchange for Terry Gray plus £10,000. Fred Robinson was the next player to put pen to paper for Town having recently signed from Doncaster Rovers.

Michael George Laverick – 'Micky' was a midfielder that Buxton signed from Southend United. His first appearance in our old home was in a friendly on August 4th 1979 against Rotherham United, in front of a Leeds Road crowd of just 939 Town won 2-0. By 1981 he had signed permanently for York City, due to Mark Lillis having taken the number seven shirt from him, the following year he returned to Town and played two games on loan before he retired from professional football altogether in May 1983.

Fredrick James Robinson – 'Fred' signed for Buxton after he had been released by Doncaster Rovers in 1979. As author of this book I can still visualise him as a no-nonsense type of defender and was Cowling's minder on the pitch. Fred ensured that no-one got past him with, or without, the ball and pulled on a Town shirt on 85 different occasions. Sadly, after snapping his cruciate ligament in 1981 he was forced to retire at the end of the season.

By the beginning of September Town were fifth in the Fourth Division on six points and had beaten Crewe Alexander both home and away in the first round of the Football League Cup. They were then faced with Grimsby Town in the second round but was knocked out of the cup having lost at home and at their place. On 13th September Brian Stanton signed for Town in a £15,000 transfer from Bury while Steve Smith was back at Leeds Road working for Mick Buxton as Chief Scout.

Brian Stanton – was a midfielder Buxton signed from Bury in 1979. He made his first team debut at Scunthorpe United on 15th September and scored our only goal that day in a 1-1 draw. He went onto make 241 appearances during which time he scored 54 goals before he signed for Rochdale in 1986. On 1st January 1983, at Leeds Road against Bradford City, Stanton scored four goals that day with his second half hat-trick coming in just six minutes. It was, until our last day in our old home in 1994, a record for the fastest hat-trick ever seen at Leeds Road.

By the end of September Town were second in the Fourth Division while Portsmouth topped the division on 16 points. Since the defeat to Grimsby at the beginning of the month Town had managed to go on a five-match unbeaten run and had thrashed Port Vale 7-1 at Leeds Road in front of a home crowd of only 4,299. By the beginning of October Mick Buxton had signed Bernard Purdie.

Bernard Purdie – signed as a utility player from Crewe Alexander for £22,000 in 1979. He was able to play in various defensive and midfield positions, but by 1982 had returned to Crewe.

Ian Robins, at this stage of the season, was the leading goalscorer of the Fourth Division with eleven goals as Peterborough's Kellock and Portsmouth's Garwood were both just one goal behind him. One player who left our club in this month, due to not being able to secure a first team place, was Jim Branagan who signed for Blackburn Rovers on 18th October. Town was top of the Fourth Division on goal difference from Portsmouth by the start of November and were two points clear of them at the top of the table by 10th November. In the FA Cup Town faced Darlington away in the first round, thanks to a Peter Hart goal, they managed a 1-1 draw. A Leeds Road crowd of 8,084 saw Town lose the replay 1-0. The night match at Leeds Road against Rochdale on 21st December was watched by Steve Kindon, who having signed for Town went on to become a true terrace hero and legend. Meanwhile, making his first appearance in goal was Andy Rankin who also went on to make a name for himself. Even today Steve Kindon's name along with all the others from this season are fondly remembered and revered by everyone who saw Town play this season. Kindon having signed from Burnley was an ideal Christmas present for all Town fans given the way that he helped to kick-start our season. "Kindon, Kindon, Kindon" was heard at every Town match from Christmas onwards, with his brawn and muscle up front completing our promotion team.

Stephen Michael Kindon – 'Steve' was a striker Buxton signed from Burnley in 1979, and what a striker he turned out to be. His transfer fee was by far the largest transfer they had paid out since Alan Gowling had signed for £65,000. His first appearance in a Town shirt was against Halifax Town on Boxing Day 1979. Travelling Town fans got their first glimpse of Kindon rampaging up and down the pitch when he came on as a second half sub in place of Robbo.

His first full appearance for Town was on December 29th 1979 at Doncaster Rovers where 7,337 fans saw Town beat 'Donny' 2-1 thanks to goals from both Stanton and Kindon. Sadly, during our 1981-82 season, Steve suffered a serious injury which forced him to retire from professional football altogether, after retiring he stayed on as Commercial Manager of Huddersfield Town.

Andrew George Rankin – 'Andy' was a goalkeeper Buxton signed initially on loan from Watford on 3rd December 1979 due to injuries to both our regular keepers, Alan Starling and Richard Taylor. Andy signed permanently for Town after his loan spell had been completed. Sadly, after 81 appearances Andy was forced to retire from professional football altogether in 1982 due to a horrific injury he received the season before. He was not only carried off the field of play that day but also later hospitalised. As author of this book I can still vividly remember down at the Valley against Charlton Athletic in a Third Division match, for the last 15 minutes of the game, Andy saved everything that Charlton threw at him. His heroics that day ensured Town won 2-1.

Having played league leaders Walsall away at Fellows Park in front of a crowd of 7,639 on 5th January 1980 Town came back with a 1-1 draw after Alan Buckley, Walsall's player-manager, had missed a penalty and Kindon had scored for Town in the dying seconds. The result kept Town in second place, just one point behind leaders Walsall, as Town jetted off to Guernsey in the Channel Islands for a change of training surroundings and played a friendly match against Vale Recreation F.C. The friendly match saw 18-year-old Paul Gibson given a first team outing at full-back. Fletcher scored our first goal and Cowling scored the second goal in the 28th minute to make the final score 2-0. On returning to Leeds Road Paul Gibson made his Leeds Road debut in a West Riding Cup match against Leeds United on 16th December 1980. Meanwhile, back In the league Town travelled down to the South Coast and lost 4-1 to Portsmouth. The match watched by a Fratton Park crowd of 19,203 was 'Pompey's' highest of the season. Town were still second in the Fourth Division, but trailed the league leaders Walsall by five points, as Portsmouth now sat just a point behind Town in third place.

Peter Hart, as Town captain, recorded his 200th Football League appearance for Town against A.F.C Bournemouth on Saturday 1st March 1980. In front of a Leeds Road crowd of 7,740 Town won 2-0. By the beginning of April Walsall were confirmed as promoted while Town, attempted to chase them down for the league title, came face to face with them on 12th April at our old home. Watched by a crowd of 17,233, our best Leeds Road crowd of the season, they all saw Brian Stanton score to earn a 1-1 draw. Just three days later on Tuesday 15th April 1980 in a re-arranged league match, that had been originally scheduled to take place on Saturday 2nd February, Town played Scunthorpe United at our old home. A quiet Leeds Road crowd of 10,900 saw them kick off and thanks to two goals from Robbo Town won the match 2-1. The relief at the end of the game was felt by everyone, so much so, that the celebrations on the pitch was as if Town had won the league already.

Digital image **a47** (left) – kind permission granted by artist George Chilvers 'Colourised by George' to replicate and display his artwork of John Hasleden and Mick Buxton on that memorable night Town beat Scunthorpe United 2-1 at our old home at Leeds Road.

With just two league matches left to play for both Walsall and Town, until the end of the season, 'The Saddlers' led the Fourth Division on 64 points while Town were second on 62 points. Newport at this point of the season were third on 57 points, Portsmouth meanwhile had dropped to fourth place on 56 points. Town beat Torquay United 4-2 in front of a Leeds Road crowd of 11,067 while Walsall, faced with Wigan Athletic away, surprisingly lost 3-0.

The final match of the season for Town was at our old home against Hartlepool United on Saturday 3rd May. In front of a Leeds Road crowd of 16,807 Town won 2-1 with both goals scored in front of our 'Cowshed' by Robbo. Not only had Town won 2-1 and clinched the title as **Champions of the Fourth Division** they had also scored a record-breaking 101 goals. Walsall meanwhile had lost their final away match of the season against Newport County 4-2 and finished runners-up to Town in the league.

At the end of the season 1979-80 with a final league placing of 1st (**Champions**) it was one of;

Played 46 games; won 27, lost 7, drew 12, goals for 101, goals against 48, Points 66

10 years of Huddersfield Town's history from 1970

1970-71 15th in Division 1
              FA Cup fourth round
            Football League Cup second round
              West Riding Senior Cup Winners

1971-22 22nd in Division 1 **(relegated)**
              FA Cup sixth round
            Football League Cup second round

1972-73 21st in Division 2 **(relegated)**
              FA Cup third round
            Football League Cup second round

1973-74 10th in Division 3
              FA Cup second round
            Football League Cup first round

1974-75 24th in Division 3 **(relegated)**
              FA Cup first round
            Football League Cup second round
              West Riding Senior Cup Winners

1975-76 5th in Division 4
              FA Cup fourth round
            Football League Cup second round

1976-77 9th in Division 4
              FA Cup first round
            Football League Cup third round

1977-78 11th in Division 4
              FA Cup first round
            Football League Cup second round

1978-79 9th in Division 4
              FA Cup first round
            Football League Cup second round
              Shipp Cup Winners

1979-80 Champions Division 4 (promoted)
              FA Cup first round
            Football League Cup second round

Town's 'Greed Decade' - Chapter 10

This new decade brought many changes, conflicts and troubles for Britain. It was also an era when mass strikes, high unemployment and riots took place up and down the country. Towards the end of the decade the age of the 'Yuppie' was born. In the footballing world it was an era when three points for a league win was awarded from the 1981 season onwards, the 100th F.A Cup Final took place and the very first Sunday Football League games were also played. It also sadly saw a rise of the hooligan element that almost ruined British football forever. The British Government went as far as actually having a 'War Cabinet', to combat hooliganism on football's terraces, by the mid-1980s. There were also some sad times when various footballing tragedies occurred.

Even after promotion and having given free transfers in the summer to Ian Holmes, Brett Mellor, Paul Gartland, Daryl and Nicky Brook finances were still tight at Leeds Road. Town started off the 1980-81 season having added only three new signings; two apprentices Ian Thompson, Stephen Stoutt and Bobby Davidson (who had actually been for two Town trials with our reserves towards the end of last season). At their own request both Alan Starling and Terry Armstrong were placed on Town's transfer list while two major transfers took place just prior to the start of the season. Peter Hart transferred to Walsall while Buxton moved swiftly to sign Micky Kennedy from Halifax Town to replace him.

Stephen Paul Stoutt- 'Steve' was a defender signed from non-league Bradley Rangers in 1980. He made less than a dozen league appearances in our Town colours before he signed for Wolverhampton Wanderers in 1985. He was voted Wolves Player of the Year in 1987 and by 1991 had retired from professional football completely.

Robert Davidson – 'Bobby' was a striker who started his Town career in 1980. He made three sub appearances before he signed for Halifax Town in August 1981, and by 1997 had retired from professional football altogether.

Michael Francis Martin Kennedy – 'Micky' was a typical no-nonsense type of midfielder who Town signed from Halifax Town in 1980. He pulled on a Town shirt on 95 different occasions during which time he scored nine goals. By 1982 he had signed for Middlesbrough for £100,000 and by 1994 had finished his professional playing career. (Sadly, Michael Francis Martin Kennedy passed away in February 2019 aged 57).

Town's first game of the season was at Leeds Road against Blackburn Rovers in the Football League Cup on Tuesday 12th August. Just before the game kicked off Mick Buxton received the Bells Fourth Division Manager of the Month Award for April. The first leg away ended in a 0-0 draw and with the second leg at Leeds Road ending in a 1-1 draw it meant that Town was knocked out of the League cup on away goals rule.
Meanwhile, on the pitch over £7,000 had been spent on installing additional drainage to help improve the playing surface at Leeds Road. Money was only spent on essential maintenance in order to free up much-needed revenue for team strengthening, but first Huddersfield Town had to earn it before they were even able to spend it. The Town supporters club was, as of this season, based upstairs above Town's souvenir shop on Leeds Road with our new supporter's secretary being Mrs Edith Hargreaves.

Peter Fletcher was injured and unable to play in the league match against Blackpool, if that weren't bad enough, Steve Kindon was injured during the Blackpool game with a depressed fracture and left the field for further medical treatment. With barely a month gone into the season Town fans saw Stanton, Brown and Hanvey carrying injuries while still performing heroics on the pitch.

One very important 'presentation' took place at half time during the match against Reading on 6th September at our old home at Leeds Road. Nellie Thompson, our Town laundress, was presented with a cheque for £800 by our 'Town Travel Club' to cover the cost to replace the washing machine which had previously been bought in Town's 1971-72 season and was no longer working.

Town beat Reading 4-1, and in doing so recorded their first league win of the season in front of home crowd of 7,312, which took them up to 16th in the Third Division. An interesting point to note which occurred during the Reading game was when Cowling took a corner from our Main Stand and 'Cowshed' corner post. Steve Death, Reading's goalkeeper, blinded by the sun fumbled the ball into the goal at the near post to give Town the lead. It's no coincidence to suggest as author of this book that this wasn't the first or last time the sun played a part in matches at our old home at Leeds Road. Bernard Purdie meanwhile had to be put in plaster due to a tear in his calf muscle after the Reading match. Steve Kindon returned to first team action, at the end of September, wearing a protective skull cap for the league match at Leeds Road against Sheffield United. Watched by a Leeds Road crowd of 14,721 they all saw Stanton score to give Town a 1-0 win.

For the first time at Leeds Road Town began recording on VHS tapes all football matches from the television gantry on the main stand. Bryan Leeming our Club Electrician and Timothy Binns were the cameramen, while the initial recordings was made for coaching purposes it soon became a way for Town fans to purchase match tapes from our Town souvenir shop.

Town's away game at Swindon Town was settled by a controversial goal. Andy Rankin having jumped and caught the ball under his crossbar, with no pressure from anyone, saw the match ref signal a Swindon goal stating that the ball had crossed the line. Just to make things even worse Dave Sutton was taken off the pitch due to a facial injury from a reckless challenge. Sutty had already headed the ball clear and his feet were almost back on the ground again when a challenge left him with a severe laceration, a broken nose and concussion with no free kick or booking awarded for the challenge on him. Even worse was to follow shortly after when Mark Lillis having deputised for Sutty in defence was sent off by the ref for a handball decision. Thanks to a Kindon penalty Town won the game 1-0 against Gillingham, in front of a Leeds Road crowd of 7,716, with just ten men on the pitch. By the middle of October Town were second in the Third Division while Chesterfield topped the league on 20 points. Faced with Northwich Victoria away in the FA Cup first round Town managed to earn a 1-1 draw. 9,849 fans who braved the downpour and torrents of rain at Leeds Road saw Town emphatically beat their non-league opponents 6-0 in the replay. Meanwhile, back in the league they were down to fifth and trailed the divisional leaders Charlton Athletic by five points.

Having beaten Tranmere Rovers 3-0 away in the FA Cup second round Town was for the first time in many years through to the third round. Even better news was that they beat Leeds United 3-1 in the West Riding Cup on 16th December. Watched by a Leeds Road crowd of just 3,611 Terry Austin on his debut scored the first goal while Cowling scored both the other two. With Peter Fletcher having to undergo a back-operation in December Buxton had signed Terry Austin from Mansfield Town for £110,000. Over 70 years of league football had been played at our old home at Leeds Road and Terry Austin was Town's highest ever record-breaking transfer in 1980.

Terence Willis Austin – 'Terry' was signed as a striker from Mansfield Town. After initially breaking into the first team he struggled to get his name on the team sheet on a regular basis, and ultimately struggled with constant game time, as he tried to live up to the hefty transfer fee Town had paid for him. By 1983 Terry had signed for Doncaster Rovers.

After beating Hull City 5-0 on Boxing Day Town were fifth in the Third Division on 33 points while Charlton Athletic still topped the division with 38 points.

On 3rd January 1981 against Shrewsbury Town in the FA Cup third round, watched by a crowd of 14,712 at Leeds Road, in severe wind and rain Andy Rankin was carried off on a stretcher with a serious head injury which resulted in him seeking urgent further medical attention. His career and life had changed in that one moment on our Leeds Road pitch. During the match Town created an unenviable record in that, after Rankin's terrible injury, Kindon went in goal only to be replaced by Lillis as goalkeeper. All three of our 'keepers' each conceded a goal during the game and to this day is a Football League record as well as unique in the history of our old home at Leeds Road.
With the injury to Rankin, Neil Freeman from Birmingham City was brought in on loan, given that our only other keeper in our squad was inexperienced 17-year-old Robert Picton.

Freeman made his first team debut at Leeds Road against Newport County on 10th January 1981. Watched by a 9,063 crowd Town won 4-1 as Stanton scored twice while Austin and Cowling each scored a goal each. Stephen Vass, a fullback, signed for Town on a free transfer from Hartlepool United after he had played a small part for them in Town's final home match last season.

Neil Freeman – was a goalkeeper Town signed on loan from Birmingham City in 1981 he had joined City from Southend United for a transfer fee believed to be around £80,000. From early January onwards Neil figured in a total of 18 league games for Town before he returned to his parent club.

After a long association with Town, Joe Walker from Sheepridge retired from his casual job with our Club. For many years Joe had helped on the pitch after both first and second team matches. At 78 years old he had decided that it was time to give up. His recollections of Town went right back to the First World War and also Town's crisis period a few years later. Joe also remembered the fan's demonstration in front of the Main Stand against the decision to move our club to Leeds. He was also amongst the Leeds Road crowd who watched the Arsenal cup-tie in 1932.

On February 7th Town beat Barnsley 1-0 in front of the highest Leeds Road crowd of the season. A record-breaking 28,901 crowd witnessed Cowling score Town's winning goal in front of our 'Cowshed'. This record-breaking attendance was Town's highest home crowd in the last twenty years and remained so for our final 23 years at Leeds Road. Barnsley were on a 20-match unbeaten run and were also in the running for promotion just like Town. The next three matches in February saw Town go without a win. 14,426 watched our away match down at Bramall Lane against Sheffield United. 'The Blades' felt the full effect of Kindon coming on as a second half sub with Town 2-0 down, because by the end of the game, Steve had scored two goals and frightened the life out of Sheffield United's entire back line. By the middle of April 1981 Town were fourth in the Third Division having beaten Charlton Athletic 2-1 away at the Valley. Rankin having returned to first team action, performed heroics for the final fifteen minutes, saved and blocked everything that Charlton threw at him. This was followed up by an emphatic 5-0 home win over Exeter City when 12,009 fans saw Stanton and Lillis both scored two goals each as Hanvey also grabbed a rare goal.

On 11th April Huddersfield Town played Millwall at our old home at Leeds Road. 13,353 fans saw Millwall beat Town 1-0 that day. Not only had Town lost the match, but towards the end of the game, the match referee had lost total control of the game and frustrations had got to players and both sets of fans. The scenes at the end of the game with both sets of fans on the pitch had to be seen to be believed and had to be controlled by horse-backed police. Even then it took some time to disperse both sets of fans as Town fans were forced back by the police towards our 'Cowshed'.

In the aftermath of the Millwall game our Town Board, at the end of the season, spent approximately £20,000 on the installation of metal perimeter fencing to three sides of our old ground. The Main Stand was the only stand to avoid this ugly and unsightly fencing. Given that our Board's focus was spending money solely on team strengthening this unexpected cost made a severe dent in Town's transfer budget for our up-and-coming season.

Ironically while carrying out some research for this book I came across an article dated 1st November 1969 when Town played a Second Division match against none other than Millwall. The title of the article was 'Don't fence us in' and it stated 'To prevent a minority of supporters from running on to the playing area it will cost the club £3,000 to build a fence. We do not want to have to build this, so we ask our youngsters to show their enthusiasm by cheering the Terriers as loud as they can and to LEAVE THE FIELD TO THE PLAYERS'.

Following the defeat to Millwall Town suffered two further away defeats in succession, against Burnley and Hull City, which effectively put paid to Town's promotion hopes for what would have been a second successive year. The 2-1 defeat at Hull City owed more to 'an assist' from the match ref Mr G. Flint than any other player on the pitch. Given that in the final minute of the game a wayward shot from City looked more destined for the Humber estuary than our Town goal. That is until the ref in trying to get out of the way of the ball it struck him which was then deflected into our net. Even more unbelievable was that the ref actually signalled for a goal.

Town's final league match of the season was against Malcolm McDonald's Fulham on 2nd May 1981 at Leeds Road. It ended in a comfortable 4-2 home win for Town and was watched by a crowd of 6,965. Barnsley had already secured a 1-0 win over Rotherham United in midweek which meant that all the promotion places had already been decided prior to Town's Fulham game. Meanwhile, Town's average league gate of 11,548 from this season onwards in 1981 was the highest at Leeds Road until Town's final day in 1994.

Third Division League Table

		P	W	D	L	F	A	Pts	
1st	Rotherham United	46	24	13	9	67	38	61	**(Champions)**
2nd	Barnsley	46	21	17	8	72	45	59	**(promoted)**
3rd	Charlton Athletic	46	25	9	12	63	50	59	**(promoted)**
4th	Huddersfield	46	21	14	11	71	40	56	

At the end of the season 1980-81 with a final league placing of 4th it was one of;

Played 46 games; won 21, lost 11, drew 14, goals for 71, goals against 40, Points 56

For the 1981-82 season it was fairly obvious to everyone on Town's terraces that the financial side of football at Leeds Road was now having a great impact on our ability to compete against teams in the Third Division. In order to be able to mount a successful promotion bid our commercial department now run by Commercial Manager Maurice Porter had to come up with new and innovative ways to create more revenue for all aspects of life at Leeds Road. After the perimeter fencing was erected the next change at Leeds Road had more to do with compliance on a safety aspect for all sports grounds more than anything else. Huddersfield Town had ramps constructed for access to and from our East Terrace.

Town signed full-back David Burke and midfielder Phil Wilson from Bolton Wanderers, who were both available on a free transfer. Meanwhile, Peter Fletcher and Dick Taylor returned from injury after missing the whole of the previous season.

Such was the cruel hand of fate that both Fletcher and Taylor were forced into premature early retirement during the season as both suffered a reoccurrence of their old injuries. Before the season had even started Fred Robinson was out injured and had sadly played his last ever game for Town. Robert Picton, our young keeper, was also out of action having sustained a broken leg in early May. It would seem that at Leeds Road our keepers over the years had suffered more injuries and broken legs than most other teams in the entire Football League.

David Ian Burke – signed as a full-back at the age of 21 from Bolton Wanderers. He went on to make 189 league appearances and was voted Town's Player of the Year in 1984. I'd like to add a memory of my own, as author of this book, that I can still vividly remember even to this day. On March 23rd 1985 in a Second Division league match against Fulham I stood on our East Terrace at Leeds Road and watched the match along with 4,842 other fans and witnessed the worst ever injury to a footballer that I had ever seen at our old ground. David Burke was in Fulham's half, almost by the East Terrace touchline, and was facing towards our 'Cowshed' goal and looked to play the ball down the touchline just as Fulham's number five Jeff Hopkins, a Welsh International no less, made a wild tackle on David Burke. I was stood almost in the middle of the East Terrace and surrounded by other Town fans we all heard the crack of bones as David went down and lay motionless on the pitch. 'Big Sam' aka Sam Allardyce, who Town had signed from Bolton Wanderers the season before, was wearing our number six shirt that day and came running from the back of our defence. He was the first player to reach both David and Jeff and took a quick look down at David. Without hesitation, Big Sam went berserk and swung a fist at Jeff Hopkins which landed on him. He started to send blow after blow with both fists down onto Fulham's number five as various players from both sides grappled with each other. Both Sam and Jeff Hopkins were by now in full flow fighting mode while the match referee Mr A. Porter tried to get all the players back under his control. Once some sort of order had been restored the ref instantly pulled out a red card to Jeff Hopkins and sent him off. He then turned around and showed a red card to Allardyce who without any further hesitation or argument ran off the pitch after Jeff Hopkins, who by now was down the players tunnel, without giving a second glance to anyone. Having left the pitch Allardyce ripped off his shirt and threw it down almost in disgust, in front of the Main Stand, then ran after Jeff down the tunnel.

David Burke meanwhile had been tended to on the pitch by St. John's Ambulance medical team and was being stretched off to the sound of 4,843 fans clapping him off. Back under the Main Stand however Sam Allardyce had attempted to get to Jeff Hopkins in the away dressing room to have 'further discussions' about the events that had just taken place on the field. David Burke later discovered that his leg was broken in two places and had nearly two years of rehabilitation and physiotherapy before he played professional football again. Thanks to John Haselden's abilities, as Physio and Head Coach, David was in very good hands. By October 1987 David had left Town and signed for Steve Coppell's Crystal Palace. Then in 1988 David Burke was joined in the first team at Crystal Palace by none other than a certain Jeff Hopkins. Whoever said football is a funny old game, wasn't far wrong. Ian Greaves, as Town Manager, once stated in 1969 something quite ironic really 'Contrary to some opinions, football is not more dirty than it ever was, even allowing for the highly competitive game which it is. To say players go around trying to break legs and maim their fellow professionals is nonsense. Yes, in the heat of the moment, people do silly, irresponsible things in any walk of life and even more so in competitive sport when blood is warmed.' I'm guessing as author of this book that on that fateful day in 1985 there was a lot of warm blood, both on and off the pitch, against Fulham.

For the very first time our new Huddersfield Town strip for the 1981-82 season had the Town crest embroidered onto both the shirt and shorts. It was also manufactured with a new type of material which was selected by Mick Buxton from the kit suppliers Barralan.

Phillip Wilson – 'Phil' was a midfielder who Town signed from Bolton Wanderers in 1981. He forged a great central midfield partnership with Steve Doyle and was part of Town's promotion winning team in our 1982-83 season. By 1987 he had signed for York City and had left professional football altogether by 1991.

Town's young players who left in this season were; Paul Gibson, Trevor Parr, Paul Wormley, Stephen Vass, Tommy Smith. While Chris Topping and Bobby Davidson, who were both experienced first team players, left Leeds Road. Four new apprentices; Mark Ratcliffe, Ian Measham, Tony White and Martin Catlow signed on at Town.

A further £2,500 was spent on sand and gravel to further improve drainage and grassroot growth on our field of dreams at our beloved old home. For Raymond Chappell our groundsman at Leeds Road it was a labour of love.

The first home league match of the new season against Exeter City ended in a 1-1 draw, thanks to Kindon's penalty. A Leeds Road crowd of 8,647 fans saw Peter Fletcher return from a season long injury to make his first Third Division appearance in Town's colours. A crowd of 6,713 at Town's next home match against Rochdale in the first leg of the League Cup first round saw Fletcher score twice as Phil Wilson scored the third, his first ever goal in a Town shirt, which earned them a 3-1 win. The second leg away against Rochdale saw Town beat them 4-2, as Fletcher scored another two goals to add to his goal tally, while Kindon and Robins both got in on the action with a goal apiece.

Against Chester City on 29th September 1981 at Leeds Road 7,747 fans and players alike stood united in silence for one minute as a mark of respect for Bill Shankly who had sadly passed away in the early hours of that morning. Leeds Road also flew its flag at half-mast in respect of his passing.

By the beginning of October Town had just seven first team players who had played every game of the season so far. Thanks to a Terry Austin goal at the open end, against Brighton in the League Cup second round first leg match at Leeds Road on 6th October, Town took a 1-0 lead down to the South Coast. A Leeds Road crowd of 9,803 had witnessed Robbo's header ruled out by the match ref, Mr Allison, for offside otherwise Town would have had a 2-0 lead to take down to the South Coast. Sadly, Town lost 2-0 to Brighton at their place and was knocked out of the League Cup.

The new Huddersfield Town Greenhall Suite was officially opened for all Town fans for that 'special occasion'. Sadly though on 17th October 1981 the Suite didn't have much cheer the day Steve Kindon played his last ever game for Town against Gillingham away. A crowd of 4,432 saw Town lose 3-2 as Kindon suffered an injury, that required an immediate cartilage operation, which ultimately ended his Town playing career.

In the FA Cup first round Town was faced with Workington away and in front of a crowd of 3,101 Robbo came to the rescue and scored Town's equalizer in a 1-1 draw. Amazingly Steve Smith at the age of 35 years old was forced back into service as an emergency left-back, for the Workington match, due to the level of injuries that Town had that day. Watched by a crowd of 7,305 in the replay back at Leeds Road Town beat Workington 5-0. Down at Chesterfield in the second round of the FA Cup on 12th December Cowling scored to earn Town a 1-0 victory. Given that at the time Chesterfield were second in the league on 34 points it was a good cup result for Town. Tim Hotte, a young 18-year-old striker, made his Town debut against Brentford on 2nd January 1982. Having replaced Robbo he teamed up with Peter Fletcher and put himself about on the pitch. He required two stitches to a wound after being struck in the face by Brentford's Jim McNicholl. A well-struck shot in the first half, which just scraped the crossbar, was as close as Hotte got to scoring on his Town debut.

Timothy Alwin Hotte – 'Tim' was a striker who started his football career with Arsenal and signed for Town in 1981. After just 16 appearances, during which time he scored four goals, Tim signed for non-league Harrogate Town in 1983.

By the time Town had faced Oxford United, on Saturday 9th January 1982, Steve Kindon had addressed Town fans over their treatment of David Cowling. He had endured 18 months of torture by certain sections of our fans and the substituting and transfer-listing of Terry Austin just before Christmas was also in Kindon's thoughts. Town faced Carlisle United away in the FA Cup third round and thanks to Peter Fletcher's first ever hat-trick, in front of a 6,345 crowd, Town won 3-2. Austin by now was back in our first team and wore our number nine shirt for the match.

The fourth round of the FA Cup saw Orient take on Town at our old home at Leeds Road. Ironically 13,623 all saw Terry Austin, wearing our number ten shirt, score Town's only goal in a 1-1 draw. The replay down at Orient's place saw Town lose 2-0, and with it a chance to play Crystal Palace in the fifth round was gone. Due to injuries to both our main keepers, Rankin and Taylor, Town brought in Brian Cox initially on loan from Sheffield Wednesday for cover. His first team debut was at Leeds Road on 23rd March. In front of a home crowd of 6,721 Brian helped Town to a 1-1 draw with Chesterfield as they sneaked in an injury-time equaliser.

Brian Roy Cox – signed initially on loan from Sheffield Wednesday in 1982 and by the summer had signed permanently for Town. He was part of Town's successful promotion winning team in our 1982-83 season and by the time he left in 1988 he had played 213 league games.

Town's league match against Newport County on 30th March 1982 at Leeds Road is a date that should always be remembered if you are a Malcolm Brown fan. He had just broken Bill McGarry's club record of 158 consecutive league games. Mally had commenced his run of league matches on 9th September 1978 and had beaten a record that had stood proudly under McGarry's name for 27 years.

In April 1982 Stanley Kinder, Town's Director and past Chairman, sadly passed away at the age of 73. Having served on Town's board since May 1964 he had also been Chairman of the Development Association since it was founded in 1970. Sadly, Tom Price, who was Town's Commissionaire, also sadly passed away in this month and by the end of the season Town fans also said goodbye to Ian Robins who had retired from professional football altogether.

At the end of the season 1981-82 with a final league placing of 17th it was one of;

Played 46 games; won 15, lost 19, drew 12, goals for 64, goals against 59, Points 57

Given the many injuries from Town's previous season the start of the 1982-83 season saw Keith Mason, Stephen Doyle, Maurice Cox and Roy Greenwood all sign for Town. Peter Valentine a young centre-back was promoted to the first team and Mark Lillis came of age and became a key figure for Town in this year. Terry Austin meanwhile transferred to Doncaster Rovers in exchange for the services of Daral Pugh.

Keith Michael Mason – was a goalkeeper that Buxton signed on a free transfer from Leicester City in 1982. He made 30 league appearances before he left professional league football altogether in 1986.

Stephen Charles Doyle – 'Steve' was a midfielder Buxton signed from Preston North End in 1982 on a free transfer. He formed a deadly midfield partnership with Phil Wilson and helped Town gain promotion. He made 158 league appearances, during which time he scored six goals, before he signed for Sunderland in 1987.

Maurice Cox – was a forward Buxton signed on a free transfer in August 1982 on non-contract terms. He played only three league games, made one Milk Cup appearance and was named sub in two other league games before he left Town in 1982 for non-league football.

Roy Greenwood - was a winger that Buxton signed on a free transfer in August 1982 from Swindon Town. He made five league appearances before he initially signed on loan for Tranmere Rovers in 1983. By the following year he had signed permanently for Scarborough.

Peter Valentine – was a centre-back that came through Town's youth ranks and made his first team debut in 1981. He pulled on our Town colours on 22 different occasions, during which time he scored one goal, before he signed for Bolton Wanderers in 1983.

Daral James Pugh – was a midfielder Buxton signed in part-exchange for Terry Austin from Doncaster Rovers in 1982. Daral made nine league appearances in our promotion winning season and was named as sub on 33 other occasions. By 1985 he had signed permanently for Rotherham United.

Town's first home league game of the season saw Maurice Cox score against Exeter City on his league debut in front of a Leeds Road crowd of 5,168. Town's next game was at home against Doncaster Rovers in the Milk Cup first round first leg. In front of a 4,430 crowd Town earned a 1-1 draw. The second leg down at 'Donny' saw Mally Brown score to send Town through 2-1 on aggregate to the second round of the Milk Cup. The next four league matches without a league win home or away, while David Hodgson emerged as Kenny Dalglish's understudy at Liverpool, saw Colin Russell's services secured by Buxton for Town.

Colin Russell – was a striker Buxton signed from Liverpool in 1982. He made 49 appearances and scored 17 goals for Town in his first season. With both Mark Lillis and Brian Stanton in deadly form, the three of them headed our goalscoring charts and helped to achieve Town's second promotion in four seasons. After a total of 64 league appearances during which time Russell had scored 23 goals he surprisingly signed for Stoke City on loan in 1983 and signed permanently for Bournemouth by the following season.

Colin Russell marked his league debut for Town by scoring both goals against Oxford United in a 2-0 win at Leeds Road in September. Three days later at Leeds Road Town hit Orient for six, as they ran out 6-0 winners, as Russell scored his third goal in his first two games. Against Oxford United In the second round first leg home tie at the beginning of October thanks to Stanton and Russell both scoring Town beat them 2-0. The second leg saw Town beaten 1-0 away but went through 2-1 on aggregate to the third round of the Milk Cup. Mark Lillis meanwhile had started a goalscoring spree at Leeds Road that began with all four goals against Cardiff City in a 4-0 rout. He then scored another five goals in Town's next three matches two away at Gillingham, two at home against Doncaster and then scored Town's only goal in a 1-0 win away down at Bournemouth. Town by this time were up to sixth place in the Third Division and were faced with our old foes Leeds United away in the third round of the Milk Cup.

As author of this book I owe a huge thank you to my former near-neighbours Mr and Mrs Winstanley who kindly agreed that a 15-year-old lad could travel with them on that fateful Tuesday night to Elland Road. We set off in their blue Bedford box van with me sat on a wooden padded seat in the back. As bumpy and uncomfortable as it was I was more than happy to travel like this. We managed to get a seat in the corner section of the home end nearest to their Kop. Seeing all the United supporters around us, I was told that if we scored it might not be a good idea to celebrate. With 24,215 home and away fans watching the match that night, I can clearly still remember that in the second half, Town played with United's Kop to their backs as our away fans were all tucked down the side of their pitch.

Lillis went on a surging run down to their goal line and lofted the ball over from the right-hand side and out of nowhere came Cowling to head high into their net to score Town's winner. Unable to contain myself I instantly jumped up and down with my arms aloft. Both Mr and Mrs Winstanley tried to pull me down and stop me from shouting out whilst all the home fans below, and most of the Kop nearest to us, were all looking at me.

Thankfully we were able to watch the rest of the game without getting lynched. The scenes at the end of the game was like we had won the Milk Cup never mind it being only the third round. Town had withstood a United onslaught, that memorable night, as 'Buxton's blue and white army' headed for home, via seventh heaven.

Meanwhile, in the league Town became unstoppable as they sat second in the division and were unfazed with Arsenal away in the fourth round of the Milk Cup by the end of November. Sadly, a harshly awarded penalty down at Highbury ended Town's Milk Cup exploits against 'The Gunners'. They scored the decisive penalty to give what many had thought that night was an undeserved 1-0 victory. Buxton meanwhile rounded off the month of November by being named Manager of the Month. Mally Brown made his 200th Town appearance on 27th December 1982 at Leeds Road against Chesterfield. He marked the special occasion by scoring a trademark penalty of his as Town won 3-1 thanks to Lillis and Russell scoring Town's other goals. A top-of-the-table clash with Lincoln City away saw Town beat them 2-1 as 11,829 fans watched on.

Town started the New Year on 1st January 1983 with a right celebration, in front of 18,438 fans they beat Bradford City 6-3. Given that at one stage of the game Town were 3-1 down it was a phenomenal match to watch. Having beaten Mossley in the first round of the FA Cup and then having beaten Altrincham in the next round Town were then faced with Chelsea in the third round of the FA Cup at Leeds Road. Watched by 17,064 fans that day Town were unlucky not to win the game and had to settle for a 1-1 draw. The replay down in London saw Town knocked out of the cup, after losing 2-0 to Chelsea.

In the league momentum was building into what many hoped was going to be another promotion winning season. By the beginning of April Town had moved up to third in the league table and by the middle of the month had hit the top of the Third Division. Promotion fever had started to hit every Town fan with everyone thinking was this to be our year. It's at this point in the book that I'd like to add a rather tragic and very moving true story from Lynne Barrett a Town fan for over 49 years. She has painstakingly gone back in time and given her kind permission for me to write her account of that dreadful day.

Having been introduced to Huddersfield Town, by her Grandfather Thomas Barrett, at the mere age of ten years old. Lynne Barrett hadn't realised at that time just how much of an impact our old home at Leeds Road and our mighty Town would have on her or on her life. But like everyone whoever stepped into our old home once she stood on our terraces, Lynne felt like she belonged, she felt like she was finally home, with everyone else in our Town family, from that very first day at ten years old she was hooked as a Town fan.

Looking forward to our last home game of the season against Bradford City on 14th May in Town's 82-83 season Lynne along with other devoted Town fans had travelled to every home and away match. Her usual routine had started like many other Town fans, during the week, with a million and one thoughts about the forthcoming weekend fixture. 'Was Town home or away', 'Where should we all meet', 'How far away is it' and 'Do we need to stay over' if it was an away match. Then excitedly 'I wonder how many fans we are taking and how are we getting there' Throughout her working week her thoughts were all about Town's next game and meeting up with fellow friends and fans.

If you were lucky and your Mum used 'Persil' washing powder, you may have been saving up those special vouchers on the box lid, so you could get there by train, for free. It was a great time to be a Town fan back then, given the warm weather had also started to pick up towards the end of the season. Lynne and her then husband Paul had many friends who were also Town fans. Three such fans were Alan Boyles, Jim Woodhead and Christopher Sunderland. Alan and Jim had watched Town for many years and although they used different modes of transport to get to home and away games, they usually ended up meeting each other at the match. Christopher or Sunny as he was known by, was a founder member and Chairman of our 'Travel Club' at the time. He regularly stewarded coaches to away games. But at this crucial point in our season when the belief was that Town were going to win promotion. It was decided that for the last couple of long-distance Town matches they'd all go by car together. Sunny had arranged stewarding on the 'Travel club' coaches and was the designated driver for this travelling group of friends. On the 16th of April, Town were playing away at Leyton Orient in North London. Town didn't have many of those trips thankfully and the long journey ahead meant they needed to be organised, so they set off in good time to allow for a couple of stops and to ensure they had plenty of time before the game. At this point of the season Town had a strong following of away fans. Being the only girl in their travelling group Lynne set herself a precedent by excitingly cooking chicken and preparing a tasty picnic for everyone on the Friday evening. She didn't want anyone to worry about finding lunch before the game, but luckily, when they arrived near the ground, they found a lovely sunny beer garden and was able to grab a pint or two to wash down their picnic. Lynne can remember it being a particularly exciting day, she can still picture the anticipation and discussions about what our Town team would be before the game. We'd beaten Orient 6-0 back in September the year before and knew this was going to be an important result. We won 3-1 that day and the long drive home for Lynne and her gang didn't feel so long as they had all enjoyed a great day out.

The following week, on 23rd April, Town played Reading at home and thrashed them 3-1. Brian Stanton and Colin Russell scored one each that day, with Lynne's favourite player Malcolm Brown scoring one from the penalty spot. Winning felt good for everyone at Huddersfield Town. The May Day Bank Holiday beckoned and with only three games left of the season, two at home then that important Bradford City fixture, the excitement for every Town fan was growing.

On Saturday 30th of April the group was set to travel down to Bristol Rovers. Lynne had spent most of her Friday night cooking chicken for their picnic, packing up a few extras which she knew the lads would like and bought Sunny a box of chocolates. He'd been so good driving them all to London two weeks earlier, and now he had to drive all the way down to Bristol. He did quite a lot of driving for work and was willing to give up those pre-match pints, so Lynne thought he deserved a little gift of appreciation. She left them on her dresser in the lounge ready for when they'd return later that evening. Everyone was up early, and the sun was shining, the long weekend looked like a great adventure.

Alan and Jim were waiting by Lynne and Paul's front gate at 8.30am, bristling with excitement, albeit a little muffled after starting off the weekend with a few pints the evening before. Sunny pulled up in his Cortina, he was smiling too. They all made themselves comfortable placing bags and coats in the car boot and choosing their seats for the long journey ahead. It was going to be a tight squeeze with Jim sitting in the front passenger seat, Alan situated behind Sunny and Lynne settling in beside Alan before Paul sat beside her and behind Jim. Off they went, all smiling, looking round to see if they could see any more cars or minibuses filled with blue and white scarves. So many Town fans would all be up early and setting off to Bristol, ready to sing and wave as they passed each other on the M6. Lynne's then husband Paul continues the story.

Everyone was enjoying 'Snooker on the radio' a quiz hosted by Dave Lee Travis on his morning breakfast show. It was about 10am when Sunny screamed "What the...." Then there was an explosion. They began being thrown around in the car as it sped out of control for over 200 metres, hitting everything in its path.

It was later learned that they had been hit by a vehicle (an Austin Princess) which had been travelling in the opposite direction. The driver had lost control at high speed, hitting the central kerb, and taken off clearing the central barrier before landing directly onto our car. This is what Sunny had seen before he took the brunt of the impact and was killed instantly. A witness at the subsequent inquest said "it came down on their car like a sledgehammer" Paul was cut and bruised and in shock but was able to force his door open and climb out of the car. He could instantly see the seriousness of the situation. Jim was conscious but trapped in his seat. The other three were all unconscious. Paul helped Jim get free and clamber out of the car. The motorway was strewn with debris and had come to a complete halt. The emergency services were thankfully on their way. Both Paul and Jim kept 'spectators' away from their car until help arrived. The police confirmed to Paul at the scene that Sunny had died. Lynne was considered the most seriously injured casualty, so they took her in the first ambulance to North Staffordshire Royal Infirmary.

14 vehicles involved, 2 dead and scores injured. Reported the Stoke Evening Sentinel – Saturday 30th April 1983.

Lynne now continues with the rest of her story. We lost our good friend Christopher, 'Sunny', that day. All of our lives were changed, for good. As the tragic event happened on a part of the M6 (J15) which was very close to one of only two hospitals specialising in Neurology, Lynne was quickly taken to the North Staffordshire Royal Infirmary, Hartshill, in Stoke-On-Trent. Due to her injuries, immediate surgery was required, and surgeons carried out an operation lasting nine hours, attending to a fractured skull together with an extradural and subdural haematoma (blood clots on the brain). The surgery was carried out successfully, but it remained unclear whether Lynne would suffer any permanent brain damage until she regained full consciousness nearly three weeks later. Lynne personally still has no recollection of anything after leaving home that day nor does she have any memory of quite some time previous to and shortly after the event. Her late Dad told her he'd asked for reassurance as to how she would be when she regained consciousness but was told he would have to wait and see. Her mum came to stay with Lynne, and as she began to wake up her mum brought her favourite salmon sandwiches to eat at the hospital. Unfortunately, due to her head injury and surgery Lynne responded by throwing them away. She didn't have the ability to understand the offer nor how to eat them. Her mum replaced them with a small teddy bear, which Lynne later nicknamed him Toody, for some reason. To this day the teddy bear still sits close beside her in her bedroom. Many friends and relatives travelled to see Lynne in Stoke and when she was well enough to be subsequently transferred to the Huddersfield Royal Infirmary to continue her recovery.
Lynne vaguely remembers realising she was back in Huddersfield, in a lift, listening to people chattering about her and her home town. Lynne can also remember it wasn't long before she became aware of the passing of Christopher (Sunny). An acquaintance working at the hospital 'let it slip', but Lynne hadn't quite grasped exactly what she had said but knew something was wrong.
The doctors had said that knowing the terrible truth of what had happened to 'Sunny' might not help her recovery in the short term, but by then she had realised that he hadn't come to visit her. it was like a bad dream hearing the dreadful news Lynne felt mentally numb. By now she was sleeping a lot but began to understand more of what people were talking about. She was taken regularly to the Occupational Therapy department at the hospital and began to learn how to do the simplest of tasks, like 'make a cup of tea'. It was challenging to remember how many steps there were to carry out the simplest of actions such as 'getting dressed' but eventually and with practice, she retained the information and remembered how to do things without help or prompting. She was still suffering from double vision and a damaged scapula to her left shoulder but the swelling on her head began to subside and the scar, in time, started to heal. Meanwhile, Sunny's funeral took place during this time.

It was very well attended Paul, Jim and Alan, who were recovering from the injuries they sustained in the car accident, including cuts and bruises from the impact and broken glass, were also able to pay their respects to their lost friend. As the days and weeks passed the loss of Sunny sank in with Lynne. Why him, why not me, why were we involved in the crash at all.

Later when they all attended the inquest, they discovered another tragic event had occurred that day. The poor lady travelling to see her husband in Scotland, on the northbound carriageway, had lost one of her three children, her son. The enormity of the tragedy just kept growing and growing.

Lynne wasn't aware that her mum, friends and work colleagues was asked lots of questions by the local newspapers and media, her mum was even interviewed by the local radio station. She had received many visitors at both hospitals and remembers her bed being surrounded by numerous vases of flowers and presents from people she hadn't even met. Friends of relatives or just other Town fans had sent good wishes and Lynne particularly remembers a fluffy white polar bear which had been sent to her by the gentleman living across the road from her Dad, in Meltham.

He had bought a new car from the 'Polar Dealership' and thoughtfully sent on his free gift for her. That meant so much to her, but at the same time reminded Lynne just how serious it had all been. Lynne is not sure who contacted who or how the arrangements were made for our beloved Town football team to come along to Huddersfield Royal Infirmary to see her. The Club was in touch with North Staffordshire Royal Infirmary, Sunny's parents and then HRI. Lynne remembers their visit came when she was able to wash and dress herself and luckily when she was able to converse with people properly again and walk around the hospital ward. The photographs of Lynne with Brian Stanton, Daryl Pugh, Brian Cox, David Burke, Colin Russell and her favourite all-time player Malcolm Brown are still her treasured possessions to this very day. She had even been able to have photographs with Mick Buxton, Steve Kindon and Peter Fletcher at the Player of The Year Celebration, held at the Masonic Hall, Huddersfield after our 79/80 season. Those times were so uplifting and was needed to help Lynne it also helped her realise just how much our club cares about its supporters. This is something that resonates throughout this book from our very early days when Chapman used to arrange collections after matches for all our ageing former players to when Chapman even attended a funeral for a former Town player. Even our Town Directors sent money to war widows during WWI. There's not been a year gone by, since we first kicked a football in anger in our old home at Leeds Road, that any grief or tragedy we have had as a Town fan hasn't been shared and felt by our Club also. We have a long history of looking after our own at Town with players making regular hospital visits to see our poorly fans and that is something that even in today's modern game still thankfully continues.

a48 (left)

a49 (right)

Digital enhanced image **a48** (above left)– Courtesy of Lynne Barrett with Town players at HRI in 1983; (L to R) Malcolm Brown, Lynne Barrett, Colin Russell, David Cowling and David Burke.

Digital enhanced image **a49** (above right)– Lynne with Town players (L to R) Brian Cox, Lynne Barrett, Brian Stanton and Phil Wilson.

On the day Paul took Lynne home she remembers walking into their lounge and seeing that box of chocolates which she had bought Sunny for driving them to the away matches. He wasn't here anymore. Lynne was 21 years old and although she had been devastated losing her Grandad shortly before her marriage in 1981, nothing prepares you for losing a friend so young. Police visited their home bringing items they had collected at the scene of the accident. The boots which she wore on the day, with their sole and heel hanging off, were in her Dad's garage. So she wouldn't see them and be upset. Paul had newspaper cuttings showing the car they had travelled in, which of course was so badly damaged it had been written off.

Sometime after the event it was decided that the four friends who had survived the accident, along with their spouses, would go to visit Sunny's parents in Hipperholme, near Halifax. His parents welcomed them all into their home, and they all spoke about Christopher long into the evening. They told stories about him, how they had first met him, how they had spent time together and how they were all doing. His parents listened attentively but having lost their only son, they were still devastated, as was to be expected.

At the end of summer in 1983 Lynne and her husband took a short trip to Scarborough, she can still remember it quite clearly as they also received the very exciting and important news that they were expecting their first baby. After only a few months back at work Lynne took maternity leave from her job on Christmas Eve 1983 and their daughter Sarah Louise was born on February 18th 1984. It was decided that her christening would be the 30th of April, one year to the very day of their dreadful car accident. They hoped that it would mark a new start for them both and although it was a happy event, that very date, in the following years, was overshadowed by the memories of that tragic day that could never be forgotten.

While writing this section of the book I find it ironic that Town played our last ever game at Leeds Road against Blackpool on 30th April 1994 – 11 years to the day exactly since Sunny was tragically taken from all who knew and loved him. One would like to think Sunny was there watching our team leave our first ever home. R.I.P. Christopher Sunderland (Sunny). Never ever forgotten.

One part of Lynne's story which has never been told before is that her yearly remembrance for Christopher Sunderland (Sunny) usually appears on her own personal social media page, but in 2020 for the first time ever, Lynne Barrett posted it on to 'Those were the days my friend'. That allowed other long time Town fans to contact Lynne, some of whom were very dear friends of hers over 35 years ago. More recently she had the chance to catch up with some members of our 1979-80 promotion winning Town team at the Canalside. Malcolm Brown immediately recognised Lynne and remembered all about that fateful day back in 1983. 'Mally' was interested to know how her life had been, and how she was, even after 36 years. Back in 1983, it hadn't been just lip service or any marketing ploy, but a sincere caring visit from our then Huddersfield Town players to one of their then young, but now older and wiser but always devoted Town fan, Lynne Barrett.

On 7th May 1983 Town were faced with playing Newport County at our old home at Leeds Road. In front of 16,509 fans Dave Cowling scored the all-important winning goal six minutes from time in front of our 'Cowshed' to secure Town's second promotion in just four years. The scenes on our terraces and on the pitch at the end of the match was of one big celebration. With both Mick Buxton and John Haselden at the helm we had taken another giant step to regaining our self-respect and Town pride back. A civic reception at the end of the season marked Town's return to the Second Division after an absence of over 10 years. For the first and only time in their entire football history it was also a season when Town went unbeaten at our old home at Leeds Road.

At the end of the season 1982-83 with a final league placing of 3rd **(Promoted)** it was one of;

Played 46 games; won 23, lost 10, drew 13, goals for 84, goals against 49, Points 82

One legendary Town player that left in the summer of 1983 was our very own Malcolm Brown. Mally signed for Newcastle United but sadly his promising career was hampered by an injury that perhaps in a selfish way helped Town to sign him again in later years. Brian Laws from Burnley was signed by Buxton as Mally's replacement while Paul Jones was signed from Bolton Wanderers. Tim Hotte, Peter Valentine, Martin Coupe and Mark Radcliffe were all given free transfers while Kevin Bird, who had been released by Mansfield, had a trial period in pre-season with Town. He made his first team debut away against Blackburn Rovers in Town's first Second Division match of the new season. Kevin Stonehouse meanwhile had signed for Town from Blackburn Rovers in our 1982-83 season and got the chance this season to stake his claim for a first team place.

Brian Laws - was a right-back signed from Burnley in 1983 and made his Town debut in our Milk Cup first leg first round home tie against Mansfield Town. He made 56 league appearances during which time he scored one goal before he signed for Middlesbrough in 1985.

Paul Bernard Jones - was a central defender signed from Bolton Wanderers in 1983 and made his first team debut in our first league match back in the Second Division against Blackburn Rovers. After playing 73 league games, during which time he scored eight goals, he signed for Oldham Athletic in 1985.

Kevin Stonehouse – was a striker Town signed from Blackburn Rovers in our 1982-83 season. He wore our number 8 shirt for Town's first match back in the Second Division against none other than Blackburn Rovers. Kevin actually scored Town's penalty to give us a second half 2-1 lead before they equalised in a 2-2 draw. After making 20 league appearances, during which time he scored four goals, he signed for Blackpool and by 1990 had finished his playing career at Rochdale. (Sadly, Kevin Stonehouse passed away in July 2019 aged 59).

The problem of 'going up' for Town in our 1983-84 season was magnified for us all at our old home by the introduction of the 'Safety of the Sports ground Act'. Along with all other First and Second Division teams Town was now the subject of a Government Home Office Order made by the then Secretary of State Leon Brittan, which was laid before parliament on 13th July 1983. This meant amongst other things that Town had to obtain a Safety Certificate in order to continue staging matches at our old home at Leeds Road. One of the immediate changes that took place was our old ground was segregated into four separate sections. This meant it was no longer permissible for any transferring of stands between games for any Town fan anymore. The open end at Bradley Mills was solely designated for visiting supporters only. Our 'Cowshed' was now only licensed to hold just 3,304 fans for every home game. Our capacity crowd for the start of the season was 26,301 which would increase to 30,459 after Town had spent approximately £75,000 on improvement works.

By the end of September Town were unbeaten in the league after six matches and was third in the league on 12 points as Sheffield Wednesday sat top of the division with 17 points. Having beaten Mansfield Town home and away in the Milk Cup first round Town was then faced with Watford in the next round. As an over-aged player Steve Doyle was called up by the Welsh Under-21 side and became the first Town player since Richard Taylor in 1974 and 1975 to win any international honour of any kind while still a Town player.

Town's Second Division match on October 1st 1983 against Chelsea ended in a 3-2 home defeat. It was our first league defeat of the season and after 33 league and cup matches the best home record in the Football League had finally come to an end. Sadly it's also remembered for all the wrong reasons too as Richard Aldridge a Chelsea supporter who had attended the match tragically lost his life just thirty minutes after the final whistle. Over three hundred letters and cards from Town fans was sent to Mr and Mrs Aldridge to offer our sincere condolences on the loss of their beloved son.

Having beaten Watford in the second round of the Milk Cup Town was then faced with Stoke City away in the next round. After a hard fought 0-0 draw against City it meant a replay back at our place at Leeds Road. In the league meanwhile Town were fifth on 24 points while Wednesday still topped the division with 34 points.

Finally, after five years of Mick Buxton and John Haselden working hard, for the greater good of our club, not just with the first team but with our whole Town set up. We had a full team of youth players on our full-time register once again. Not since the days of Ian Greaves and his backroom staff had Town enjoyed that luxury. We were slowly turning a corner in that Huddersfield Town was in the process of producing our own players once again.

For Town's Milk Cup third round replay against Stoke City on Tuesday 22nd November 1983, making her third appearance of the season was Maggie the prize cow. As representative of Hildale Farms Dairy who were Town's match sponsors Maggie and her herdsman Peter once again tried to help Town to another Milk Cup win. Sadly, the tactics employed by Stoke for the match 'earned' them a 2-0 win and Town was out of the Milk Cup, and it would be the last Town fans saw anything of Maggie. David Burke made his 100th Football League appearance against Fulham in this month while David Cowling celebrated his 200th Football League appearance in our Town colours against Cardiff City towards the end of the month.

In early December Town was up against the likes of Keegan, Beardsley, Waddle and McDermott as they were faced with Newcastle United away. In front of 25,747 fans Town suffered a heavy 5-2 league defeat. Ironically watching from the stands that day was our former number two Town legend Mally Brown who was out injured for Newcastle. Alongside Mally in the stands was Town's new number two Brian Laws who was himself out injured also after just having had a cartilage operation.

Watched by only 7,889 at Leeds Road just before Christmas Town managed a 2-2 draw against Middlesbrough. Thankfully for Town's next league match away against Leeds United on Boxing Day Colin Russell scored first, then Mark Lillis scored with a trademark header, Town won 2-1 in front of a crowd of 23,614. The day after in front of Town's highest home crowd of the season so far 23,497 fans saw Town defeated 3-1 against Manchester City. Ground record takings of £47,000 was generated from just the City match alone giving Town some very much needed revenue.

In the New Year having drawn First Division Q.P.R at home in the FA Cup third round, thanks to goals from Mark Lillis and Kevin Stonehouse, Town won 2-1 against Terry Venables's Q.P.R side. Drawn at home against First Division Notts County, in the fourth round of the FA Cup, after two match postponements due to severe snow. Having finally kicked off and despite another goal by Kevin Stonehouse in front of crowd of 13,634 Town lost 2-1 and was out of the FA Cup after Mark Lillis had a goal disallowed. Steve Stoutt meanwhile had made his first team appearance in our Town colours wearing our number two shirt. By early February Town found themselves with yet more injuries as both Cowling and Lillis had been injured during the Notts County match and missed the 3-1 away defeat down at Chelsea. Brian Cox was the next injured Town player having suffered a depressed fracture of the cheekbone in a league match against Oldham Athletic at Leeds Road. Mark Lillis once again donned our keeper's jersey as a makeshift keeper to cover for our injured goalie. Liam Robinson made his first team debut for Town, wearing our number nine shirt, at the end of February against Derby County away whilst Keith Mason took over the keeper's shirt from the injured Brian Cox.

Spencer Liam Robinson – Liam was a striker Town signed from Nottingham Forest in 1983. Having pulled on our Town shirt on just 21 occasions, during which time he scored two goals, by 1986 having signed initially on loan at Tranmere he signed permanently for Bury at the end of the season.

Unbelievably Town had to wait from the beginning of the New Year until 24th March 1984 before they recorded another win in the league. A 3-0 Leeds Road win over Cambridge United was watched by a crowd of 6,037. Mel Eves and Peter Eastoe had recently signed for Town on loan and made their first team debut. Mel scored two of Town's three goals against Cambridge United with the third goal coming from a Paul Jones penalty.

Mel Eves – was a striker Town signed on loan from Wolverhampton Wanderers in 1984. He stayed until the end of the season and appeared in seven league games, during which time he scored four goals, before he signed for Sheffield United at the end of the season.

Peter Robert Eastoe – was a striker Town signed on loan from West Bromwich Albion in 1984. Once the season had finished he went back to his parent club.

A 16,270 crowd at Leeds Road at Easter witnessed a 2-2 home draw with our old adversaries Leeds United. Thanks to goals from Mel Eves and Steve Doyle it gave Town a 2-1 lead but as was the case in this season another Town player suffered a facial injury. Keith Hanvey suffered a depressed fracture of the cheekbone six minutes from the end of the game and ultimately Town hung on for a 2-2 draw. Dave Sutton was our next Town player hit by injury in the next league game away against Manchester City. He suffered a double fracture of his right leg in a tackle with Derek Parlane as Town ran out 3-2 winners at Maine Road. By the end of April Town was eleventh in the Second Division on 54 points while Sheffield Wednesday topped the league on 81 points. At the beginning of May 18,488 fans saw Town take on Sheffield Wednesday at Leeds Road. With a makeshift team Town lost the match 1-0 as Paul Jones was voted Town's Player of the Year and also won the Supporters Player of the Year Award (which was the first time that this had ever happened).

Town's last home match of the season on Monday 7th May 1984 was against Newcastle United. It was to be Kevin Keegan's swansong before his retirement from professional football altogether. 25,101 fans filled our old home at Leeds Road for Keegan's special occasion, as it was Keegan was a no-show on the day. With the help of Graham Cooper playing his first league match in Town's colours he managed to get Town into a 2-0 half-time lead. Both of the goals came at the open end with Cooper scoring a cracker with his head for his first ever league goal. The second was another Cooper header, but went in off Newcastle's Steve Carney, and was attributed as an own goal. By half-time the 'Geordies' in our ground had started to run riot and some were seen climbing the floodlights in the away end. West Yorkshire Police had a novel way of keeping the Newcastle fans up there. They used a hose and plenty of water to drive them all back up until they were all arrested for trespass at the end of the match. By the end of the match Newcastle's Peter Beardsley and David Mills had both scored to make the full-time score 2-2.

At the end of the season 1983-84 with a final league placing of 12th it was one of;

Played 42 games; won 14, lost 13, drew 15, goals for 56, goals against 49, Points 57

Town's second season back in the Second Division, in our 1984-85 season, saw two new faces added to our squad Sam Allardyce and Dale Tempest. Big Sam had signed for Town on a permanent deal while Dale had signed initially on loan before a permanent transfer took place at a later stage. After six years of hard work and endeavour Keith Hanvey sadly left Town before the start of the season and signed for Rochdale. Steve Stoutt, Peter Butler Ian Measham and Julian Winter all broke through into the first team in this season. Diahatsu was our second shirt sponsor following the Club's previous two years with Central Garage, Mirfield.

Samuel Allardyce – 'Big Sam' was signed by Town as a defender on a free transfer from Coventry City. He once again formed a defensive partnership with his former Bolton colleague Paul Jones, at the heart of Town's defence. By 1985 he had signed for Bolton Wanderers in a £15,000 transfer.

Dale Michael Tempest – was a striker signed initially on loan from Fulham before he signed permanently for Town. After pulling on our Town colours on 72 different occasions, during which time he scored 29 goals, he signed for Belgian side Lokeren in 1986.

Graham Cooper – was a midfielder who was born in Huddersfield and started his Football League career at Town in 1983. He made 61 league appearances, during which time he scored ten goals, before being transferred to Wrexham in 1987 for £25,000. By 1992 he had left professional football altogether.

The first league match of the 1984-85 season began with Oxford United at Leeds Road, the match was watched by a crowd of just 6,184 and ended in a 3-0 defeat for Town. Julian Winter and Peter Butler were both given a run out in this match due to overnight injuries to some regular first team players. Dale Tempest meanwhile had his nose broken and had to undergo an operation which left him out of action for three weeks from the middle of September.

Julian Winter – was a defender who started his football career at Town in 1984. He made 89 league appearances, during which time he scored five goals, before he signed on loan for Scunthorpe United in 1988. By the start of the following season Julian had signed permanently for Dave Bassett's Sheffield United team. Just a week before the season was due to start Julian Winter sustained a career-ending ligament injury. After ten operations in just four years, he was forced to retire from the professional game. In March 2016 he became Chief Executive at Huddersfield Town and was appointed a Town Director by November of that same year. By early March 2020, after tendering his resignation towards the end of 2019, Julian Winter had left our club.

Peter James Butler – was a midfielder who started his Football League career at Town in 1984. He wore our Town colours as a first team sub on a handful of occasions before he went on loan to Cambridge United in 1988. Having signed permanently for Southend United by 1992 he came back to Town on loan and played seven league games. Then having gone back to his parent club at Southend Peter Butler was signed by West Ham United in 1994.

Three league games of the new season had been played and Town were 12th in the Second Division on four points having beaten Brighton 1-0 at the Goldstone Ground thanks to a goal from Julian Winter. Steve Stoutt made his first team debut against 'The Seagulls' wearing our number six shirt. By the beginning of September Brian Stanton, after twenty weeks out on the side lines injured, resumed training. In what was initially thought a groin problem he was diagnosed with another medical problem which had kept him out of first team action since the 1-0 defeat against Second Division Barnsley on April 7th. Brian was in good company given that Mark Lillis was also out injured.

On 8th September Town suffered a heavy 5-1 defeat at the hands of Shrewsbury Town in front of a Leeds Road crowd of 4,980. The very next league match in front of a Maine Road crowd of 20,201 saw Town lose 1-0 to Manchester City. First Division Sheffield Wednesday was Town's second round first leg Milk Cup match opponents. Watched by a crowd of 16,139 at Hillsborough they all saw Town beaten 3-0. By the end of the September Town had lost 1-0 to divisional leaders Birmingham City. Mark Lillis had returned from injury to our starting line-up and wore our number nine shirt at St Andrew's while Brian Cox reclaimed his keeper's shirt after recovering from a fractured cheekbone.

Town's second round second leg Milk Cup match at Leeds Road against Sheffield Wednesday on 9th October was watched by a crowd of 7,163. Thanks to goals from Paul Jones and Mark Lillis they managed a much-needed moral boosting 2-1 home win. While they may have been knocked out of the Milk Cup it was still nonetheless Town's first win, home or away, in eight games.

The very next league match against Wimbledon was watched by a lowly Leeds Road crowd of 5,001. They all saw Town win 2-1 thanks to goals by Steve Doyle and Dale Tempest who had just returned to first team action after undergoing an operation. The next home league match at Leeds Road on Saturday 20th October was against, our old adversaries, Leeds United. The day is best remembered for more than just the football that took place that day. Watched by a crowd of 15,257 about sixty-five arrests were made in both the away end and in the East Terrace as fighting broke out before, during, and after the match. Thanks to a Mark Lillis headed goal in front of our 'Cowshed' Town beat United 1-0.

In the middle of November Brian Stanton, having just returned from injury, scored at Notts County in a 2-0 win whilst Dale Tempest scored Town's other goal that day. After an unbeaten run of nine league games, since the Fulham defeat, it took Portsmouth away on December 15th before Town suffered another league defeat. By this time Town were eighth in the Second Division on 31 points just nine points off divisional leaders Blackburn Rovers. Paul Jones had started his 55th league game for Town against 'Pompey' and it was also his 500th Football League appearance.

By January 1985 with crowd disorder in football at the top of most daily newspaper reports and with ongoing debates in British politics. Huddersfield Town elected in conjunction with the police to install CCTV cameras to monitor and record crowd disorder in close-up in all parts of our ground at Leeds Road. This included the Main Stand and the cameras were also used close to our ground both before and after matches. Town's first league game of the New Year in 1985 against Grimsby away saw Town suffer a heavy 5-1 battering at the hands of 'The Mariners'. Thankfully four days later against Wolverhampton Wanderers in the FA Cup third round thanks to a Dale Tempest goal Town managed a 1-1 draw in front of a Molineux crowd of 8,589.

After Town's first promotion and after reviewing the last few years of our Town's history I can see that we went from an average of 11,548 in 1980-81 down to 7,363 at this point in 1985. Quite why this was for, as author and a Town fan, I can only hazard a guess. It seems strange that after moving 45 places up the Football League Town's average home crowd had drastically reduced match by match.

The FA Cup third round against Wolves at Leeds Road was watched by a crowd of 7,055. Thanks to two goals from Mark Lillis with one coming from the penalty spot, and Dale Tempest who scored our third goal, Town ran out 3-1 winners. Luton Town away was the next destination in the FA Cup fourth round. Due to an injury to Dale Tempest, who was rested for this game and with both Cowling and Cooper injuring themselves before the start of this match Town struggled before they had even kicked off. After only 30 minutes of the match, Brian Laws was sent off and from the resultant free kick, Town went 1-0 down. From then on it was an uphill battle with 10 men on the pitch, two of whom weren't fully fit, against a First Division team Town lost the match 2-0.

Sadly in February 1985 Maureen Brown passed away. Along with her husband Derek they ran our Town Souvenir Shop and at the time of her passing she was also Treasurer of our Supporters Club.

By the middle of March, Town having lost 5-1 away to Shrewsbury saw Town's new signing, defender Simon Webster, wear our number five shirt.

Simon Paul Webster – was a defender signed initially on loan from Tottenham Hotspur in 1985. He made 118 league appearances in our colours before he signed for Sheffield United in 1988. During his spell at United he broke his leg in two places and was out of action for quite a while. Within weeks of signing for West Ham United in 1993 Simon had his Sheffield United injury re-inflicted on him in a training ground tackle by Julian Dicks. By 1995 Simon Webster had left professional football altogether.

Saturday 23rd March 1985 saw David Burke suffer a break to both his tibia and fibula after a horror tackle from Jeff Hopkins in a home match against Fulham. With Brian Stanton also recovering from having had a hernia operation, and Paul Jones also out of action as well, our treatment room looked like something out of an A and E department.

Huddersfield Town created a Huddersfield Town Patrons Association during the season with none other than Lord Wilson as our Vice-President. Bill Boothroyd of Mirfield became our first ever secretary for the Patrons Association as some other local born celebrities were also given vice-presidency; Roy Castle, Derek Ibbotson, Anita Lonsbrough and MP Barry Sheerman.
Our Town Directors gave a 'declaration of intent' to, in due course provide a full shareholding in our club to all patrons just like our Town saga in 1919-20 when local townsfolk bought shares in our Club.

On Saturday 11th May 1985, our 'Cowshed' was taken over by Portsmouth supporters as Town handed them both ends of our ground due to the travelling numbers from 'Pompey'. 13,290 fans saw Town beaten 2-0 but due to other results going against Portsmouth they weren't promoted to the First Division. Mark Lillis sadly, signed for Manchester City at the end of this season for £132,500 after his fee had been set by a tribunal.

At the end of the season 1984-85 with a final league placing of 13th it was one of;

Played 42 games; won 15, lost 17, drew 10, goals for 52, goals against 64, Points 55

The 1985-86 pre-season saw a return of Town legend Mally Brown along with new signings; Terry Curran, Ian Bray, David Cork, Joey Jones and Paul Raynor. They were also some changes in our old home too, the Main Stand now had a physical barrier down the centre of the gangway which separated the southern block from the rest of the stand seats.

Edward Terence Curran – 'Terry' was a winger Town signed in 1985 from Everton. He made 33 league appearances in a mighty blue and white shirt during which time he scored seven goals before he left in 1986 to sign for Greek side Panionios.

Ian Michael Bray – was a defender Town signed on a free transfer in 1985 from Hereford United. He made 87 league appearances during which time he scored one goal. Town's 1987-88 season saw Ian out injured and was out of the side for the following season also. Ian signed permanently for Burnley in 1990 and after two more seasons in 1992 he retired from football completely.

David Cork – was a forward signed from Arsenal in 1985. He made 104 league appearances for Town during which time he scored 25 goals. In 1988 David left Town briefly to go on loan to W.B.A. and by the start of the 1988-89 football season had signed permanently for Scunthorpe United.

Joseph Patrick Jones – 'Joey' was signed as a left-back from Chelsea in 1985. He went on to become Player of the Year in his first full season with Town. His committed attitude and pre-match fist-clenching, as he ran out in front of Town fans, adhered himself to all Yorkshire folks in no time at all. After just two seasons, having played 67 league games and scored three goals, Joey signed for Wrexham in 1987.

Paul James Raynor – was a midfielder signed from Nottingham Forest in 1985. After 38 league games, during which time he scored nine goals, he signed for Swansea City in 1987.

The first league game of the season against Millwall, on Saturday 17th August, saw Town come back from 2-0 down at half-time to win the match 4-3. 6,603 fans at Leeds Road witnessed Dale Tempest become the first Town player ever to score a hat-trick on the opening day of the season, while Simon Webster scored Town's other goal. Pitched against Shrewsbury Town in the Milk Cup second round Huddersfield Town won 3-2 at Leeds Road. The away leg at Shrewsbury in mid-October saw Town lose 2-0, and ultimately knocked out of the cup 4-3 on aggregate. By mid-November Town was struggling in the league and by the middle of December was next to bottom in the Second Division.

Town's FA Cup third round match at Leeds Road against Reading at the beginning of January 1986 ended in a goalless draw. The replay down at Elm Park saw Town knocked out of the FA Cup, having lost 2-1 to Reading. Towards the end of February Town moved up to 16th place in the Second Division on 34 points while Norwich City were the divisional leaders on 61 points. More worryingly was the fact that Town were just six points off a relegation place.

Thursday 27th March 1986, transfer deadline day, saw Town sign a then young unknown striker from Chelsea for £10,000. Unbeknown to Town fans he would go on to become a terrace favourite. Meanwhile, Ian Measham joined Fourth Division Rochdale on a month's loan and Brian Stanton also started a month's loan out at Wrexham. Peter Butler meanwhile was into his third month on loan at Cambridge United.

Monday 31st March 1986 saw 2,000 travelling Town fans descend on Oakwell to see Town take on Barnsley in a league match. Wearing Town's number nine shirt and making his first team debut was our new signing Duncan Shearer. 5,746 fans saw Shearer score his very first Football League hat-trick, in a very much needed, 3-1 away win. Duncan added his name to that of our previous Town league hat-trick debutant Dale Tempest who had scored his hat-trick in a West Riding Cup tie at Halifax in our 1984-85 season. Arnold Rogers had achieved his feat in his second league appearance back in November 1946 when Town beat Charlton Athletic 5-1 with Albert Bateman and Jimmy Glazzard scoring Town's other two goals. So until Shearer's hat-trick the only other Town player who held the record for scoring on his league debut was that of Bob Kelly. He had achieved his record by scoring three times in a 4-3 victory over Sheffield Wednesday on 12th February 1927. By the end of March 1986 Town's Joey Jones became the then most capped international player in the history of the Welsh Football Association, having earned a total of 72 Welsh caps, his first cap having been won back in 1975.

In Town's next League match at Leeds Road, against Stoke City, in front of a crowd of just 5,750. Duncan Shearer added another two league goals to his previous hat-trick. With his first goal coming from about 45 yards out Shearer lobbed their keeper, Peter Fox, from just outside the centre circle. Without the aid of any weather condition Shearer planted the ball firmly into the open end Bradley Mills net for his first ever Leeds Road goal as Shearer scored his second goal in front of our old 'Cowshed' in the second half.

Duncan Nichol Shearer – was a striker that was signed by Buxton in March 1986 to try to help fight off the threat of relegation. Not only did Town manage that this season, but Duncan turned out to be a goal scoring legend. Having signed for £10,000 from Chelsea, he played 80 league games, during which time he scored 38 goals, and was Town's top goalscorer for both our 1986 and 1987 seasons. He was named as the team's Player of the Year for 1987. By the end of the following season Duncan Shearer unable to save Town single-handedly, from the very real threat of relegation, was sold to Swindon Town for a then Club record fee of £250,000.

By the end of March 1986 Town had appointed two new Directors to our Leeds Road Board. It was the first Boardroom shuffle in four years as both Roger Fielding and Geoffrey Headey was added to our list of Town Directors. It was also stated that given our average attendance figures this season Huddersfield Town was expected to make a financial loss. With just 5,000 hardcore Town supporters, of which only 2,000 were season ticket holders in this season, Town struggled both on and off the pitch.

Our last match of the season was against none other than Dave Bassett's Wimbledon, with the 'Don's' needing to win to earn promotion to the First Division. It was a game that had a huge financial significance for Wimbledon. In front of a crowd of 6,083 Town struggled to compete with their game plan. By the second half with the score still 0-0 Terry Curran was sent off for a foul on John Fashanu. He was the first of two Town players that was sent off that afternoon. From the resultant free kick, Laurie Sanchez scored the all-important goal for them. Just nine years after being elected into the Football League Wimbledon, against all the odds, had achieved promotion to the First Division.

At the end of the season 1985-86 with a final league placing of 16th it was one of;

Played 42 games; won 14, lost 18, drew 10, goals for 51, goals against 67, Points 52

For the 1986-87 season Greenall Whitley of Warrington took over from Daihatsu as Town's shirt sponsor. 'Greenall Beers' was the familiar sight on our shirts as Town fans travelled around the country following our mighty Terriers. Keith Hanvey had returned in this year, and took over from Steve Kindon, as our Commercial Executive with Maurice Porter still continuing as our Commercial Manager. It's at this stage of our Town history in our old home at Leeds Road, that both Steve Kindon and John Haselden, who was our First Team Coach and Physiotherapist, left our club. Four Town players who left on a free transfer in this season were; Terry Curran, Brian Stanton, Ian Measham who went to Cambridge United and Andrew Watson who moved to Exeter City. Liam Robinson at £7,000 and Peter Butler at £10,000 both signed for Bury. Dale Tempest also left and signed for 'Sporting Club Lokeren' of Belgium in a £30,000 transfer. Gary Worthington, nephew of Frank Worthington, signed from Manchester United and Andy Thackeray signed from Manchester City. While both David Burke and Graham Cooper were once again fit to play for Town.

Given that Town had lost in excess of £100,000 last season signings was something of a rare commodity, if at all, this season. The first league match of the new season saw Town play Sunderland at Leeds Road on 23rd August 1986. A crowd of 9,937 saw Town lose 2-0 to 'The Black Cats'. As of this season the League Cup had a new name for the trophy. 'Littlewoods Challenge Cup' was now the name for the original "Viscountess Furness Football Cup" which dated back to 1895.

Town's first ever Littlewoods Cup first round first leg tie at Leeds Road was against Halifax. Watched by a meagre crowd of 2,636 Town ran out 3-1 winners. Back to our league form and Town suffered a second successive league defeat, down at the Hawthorne's, at the hands of W.B.A. The Littlewoods Cup second leg against Halifax at the Shay saw Town go 2-0 down after just 45 minutes. By the second half Town had come out and started to batter the Halifax goal with shots galore. Paddy Roche in the Halifax goal had the game of his life and saved almost everything that Town threw at him. Thankfully David Cork and Duncan Shearer both scored to send Town through 5-3 on aggregate, after extra-time. Having played Blackburn Rovers in the Full Members Cup first round at Leeds Road Town lost 2-1 after extra-time. Simon Trevitt made his first team debut wearing Town's number two shirt while Andy Thackeray was named as a sub. After 158 league appearances Stephen Doyle signed for Lawrie McMenemy's Sunderland side on Monday 15th September 1986. Town immediately swooped and signed Ian Banks from Leicester City.

Wearing our number four shirt Ian made his first team debut against Oldham Athletic at Leeds Road on Saturday 20th September 1986. Given that Oldham Athletic at this point in the season were top of the division and had not conceded a single goal while Town had struggled to keep a clean sheet all season. The final result of 5-4 to Town was a complete shock to many in the 7,368 crowd. It was more surprising given the fact that Town had spent most of the game with only ten men on the pitch against 'The Latics'.

Town's Littlewoods Challenge Cup second leg first round match down at Highbury against Arsenal saw 'The Gunners' win 2-0. Graham Mitchell wearing our number eight shirt had made his first team debut in front a 15,194 North London crowd. Town having drawn 1-1 against Arsenal in the second leg at Leeds Road was knocked out of the cup.

Andrew John Thackeray – 'Andy' was a local born Huddersfield lad who started his football career with Manchester City. He signed for Town as a defender in 1986 and made two league appearances before he signed for Newport County in 1987.

Ian Fredrick Banks - signed as midfielder from Leicester City for £40,000 in 1986. He made 86 appearances for Town, during which time he scored 18 goals, before he signed for Bradford City in 1988.

Simon Trevitt – started his football career as a defender with Town in 1986 wearing our legendary number two shirt. He made a total of 272 appearances, during which time he scored four goals, before he signed for Hull City in 1996 for £20,000. By 1998 he had retired from professional football altogether.

Given that hooliganism was by now starting to affect football in a way that could not be ignored clubs looked at different ways in which they could combat the threat themselves. For Luton Town this meant they were forced to withdraw from the Littlewoods Cup for refusing an application from Cardiff City for their allocation of cup tickets.

Town were rock bottom of the Second Division by mid-December. A 4-0 defeat away at Millwall, watched by just 3,515, cemented Town's place at the bottom of the league. A 2-1 defeat at the hands of Crystal Palace in front of a Leeds Road crowd of just 4,181 on 20th December was the catalyst, to the devastating news just three days later, of Mick Buxton's sacking. Such was the shock of the 'Buxton era' ending, after just over eight years, that even the local newspaper ran a front-page headline announcing the news. Town Coach Steve Smith took over as Caretaker Manager and almost immediately Town won 2-1 away against Blackburn Rovers on Boxing Day. Town then went on to beat Bradford City 5-2 in front of our highest home crowd of the season as 10,003 home and away fans all saw Duncan Shearer score four goals while Ian Banks chipped in with a goal.

By the start of 1987 Town were up to 19th in the Second Division and was faced with having to replay Norwich City in the FA Cup third round, after a 1-1 draw down at Carrow Road. Steve Smith moved quickly to secure striker Peter Ward's signature from Chester-le-street in January. He played 24 league games, during which time he scored three goals, before he signed for Rochdale in 1989.

The FA Cup replay at Leeds Road against Norwich City was watched by a crowd of 8,970 and saw Town beaten 4-2 by 'The Canaries'. By the end of January Town were once again bottom of the Second Division as Steve Smith's position as Town Manager became permanent. Thankfully by mid-February our Club had once again allowed Town fans to move stands from our East Terrace to our 'Cowshed'. They agreed to open the gate which separated both stands, but it was decided that the gate was to be opened for only five minutes from kick-off and only opened again for the half-time interval.

In March Andy Dibble, a Welsh U-21 goalkeeper, was signed from Luton on a month's loan and made five appearances wearing our Town colours. Willie McStay was signed from Celtic and made five appearances before he left for Notts County. By the end of April Town were next to bottom of the Second Division, two points off safety, and had to win our final match of the season at Leeds Road against Millwall to avoid relegation. Thanks to a 3-0 home win Town ensured their own safety as they finished three points and three places away from relegation. Anyone who was there that fateful day will never forget the sight of Joey Jones as he charged up field and punched the air after scoring. Sunderland was relegated via the play-offs while Grimsby and Brighton were also relegated after finishing in the two bottom places.

At the end of the season 1986-87 with a final league placing of 17th it was one of;

Played 42 games; won 13, lost 17, drew 12, goals for 54, goals against 61, Points 51

Steve Smith's first full season in charge as Manager saw him sign Mark Barham from Norwich City and Andy May from Manchester City. Roger Fielding was now Town's Chairman with Keith Mincher given the task of coaching both our reserve and youth teams. Gary Worthington had been released at the end of last season and Paul Wilson had signed for Norwich City while Phil Wilson had signed for York City.

Mark Francis Barham – was a midfielder Town signed from Norwich City in 1987. After pulling on our Town colours on 29 occasions, during which time he scored one league goal against Birmingham City in February 1988, he signed for Middlesbrough at the end of the 1988 season.

Andrew Michael Peter May – 'Andy' was a midfielder Town signed from Manchester City in 1987 and during his first season at our club went out on loan to Bolton Wanderers. By 1990 Andy had signed permanently for Bristol City.

Lee Martin, Junior Bent, Paul France and Carl Madrick, having appeared regularly for our reserves, all got their chance and made a claim for a first team place in this year. While Gordon Tucker was signed from Derby County and made his first team debut this year.

Lee Brendan Martin – was a goalkeeper who started his football career with Town in 1987. He made 63 appearances and was voted Player of the Year in 1990. Having signed for Blackpool in 1992 he was ironically present, albeit in the Blackpool side, when Town played our last ever league match at Leeds Road on 30th April 1994. By 2003 Lee had been appointed Town's physio, a position he held for five seasons, until he left in July 2008.

Junior Antony Bent – was a winger who started his football career with Town in 1987. He pulled on our Town colours on 41 different occasions, during which time he scored seven goals, before he went out on a short-term loan to Burnley in 1989. By the summer of 1990 he had signed for Bristol City in a £30,000 transfer.

Michael Paul France – was a defender who started his football career with Town in 1987. He made seven league appearances before he signed for Bristol City in 1989. After retiring from football, in later life, he became our Football in the Community Officer at Huddersfield Town. He was also Manager of Sporting Pride which was based in Huddersfield Town centre.

Carl James Madrick – was a midfielder who started his football career with Town in 1987. He pulled on our Town shirt on eight different occasions and scored his only goal in a 1-0 win over Manchester City on April 2nd 1988. He signed permanently for Peterborough United at the end of the 1988 season.

Gordon Tucker – was a defender signed from Derby County in 1987 and after pulling on our Town shirt on 41 different occasions he signed for Scunthorpe United in 1989.

With a major change in both our home and away shirt, it was hoped by many that it would signal a change in Town's fortunes as 'Greenall Beers' also agreed to extend their shirt sponsorship for another season. Our new strips was designed and manufactured by 'Matchwinner' who were based in Scotland. The home shirt had a white panel on the chest with much thinner blue and white stripes. Our away shirt for the first time ever in our entire footballing history was black and yellow checked shirts, black shorts with yellow trim and yellow socks. (This kit is now best remembered for a record-breaking league defeat at Main Road).

Town's first league match of the new season on Saturday 15th August 1987 was against Crystal Palace. In front of a home crowd of 6,132 at Leeds Road Town drew the game 2-2. The following Tuesday away at Rotherham in the Littlewood's Challenge Cup first round first leg Town managed, thanks to a hat-trick from Duncan Shearer, to draw 4-4. The away trip down to Plymouth Argyle on 22nd August saw Town defeated 6-1 with our consolation goal coming from Peter Ward. This was then followed by a 3-1 home defeat at the hands of Rotherham United in the second leg Littlewood's Challenge Cup match. In front of a Leeds Road crowd of just 4,528 Town was knocked out of the cup.

By 1st September 1987 parts of our old home at Leeds Road was converted to 'Members Only Sections'. The areas that this plan covered was; our 'Cowshed', outer centre of Main Stand and wing stand of Main Stand. Five league games without a win and by the middle of the month Town was bottom of the Second Division. As the month came to a close after a defeat to Bradford City it left Town marooned at the very bottom of the Second Division. Steve Smith remained as Team Manager while Jimmy Robson went back to his old position as Reserve Team Coach.

Stan Ternent was approached but turned down the offer to become Town's Assistant Manager as both Keith Mincher and Chief Scout Tony Fawthorp were asked to relinquish their positions. By the beginning of October Steve Smith had tendered his resignation as Manager and asked if he could revert to his previous job of Chief Scout and Youth Team Coach, his request was granted. Town by then was rooted firmly to the bottom of the Second Division six points adrift of safety after only 10 league games and was looking for a Manager and Assistant Manager.

By the middle of October 1987, after a 3-2 away defeat down at Reading. The footballing world was informed that Malcolm MacDonald had been persuaded, by Town Chairman, Roger Fielding, to join us as our new Huddersfield Town Manager on a three-year contract. MacDonald's opening statement to the local press was 'Who's coming with me to the First Division'. After three further league defeats, two away both by 3-2 score lines and a 2-0 home defeat against Hull City, Malcolm MacDonald brought in, on loan, defender Steve Walford from West Ham United. By the third game of Steve Walford's short Town career on Saturday 7th November 1987 the most humiliating and most embarrassing Town score line from Maine Road read:-

Manchester City 10 Huddersfield Town 1.

It's still the biggest ever Football League defeat that Huddersfield Town have had recorded against us in our entire football history. Nearly 1,500 loyal Town fans, my self-included, had travelled the 40 miles over the Pennines to be largely crammed into one corner of their ground with some of us also behind one of the goals. The fact that we sang our hearts out and did everything we could to lift the mood was no reflection on any Town fan that fateful day. Town played Leicester City in the Simod Cup first-round three days later and lost 1-0 down at Filbert Street. By late November Eoin Hand, having newly returned from Saudi Arabia, teamed up with Malcolm MacDonald and became Town's Assistant Manager.

By the beginning of December Town had finally managed to haul ourselves off the bottom of the Second Division having leapfrogged over Reading by one point. Chris Hutchings signed for Town in this month from Brighton and Hove Albion while Steve Walford extended his loan for another month. Just before Christmas Town moved up to third from bottom of the league on 19 points as Shrewsbury and Reading sat below us in the Second Division.

The start of the New Year saw Town once again firmly rooted at the bottom of the Second Division and faced Manchester City in the FA Cup third round. After a 2-2 draw in front of a 18,102 crowd at Leeds Road Town were faced with a replay a week later at Maine Road. Keen to lay a few ghosts to rest, ten to be precise, a crowd of 24,565 saw a 0-0 draw. Town were then faced with a second replay against City at the end of January. In front of a Leeds Road crowd of 21,510 it finished 3-0 to Manchester City which saw Town knocked out of the FA Cup for another season.

In February Seamus McDonagh, a 35-year-old goalkeeper, signed on loan from Neil Warnock's Scarborough while Vincent Chapman a left-back from Tow Law also signed in this month. Portsmouth's central defender Malcolm Shotton signed for Town, for a reputed fee believed to be £70,000, as Willie McStay joined Notts County. By the end of March, after losing his place in the first team to Malcolm Shotton, Simon Webster signed for Sheffield United. After 331 league games David Cowling had his Town contract cancelled by mutual agreement while Andy May moved across to Bolton on loan. More shocking news filtered through when our Club Chairman, Roger Fielding, resigned as both Chairman and Director in March. Having only occupied the office of Chairman for nine months and only been a Director of our Club since 17th March 1986 Roger Fielding took up residence in the Isle of Man as a tax exile. Vice-Chairman Joe Christie also resigned having been a member of our Leeds Road Board for just over 20 years. Thankfully Keith Longbottom stepped back into the hot seat as Chairman while Geoff Headey, our newest member of the Board, became Vice-Chairman.

By the end of March Town were still rock bottom of the Second Division and was eight points adrift of next to bottom of the table Reading who were on 32 points. If that weren't bad enough Ian Bray in a league match against W.B.A received a compound fracture of both his tibia and fibula in his left leg and was rushed to hospital where he underwent surgery to have metal plates fastened to both his bones.

Just when you thought things couldn't get any worse on Tuesday 19th April 1988 Town took to the field against Oldham Athletic at our old home at Leeds Road in a re-arranged league match. What should have been a routine Second Division game was brought to the attention of the media world, weeks afterwards, when a FA Commission headed by Mr L. A. M Mackay, Chairman of the FA Disciplinary Committee investigated an assault on one of the match-day linesmen. The assault had taken place during the match on our East Terrace side of the ground between our 'Cowshed' and the halfway line and overshadowed the 2-2 draw which was watched by a crowd of just 5,547.

Town's 4-0 league defeat against Hull City at Boothferry Park on Saturday 23rd April 1988 finally sealed our fate for this terrible season. Relegation with three league games still left to play was a devastating blow to all Town fans. By the end of the month Malcolm MacDonald had resigned with an official statement from our Town Board citing the following;
"Malcolm MacDonald feels that the recent change of Chairman, financial constraints and policy changes have led to a difference of opinion as to the future of the running of the Club. The Board has accepted his resignation and wishes him well for the future. The position will be advertised. In the meantime the current staff will carry on the day to day running of the Club".

And with that Malcolm MacDonald was gone.

For me, as author of this book, I have to say this was, and still is, the worst season I have ever seen our Town team have. To have finished rock bottom of the Second Division having won only six games all season and having conceded 100 goals in the process was bad enough but to see that we finished 19 points adrift of safety, 14 points behind second from bottom Reading, was nothing more than embarrassing.

At the end of the season 1987-88 with a final league placing of 23rd (**relegated**) it was one of;

Played 44 games; won 6, lost 28, drew 10, goals for 41, goals against 100, Points 28

While carrying out some research for this book, I came across an article that was published in the local press. After thirteen years of negotiation Town finally signed a new lease for our ground with the local council on 13th July 1988. It guaranteed that a football ground would remain at Leeds Road for the next 125 years. (Sadly, as we all know by 1994 that was not to be exactly true).

Town's Commercial Manager, Maurice Porter, in the close season left and began working for Leeds Rugby League club as Tony Flynn took over his role at Town. Eoin Hand stepped forward and became our new Manager while Peter Withe became Player-Coach and Derek Mann joined our backroom staff (but had left by the end of this season). The first player Eoin Hand signed was Ken O'Doherty a central defender from Crystal Palace. This was shortly followed by Town signing a virtual unknown striker from Southampton, Craig Maskell, not only did he very quickly establish himself in our first team, but he also wrote his name as a true legend into our record books with his natural goalscoring abilities. By 22nd June our record transfer receipts was smashed when Town sold Duncan Shearer to Swindon Town for £250,000. Goalkeeper Steve Hardwick signed for Town on a free transfer from Oxford United as Micky Holmes, a midfielder, was also signed on a free transfer from Wolves.

Town also took on over half a dozen new trainees; Jason Byrne, Simon Charlton, Kevin Donovan, John Hildith, Chris McKee, Karl Rainton and goalkeeper Robert Wraight. Meanwhile, Ian Bray after his injury last season had to undergo a bone graft on his left leg and had to be put back in plaster.
By 14th July Steve Smith after a very long and distinguished Town career left Leeds Road. The following day Chris Marsden signed for Town from Sheffield United as Ian Banks left and signed for Bradford City. By the end of July Kieran O'Reagan became Town's seventh summer signing as Graham Cooper signed for Fourth Division Wrexham. By the beginning of August Brian Cox had left and signed for Mansfield Town.

For the start of the 1988-89 season our East Terrace had a new look to it in that all the gaps in the pitch perimeter fencing were now filled with safety gates which could readily be opened by Stewards in an emergency. The installation was due to be completed in Town's longer-term plans but due to the incident during last season's Oldham match when a Town fan entered the field of play the work was brought forward. The Town fan who assaulted the linesman was convicted in Crown Court and ultimately banned from attending all matches at Leeds Road for life. This brought the total of Town "life bans" at the time to four.

Kenneth Brendan O'Doherty – 'Ken' signed as a defender for Town in 1988 from Crystal Palace and earned a Republic of Ireland U21 cap while at Town. As author of this book I remember him having some of his teeth knocked out by Cardiff City's new striker Cohen Griffith during a league match, Ken refused to be subbed off, and only left the field at the final whistle. By 1992 Ken had signed for Shelbourne.

Craig Dell Maskell – was signed as a forward from Southampton for £50,000 in 1988 and wrote his name into Town's history books in his very first season. At Leeds Road against Wigan Athletic he scored his 33rd goal of the season and broke a post-war goalscoring record set by Jimmy Glazzard in 1955. In his second season with Town, even though Maskell was transferred-listed, at his own request, for most of the season he was still top goalscorer. He became only the third Town player to ever score four goals, in a 5-1 away victory against Cardiff City in our 1989-90 season, equalling the feat of Charlie Watson at Burnley (1924-25 season) and George Brown at Chesterfield (FA Cup 1929). During the close season of 1990 Maskell signed for Reading for £250,000.

Steve Hardwick – was signed as a goalkeeper from Oxford United in 1988 and after 109 league appearances for Town he had retired from professional league football altogether by 1991.

Michael Arthur Holmes – 'Micky' was signed as a midfielder by Town from Wolves in 1988. He played three league games before he signed for Cambridge United the following season. While at Northampton Town in 1993, at the young age of 29, his football career was ended due to a back injury he sustained in a car crash.

Christopher Marsden – 'Chris' was signed as a midfielder from Sheffield United in 1988. After pulling on a Town shirt on a 155 different occasions he signed for Wolves in 1994. He was forced to retire while at Sheffield Wednesday in 2005 after he suffered a hamstring injury.

Kieran Michael O'Regan – was signed as a midfielder from Swindon Town in 1988 with his transfer fee decided by a tribunal. After 187 league appearances during which he had scored 25 league goals, as well as standing in as keeper, Kieran left Town in 1993 and signed for West Bromwich Albion. After retiring from professional football altogether in later years Kieran returned to Huddersfield Town, along with Paul Ogden, and worked as a BBC Radio Leeds football commentator.

Town's first Third Division match of the season on Saturday 27th August saw them lose 1-0 away at Brentford. In an ironic twist of fate our first leg first round Littlewoods Challenge Cup tie was away against Scunthorpe United. With Micky Buxton as their Manager and with Dave Cowling in their side in front of a crowd of 3,820 Scunthorpe United beat Town 3-2. Julian Winter now free of injury moved to Scunthorpe United, on a month's loan, to link up once again with Buxton. Carl Madrick, after his goal against Manchester City last season, was given a free transfer after spending time with Peterborough United on trial. Whilst Mick Byrne signed for Town as a forward from Shamrock Rovers for approximately £20,000 in this month.

Malcolm Shotton having only signed for Town in February in this year and been made captain by September 1988, after just 16 games in which he had scored one goal, left and signed for Barnsley. Andy Duggan signed for Town from Barnsley in the same week as Chris Hutchings became our new Club captain. David Cork, who was out of contract, joined West Bromwich Albion on a temporary basis. Meanwhile, Peter Ward unhappy about not gaining a first team place asked to be placed on the transfer list.

Michael Byrne – 'Mick' sign for Town in 1988 and pulled on our Town shirt on 60 different occasions during which he scored 11 goals. By 1989 he had signed a short-term loan for Irish side Shelbourne before he finally left in 1990 to go back to Ireland and play for Shamrock Rovers.

Andrew James Duggan – 'Andy' was signed as a defender from Barnsley in 1988. After 29 league appearances he signed for Rochdale in 1990.

Christopher Hutchings – 'Chris' was signed as a defender from Brighton and Hove Albion in 1987 and became Town captain. After pulling on our Town shirt on 124 different occasions, during which time he scored 10 goals, he signed for Walsall in 1990.

Town's Littlewoods Challenge Cup match at home against Scunthorpe United in front of a crowd of 4,237 was settled after extra-time as United went through 5-4 on aggregate. Town's physio George McAllister, who had come in after John Haselden, left our club as Town suffered a heavy 5-1 league defeat at the end of October down at Bristol Rovers.

By the beginning of November, after 13 league matches, Town was in the bottom half of the Third Division, eleven points off the top and ten points from the bottom of the division. Whilst Mark Barham after struggling with injuries throughout his time at Town moved onto Middlesbrough.
Town was faced with Rochdale in the first round of the FA Cup, a 6,178 home crowd saw Andy May score in a 1-1 draw and force a replay. Mike Cecere signed for Town during the month of November while promising full-back Simon Charlton, son of our former Town player Wilf Charlton, stepped up another rung in the England international ladder having previously played for the Under-15 and Under-16 level.

Michele Joseph Cecere – 'Mike' was signed as a striker from Oldham Athletic in 1988 and made 50 league appearances, during which time he scored eight goals, before he left in 1990.

At the end of November Town's FA Cup first round replay against Rochdale in front of a Deepdale crowd of 5,645 saw them win 4-3 and go through to the next round. For the first time ever Town played in the Sherpa Van Trophy and was drawn against Scunthorpe United and Halifax Town in the preliminary round. A 1-0 win at Leeds Road over Scunthorpe United saw Town take on Halifax Town away at the Shay on 19th December. A 1-0 defeat was good enough to get Huddersfield Town through to face Grimsby Town in the next round. In the second round of the FA Cup against Chester City at Leeds Road a goal by Kieran O'Reagan earned Town a 1-0 victory and took them through to the next round. By the start of the New Year Town took on Sheffield United in the third round of the FA Cup. A 1-0 defeat in front of a Leeds Road crowd of 15,543 signalled the end of Town's cup run for another season.

Meanwhile, the British Government in trying to defeat a small minority of football hooligans from the sport attempted to bring about a National Membership Scheme to control and restrict entry to all Football League matches at an estimated cost in this year of approximately thirty-four million pounds. Thankfully the legislation for the proposed 'Football Spectators Bill' part 1 and 2 didn't get through Parliament. As a matter of interest at Leeds Road over the last three to four seasons during league matches 126 arrests had been made against an average league attendance of 6,833. Only 43 of the 126 arrests had been inside our old ground. Fifteen of the 43 arrested was for possession of, or being the worse for, drink. While two was for entering the ground while being the subject of an Exclusion Order. The remaining 26 was little more than one per game throughout an entire season.

Having reached the Sherpa Van Trophy Area quarter-final Town was faced with Scarborough at Leeds Road on Tuesday 21st February. Watched by a Leeds Road crowd of 4,665 Town lost 2-1 and was knocked out of the Sherpa Van Trophy whilst Mark Smith signed for Town from Rochdale.

Mark Cyril Smith – was a winger Town signed from Rochdale in 1989 and made 100 appearances, during which time he scored 13 goals, before he signed for Grimsby Town in 1991.

Town suffered a 5-1 defeat at Bramall Lane at the hands of Sheffield United in March 1989. Given that by this stage of the season Town were tenth in the Third Division on 46 points, while Sheffield United sat third on 56 points a shot at the play-offs up to the 5-1 drubbing was considered an outside possibility. It was no April Fool's joke when Town recorded their biggest away league win of the season having beaten Bury 6-0 at Gigg Lane on 1st April 1989. By mid-April George Mulhall had taken up the position of Youth Team Coach as Town failed to win any of their final seven league matches of this season. It was during this run that Town suffered a 6-1 defeat, the heaviest defeat of our entire season, away at Ashton Gate against Bristol City. In our final match of the season at Leeds road against Wigan Athletic Craig Maskell scored his 33rd record-breaking goal of his season.

At the end of the season 1988-89 with a final league placing of 14th it was one of;

Played 46 games; won 17, lost 20, drew 9, goals for 63, goals against 73, Points 60

Just before the start of the 1989-90 season Eoin Hand signed Robert Wilson from Fulham, Dudley Lewis from Swansea and Ifem Onuora from non-league football and Gary Leake from W.B.A. Town then released four players on free transfers; Paul France who signed for Bristol City, Ian McInerney who signed for Stockport County, Peter Ward and Vince Chapman who were both signed by Rochdale. While Julian Winter and Gordon Tucker decided after their contracts had expired to seek 'pastures new' Julian signed for Sheffield United and Gordon signed for Micky Buxton's Scunthorpe United.

On the non-playing side of Town both Jack Johnson and Fred Kershaw had notched up over 130 years' service to Huddersfield Town in which they were familiar figures to generations of Gatemen, Stewards and Match Officials at our old home at Leeds Road. Both were commemorated on their retirement with a life membership of Huddersfield Town.

Robert James Wilson – was a midfielder Town signed from Fulham in 1989 he made 52 league appearances, during which time he scored eight goals, before he signed for Rotherham United in 1991.

Dudley Keith Lewis – was a defender signed from Swansea City in 1989. He made a total of 44 appearances in our Town colours before he signed for Wrexham in 1991.

Ifem Onuora – 'Iffy' was a striker who played non-league football for Bradford University Football Club when Town signed him on professional terms in 1989. Every Town fan that stood on our terraces saw Iffy as being possibly 'the new Steve Kindon'. After 115 league appearances during which time he had scored 30 goals Iffy signed for Mansfield Town in 1994. This wasn't the end of his career with Town by 25th March 2004, after signing professional terms with Town once again, he scored an important goal in our semi-final play-off against Lincoln City. By July 2004 after a short stay at Walsall as Player/Coach Iffy retired from professional football altogether.

Gary Leake – was a goalkeeper Town signed from W.B.A in 1989. He was forced to give up football completely at the age of 21, due to numerous injuries, latterly a cruciate ligament injury.

As a result of an interim report, issued by Lord Justice Taylor, the Licensing Body for our Safety Certificate for our old home at Leeds Road had some uncertainty as to the safety of our 'Cowshed' roof. It was mutually agreed by both Club and the Licensing Body that our 'Cowshed' was temporarily closed for the first two home games of the 1989-90 season. Additional changes to our old home at Leeds Road were needed to comply with the Taylor report which was expected to exceed £80,000. One final safety measure that was put in place whilst the work was carried out was that Leeds Road was limited to a capacity of just 14,000 spectators.

One 'new signing' in this year which brought a smile to many a Town fan, and still does to this very day, was our 'larger than life' Terrier who was given his first ever name 'Huddson'. In later years in our new home at the John Smith's Stadium we all know him as simply 'Terry the Terrier' along with his female sidekick 'Tilly the Terrier'.

Town's opening league match against Swansea City was watched by a Leeds Road crowd of 5,775 and thanks to a goal from Mike Cecere Town won 1-0. A 1-1 draw against Doncaster Rovers in the Littlewoods Challenge Cup first round first leg at home coupled with a 2-1 win in the second leg down at their place meant Town were faced with Nottingham Forest in the next round. Having drawn 1-1 away against Forest the second round first leg was all still to play for at Leeds Road. After extra-time the match ended in a 3-3 draw and ultimately due to the away goals rule Town was out of the Littlewoods Cup for another season.

A run of eight games undefeated came to end when Town's first league defeat of the season, against Tranmere Rovers away, was a 4-0 drubbing. At the time Town were eighth in the Third Division on 12 points while Bristol Rovers were the divisional leaders on 16 points. Town lost their unbeaten home record for this season, against Cardiff City, on Saturday 7th October. A 3-2 defeat was watched by a lowly Leeds Road crowd of just 5,835. During the game Ken O'Doherty suffered a loss of three of his teeth in an accidental aerial battle with Cardiff City's Cohen Griffith and had to wear a gum shield and was wired up for six weeks after his injury.

Town's preliminary round group five game in the Leyland DAF Trophy against Doncaster Rovers at Leeds Road on 7th November was watched by a lowly 1,714 crowd and ended in a 2-2 draw. The next cup game was the FA Cup first round at Hartlepool United. Watched by a 3,160 crowd Town won 2-0 thanks to two goals from Mike Cecere. Having won 2-0 in the second round at Chesterfield Town were faced with Grimsby in the next round. Before that though Town had to face Grimsby away in a preliminary round group five game in the Leyland DAF trophy. A 3-3 draw was enough to send Town through to the first round where they were drawn against Rotherham United.

Town fans had good reason to celebrate at Leeds Road on Boxing Day, not just with the fact that Town had played Bury and won 2-1. Our old 'Cowshed' had reopened which gave fans the chance once again to enjoy the view of our old home as the Bristol City game brought to a close another decade of football for everyone at Town. A decade that, like most others, had been full of its ups and downs with our own memories of the good and bad times. It had started positively with our record-breaking Fourth Division Championship success. Then having achieved promotion to the Second Division a few seasons later a serious challenge on achieving promotion to the First Division sadly never materialised. Instead, it signalled the end of the Buxton era and various management changes, culminating in Malcolm MacDonald's reign, could not prevent us from slipping back into the Third Division. With the dawning of a new decade almost upon us the exciting prospect of becoming a proposed multi-million-pound leisure complex subject to planning approval was a step nearer due to our days in our old home at Leeds Road being sadly numbered. The start of a new decade began with a 2-2 draw against Blackpool at Bloomfield Road. In atrocious weather Town managed to score a last-minute equaliser that kept them sixth in the Third Division just six points off Neil Warnock's Notts County team who were the divisional leaders. In front of a Leeds Road crowd of 9,901 Town beat Grimsby 3-1 in the FA Cup third round. This was then followed by a 3-0 away defeat in the Leyland DAF Trophy against Rotherham United. In front of a Selhurst Park crowd of 12,920 Town lost 4-0 in the FA Cup fourth round against Crystal Palace. The Final Report of Lord Justice Taylor at the start of this new decade brought much criticism of the Government's plan to introduce a compulsory membership card scheme. This then forced the British Government to back down on that particular section of the 'Football Spectators Act' although the legislation remained on the stature book. Probably the most far-reaching recommendation concerned the move to all seater-stadia for all Football League and Scottish clubs in the next ten years.

It also recommended that all First and Second Division clubs reduced their present standing capacity by 20% per year starting in August 1990. Thus by the start of the 1994-95 season all such clubs had to be all-seater. The ramifications of Taylor's Final Report was fundamental in the decision that Town had to move to a new stadium in order to survive as a Football League Club in the 21st century. By the start of our 1994-95 season life as a Town fan was vastly different to the life we all had in our old home at Leeds Road.

After a 1-0 defeat against Fulham in front of a Leeds Road crowd of just 4,780 fans. A large crowd of Town fans demonstrated outside our Leeds Road ground as a group of businessmen declared their intent to take over our Club from the present Chairman and Board of Directors. By the end of the season, instead of a play-off place, Town had to be content with finishing eighth, four points off the last play-off place.

At the end of the season 1989-90 with a final league placing of 8th it was one of;

Played 46 games; won 17, lost 15, drew 14, goals for 61, goals against 62, Points 65

10 years of Huddersfield Town's history from 1980

1980-81 4th in Division 3 — FA Cup third round
Football League Cup first round

1981-82 17th in Division 3 — FA Cup fourth round
Football League Cup second round

1982-83 3rd in Division 3 **(promoted)** — FA Cup third round
Milk Cup fourth round

1983-84 12th in Division 2 — FA Cup fourth round
Milk Cup third round

1984-85 13th in Division 2 — FA Cup fourth round
Milk Cup second round
Northern Intermediate League Championship winners

1985-86 16th in Division 2 — FA Cup third round
Milk Cup second round

1986-87 17th in Division 2 — FA Cup third round
Littlewoods Challenge Cup second round
Full Members Cup first round

1987-88 23rd in Division 2 **(relegated)** — FA Cup third round
Littlewoods Challenge Cup first round
Simod Cup first round

1988-89 14th in Division 3 — FA Cup third round
Littlewoods Challenge Cup first round
Sherpa-Van Trophy Area quarter-finalist

1989-90 8th in Division 3 — FA Cup fourth round
Littlewoods Challenge Cup second round
Leyland DAF Trophy first round

Town's 'Football's coming home Decade' - Chapter 11

This new decade brought many changes in the world as millions watched on as Nelson Mandala finally walked to freedom and Gazza's tears, at England being knocked out of the World Cup at Italia 90, had a nation crying with him. It was an age when the world got smaller with the invention and introduction of both the mobile phone and the worldwide web, even if you had to listen to a dialling tone while waiting to call-up the internet. It was an era where you could get to France on a train under the sea.

In football, it signalled the restructuring of all the Football Leagues and with it the birth of the Premier League by the mid-nineties. We all saw a nation sing 'Football's coming home' (for the first time-in 1996) and saw a change in British politics as our nation heard 'Things can only get better' as an election anthem. Towards the end of the decade it was a case of partying like it's 1999 while trying to avoid the doom-mongering about the Y2Bug. A computer flaw that would create havoc when dealing with dates beyond 31st December 1999 (which coincidentally never happened).

For Town fans in this new decade it was a time when we all shed tears of sadness and also shared those of happy ones too. It saw the end of one historical Town era and the dawning of another and with it much cause for celebration.

During pre-season of the 1990-91 season Town fans saw our crowd favourite Craig Maskell leave for Reading, in a £250,000 transfer, with his transfer fee having to be set by a tribunal. Iwan Roberts signed for Town from Watford in a £275,000 record-breaking deal. Town also signed Gary Barnett from Fulham with his fee having to be decided by a tribunal. Neil Parsley then signed for Town on a free transfer while David Campbell signed after being on trial from Bohemians.

Meanwhile, behind the scenes at our old home at Leeds Road Paul Fletcher was settling into the hot seat as Commercial Executive given that Keith Hanvey had left our club at this point. Greenalls were once again our main club sponsors for the season. Chris Hutchings left our club and joined Walsall whilst Ian Bray left after not having his contract renewed, and in doing so, was the last remaining player from our Buxton days. Young defender Aidey Boothroyd left and signed for Bristol Rovers while just a few miles down the road Andy May under 'freedom of contract' signed for Bristol City.

Iwan Wyn Roberts – was a striker signed from Watford in 1990 for a record-breaking fee of £275,000. It broke the previous record transfer of Terry Austin's by a considerable margin. Iwan broke Town's goalscoring record in the 1991-92 season, by banging in 34 goals in all competitions to break the post-war record of Craig Maskell's, set just three seasons earlier. Iwan went on to score half a century of goals in 142 appearances for Town before he signed for Leicester City in November 1993 for a record-breaking £300,000 transfer deal.

Gary Lloyd Barnett - was a midfielder signed from Fulham in 1990. He made 92 league appearances before he signed for Leyton Orient in 1993.

Neil Robert Parsley - was a defender signed from Leeds United in 1990. He made 55 league appearances before he signed for West Bromwich Albion in a £25,000 transfer in 1993.

David Martin Campbell – was a defender Town signed from League of Ireland side Bohemians in 1990. Due to a series of disabling injuries this side of the Irish sea he made only handful of league appearances before he left for Ireland and signed for Shamrock Rovers in 1992.

Behind the scenes at Boardroom level the appointment of Graham Leslie back in the middle of May had been the first addition to our Board of Directors since current Vice-Chairman Geoff Headey and Roger Fielding had joined Town three years ago.

Clifford Senior left our Town Board and took up the position of Life Vice-President, he was only the third person in Town's history to be afforded his new title, the others were Sir Emmanuel Hoyle and Amos Brook Hirst. 19-year-old Neil Edwards signed on loan to cover for our injured goalkeeper, Lee Martin, who had been ruled out of action for a month. Peter Maguire after three sub appearances last season headed west along the M62 to sign on a month's loan for Stockport County.

The opening day Barclays League fixture against Southend United in front of a Leeds Road crowd of 5,219 all saw Town lose 2-1. The first leg first round League Cup match against Bolton Wanderers ended in a 3-0 defeat in front of a Leeds Road crowd of just 4,444. The second leg at Bolton in September saw Town lose 2-1 and ultimately dumped out of the League Cup.
Four days later Town beat the very same Bolton Wanderers team 4-0 in a league match at Leeds Road. Keith Edwards scored a hat-trick and in the process, with his first goal, it took him to his 250th league goal. Iwan Roberts in his fifth game of the season for Town finally scored his first goal of the season in the Bolton game. Appearing in Town's number six shirt for the Bolton match was Peter Jackson our new signing from Bradford City.

Sadly, on the same afternoon as Keith scored his 250th league goal York City footballer David Longhurst tragically died. As a mark of respect for David, Keith kindly donated the match ball, which had been signed by the entire Town squad. Keith's kind generosity raised £500 in an auction for the David Longhurst Memorial Fund.

Peter Allan Jackson – 'Jacko' was a central defender Eoin Hand somehow had managed to sign from Bradford City. After playing in all four of the divisions with Bradford City and Newcastle United he signed for Town in 1990 and went on to become captain and also Reserve Team Coach. After racking up 152 league appearances he signed for Chester City in 1994.
By October 1997 Jacko was back at Town, but this time as Manager. In 1999 Jacko was replaced by Steve Bruce as Manager, a decision which was made by our new owner Barry Rubery. By 2003, after emerging from administration, and stuck firmly in Division Three Peter Jackson was back as Town Manager once again. In his first season back he led Town to promotion via the Play-offs. The following season saw Town just miss out on the Play-offs and in his third season saw Town finish in the League One Play-offs. On 6th March 2007 Jacko left Town after having his contract as Manager cancelled by mutual consent. Peter can still often be seen on a match day down at our John Smith's Stadium hosting events in our Legends bar.

Jimmy Firth our Supporter's Club President who had been connected with Town from our early days and was Chairman of our Supporters Club until the mid-70's sadly passed away aged 94. Eric Simpson who had been a Director of our club from 1974 to 1977, during that time he had spent a period as Town's Vice-Chairman, also sadly passed away in September.

Town beat Altrincham 2-1 in the first round of the FA Cup in November but lost 2-0 to Blackpool in the next round at Leeds Road the following month. In the Leyland DAF Trophy Town having drawn 1-1 with Bradford City and lost 4-1 against Hartlepool was out of the competition for another season. Gary Barnett suffered a fracture to his right fibula in our New Year's Day clash with Wigan Athletic and didn't resume first team training until the end of February. Meanwhile, Peter Withe after 2½ years as Player-Coach, in which he figured in 38 league games as both striker and his latest role of sweeper, departed from Leeds Road and took up an offer of First Team Coach with his previous club Aston Villa. Town meanwhile completed the loan signing of Phil Stant from Notts County in January as Keith Edwards left for Plymouth Argyle.

Phillip Richard Stant – 'Phil' signed on loan for a month from Notts County and played five league games during which he scored one goal, at home, against Swansea City before going back to his parent club.

By the middle of March Town had moved up to sixth in the Third Division on 52 points while Southend United topped the division on 64 points. Ian Ross meanwhile started as First Team Coach and Assistant to Eoin Hand in this month while Jimmy Glazzard our former Legend had accepted an offer to become one of our Patron's Association's new Vice-Presidents. Jimmy, a true gentleman and having been a terrace-side season ticket-holder for many years, accepted the role with much gratitude. Sadly, Simon Charlton suffered a broken leg against Chester City at Leeds Road and was out of action until the following season.

Simon Thomas Charlton – was a full-back who started his football career with Town in 1989. He made 122 league appearances for Town wearing our number three shirt and scored his one and only goal in the League Cup second round first leg 2-1 away win against Sunderland. By 1993 Simon had signed for Southampton in a £250,000 transfer.

Town's playing form for the last seven league games of the season saw four defeats and just one victory, this ultimately cost Town dearly as they missed out on the play-offs by six points. Town were also awarded a record 14 penalties in this season, but only managed to score nine of them. So, the record of eleven penalties scored in a season which was set in Town's 1983–84 season remained historically intact.

At the end of the season 1990-91 with a final league placing of 11th it was one of;

Played 46 games; won 18, lost 15, drew 13, goals for 57, goals against 51, Points 67

Having signed Tim Clarke from Coventry in 1991 he went on to earn an amusing nickname for himself from our Leeds Road terraces.

Timothy Joseph Clarke – 'Tim' was a goalkeeper who made 70 league appearances for Town and in the process 'earned' himself the amusing nickname of 'Coco'. It was chanted by Town fans on our terraces and was acknowledged with great affection and good humour by Clarke. His nickname came about when opponents centered the ball from the wing into his penalty area and 'Coco' more often than not made a mistake that caused us all on the terraces to have a heart-in-mouth adrenalin rush. Having signed on loan for Rochdale by the end of 1993 he then moved onto Altrincham before finally ending back up in professional football with Shrewsbury Town.

Town drew 1-1 at Bolton Wanderers in the first league match of the 1991-92 season. By the time our team took to the field at Darlington for the first round first leg League Cup match, on Tuesday 20th August, new signing Phil Starbuck was wearing the number ten shirt.

Philip Michael Starbuck – 'Phil' was originally a striker, who also played as a winger, before he became an attacking midfielder. Town somehow had managed to sign him from Cloughie's Nottingham Forest side in 1991. As far as I can research from his Forest days he is the only player in their entire football history to have scored on both his away debut and home debut in 1986.
Phil got off to a flying start in his first season with Town in 1991 and scored eight goals in his first ten games in our colours. Straight away all Town fans on the terraces knew we were seeing another legend in the making. He became Town captain, but sadly with a change of Manager from Eoin Hand to Ian Ross it was also a period in time when he was constantly being benched by our new Manager.

His answer to that was simply to get off the subs bench and once on the pitch score for Town. On 12th April 1993 having yet again appeared as a substitute Phil set a record at the time for the fastest goal scored by a sub when he scored against Wigan Athletic, just three seconds after coming on.

As author of this book I can distinctly remember him having come on to a massive cheer as Town was about to take a corner down at our 'Cowshed'. Starbuck ran to the near post and glanced the ball into the far corner of Wigan's net with his first touch of the ball. (Seeing his obvious reaction to scoring that day, I could only hazard a guess as to what he was actually thinking). Phil went on to captain Town to Wembley and should always be remembered for scoring the last ever goal at Leeds Road in 1994. After having had the good fortune of having had the luxury of Phil's company, while I was fundraising for Alzheimer's Society a few years ago, I have to say that he is a true gentleman. Hearing his stories of the old days under Cloughie at Forest was genuinely heart-warming for me as well as hearing about his old days with us all at Town.

Phil Starbuck and John O'Mahoney photographed in Huddersfield in 2018 raising valuable funds for Alzheimer's Society.
Digital image **a50** (left)

Phil Starbuck (above) generously supporting Alzheimer's Society in June 2018 - photographed meeting up just outside the town centre of Huddersfield as part of a fundraising scheme on social media platform 'Those were the days my friend'.

Town's new club shop at Leeds Road was officially opened by former legends Frank Worthington and Trevor Cherry. It was inundated with Town fans desperate to buy our new red and black Gola away shirt. The new design on our away shirt was a sell-out with fans, given that we bought five times more away shirts than our home shirt sold this season.

Digital image **a51**- (left) John O'Mahoney's old photograph of Leeds Road showing our old Town club shop in 1995

Ken O'Doherty had moved to Exeter City on loan, with a view to a permanent transfer by the end of August, while Graham Mitchell and Peter Jackson had by now established themselves as Town's regular defensive duo. In September Town played Bury away in a league match and by half-time Town was 4-0 down. In a remarkable turn-around of events in the second half, with two goals each from Phil Starbuck and Iwan Roberts, Town drew the match 4-4. It had only ever happened on two other occasions, in a Division One game against Derby County at the Baseball Ground in front of a 24,600 attendance on 16th April 1927 and in a Division One game on 8th November 1947 against Manchester United at Maine Road in front of a 59,772 attendance, given that Old Trafford had been bombed during the war.

Graham Mitchell – was a defender who started his football career with Town in 1983 and signed professionally in 1986. During his time with Town he played in various positions from defence to winger and even as a striker. By 1993 he had gone out on loan to Bournemouth and by 1994 after 310 games for Town in all competitions, during which time he scored five goals, he signed for Bradford City. By 2002 Graham was back at the Club coaching in our football academy and by 2009 had held various roles; Caretaker Assistant Manager, Caretaker Manager (In Gerry Murphy's absence), Reserve Team Manager, U18's Coach, and at one point was the Head of Town's Academy following Gerry Murphy's retirement. He left the role of Head of Academy in November 2011 and thereby ended a 28-year association with Town that first began in Mick Buxton's era.

By the end of September Town hosted a Frank Worthington Testimonial match with a host of international stars who appeared in a Denis Law international line-up. 6,000 fans attended at our old home at Leeds Road and paid tribute to a true Town legend as the game ended in a 4-4 draw. Having played Leyton Orient down at their place Town came away having not only lost 1-0 but ultimately saw their unbeaten Barclays League record come to an end for this season. Then having beaten Darlington 4-1 on aggregate in the first round of the League Cup, and comfortably disposed of Sunderland 6-1 on aggregate in the next round, Town was faced with Swindon Town in the third round. In front of a Leeds Road crowd of 10,088 Town were out of the League Cup having lost 4-1 to 'The Robins'. Group 6 of the preliminary round of the Football League Trophy saw Town go through to the first round after a 1-0 win over Wigan Athletic and a 1-1 draw with Scarborough.

Sadly Fred Elms, after working at Town for more than 40 years as Town's Maintenance Foreman, passed away on Tuesday 15th October 1991 aged 71. Fred, who had joined the staff in 1951, was originally brought in by contracts to help rebuild the West Stand which had been gutted by fire. On completion of the stand he joined Town full time and made anything from our first team posts to a table tennis table for Bill Shankly which was still used by Town players this season. Fred Elms received official recognition in the form of an award from the Club for his outstanding achievements and devotion to Huddersfield Town.

Having seen Keith Edwards leave our Club for Plymouth, Town were quick to sign Frank Stapleton on non-contract terms towards the end of October. He was named as a sub in Town's 4-1 cup defeat to Swindon Town while his first team debut came at Stoke City. Wearing our number eight shirt that day he helped Town to a 2-0 win which took them up to fourth place in the Third Division. By early December Frank Stapleton had been appointed Bradford City's new Manager.

Faced with playing non-league Lincoln United in the FA Cup first round it's interesting to know that in August of this year United were not even sure if they could afford to take part in the competition. So tight was the budget at the little Central Midlands League Club that the £75 FA Cup entry fee presented a major problem. Their club committee was about to go for the cheaper options of the FA Trophy and FA Vase, but they were persuaded to go for the big one. After surviving a protest from Leek Town about playing an ineligible player in the fourth qualifying round they hoped to make over £10,000 from their trip to our old home at Leeds Road. Watched by a Leeds Road crowd of 6,763 fans they were all in for a football treat as Town ran out 7-0 winners and faced Rochdale away in the second round. Having beaten 'The Dale' 2-1 Town were then drawn at home against Millwall in the third round. In front of a Leeds Road crowd of 10,879 Town were knocked out of the cup having lost 4-0 to the South East London club.

Saturday 18th January 1992, having played Peterborough United, was a day to celebrate for Huddersfield Town given that it was their 3,000th Football League game. Hugh Turner at the age of 87 years old, as a former player, along with 8,763 fans was at Leeds Road to help celebrate the occasion and saw Town draw 0-0 with 'The Posh'.

It had taken Town 28 years to complete the first one thousand league games on October 22nd 1938, another 31 years to complete our second thousand league games on August 23rd 1969 and just 23 years to get to our 3000th league game on 18th January 1992. A grand total of eighty-two years in which our old home at Leeds Road had seen many triumphs and many despairing days. Memories in time in which they were not only crowned 'Champions' of England and the best team in the world but had also suffered the humiliation of playing in all four divisions, backwards.

The 3000th league game was also a special event for our old ground too as it marked the start of the removal of the fencing at Leeds Road. With the removal of two sections of segregation fences and the perimeter fencing it allowed Town to increase the capacity of our East Terrace to above the 7,000 limit, which had been set previously due to the Taylor report.

The original first round tie against Blackpool in January for the Football League Trophy was abandoned at half-time due to fog at Leeds Road and had to be re-scheduled for Tuesday 21st January. At the final whistle with the score at 1-1 the match had to be decided on penalties. Thanks to Mitchell, O'Regan and Wright, who all scored for Town, they won the penalty round 3-1. By the end of the month Eoin Hand had managed to secure the services of both Nigel Callaghan on loan from Ron Atkinson's Aston Villa and Neil McNab on loan from Tranmere Rovers.

Mark Andrew Wright – was a defender Town signed initially on loan from Everton. He made ten first team appearances in his first season, while most of his time was spent on the sub bench. Having signed permanently for Town the following season he made a further 15 league appearances before he signed for Wigan Athletic.

Nigel Callaghan – was a winger who Town signed from Aston Villa on loan. After eight league games he went back to his parent club and was given a free transfer by Ron Atkinson at the beginning of March. By the end of the season he had left professional football altogether.

Neil McNab – was a midfielder signed from Tranmere Rovers on loan. By the middle of March he had gone back to his parent club.

By the end of January Town were fifth in the Third Division, on 45 points, just seven points behind the divisional leaders Brentford. Iwan Roberts had scored 23 goals at this point in the season and was Town's leading goalscorer with Phil Starbuck having scored ten goals. Kevin Donovan was allowed to leave Town to go on loan to Halifax Town while Chris Billy made the breakthrough wearing Town's number seven shirt. Off the field of play George Calligan became Town's first ever Ground Safety Officer. His remit at Leeds Road was to meet the tough guidelines that had been laid down for safety at all football grounds.

Kevin Donovan – was a midfielder who started with Town in 1988 after coming through our ranks. He made 11 league appearances during which time he scored one goal. Having gone out initially on loan to Halifax Town in February he signed for West Bromwich Albion in a £70,000 transfer. By 2006 Kevin had retired from professional football altogether.

Christopher Anthony Billy – 'Chris' was a midfielder who started his football career with Town in 1991. He made his first ever Town appearance on Friday 7th February 1992 when he came on as a second sub against Stockport County, having replaced Nigel Callaghan, which ended in a 0-0 draw. Having scored the winning goal at Wembley in the Second Division Play-Off Final against Bristol Rovers he signed for Plymouth Argyle in August 1995.

Having beaten Bury 2-1 in the Area Quarter-Final of the League Trophy Town were then faced with Burnley in the Area Semi-Final. Our league form at this time was a cause for concern for many on our terraces, given that it had taken from the New Year until the Hartlepool game in the second week of February before anyone at Leeds Road saw the first league win of the year. By the beginning of March Eoin Hand was relieved of his managerial duties and was replaced by his Assistant Ian Ross.

On 10th March 1992 a young up and coming striker made his first ever appearance for Town as a sub in place of Gary Barnett. His name was none other than Andrew David Booth, who would in time be simply known as 'Boothy' by everyone on our terraces. He was a striker who had started his football career in our youth ranks and went on to become a true legend in every way possible.

(As author of this book I have tried to recap as best I can all of his time with Town).

08/01/1983 – Boothy is Town mascot for the FA Cup third row tie against Chelsea at Leeds Road
1989 - Signs schoolboy forms with Town.
10/03/1992 - Makes his first team debut as a sub for Gary Barnett away at Fulham.
03/11/1992 - Scored his first goal for Town away at Blackpool in Second Division (2-2 draw).
10/10/1994 - Scored his first professional hat-trick in a 3-0 away win at Plymouth Argyle.
12/11/1994 - Scored his first goal in the FA Cup away at Doncaster Rovers.
25/04/1995 - Earned his first England U21 cap against Latvia.
07/06/1995 - Won his second England U21 cap and scored his first goal at Turf Moor in a 4-0 win.
28/05/1995 - Scored at Wembley and provided an assist for Chris Billy's winner in a Play-Off Final.
10/10/1995 - Won his third and last England U21 cap against Norway and scored his second goal.
02/12/1995 - Made his 100th league appearance in a 1-0 defeat at Port Vale.
08/07/1996 - Sheff Wed signed him for a record £2.7 million pounds.
22/03/2001 - Boothy returned to Town for £200,000.
31/03/2001 - Received a standing ovation on his second Town debut and scores in a 4-1 win.
03/05/2003 - Made his 200th league appearance in a 1-1 draw at home to Oldham Athletic.
08/05/2004 - Scored his 100th goal during our heart-breaking 1-1 draw at Cheltenham Town.
09/04/2005 - Scored against Doncaster United at Galpharm Stadium to put him 4th in the all-time goal scorers list for Town, overtaking Les Massie.
18/04/2006 - Made his 300th appearance for Town in a 2-1 home defeat against Chesterfield.
25/07/2006 - Awarded a well-deserved testimonial against Real Sociedad which finished 0-0.
22/04/2009 - Announced his intention to retire at the end of the season.
25/09/2009 - Scored his 149th goal at our Galpharm Stadium and in last five minutes is subbed off to a standing ovation from Town and Brighton fans.
02/05/2009 - Scored his 150th goal against Leyton Orient in his final appearance in a Town shirt.

And with that a true legend that is Andy Booth came to the end of his 20-year professional football career which included the most amazing Town career. It was a fitting and apt way that he chose to end his career in Town's centenary season. After 452 appearances and 150 goals we had lost one of our very own from our field of dreams but gained an amazing Club Ambassador off the field that is Andy Booth, quite simply 'Mr Huddersfield Town'.

Town meanwhile had dropped out of the promotion race by the end of March and were down to eighth place on 59 points in the Third Division while Stoke City topped the division on 68 points. Simon Charlton, Chris Marsden and Iwan Roberts meanwhile was all included in the P.F.A's Third Division side. It had been a good while since Town had one player in a P.F.A side so to have three in one season, more than any other Third Division Club, was a great accolade.

Iwan Roberts broke Craig Maskell's post-war goalscoring record when he scored his 34th goal of the season in Town's 1-0 win over Swansea City on 25th April. The final league match of the season saw Torquay United beaten 4-0 at Leeds Road thanks to two goals from Phil Starbuck, a goal from Iffy Onuora and a record-breaking 35th goal for Iwan Roberts. The result saw Town finish third in the Third Division and head off into the play-off against Peterborough United.
The first leg of the semi-final play-off on 11th May saw Town come away with a 2-2 draw. The return leg was watched by a 16,107 crowd at Leeds Road, and they all saw Peterborough win 2-1. Phil Starbuck scored Town's first ever Leeds Road play-off goal in the opening minutes of the match but having lost 4-3 on aggregate to 'The Posh' they were out of the Play-offs. Huddersfield Town did actually play in the Second Division, the following season anyhow, due to the formation of the new Premier League.

At the end of the season 1991-92 with a final league placing of 3rd it was one of;

Played 46 games; won 22, lost 12, drew 12, goals for 59, goals against 38, Points 78

During the close season of 1992 19-year-old Kevin Lampkin and 22-year-old Tony Elliott both signed for Town while Mick Lyons was appointed Town's new coach.

Kevin Lampkin – was a central defender signed from Liverpool who played in various positions in Town's first team during the season. By 1993 he had signed permanently for Mansfield Town.

Anthony Robert Elliott – 'Tony' was a goalkeeper signed from Hereford United. He made 15 league appearances for Town before signing for Carlisle United in 1993.

With millions of pounds being invested on upgrading football grounds up and down the country to meet the requirements of the Taylor Report. Little work had been done at our old home at Leeds Road as the new season got underway. The first all-purpose all-seater stadium, on the land just across from our old home at Leeds Road, was being planned for and under constant review with a view to commencing construction in March 1993 for both codes of football. Something back in 1905 wasn't even thought as feasible by Rugby's Northern Union.

Town's first league match of the newly reformed Second Division at Bolton Wanderers was watched by a crowd of 7,897 and ended in a 2-0 defeat. In the League Cup Town travelled up to the North East for their first round first leg match against Sunderland. Thanks to goals from Phil Starbuck, Neil Parsley and Iwan Roberts Town won 3-2. Town's third goal scored by Roberts was his 50th goal in just over 100 appearances. The first home league match of the season against West Bromwich Albion saw Town lose 1-0 in front of the Y.T.V cameras and a 7,947 Leeds Road crowd. Prior to the start of the W.B.A game Iwan Roberts was presented with the coveted Adidas/Shoot Golden Shoe Award, as joint top scorer in the Third Division with 24 League goals, he shared his award with Dean Holdsworth of Brentford.
The second leg of the League Cup first round against Sunderland ended in a 1-0 defeat. A Leeds Road crowd of 6,737 saw Town lose the match, but they still went through to the next round on away goals rule.

For the first time ever in their illustrious rugby history Fartown took to the field at our old home at Leeds Road on Sunday afternoon August 30th for a 3.30pm kick-off. Two sides of our old ground were open for the game the Main Stand and the East Terrace. For Raymond Chappell, Town's Groundsman, it meant working all day and most of the night to prepare our field of dreams for both the football and rugby games in August 1992. Stories of Ray's are legendary with a classic he often tells is that of the time when our Town team asked him to paint the goalposts blue for a league match against Oxford United, because they couldn't see the goal due to snow that was still sat on the Bradley Mills open terrace. The match ref on inspection of the goalposts told Ray in no uncertain terms to paint them back to white again. Raymond Chappell was someone over the many years at Leeds Road I got to know as author of this book and at the John Smith's Stadium in 2018 I enjoyed meeting up with him once again.

Digital image **a52** (left) - Raymond Chappell and John O'Mahoney photographed on John O'Mahoney's personal mobile phone at the FA Cup fourth round match against Birmingham City in January 2018.

By the beginning of September Town was up against Bradford City in a league match at Leeds Road with the kick-off scheduled for 1.15pm. Yorkshire Television featured Town live for the very first time at our old ground with the commentary covered by John Helm and his Y.T.V colleagues. As is often the case when the TV cameras arrive, in front of a crowd of just 5,583, Town lost the game 2-1. Phil Robinson was bought in on loan from Notts County and wore our number eight shirt for the City game.

Philip John Robinson – 'Phil' was a midfielder who was signed initially on loan from Notts County in 1992. He made 74 league appearances, during which time he scored five goals, before he signed for Chesterfield at the start of the 1994-95 season.

Two keen Huddersfield Town supporters and Town Patrons sadly passed away in September. Mary Wright was a member of our '92 club and was also a Committee Member of our Supporters Club. She had worked tirelessly in helping to run our travel section and had travelled many thousands of miles herself watching Town over the years. This was then followed by the news of Frank Mellor's sad passing. Off the field at Leeds Road Heidi Vettraino was appointed as Town's new Commercial Executive.

After the worst start to a football season in our entire football history at Leeds Road Town were pointless until the middle of September when a crowd of 4,411 watched Peter Shilton's Plymouth Argyle lose 2-1 at Leeds Road. (Meanwhile off the field Town's new £14 million Stadium took another step forward when formal Government approval for the scheme was granted).
Town were faced with Kenny Dalglish's Blackburn Rovers in the second round first leg of the League Cup. Watched by a Leeds Road crowd of 11,071 Iwan Roberts scored to earn Town a 1-1 draw. The game down at Ewood Park saw Blackburn win 4-3 thanks to an Alan Shearer hat-trick. The result meant Town was out of the League Cup 5-4 on aggregate. In October Rob Dewhurst came on loan from Blackburn Rovers and played seven league games for Town before he headed back to his parent club.

After ten league games Town were still bottom of Division Two on four points while West Bromwich Albion topped the division on 22 points. Our injury list was horrendous, and Town had to rely on some of our young reserves to fill places in the first team squad while Simon Ireland and Jon Dyson were called up to the first eleven.

Simon Piers Ireland – was a winger who after being out on loan at Wrexham last season got his chance in 1992 to have an extended run in our first team. He starred in our League Cup match away at Blackburn Rovers and was named Town's Man of the Match. After a Town career which had begun in 1990, during which time he had played ten league games, he signed for Blackburn Rovers after they had spent two years scouting him.

Jonathon Paul Dyson – 'Jon' was a defender who started his Town career in our junior ranks in 1990. After a 13-year career with Town, during which time he made 184 league appearances and scored nine goals, he left professional football altogether and signed for Nuneaton Borough in 2003.

Town's first away win in the league was a 3-2 win against Hull City on 17th October in front of a crowd of 4,705. Meanwhile, Town's shareholders had approved the proposed move from our old home at Leeds Road to a new Stadium. An agreement was reached at a shareholders meeting that Town would sell off our current site and take a 150-year lease on the proposed Stadium complex. New Town Associate Chairman Graham Leslie stated that with our other two partners at the Local Council and Fartown they needed to create a funding base. The reality of the problem at Town was that the Club was faced with having to spend two million pounds at Leeds Road over the next three years and around four million pounds by the year 2000. This was considered by our Town Board as simply not viable to keep our old home running.

By the end of October they had put on a real horror show at Edgeley Park as Stockport County ran five goals past Town without reply. Watched by a crowd of 5,405 it was the heaviest defeat of Town's season. Faced with Scunthorpe United away in the first round of the FA Cup Town managed to secure a 0-0 draw. The replay at Leeds Road saw Town beat 'The Iron' 2-1 thanks to two goals from Gary Barnett. At the start of December Town was faced with playing Bradford City away twice in three days. In the second round of the FA Cup Town beat them 2-0 while in the Football League Trophy Town managed a 0-0 draw in a first round group two game. A week later at Leeds Road against Halifax Town in the second match of the group stage Town blasted five goals past 'The Shaymen' to take them through to the next round of the Football League Trophy.

Iain Dunne made his first team debut in Town's FA Cup second round match at Bradford City and wore the number ten shirt. He crowned his debut by scoring his first ever Town goal while Kieran O'Regan scored Town's second goal from a penalty.

Iain George William Dunne – Iain, or 'Dunny' as Town fans knew him more affectionately by was initially given a contract for a season at Town. He scored the first ever golden goal in British Football in the Football League Trophy second round against Lincoln City on 30th November 1994. Thanks to Dunny, Town won the match 3–2 in extra time. To mark the occasion Iain was presented with a commemorative trophy and became a 'cult figure' with everyone on the terraces and had a song dedicated to him that, even to this day, resonates with Town fans across all ages.

Iain Dunn,
Iain Dunn,
Iain, Iain Dunn
He's got no hair,
But we don't care.
Iain, Iain Dunn.

More importantly who could ever forget Iain coming on as a second half sub for Gary Crosby at Wembley in Town's 1994-95 play-off final against Bristol Rovers. Within twenty seconds of coming on, with his fourth initial touch of the ball, he had sent over a cross for Boothy to head on only for Chris Billy to pop up and score the winning goal. By 1997 Iain had sadly signed for Chesterfield United. To this day his 'cult hero status' still remains at our John Smith's Stadium.

Off the pitch Alfred McAlpine was appointed as the major contractor for the construction of our new Stadium after an initial list of 38 contractors had been whittled down. Town played Chester City at Leeds Road on Saturday 19th December and for Peter Jackson it was a special occasion as it was his 100th league game in a Town shirt. Sadly, watched by a home crowd of just 4,626 the game ended in a 2-0 defeat for Town.

Given our chronic injury problems this season it gave some young Town players an early chance to experience first-team football. In my opinion as author of this book had Town not resurrected our youth team policy back in the 1980s they would have seriously struggled this season. As someone famous once said it had been an 'Annus horribilis' year and 1993 for Town could only get better, surely.

Faced with playing Gillingham away in the FA Cup third round at the start of the New Year Town managed a hard-fought 0-0 draw. In front of a Leeds Road crowd of 5,144 Town won the replay 2-1 thanks to a goal each from Phil Robinson and Iain Dunne. Meanwhile, off the field of play Mick Lyons, who had joined as coach in the summer, was dismissed while Ian Ross led the coaching activities assisted by George Mulhall and Wayne Jones.

Town started January rock bottom of the Second Division on 13 points after 20 league games but had three or four games in hand to catch up with the rest of the division. Given that Town were at this point of the season eight points off safety games in hand meant nothing without points.

Up against Doncaster Rovers in the second round of the Football League Trophy Town won 3-1 in front of a lowly crowd at Leeds Road of just 1,535. Three successive away ties in the FA Cup was played and won before Town was rewarded with a home tie against First Division Southend United in the fourth round. In front of a Leeds Road crowd of 7,961 Town lost 2-1 and was knocked out of the FA Cup.

Simon Charlton meanwhile reached his 100th league appearance for Town against Hartlepool United on Wednesday 27th January 1993. He had reached the landmark less than three years after making his first team debut. With just 4,153 present at Leeds Road they all saw Town beat Hartlepool United 3-0. Then having beaten Bolton Wanderers 3-0 in the League Trophy Area Quarter-Final in front of a lowly 2,996 Leeds Road crowd Town was up against Wigan Athletic in the Area Semi-Final. Peter Jackson played his 500th league game of his career for Town against Bolton Wanderers on Saturday 6th February 1993 and thanks to a Kieran O'Regan penalty Town drew the match 1-1. By the middle of February Town were second from bottom of the Second Division and had a meagre 21 points on the board. Town still had games in hand at this point of the season, but they were still eight points adrift of safety.

Off the field of play Town welcomed Malcolm Asquith and David Taylor on to the Board of Directors. Malcolm was a founder member of Town's President's Club, along with his father John, as was David Taylor. Coupled with the new arrivals Town fans saw the departure of former Chairman Keith Longbottom, Leslie Thewlis, Brian Buckley and Charles Hodgkinson. It was a precarious time for a new Chairman to take over just after Christmas given that Town was sitting near the foot of the division, saddled with financial constraints and beset with injuries.

Huddersfield Town was about 18 months away from a commercial lifeline with a facility to attract families and corporate facilities in order to secure a financial future for our Club in a new Stadium.

Graham Leslie's main task on taking over as Town Chairman was to tackle the one million pound debt that had accumulated. Steps were taken to keep our club alive, and along with a major share issue, it aided our immediate situation. A stark reality in this season was that crowds of 9,500 and 10,000 was needed just to break even at Leeds Road.

Town lost the Football League Trophy Area Semi-Final 5-2 away to Wigan and due to the backlog of games was faced with having to play nine games in 28 days in March, with six of them at Leeds Road. In an effort to strength Town's defence Mark Smith was brought in on loan from Notts County while Wayne Jones left Town and took up a coaching appointment at Notts County. Thankfully Town appointed a very worthy and very much still admired successor in Mick Buxton who kindly agreed to re-join the Club. His official title given to him at Town was as Physiotherapist but as we would soon see on our field of dreams, from now until the end of the season, his managerial tactics were still very obvious to us fans on the terraces.

Terry Fisher having only been appointed to our full Board of Directors last August as an Associate Director now stepped in to take over as Chairman due to Graham Leslie's ill-health. In our final 17 matches of the season Town lost only three league games and managed to avoid relegation just 47 days after Mick Buxton had come in when Town sat looking up at the rest of the division. How a team that finished in the Play-offs last season then struggled to survive in the same division this season still surprises me, as author of this book, even to this very day.

At the end of the season 1992-93 with a final league placing of 15th it was one of;

Played 46 games; won 17, lost 20, drew 9, goals for 54, goals against 61, Points 60

Mick Buxton sadly left Town after the last ball had been kicked at the end of the season and Ian Ross quickly followed him out of our old home at Leeds Road. Meanwhile, Neil Warnock walked through our main reception doors at Leeds Road in the summer of 1993 and was announced as Town Manager for the start of the season along with his new backroom staff; Assistant Mick Jones, Physio Dave Wilson and Kevin Blackwell. With Simon Charlton (£250,000) and Kieran O'Regan (£25,000) departing from Town in the summer. Neil's first job as Manager was to sign Steve Francis as goalkeeper. Mark Wells and Richard Ward were then signed by Warnock from Notts County. Richard Ward didn't figure in any league game for Town before he departed at the end of the season.

Stephen Stuart Francis – 'Steve' was a goalkeeper Town signed from Reading in 1993 for £150,000 with his fee having to be set by a tribunal down at Millwall's ground in South East London. Reading had initially wanted £400,000 for him, while Town had offered just £45,000, given that Reading had to pay fifty percent of any fee to Steve's previous club Chelsea.
Steve became a Town favourite and was our number one keeper for the next four seasons. By 1995 he had played a major part in our promotion winning Play-off season after coming to Town's rescue as the last line of our defence on many occasions. In my opinion as author of this book the term 'safe as houses' definitely applied to Steve when he was faced with having to make a vital save for Town. After 186 league appearances Steve signed for Northampton Town in 1999.

Mark Anthony Wells – was a defender signed from Notts County in 1993. He made 21 league appearances for Town, during which time he had scored four goals, then signed for Scarborough in 1994.

Town's first league game of the new season kicked off against Reading. A Leeds Road crowd of 6,415 saw Town lose 3-0. Their next game was against Scarborough in the Coco-Cola Cup first round first leg.

A Leeds Road crowd of 2,822 witnessed a 0-0 draw. The first away game for Town was a short journey over to Rotherham's place at Millmoor. In front of a crowd of 5,540 visiting Town fans were all treated to a 3-2 away win after they had initially fallen behind in the game. Phil Starbuck wore our number four shirt and played as a sweeper due to injuries in our team while Stuart Hicks made his Town debut wearing our number five shirt. The second leg away at Scarborough saw Town finish 3-0 winners on the night and go through to the next round of the Coco-Cola Cup

Stuart Jason Hicks – was a defender signed from Doncaster Rovers for £10,000. He scored his only league goal in a 1-0 win over Fulham and by 1994 had signed for Preston North End.

The league match against Exeter City on 11th September was unique given that Town fans for the first time in many years were able to watch the game from a part of our ground that had been closed off to home fans for the last 15 years. The Bradley Mills open end terrace was now able to be occupied by home supporters instead of visiting supporters. It was a decision partly based on the fact that for Town fans it was our very last season in our old home at Leeds Road and was a move welcomed by everyone. Sadly, someone forgot to tell Exeter City about the occasion given that they managed to secure a 1-0 win over Town in front of a home crowd of 5,266.
Town's second leg Coco-Cola Cup match against Arsenal on Tuesday 21st September was another unique game. For the first time ever, Town fans saw squad numbers used by a Premiership team at our old home at Leeds Road. Sadly that is all our fans did see of 'The Gunners' as they shot Town down 5-0.

Given the league defeat to Exeter City Neil Warnock moved quickly and signed Andy Williams on loan from Notts County for a month. This loan deal enabled Phil Starbuck to move from sweeper to striker in a 4-4-2 line-up against Port Vale. Liverpool defender Steve Harkness was then signed on loan for a month and made his Town debut against Fulham. The Autoglass Trophy group five home game against Doncaster Rovers saw Town win 3-1 in front of a Leeds Road crowd of just 1,069. While the second round second leg Coco-Cola Cup match down at Highbury against Arsenal was a chance for Town to show the Premiership club our Terrier side. Thanks to a goal from Dunny Town came away with a respectable 1-1 draw, but it wasn't enough to win the round.

Steve Francis at this point in the season had already seen various defensive line-ups in front of him. So when Town played Burnley on Saturday 23rd October, in front of a 12,011 Turf Moor crowd, the cheers from Town's loyal travelling clan rang in his ears as a fitting tribute for his 300th league appearance. He marked his special occasion by saving a penalty from Burnley's David Eyres which helped to earn Town a 1-1 draw thanks to a Phil Starbuck goal.
By the end of October Warnock had signed full back Jonathan David Witney for £5,000 from Winsford United. In his first professional league game of his career while wearing the number three shirt 'Jon' helped Town to keep a clean sheet as they beat Bristol Rovers 1-0 at Leeds Road. Another player who made his debut this season was Rodney Rowe. Wearing our number seven shirt he scored to earn Town a 1-1 draw away at Rotherham United in the final group 5 stage of the Autoglass Trophy.

Having beaten Telford United in the FA Cup first round after a replay on Tuesday 23rd November Town were through to play Port Vale in the next round. Town's FA cup replay against non-league Telford United was the very last cup-tie to be played at Leeds Road. 3,517 fans braved the freezing conditions and saw Peter Jackson score Town's last ever FA Cup goal in a 1-0 win.

Rodney Carl Rowe – was a striker who started his football career with Town in 1993. As author of this book I must add that I saw him score a memorable goal, prior to him making his first team debut, in a reserve game against Scunthorpe United.

I would say it could have been a contender for the goal of the season at our old home at Leeds Road. He collected the ball in midfield, drew the defence, and delivered an inch perfect pass to Chris Billy. Rowe continued his run into the penalty area and when Billy knocked over his cross Rodney sent a powerful header beyond the hapless United keeper. After a Town career which lasted until 1997 Rodney Rowe signed for York City.

The second round Autoglass Trophy match against Preston North End at the end of November was a hard-fought 0-0 draw. The game had to be decided by penalties so Town having successfully scored all five of our penalties was through to the next round. One of Town's penalties was scored by our new signing, midfielder Darren Bullock, who wore the number eight shirt.

Darren John Bullock – 'Bully' was a central midfielder who Town signed from Nuneaton Borough for £40,000 in 1993 with an extra £20,000 to be paid after he had played 50 league games. He was a no-nonsense midfielder who as author of this book I thought he was very much like our former Town players Jimmy McGill and Mick Kennedy. All of them would have tackled a shire horse on grass, if they had to, given their aggressive tackling style of play.

In regard to Bully who could ever forget our Autoglass Trophy Area Final against Carlisle United in 1993. Having led 4-1 from the first leg Town just had to ensure that we didn't lose the match 3-0 or more to get through to a Wembley Final for the first time in 56 years. With Carlisle United scoring twice in 90 seconds just before half-time. Town had a true battle on our hands to stay in control of the game. That was when Bully after being treated for an injury was carried off from our Leeds Road pitch on a stretcher. In my opinion as author of this book if he hadn't left the field through injury the danger was he may well have been sent off. Thankfully Town hung on to win the round and went through to Wembley.

Darren became a legend with everyone on the terraces as he helped Town win promotion as play-off winners. His winning penalty down at Brentford to get Town to a play-off final was a moment we all savoured and to this day it's never been forgotten. Nor could anyone forget his handstand walk to celebrate with Town fans behind the goal at Griffin Park after the match.

After promotion, he relished his position in the centre of our midfield and helped Town to reach the FA Cup fifth round and finish eighth in Division One. By 1997 Bully had sadly signed for Swindon Town in a £400,000 transfer.

Next through Town's doors was midfielder Richard Logan who signed from Northern Premier League side Gainsborough for a nominal fee. Richard scored our only goal in the Autoglass Trophy final against Swansea City at Wembley. By 1996 he had signed for Plymouth Argyle.

After the defeat against Port Vale in the second round of the FA Cup in December Town made another legendary signing when Ronnie Jepson agreed to sign in a £70,000 transfer from Exeter City.

Ronald Francis Jepson – better known as 'Ronnie' or Rocket Ron' signed as a striker for Town in 1993 and went on to form a deadly partnership with Andy Booth. Ronnie scored five goals in his first season and went on to become a true legend as well as having scored twice in a 4-2 home win over Hull City in our Yorkshire Electric Cup final he helped Town win promotion. After scoring 42 goals in 125 appearances Ronnie signed for Bury in a £40,000 transfer in 1996.

1994 was the dawning of a new beginning for all Town fans and almost the end of an era for our old home at Leeds Road. Meanwhile, in the Autoglass Trophy Town took another step towards Wembley when they faced Crewe Alexander on Tuesday 11th January at Leeds Road.

Watched by a lowly crowd of just 2,287 they all saw Starbuck score twice while Town's third goal came from none other than our very own Andy Booth.

Town's league game down at Bath's Twerton Park ground against Bristol Rovers on 29th January 1994 featured a very special guest. Joe Walter who at the time was aged 98 and was considered to be Town's oldest surviving player. Joe, a wing-half had played for our great Huddersfield Town side that was crowned 'Thrice Champions' in the 1920s. He had signed from Bristol Rovers and saw his wage double from £4 to £8 a week. After leaving Town he ended up back in the West Country and completed his playing career with Bath City. So it was ironic and totally apt that he was Town's guest of honour both away and at Leeds Road in our final farewell year.

Thanks to a single goal by Dunny against much fancied Stockport County, in the Area Semi-Final Autoglass Trophy at Edgeley Park, Town went on to the Area Final and had to face Carlisle United in the first leg at Leeds Road. Stockport County were at the time second in the Endsleigh Division Two table while Town was closer to relegation than any promotion place. So Town's win in the Autoglass Trophy was made that bit more enjoyable given that they had lost 3-0 to Stockport County in the league less than two weeks previous.

Gary Clayton was Town's ninth signing of this season by Warnock. He was signed for £20,000 from Cambridge United, and it was the second time that Clayton had been signed by Warnock after previously signing for Neil at Burton Albion. After pulling on a Town shirt on 24 different occasions Gary signed for Plymouth Argyle, along with Chris Billy, in August 1995 for a joint transfer fee of £125,000.

Town's Area Semi-Final Autoglass Trophy match at Leeds Road on Tuesday 8th March 1994 was watched by a crowd of 10,552. At the final whistle hundreds of Town fans ran onto the Leeds Road pitch and carried Jacko off shoulder-high after he had played an amazing game. Thanks to goals from Starbuck, Dunne, Bullock and Jackson it helped Town to take a 4-1 lead to their place. Town lost the second leg up at Carlisle 2-0 but still managed to reach Wembley 4-3 on aggregate. While it seemed Town were destined to play the Autoglass Final against Swansea City Town fans on the terraces were also mindful that we weren't yet safe in the league from the real fear of relegation.

In a season that saw many new faces, within our Town team, we also saw a young 18-year-old Simon Baldry make his first team debut. Along with new signings Pat Scully and Tom Cowan they were very much needed to help maintain our league status as well as our first Wembley showing since 1938. Their first team debut came in the league at Leeds Road against Plymouth Argyle on Saturday 26th March.

Simon Jonathon Baldry – was a winger who came through our youth ranks and went on to win various awards while at Town including Player of the Year award. In the very same year he signed his first ever professional contract with Town he also became the youngest player to ever play in a Final at Wembley. No-one can ever forget Baldry scoring the first goal at our 'Cowshed' end in the final ever league game at Leeds Road against Blackpool on 30th April 1994. He also scored another memorable goal which to this day is still fondly remembered by all who were there on 18th April 1998. Against W.B.A Baldry scored the only goal of the game to save Town from relegation in our 1997-98 season and was substituted five minutes from the end of the game to a rousing emotional applause from every Town fan in the Stadium. But for injuries Simon could have possibly gone on to even more footballing glory. While undergoing a medical with a Premiership club he became injured and the deal was ultimately called off. Simon finally signed for Notts County in 2003.

Patrick Joseph Scully – 'Pat' was a defender signed from Southend United for £100,000 in 1994. He went on to become a key figure at the centre of our defence and was a part of our promotion winning team just twelve months later. By 1996 he had left Town to go back to Ireland where he signed for Shelbourne.

Thomas Cowan – 'Tom' was a left-back signed initially on loan from Sheffield United in 1994. It were rumoured at the time of his loan Dave Bassett valued Tom in the region of £250,000. By July 1994 Tom had signed permanently for Town in a £200,000 transfer. After helping Town to achieve promotion and having played in our Autoglass Trophy Final team Tom signed for Burnley in 1999.

Heading into the final part of our season and Town had four consecutive home games, prior to our Wembley Final, in which to ensure our Second Division safety. It was vitally important for everyone at Town that we secured our status in the league given that we were about to kick-off in a brand-new Stadium next season. Thankfully Town went unbeaten and did enough to secure our safety for another season. The game against Cardiff City which was originally scheduled to be played on Tuesday 28th December 1993 was actually played on Tuesday 19th April 1994 and was the last ever evening kick-off in which our old home lit up Leeds Road. Having won 2-0 against 'The Bluebirds' it was a fitting end to our Leeds Road days that our last ever goals under floodlight was scored by Andy Booth.

The Wembley Final down in London was Town's first appearance for 56 years. With the scores equal at 1-1 on 90 minutes, thanks to Richard Logan's headed goal. The game went into extra-time and with neither side unable to break the deadlock it had to be settled with penalties. Sadly the only penalty that Town converted that day was scored by Pat Scully as Town lost 3-1.

And so it was on 30th April 1994 at our old home at Leeds Road against Blackpool that Town's last ever league match took place. For many of us on the terraces, myself included, it was a heart-breaking day. From my days in our old 'Cowshed' back in 1979, as a young 12-year-old lad, to finally be stood on our Bradley Mills open end in 1994, some 15 years later, as a grown man. To have to watch our last ever league game being played out as the clock ticked away, minute by minute, was a truly devastating feeling for me. As I waited for the ref's whistle, to signal the end of time, I looked out onto our field of dreams and all the memories I had of years gone by came flooding back to me in an instant. Looking around at all my fellow Town fans I saw kids held high on their dad's shoulders as our older Town fans leant against the crush barriers. It seemed to me that we were all united in the same deep thought as I saw the look on their faces. Grown men had tears in their eyes as I glanced across the Bradley Mills terracing and looked across to the new Stadium where our future Town days were going to be. On hearing the ref's final whistle it brought to an end our days at Leeds Road. Looking around I saw Town fans who had endured many more years than I had succumbed to their emotions as their thoughts were clearly with all their loved ones, past and present. It made me emotional to think that we could no longer call Leeds Road our home and that in time the only things we would have left of our days here was to be our memories and the remembrance of where we all used to stand.

Long after the final whistle had gone and the dust had settled, Huddersfield Town fans were still scattered all around our old home. We all stood there like we were all mourning the passing of a loved one. My thoughts were those from my childhood and the passing of a good friend, in later life, from a dreadful disease. Given what he faced he didn't let it stop him from cheering Town on every home game. For me having left our old home that last final time, on that fateful day, was like leaving a part of me behind. To this day I still wish I could have just one more day in our old home with all our past and now much older present Terriers, both on and off the field of play.

The final curtain call for this season was brought down when Town played Brentford away on May 7th 1994. Thanks to Iain Dunne scoring twice it gave us all a chance to be able to sign off our Leeds Road days on a high with a 2-0 win.

At the end of the season 1993-94 with a final league placing of 11th it was one of;

Played 46 games; won 17, lost 15, drew 14, goals for 58, goals against 61, Points 65

Digital image **a53** (left) - Personal old photograph of John O'Mahoney's of our old home at Leeds Road at the start of the demolition in 1995 (Taken of the open end).

Digital image **a54** (left) - Personal old photograph of John O'Mahoney's of our old home at Leeds Road at the start of the demolition in 1995 (Taken on the pitch of the open end and the Main Stand).

Digital image **a55** (left) - Personal old photograph of John O'Mahoney's of our old home at Leeds Road during the demolition in 1995 (Taken from the corner of the open end and the corner of where our East Terrace once stood).

Digital image **a56** (left) - Personal old photograph of John O'Mahoney's of our old home at Leeds Road during the demolition in 1995 (View from the Main Stand during the demolition process).

Digital image **a57** (left) - Personal old photograph of John O'Mahoney's of Leeds Road during construction (The view during the building process of the new Leeds Road Retail Park).

Digital image **a58** (left) - Personal old photograph of John O'Mahoney's of Alfred McAlpine Stadium during construction (The view from the nearby banking during the building process of our new Stadium).

Digital image **a59** (left) - Personal old photograph of John O'Mahoney's of Alfred McAlpine Stadium during construction (The view from the nearby banking during the building process of our new Stadium).

Digital image **a60** (left) - Personal old photograph of John O'Mahoney's of Alfred McAlpine Stadium during construction (The view of the South Stand during the building process of our new Stadium).

With the move to the new Alfred McAlpine Stadium for the start of the 1994-95 season many Town fans hoped it would signal a charge up the Second Division table. Warnock, having signed Paul Reid from Bradford City for £70,000 in pre-season, set about with an intent to attack the division with promotion in mind as Town exchanged Iffy Onuora for Kevin Gray at Mansfield Town.

Paul Robert Reid – 'Reidy' was a midfielder Town signed from Bradford City in 1994 for £70,000 and was part of our promotion winning team in 1995 before he signed for Oldham Athletic in 1997.

Kevin Gray – was a defender Warnock signed from Mansfield Town in a straight player exchange for Iffy Onuora. Kevin made his first team debut wearing our number five shirt in a league match against Oxford United on Saturday 3rd September 1994. During his time with Town, he was subjected to a legal battle with a Bradford City player over a footballing incident. Having made 214 league appearances, during which time he scored six goals, Kevin signed for Tranmere Rovers in 2002.

Town's first league game of the season was against Blackpool at Bloomfield Road and was played out in front of a large travelling Town following which boosted the crowd to 8,343. Thanks to two goals each from Paul Reid and Ronnie Jepson Town ran out 4-1 winners. The next game up was Scunthorpe United away in the Coco-Cola Cup first round first leg. Even with a rare Pat Scully goal Town still lost 2-1 in front of a 2,841 crowd.

The first ever Football League match at our new home at the Alfred McAlpine Stadium on Saturday 20th August 1994 saw a crowd of 13,334 attend as Town went down 1-0 against Wycombe Wanderers. Pat Scully personally marked the special occasion by getting sent off. Three days later at our new home in the Coca-Cola Cup second leg against Scunthorpe United, thanks to two goals from Rocket Ron and one from Reidy, Town won 3-0 on the night and were through 4-2 on aggregate to the next round. Wearing Town's number fourteen shirt against 'The Iron' was Craig Whittington who made an appearance as a second half sub.

Craig Whittington – was signed as a striker by Warnock in 1994 for £40,000 after he saw him play for Scarborough in a pre-season game against Town. Craig made his first team league debut at the Alfred McAlpine Stadium against Leyton Orient on Tuesday 30th August 1994. He was subbed off for Iain Dunne in the second half and never played for Town again. By 1995 Craig had signed for Rochdale on a season long loan and by the following year had signed permanently for Crawley Town.

Town finally managed to win their first piece of silverware in fifteen years having defeated Hull City 4-2 in the Yorkshire Electric Cup Final at the beginning of September. A home crowd of just 5,096 watched on as Phil Starbuck, having come on as a late sub in the game, scored a late goal and was told by our captain Reidy to go up the steps and collect the trophy. Once all the photographs had been taken after the game, our players disappeared down the tunnel as Starbuck, having collected the trophy, displayed the cup in front of our very own Kilner Bank Stand on his own. By the following Saturday Andy Booth had netted his first ever senior hat-trick, down at Plymouth Argyle, as Town won 3-0. It was Boothy's sixth goal in four league matches. Our Town Board then loudly declared that it would take over one million pounds to prise the highly-rated marksman away from our Club. Peter Jackson, meanwhile, in his testimonial year was allowed to sign for Chester City.

Town was rewarded with a second round Coco-Cola Cup tie against Premiership Southampton at Leeds Road. Having lost the first leg 1-0 the second leg down on the South Coast saw Town knocked out of the competition altogether, having lost 4-0. Neil Warnock far from finished in the transfer market signed Gary Crosby on a free transfer from Nottingham Forest.

Gary Crosby – was a midfielder that Warnock managed to sign from Forest in September 1994. Having made nearly three dozen league appearances and having made an appearance in Town's 1995 play-off Wembley Final he signed permanently for Rushden and Diamonds in 1997.

With a 2-1 away win over Bradford City and a 3-0 home win over York city in the first round group seven Auto-Windscreens Shield Trophy matches Town was through to the next round. Unbelievably having been overlooked for the September Manager of the Month Award, which was won by Brighton's Liam Brady, Warnock set about the month of October by beating Brady's 'Seagulls' 3-0. The result put Town on top of the division for the first time this season, not since April 1983 had they topped a division, and it would be sometime before they were knocked off as they went through the month unbeaten at league level. Tom Cowan having got himself sent off in a 3-0 away league defeat at York City at the start of November saw Town sign left-back Paul Williams on loan from Coventry City. (Paul, having made his debut in a 1-0 home win over Brentford played nine league games in two loan spells in 1994 and 1995). By the end of November after drawing 1-1, down at Bristol Rovers, Town slid down the league table into second place just as the rumours had started about Liverpool's supposed interest in Boothy. Pat Scully for the second time this season had been sent off at Bristol Rovers as Town took to the field at Twerton Park for the very first time in our red Panasonic-sponsored shirts. On 30th November Iain Dunne scored the first ever sudden-death extra-time goal in an Auto-Windscreens Shield match, against Lincoln City, after coming from behind to win 3-2.

Lincoln City extracted revenge on Town by beating them 1-0 in the second round of the FA Cup at Sincil Bank in early December. The next league game down at Wycombe Wanderers saw Town lose 2-1 against a 10-man home team. With them only managing a home draw against Blackpool just before Christmas Warnock reacted to Town's slip from the top of the division to fourth place by planning a record transfer swoop. Lee Duxbury and Lee Sinnott were signed, from our local rivals Bradford City, in a £500,000 package deal which also saw long-serving Graham Mitchell transfer across to Valley Parade.

Both new signings made their debut in the Boxing Day clash with Hull City as did our loan signing from Notts County, Chris Short. The new faces in the team that day were unable to influence any part of the Hull City game, given that Town lost 1-0.

Lee Duxbury – was a midfielder signed from Bradford City. After 29 league appearances, during which time he scored twice, he returned to Bradford City for the following season.

Lee Sinnott – was a defender signed from Bradford City. After three seasons with Town, during which time he made 86 league appearances and scored one goal, he signed for Oldham Athletic in 1997.

Christian Mark Short – 'Chris' signed on loan for Town in December 1994 and played half a dozen games before he went back to his parent club at Notts County. By the following year had signed permanently for Sheffield United.

Andy Booth scored a truly spectacular goal in a 1-0 home win, in front of a 15,557 crowd, on Tuesday 27th December 1994 against Rotherham United. By the start of the New Year Phil Starbuck had sadly signed for Sheffield United and Lee Duxbury made sure 1995 started with a right bang in front of a home crowd of 12,748 as he netted a last-gasp goal in a 2-1 win over Shrewsbury Town. An unbeaten home run by this time had extended to 11 matches and Town was challenged by Warnock to continue it against a Crewe side as our under-soil heating was used for the first time since we had moved to our new home. Sadly, it was the only thing that got going on the pitch that day as Town lost 2-1. The Auto-Windscreens Shield match against Bury fell victim to the weather and had to be postponed because of water-logging.

Meanwhile, a visit to the McAlpine Stadium by Kevin Keegan for a reserve fixture, he had just sold Andy Cole to Manchester United for seven million pounds, was accompanied by further rumours of Boothy going to Newcastle United while Ian Lawson signed professional forms with Town. Following the goalless draw down at Cardiff Warnock took our squad to Jersey, to a training camp, in readiness for the Auto-Windscreens Area Quarter-Final home match with Bury. Sadly, Town lost the match 2-1 and was knocked out of the competition.

By February Town announced a profit of £373,000 on their previous season. Also, in this month Darren Bullock went on the transfer list while Boothy grabbed his 20th goal of the season in a 1-1 home draw with Bristol Rovers. With Bully recalled to our midfield, alongside Lee Duxbury, Boothy scored down at the Racecourse Ground which gave Town a 2-1 win over Wrexham. It gave Boothy the perfect platform to celebrate his call up to the Endsleigh League U21 representative side in Italy where he scored in a 3-2 win in Andria, near Bari.

At this point of the season Town had nine players who were just a booking away from suspension. It certainly didn't stop them though from recording a 5-1 mauling of Cardiff City at the McAlpine Stadium. The next home match against Brentford was Ronnie Jepson's 50th league game in a Town shirt. Sadly 'The Bees' hadn't read the script correctly and managed to earn themselves a 0-0 draw. Having followed that up with another goalless draw, against Brighton, Town had by now started to slide down the league table. Our five-man Board meanwhile announced ahead of their annual meeting that they had bought 55,000 shares belonging to former Chairman Graham Leslie.

It took the 3-0 home win over York City at the end of February before Town fans were able to enjoy a return to the top of the division. Strangely enough though Warnock still never featured in any Manager of the Month Award given Town's results so far this season.

By the beginning of March in front of a home crowd of 17,404 Town was lucky to secure a 0-0 draw with Bradford City after Tom Cowan had been sent off. This was then followed by a 3-1 away defeat down at Oxford United. Just four days later in a home match against Chester City Ronnie Jepson scored to put himself and Andy Booth into the record books, as the first strike force for 67 years to score 20 goals apiece in a season, as they ran out 5-1 winners over 'The Seals'. Tom Cowan was suspended for four matches and had to undergo a left-knee cartilage operation before the league game down at Leyton Orient. Warnock with no money to spend, without first making a sale, signed former Oldham and Manchester City forward Paul Moulden from Birmingham City on transfer deadline day. Meanwhile, Jon Witney had gone to Wigan and Rodney Rowe had signed for Bury.

Paul Anthony Joseph Moulden – signed as a striker from Birmingham City and played just two league games before he signed for Rochdale at the end of the season. He made his Town debut against Peterborough United after coming on as a sub for Iain Dunne. His final appearance was against his former club Birmingham City, just over a month later.

Town were faced with Peterborough United at our McAlpine Stadium on 1st April. Not since our ill-fated semi-final play-off of 1992 had they had any chance to avenge our Leeds Road defeat against them. In front of a home crowd of 11,324 Town fans saw 'Bully' score, but it was no April Fool's joke to see Town beaten 2-1 and ultimately our championship challenge start to fade. Swansea were next up at the McAlpine Stadium with a home crowd of 10,105 Town won 2-0 thanks to two goals from Gary Crosby. Andy Booth and Tom Cowan meanwhile was both elected to the PFA Second Division representative side. By the middle of the month, with Gary Crosby out injured, Town were faced with Rotherham United away. It was a controversial game in which Lee Sinnott was sent off as Town desperately hung on for a 1-1 draw. It was also a battle for Town in our next league game against Hull City at the McAlpine Stadium as they came from behind to earn a 1-1 draw, thanks to Lee Sinnott's first goal for Town, on Easter Monday.

Having successfully contested Lee Sinnott's red card at Millmoor he was unable to keep our Championship hopes from fading badly at Gay Meadow in a rain-ruined 2-1 defeat, down at Shrewsbury Town. A point was still needed to clinch a play-off place when Town travelled down to Cambridge United at the end of April as Birmingham and Brentford were left to scrap it out for the title. In a hard-fought match 5,188 fans at the Abbey Stadium saw them come away with a 1-1 draw thanks to Boothy's goal which ensured our place in the Play-offs. Andy Booth signed off from Town with his 28th goal of the season down at Cambridge United to earn his England U21 cap. Having played 22 minutes as a substitute in the UEFA Championship qualifier in Latvia he set up the only goal to crown a memorable first full season at league level.

The final league match of the season against Birmingham City on 6th May 1995 at the McAlpine Stadium was an all-ticket sell-out crowd. A pre-match announcement of a £250,000 three-year shirt sponsorship with Panasonic was made as our Town players took to the field in their new-look kit. Having won the match 2-1 Birmingham City were crowned Second Division Champions. The sell-out City crowd took our aggregate attendance for 23 matches at the McAlpine Stadium to 268,390, an average of 11,629. This was an increase of 5,000 from our last ever season at Leeds Road. Not only were Town the second-best supported home side in the division they were also the second-best supported away side having amassed an aggregate attendance of 151,275 from 23 away games.

Our first leg play-off semi-final, at home against Brentford, on Sunday 14th May 1995 finished in a 1-1 draw, thanks to a goal from Chris Billy. Lots of Town fans thought we had blown our best chance as we all set off for the second leg down at Griffin Park on Wednesday 17th April. An early goal for Brentford did nothing to help any Town fan with their nerves thankfully though on 30 minutes, Boothy doing what he does best, came to the rescue and scored our equaliser after Darren Bullock had battled in their penalty area to win the ball. An epic battle began with both Brentford and Town going all out for the winner. After extra-time had been played-out penalties were needed to decide the biggest game Town had played in since we had last won promotion back in 1983.
First up to take their penalty was Martin Grainger for Brentford. It was left to Rocket Ron to blast our first penalty home to make it 1-1. Robert Taylor was up next for Brentford and without any hesitation made it 2-1. Next up for Town was Pat Scully, with many fans crossing their fingers hoping to see him score, the feelings we all had when we saw Barry Dearden save his penalty was one of sheer devastation.
Many fans, myself included, thought that this was the defining moment in the game. Then up stepped Denny Mundee only to see Steve Francis save his penalty to keep Town in the game. Lee Sinnott having scored his penalty then saw Simon Ratcliffe step up next for Brentford, who dispatched his penalty with ease, to make it 3-2 on the night. Lee Duxbury showed no sign of nerves as he hit his penalty with confidence to make it 3-3. Jamie Bates, Brentford's captain, took their last remaining penalty but thanks to another fabulous Steve Francis save Town had a chance to win the round with our final penalty on the night. Who better to take it than our own 'Man of the Match' Darren Bullock who having fought and battled his way through the game with his never-say-die attitude, had helped Town to stay in the game, now everything rested on his shoulders with the final spot kick.

Without much ado Bully ran at the ball and hit it for everything he was worth, while every Town fan held their breath. The second the back of the net bulged the celebrations began like we had won the final already as all our players set off running from the other side of Griffin Park to celebrate with the Town fans in the away end. As author a lasting memory I have of that night is of Bully walking on his hands behind the goal as fans and players alike celebrated carnival style well into the night. Even Reidy who was out injured was there in the away end and got involved to celebrate the fact that Town had won 4-3 on penalties.

Town was faced with playing Bristol Rovers in the play-off final down under the Twin Towers at Wembley. With the Stadium filled with both sets of fans they all witnessed an epic battle on the pitch with some Town fans mindful of the fact that they had already lost three FA Cup Finals (1928, 1930, 1938) and last year's Football League Trophy Final at Wembley.

Both sides started the game with the notion of not conceding an early goal. Just before half-time Rocket Ron from an overhead kick sent a ball over in the penalty area in the hope that someone in a Town shirt might get on the end of it. Thankfully Boothy managed to get his head to the ball and nudged Town 1-0 in front. The joy was short-lived however as Rovers danger man Marcus Stewart, almost at the stroke of half-time, managed to score to put Bristol Rovers level at 1-1. Within nine minutes of the second half Warnock made his first change of the game having sent on Jon Dyson and subbed Simon Trevitt off. The game looked to be going to a stalemate and into extra-time when in the 80th minute Warnock pulled off a master-stroke having sent on Iain Dunne as our second sub and subbed Gary Crosby off.

Steve Francis immediately knocked a long ball down the field to Boothy, who laid the ball off to Dunny out on the wing, who after being on the pitch for less than 60 seconds controlled the ball with just his fourth touch then sent over a cross into the Bristol Rovers penalty area. Boothy managed to head the ball towards the Rovers goalmouth, which was beyond the head of Rocket Ron, but it weren't beyond Chris Billy's. He swooped and headed the ball to the side of Rovers keeper Brian Parkin who was heading in the opposite direction. The ball flew into the corner of the net and gave Town a 2-1 lead. The match was far from over though as Stewart, who had been a danger throughout the game, drove Rovers forward constantly. From one of his relentless attacks, from about 35 yards out, Stewart let out a thunderous shot that flew towards our goal. Thankfully, with Francis well and truly beaten, it hit the crossbar and flew back into the penalty area only for Marcus Browning to miss with the follow-up. Town fans, myself included, all had our hearts in our mouths as the minutes slowly ticked down. With a constant barrage of wolf whistles from all the travelling Town fans we all urged the ref to blow his whistle. A long punt up field from their keeper in a last-ditch attempt to equalise was thankfully the last kick of the game as the ref finally blew his whistle. It was the signal for all Town fans in Wembley Stadium to go crazy as the realisation set in that we had taken another giant step forward in gaining some self-respect back after all the years spent in the depths of football's basement.

At the end of the season 1994-95 with a final league placing of 5th (promoted) it was one of;

Played 46 games; won 22, lost 9, drew 15, goals for 79, goals against 49, Points 81

The 1995-96 pre-season saw Neil Warnock and Mick Jones depart our McAlpine Stadium and was replaced by Brian Horton as Town Manager while Dennis Booth took on the role of First Team Coach. With the new Manager came a different style of play with more football played on the ground and involved a lot more passing of the ball, unlike Warnock's style of play.

Town marked the official opening of the Alfred McAlpine Stadium on Saturday 5th August 1995 with a friendly match against Blackburn Rovers. It was quite fitting and apt that our Huddersfield born legend Andy Booth continued where he left off last season by scoring first as Blackburn Rovers came from behind in a 1-1 draw. Town only had two new faces to our new-look playing staff for the start of this season.

Tony Norman was signed on a free transfer from Sunderland while Paul Dalton, who was out of contract at Plymouth Argyle, trained with Town with a view to a permanent move back up north. Simon Collins meanwhile featured more for the first team this season.

Anthony Joseph Norman – 'Tony' signed for Town as a goalkeeper in 1995 and by 1997 had retired from professional football altogether.

Paul Dalton – was a winger Town signed in 1995 for a transfer fee of £125,000 from Plymouth Argyle with Chris Billy offered as part of the deal. After an initial loan spell at Carlisle United Paul signed for non-league Gateshead in 2000.

Simon Jonathan Collins – was a defender who started his football career with Town in 1992. He made 24 league appearances during which time he scored three goals. By 1997 Simon had joined Warnock down at Plymouth Argyle.

The first league match of the new season in Division One saw Town play Oldham Athletic. With Lee Sinnott installed as skipper, due to Reidy's injury, in front of a 10,259 away crowd at Boundary Park Town were beaten 3-0. Three days later, on Tuesday 12th August 1995, Town now playing in our all yellow Super League designed third strip faced Port Vale at our Alfred McAlpine Stadium in the Coco-Cola Cup first round first leg. In front of a home crowd of 5,363 they went down 2-1 as Paul Dalton grabbed his first goal of his Town career. The new Super League design was Brazilian yellow with blue trim and had been forced on Town due to their first-choice strip clashing on many occasions last season. Having gone back to basics in footballing terms a 10,556 crowd at our McAlpine Stadium saw the first league win of the season as they beat Watford 1-0. Our second leg Coca-Cola Cup match down at Port Vale saw Town win 3-1 on the night. The game against Birmingham City at the end of August was a milestone for Rocket Ron who in his 68th league match for Huddersfield Town had reached his 200th league appearance of his football career. Watched by a McAlpine crowd of 12,305 they ran out 4-2 winners as Jepson scored a goal to celebrate his special occasion. Tom Cowan marked the Birmingham game in his own way by getting sent off in the 70th minute.

By the start of September having lost 2-1, down at the Valley against Charlton Athletic, Town sat mid-table in the Division. Already Horton was in desperate need of some new faces to add to our squad at this point of the season. Pat Scully's 57th league appearance for Town down at Crystal Palace was his 200th league appearance of his football career. Pat helped mark the occasion by securing a 0-0 draw in front of a 15,645 crowd as Town sat seventh in Division One, on 13 points, while Leicester City were joint top leaders of the division, on 17 points, along with Millwall.

The Coca-Cola Cup second round first leg match against Barnsley saw Town win 2-0 in front of a home crowd of 8,264. Having beaten 'The Tykes' twice already at the McAlpine Stadium this season the second leg away at Oakwell saw Town beaten 4-0 and ultimately knocked out of the cup 4-2 on aggregate.

Andy Booth capped off a great month for himself by scoring the winner down at West Bromwich Albion in a 2-1 Town win and then by getting called up to the shadow party for the England U21 international that was due to take place the following week. By the beginning of October Town were fifth in the league on 16 points just four points behind the leaders Leicester City. By mid-October Lee Makel had made his Town debut in a 3-1 defeat down at Reading.

Lee Robert Makel – was a midfielder signed from Blackburn Rovers for £300,000. After pulling on our Town shirt on 79 different occasions, during which time he scored five goals, he signed for Heart of Midlothian in March 1998 for £75,000.

Andy Booth meanwhile had scored for the England U21's as Town's McAlpine Stadium was chosen to host the Endsleigh Football League match against the Italian League. Brian Horton had double reason to celebrate as he had been chosen to manage the Endsleigh Football League team while both Lee Makel and Andy Booth were chosen to represent the Endsleigh Football League.

Lee Makel was voted 'Man of the Match' and scored the only goal for the Endsleigh League in a 1-1 draw. Town's Board meanwhile had turned down a £2.5 million pound bid from Crystal Palace for Andy Booth by the end of October. Amongst the many faces seen in the Town Director's box the night Town hosted the international match was David Pleat and his Assistant Ritchie Barker. As Town ended the month of October in Division One in 13th place on 18 points Steve Jenkins signed for Town after lengthy protracted negotiations had taken place. Steve a newly capped Welsh international was signed from Swansea City for a fee set by a tribunal in London for £275,000. He made his debut at the McAlpine Stadium against Norwich City and marked the occasion with a goal to give Town a much needed 3-2 home win.

Stephen Robert Jenkins – was a player who was able to play as a left-back/right-back in central defence or even midfield. He followed other ex-Town players Ray Mielczarek, Dick Krzywicki, Joey Jones and Iwan Roberts who had all previously played for Wales while still a Town player. After 257 league games for Town, during which time he became captain and a firm favourite with us on the terraces, Steve signed for Cardiff City in 2003.

Having drawn 1-1 down at Portsmouth, then scraped a 0-0 draw away at Millwall, Town was faced with playing in-form Leicester City at the McAlpine Stadium on Tuesday 21st November. Playing for Leicester City that day was none other than Iwan Roberts and in front of a 14,300 home crowd Town won 3-1 thanks to two goals from Bully and one from Paul Dalton.
For some unknown reason at the beginning of December after a seven-match unbeaten run Town lost 1-0 away against bottom club Port Vale as Andy Booth's 100th league appearance was spoilt by the 'Valiants'. Town bounced straight back with a 2-0 win over Sheffield United at Bramall Lane five days later and beat West Bromwich Albion 4-1 at the McAlpine Stadium nine days before Christmas.
Up against Blackpool in the FA Cup third round 12,424 fans saw Rocket Ron score twice to secure a 2-1 home win to earn Town a home tie against Peterborough United in the next round.
The FA Cup fourth round meeting against 'The Posh' was a chance for all Town fans to see them go through to the next round for the first time in 24 years. It was also a further chance to avenge the bitterness of our Play-off defeat in 1992. Peterborough started the game in great form and could have been two up by the half-time whistle but thanks to a goal each from both Bully and Boothy, in the second half, Town were through to the fifth round of the FA Cup.

Up against Premiership opposition in the last 16 of the FA Cup Town was faced with Wimbledon. In front of a McAlpine Stadium crowd and the Match of the Day cameras Town were seconds away from winning as 'The Dons' somehow managed to hang on and scored in the dying seconds of stoppage time to secure a 2-2 draw. Town was faced with a replay, down at Wimbledon's shared home with Crystal Palace, at Selhurst Park. Ian Lawson made his first appearance in our first team squad when he was given the number twelve shirt for the Charlton home match. Having scored 23 goals for the juniors and one for the reserves it was felt by Horton that the next step in his career was with the first team as Town drew 2-2 with 'The Addicks' at the McAlpine Stadium.

Ian James Lawson – is the son of former Town player Jimmy Lawson. He started his football career with Town as a striker in 1993 and made 13 league appearances, during which time he scored five goals, before he signed for Bury in 1999.

The FA Cup fifth round replay down at Wimbledon on Wednesday 28th February 1996 saw Town knocked out of the cup after losing 3-1. After a run of seven undefeated league games their promotion hopes was severely dented after losing 3-2 away to the divisional leaders Derby County at the beginning of March.

Thanks to an early second minute goal from Boothy Town struck first but was 3-1 down before our new loan signing, winger, Ben Thornley put the frighteners on title favourites Derby. He scored our second goal of the game in the 81st minute with a far post header from a Lee Makel cross. Having thrown everything at Derby to equalise Town was denied a late penalty as Andy Booth was stretched off after seeing Chris Powell fall on his ankle to stop him from scoring.

Benjamin Lindsay Thornley – 'Ben' was a winger who first signed on loan for Town in February 1996. Then having signed from Manchester United for the start of the 1996-97 season he made 77 league appearances in our Town colours, during which time he scored five goals, before he signed for Aberdeen in 2001.

In the very next league match at the McAlpine Stadium Town got back to winning ways against Luton Town with a 1-0 win. Having seen Rob Edwards, our new signing, score the only goal in the game it was a moment to saviour for all Town fans given that it was our 100th goal in just 54 competitive first team matches since the opening of the McAlpine Stadium.

Robert Edwards – 'Rob' was a defensive midfielder signed from Crewe Alexander for £150,000 in March 1996. He made 109 league appearances during which he scored 14 goals in his first spell with Town. Having signed for Chesterfield in 2000 just three years later Rob was back in a Town shirt and continued his career at the McAlpine Stadium for another two seasons. After a further 32 league games, during which time he scored three memorable Town goals, Rob's final Town appearance came in 2005 and saw him given a standing ovation as he was clapped off our McAlpine pitch by both fans and players alike during the Swindon game.

Mark Ward – was a winger who signed on a free transfer from Birmingham City. Having signed until the end of the season he made a handful of league appearances in our Town colours before he signed for Ayr United in the summer of 1996.

After a 3-0 home win over Millwall in April, for the final four league games of this season, Town did not register another league win. It ultimately consigned them to a league placing outside the Division One play-offs.

At the end of the season 1995-96 with a final league placing of 8th it was one of;

Played 46 games; won 17, lost 17, drew 12, goals for 61, goals against 58, Points 63

Town started the 1996-97 season with three new faces in our squad having sold Andy Booth to Sheffield Wednesday for a record club deal of £2.7 million pounds, and allowed Jepson to sign for Bury, in the close season. Brian Horton invested the money in signing prolific Bristol Rovers striker Marcus Stewart for a club record £1.2 million pounds, Barnsley's Andy Payton for £350,000 and Blackpool's defender Andy Morrison for £500,000. Physio Dave Wilson retired due to ill-health in this year as 43-year-old John Dickens carried on Dave's good work.

William Marcus Paul Stewart – Marcus was a striker that having terrified our defence previously at Wembley was well remembered by many Town fans still. Having completed his transfer for a club record £1.2 million pounds Marcus went on to pull on our Town shirt on 160 different occasions, during which time he scored 68 league goals, before been sold to Ipswich Town in the final run-in of our 1999-2000 season. Stewart helped Ipswich Town to reach the Premier League while our club fell away from the promotion race at the final hurdle.

Andrew Paul Payton – 'Andy' was a striker signed from Barnsley for £350,000 in 1996. He made 42 league appearances, during which time he scored 17 league goals, before he signed for Burnley in part-exchange for Paul Barnes in 1998.

Andrew Charles Morrison – 'Andy' was a defender signed from Blackpool for £500,000 in 1996. He soon became captain and scored within the first five minutes of his debut against Charlton Athletic.
Andy earned the respect of all fans with his braveheart style warrior performances, but a knee injury restricted his appearances in his first year with Town as Sam Collins stepped in to cover for his absence. It was April 1997 before Andy resumed his playing career again and by 1998 had signed for Manchester City for £80,000. Having been made captain at City he retired from professional football in 2001 due to an injury.

The first league match of the new season saw Town beat Charlton Athletic 2-0 in front of a 11,858 crowd at the McAlpine Stadium. Huddersfield Town said farewell to Chief Executive Paul Fletcher as he left our McAlpine Stadium and started work on a similar project in his native Lancashire. He was tasked with working on Bolton's new thirty million pound stadium to replace Burnden Park.

Town were faced with playing Wrexham in the Coca-Cola Cup first round and in the first leg at home ran out 3-0 winners, thanks to a Marcus Stewart hat-trick. The second leg down at the Racecourse Ground saw Town beat them 2-1 on the night. The league game against Ipswich Town away on Saturday 7th September saw another Town new signing, Wayne Burnett, make his first team debut in a 3-1 away win. It was their first away victory since Darren Bullock had scored the only goal of the game against Watford, 238 days ago.

Wayne Burnett – was a midfielder signed from Bolton Wanderers for £150,000 after an initial loan period. He would be best remembered by many fans, I am sure, for his wonderful goal against Bradford City having scored from just inside Town's own half in a League Cup tie. At the time of his goal, the tie was balanced at 2–2 on aggregate until Burnett's stunning goal in the 77th minute put Town through to the next round. By 1998 Wayne went on loan initially to Grimsby Town before he signed permanently for 'The Mariners'.

Finally, after an absence of two years fans saw the return of our great Town Terrier mascot 'Hudson' at the McAlpine Stadium. The original Hudson was rumoured to be under the weather, after a visit to the vets, actually it was because the 'man inside' had moved to Scotland. Our new Hudson was none other than 16-year-old Mark Tague. Thanks to a Tom Cowan goal our second round first leg Coca-Cola Cup match at home against Colchester United ended in a 1-1 draw. Town went on to win the second leg second round 2-0 and was through to the next round.

The start of October saw Town 11th in Division One on 13 points while Bolton topped the division with 23 points. By the middle of the month, they had suffered a humiliating 6-0 defeat down at Swindon. The manner in which Town had conceded six goals in just 19 minutes was frightening while the injuries at this stage of the season was starting to seriously affect their ability to field a first team eleven. Michael Williams a midfielder was signed on loan from Sheffield Wednesday after the 6-0 debacle at Swindon. He made his first team debut at the McAlpine Stadium against Southend United wearing the number four shirt and helped Town to a 0-0 draw.

The third round Coca-Cola Cup match up at the Riverside Stadium against Middlesbrough saw Town heavily beaten 5-1 in front of a 26,615 crowd. Over 5,000 travelling supporters were willing them on that night, but it was to no avail.

Simon Davies was then loaned from Alex Ferguson's Manchester United and made his debut at the McAlpine Stadium in a 3-3 draw against Bradford City. Thanks to goals from Gary Crosby, Paul Dalton, and Ian Lawson they fought back from 3-0 down.

The club's annual accounts which was issued to our shareholders in this month showed a loss of £512,794 for the past year. The deficit was attributed to our transfer activity with our gate receipts going through the two million pound barrier for the first time in the history of the Club. Having spent well over a million pounds on the purchase of Paul Dalton, Lee Makel, Steve Jenkins and Rob Edwards our Chairman Geoff Headey felt that to achieve a trading profit before transfers meant that Town was on a solid financial footing. At this point in the season the plans for the fourth stand at the North End of our Stadium start to come to fruition as building work was scheduled to commence shortly.

By the middle of December Town sat 17th in the league on 28 points while Bolton led the division on 42 points. Having suffered with many injuries, up to this point of the season, Town had used over 30 players at first team level with Tom Cowan being the only player to have played every game so far this season.

At the start of the New Year faced with Q.P.R away in the FA Cup third round Town, thanks to a Gary Crosby goal, drew the match 1-1 to earn a replay. Given the fact that Town had lost Tony Norman to an injury during the match they did well to hang on until late in the game, when Q.P.R finally equalised, as Tom Cowan deputised as our stand-in keeper. With Steve Francis back between the posts our luck in the FA Cup ran out at the McAlpine Stadium as Q.P.R won the replay 2-1. Ironically Tom Cowan was ruled out of this game due to having to serve a two-match suspension and thereby his ever-present record had ended.

Alan Miller from Middlesbrough was then brought in on loan due to injuries to both Steve Francis and Tony Norman. Thankfully Alan Miller wasn't needed as Steve Francis returned from injury to face Manchester city at the McAlpine Stadium.

The plans for the completion of the North Stand at the McAlpine Stadium had now been finalised and work on the eleven million pound project had started in earnest. The funding for the project had come from a Sports Council National Lottery Grant of £5.5 million, £1.83 million from Kirklees Council, £1.66 million from the Government regeneration agency English Partnerships, a total of £1.2 million from Huddersfield Town with additional finances from the Huddersfield Giants Rugby League Club. The completion of the North Stand would see the McAlpine Stadium become a forty million pound leisure complex.

Sadly five-year-old Town fan Aimee Drew lost her battle against cancer in January 1997 after suffering immune problems since birth. Aimee loved her football and often came to watch Town with her Dad (the man with the giant red and yellow cards) Uncle and Grandad. The first match she watched was from her pram, behind the away goal at Rotherham, in the 1993-94 season.

Marcus Browning was signed by Brian Horton from Bristol Rovers for £500,000 on 14th February 1997. He made his debut at the McAlpine Stadium against Bolton Wanderers on Saturday 22nd February as Town lost 2-1. Darren Bullock and Rodney Rowe meanwhile had both departed Town for pastures new. Rodney Rowe was the first to leave for York City and scored a spectacular goal on his home debut in a 3-1 win over Preston. Bully, meanwhile, signed for Swindon Town 24 hours later in a £400,000 transfer and just 13 minutes into his first team debut scored in Swindon's 3-1 win over Birmingham City. Simon Collins also left having signed for Plymouth Argyle and Iain Dunne was the fourth player to leave having signed for Chesterfield in a £35,000 transfer.

Marcus Trevor Browning – was a defensive midfielder who Brian Horton signed in 1997 from Bristol Rovers for £500,000 and by 1999 had signed for Gillingham in a £200,000 transfer.

Darren Edmondson and Lee Glover both signed in March this year and was in the starting line-up for the home league match against Oxford United. Darren had signed from Carlisle United in a £200,000 transfer, with an additional £25,000 to be paid to Carlisle on completion of him having played 25 league games. Lee signed on loan, from Rotherham United, until the end of the season. With both Darren and Lee starting against Oxford United it took our total of Town players used in this season to 32 which equalled the highest ever figure for a season set when Bobby Collins was Manager.

Darren Stephen Edmondson – was a player Horton signed from Carlisle United that could play at full back, central defence or midfield. He had a difficult time at Town and struggled to settle into our first team. As author of this book, I can clearly remember one particular match against Ipswich Town when Edmondson played the ball back to our keeper only to see the ball go through Steve Francis's legs and end up as an own goal. After just 43 occasions when he pulled on a Town shirt Darren signed for York City in 2000.

Edward Lee Glover – Lee was a forward Town signed on loan from Rotherham United in 1997. He made just 11 appearances before he went back to his parent club. On his return to Rotherham United at the end of the 1997 season he found out that the 'The Millers' had been relegated.

Dave Wilson our former Town Physiotherapist sadly passed away aged just 48 on 10th March 1997 at Huddersfield Royal Infirmary. He had sadly been forced to retire through ill-health while at Town last summer. Prior to his passing he was often seen at our McAlpine Stadium on match days watching our beloved Town team, from the touchlines, having first being brought to our club by Neil Warnock in 1993. When Neil and Mick Jones both left for Plymouth Dave stayed loyal to everyone at Town and formed an attachment to Huddersfield Town Football Club, the players, supporters, staff and his many friends that he had made in the area.

Having lost 3-1 to Portsmouth in a bizarre last four minutes of madness Town fans let their feelings be known at the McAlpine Stadium at the final whistle as they languished towards the foot of the division and were dicing with possible relegation. 16-year-old Delroy Facey came on as a 77th minute substitute in the 'Pompey' game and became our 33rd player to represent Town in first team matches this season, a new club record. He was also the fifth youngest player in Town's history to have played senior football in the first team. The others were Denis Law in 1956, Derek Parkin in 1964, Billy Legg in 1965 and Peter Hart the youngest ever Town player at 16 years and 229 days old in 1974 against Southend United.

David Beresford arrived on transfer deadline day from Oldham Athletic in a £350,000 transfer while Paul Reid, our former captain, made the reverse journey to Boundary Park in a £100,000 transfer.

David Beresford – was a midfielder Horton signed who after being sent out on loan a few times finally left Town in 2001 and signed for Hull City on a free transfer.

By the middle of April Town found themselves down in 20th place in Division One on 49 points, just two places off a relegation place. By the end of April, with our last match of the season down at Southend United, they had to field more youngsters in our first team. It was a carnival atmosphere for 600 Town fans down at Roots Hall given that there was non-stop singing, conga's, shirt waving and even bare torso's as Town managed to secure another season in Division One having condemned United to a 2-1 defeat, and ultimately for 'The Shrimpers' relegation.

A record-breaking 37 different Town players had been used by the time the final whistle had sounded for the season at our McAlpine Stadium. The final league match was a chance for Town to showcase their newly sponsored Pony home shirts against Swindon Town.

For our Town Chairman Geoff Headey, the Swindon Town game was also his last in his two-year tenure. Malcolm Asquith as of 1st July 1997 became our new Town Chairman while David Taylor became our Vice-Chairman. In Geoff Headey's time as Chairman, in his two years in the chair, he had presided over our club spending a total of £4.25 million pounds. It was the most that they had spent in a two-year period in our entire history up to this point in 1997.

At the end of the season 1996-97 with a final league placing of 20th it was one of;

Played 46 games; won 13, lost 18, drew 15, goals for 48, goals against 61, Points 54

In the pre-season of 1997-98 Town played seven friendlies resulting in three wins, two draws and two losses. Horton signed Alex Dyer but had to wait for international clearance before he got to make his first team debut for Town.

Alexander Constantine Dyer – 'Alex' started his football career as a left-winger but also played as a midfielder as well. Having signed for Town in 1997 from FC Maia (Portugal) he made his Town debut as a striker wearing our number ten shirt in the away game at Swindon Town. Having made a total of eight league appearances in which he scored his only goal, and Town's winner, in the Coca-Cola Cup second leg first-round match against West Ham United on Tuesday 16th September 1997 Alex signed for Notts County in early 1998.

The opening league match of the 1997-98 season saw Town beaten 2-0 away to Oxford United. The only other two signings Town fans saw for the start of this season was midfielder Chris Hurst who signed from Emley for £30,000 and finally 'Terrie' Town's new mascot.
The new name had been given to our larger-than-life Terrier. 'Terrie' brought some much-needed cheer to our West Yorkshire derby against Bradford City in the Coca-Cola Cup first round first leg at our McAlpine Stadium as Town ran out 2-1 winners. Then having drawn 1-1 at Bradford City in the second leg Town went through to the next round of the cup.
Town's injury jinx continued into this season as Dean Williams had to be drafted in as goalkeeper cover, for the injured Derek O'Connor. By the time Town had taken on and beaten West Ham United 1-0, in the Coca-Cola Cup second round first leg match at the McAlpine Stadium, in the middle of September, they were still without a win in the league. Having played six matches Town were rock bottom of Division One on three points whilst Bradford City topped the division with 14 points. For the Wolves match, towards the end of September, Town had already used 25 players in our opening twelve league and cup outings, and it looked like it was going to be a repeat of last season on the field of play. The second leg down at West Ham United in the Coca-Cola Cup saw Town lose 3-0 and was dumped out of the cup for another season.
Friday 3rd October 1997 saw Town take to our McAlpine Stadium pitch and line up against Nottingham Forest in a televised league match. It was a significant date in our season given that it was the last time Brian Horton sat in our dugout as Manager. Having dropped Steve Francis in favour of Derek O'Conner, and having lost 2-0 to Forest, Town sat rooted firmly at the bottom of Division One. Brian Horton was relieved of his duties just two days after the Forest defeat.

By the time Town had taken to the field for the re-arranged league match against Charlton Athletic on Tuesday 14th October they had a new management structure in place.

At a press conference at the Banqueting Suite at the McAlpine Stadium at 11am on Tuesday 7th October 1997 Peter Jackson, our former Town player, was proudly presented as our new Manager along with Terry Yorath as Coach.

The first appointment the new management duo made was the signing of another former player Terry Dolan as Reserve Team Coach. Their first job was to set about signing some new Town players. Tom Cowan was out for the season with an injury that required an operation. Marcus Browning was still unfit from the start of the season, David Beresford had to undergo an operation and Andy Payton, Thomas Heary and Lee Makel was all out injured. So Barry Horne and Lee Richardson became our latest signings from our new management duo.

Barry Horne – was a midfielder who was signed from Birmingham City on a free transfer by Jackson and Yorath. By the end of his Town career he had become a firm favourite with every fan on the terraces at the McAlpine Stadium. After pulling on a Town shirt on 73 different occasions Barry signed for Sheffield Wednesday in 2000.

Lee James Richardson – was a midfielder who was signed from Oldham Athletic for £65,000. After playing 29 league games, during which time he scored three goals, Lee signed for Scottish club Livingston in 2000.

Vince Bartram signed on loan for Town from Premier League club Arsenal. With David Seaman blocking his route to 'The Gunners' number one shirt Vince played twelve games for Town, before he returned to his parent club in December 1997, while newly signed Chris Hurst went out on loan to Halifax Town. Saturday 1st November 1997 is a date that should now be etched into the minds of all Town fans. Against the odds and with everyone inside the McAlpine Stadium willing and urging Paul Dalton, late on in the game, to shoot from about 45-50 yards out Town finally won their first league match of the season against Stoke City 3-1, in front of a crowd of 10,916. The name of Wayne Allison meanwhile was added to the list of Town signings this season.

Wayne Anthony Allison – was a striker signed from Swindon Town on Monday 10th November 1997 for £800,000. After playing 71 league games, during which time he scored 17 goals, and having won the admiration of fans up and down our terraces, Wayne better known as 'Chief' to all Town fans signed for Tranmere Rovers for £300,000 in 1999.

Town followed up their first league win of the season by beating Manchester City 1-0 on Friday 7th November to secure their first away win of the season. Just 24 hours after the win over City Grant Johnson signed from Dundee United. Not long after that Town signed David Phillips from Nottingham Forest on a two-year deal. He made over fifty appearances during which time he scored a handful of goals before he signed for Lincoln City in 1999.

Ian Grant Johnson – was a midfielder signed from Dundee United for £90,000 in 1997. He made 64 league appearances, during which time he scored five league goals, before he left briefly for Clydebank and then signed permanently for Alloa Athletic in 2000.

The league match against Reading in the middle of November was Grant Johnson's first appearance in a Town shirt. Given that he appeared as a second half sub at the McAlpine Stadium he became the 31st player to appear in our first team this season. The 1-0 win over Reading saw Town still rooted at the bottom of Division One on 14 points.

In December Town signed Newcastle United goalkeeper Steve Harper on loan for the rest of the season. He was the fourth goalkeeper this season that wore the number one shirt making him the 32nd player used in 27 league and cup matches by Town. His first appearance in a league game was a 2-0 away win at West Bromwich Albion on Saturday 20th December as Town ended the year by drawing 1-1 against Bradford City at their place.

Town started 1998 with a right bang, winning 5-1 at home against Oxford United and then went down to the South Coast to take on Bournemouth in the FA Cup third round. Thanks to a Marcus Stewart goal Town won 1-0 and faced Wimbledon at home in the next round. The FA Cup fourth round match at the McAlpine Stadium saw 'The Dons' win 1-0 in front of a 14,533 crowd. They all saw Town denied a penalty after an action replay on television later proved that Wimbledon's Dean Blackwell did indeed handle the ball to block Andy Morrison's would-be equaliser, while the ref ruled it away as unintentional handball.

Town carried out a player-exchange swap with Burnley for Andy Payton in return for signing Paul Barnes, and he became the 33rd player to figure for this season when he appeared as a sub against Birmingham City.

Paul Barnes - was a striker who signed for Town and made 13 league appearances, during which time he scored two goals, before he signed for Bury for £40,000 just a year later.

Alex Smith was the next player to sign on a free transfer from Swindon Town. He was a defensive midfielder and made his first team debut in a 3-0 defeat away at Nottingham Forest and by the end of the season had signed for Chester City. Julian Watts was another player that Town signed on loan from Leicester City this season. Julian played in eight league matches before he went back to his parent club.

Terry Yorath while not under contract at Town, after speaking to Sheffield United, turned down the offer to join 'The Blades' and pledged his commitment to both Jackson and Town. Thankfully it wasn't long after that both Peter and Terry both signed two-year deals with Town which kept them both at our club until 2000. It was welcoming news to all Town supporters given the way the season was going.

Having lost 3-1 at home to Manchester City at the beginning of March Town immediately followed this up by winning 2-1 at Stoke City, after the win Town was third from bottom of the Nationwide Football League Division One. A 3-0 win over Tranmere Rovers on Saturday 14th March 1998 was the perfect start to ensuring our survival. This was then followed up with a very much needed 2-0 away win over relegation favourites Reading as both Martin Neilson and Sean Hessey came off the Town bench to make their first team debuts, making it 37 players they had used this season. On the final Saturday of March thanks to a goal from Kevin Gray it secured a 1-1 home draw against Q.P.R.

Peter Jackson pulled on our famous blue and white shirt for the final time ever and took to the field against West Bromwich Albion in a Pontins League reserve fixture. At the final whistle he finally hung up his football boots forever but not without first rewarding a lucky Town fan with his shirt as he threw it into the crowd at the end of the game. 5,012 fans saw Jackson say his last goodbyes as a Town player at the McAlpine Stadium. It was a fitting end to his playing career as he marked the occasion having scored from the penalty spot to put Town ahead as they ran out 5-1 winners on the night.

Saturday 4th April saw Town take on Bury away at Gigg Lane and thanks to two goals from Lee Richardson they came away with a much needed 2-2 draw. This was then followed up the week after by a 2-0 home win over Crewe Alexander. With just four games to go the impossible from earlier in the season had started to become a real possibility 'The Great Escape' was on.

Very much against the script Town travelled back from Carrow Road having suffered a heavy 5-0 defeat against Norwich City. The 'Great Escape' had come down to our last home match of the season against West Bromwich Albion on Saturday 19th April, it was a game we just dared not lose.

11,704 fans gathered at the McAlpine Stadium and watched on as Town managed, thanks to Simon Baldry's precious goal, to secure Division One safety with a 1-0 win. The goal celebrations was as if we had won the league never mind just survived the division. Town lost the last two league games of the season 3-0 away to Portsmouth, and 4-0 at home against Port Vale. The match against Port Vale was joyous for both teams given that Port Vale with their away win had survived their own 'Great Escape'. With Huddersfield Town already mathematically safe, from the threat of relegation, it was a carnival atmosphere for both teams.

Town was able to look forward to the completion of the fourth stand as Panasonic, Town's official sponsors, signed up for a new three-year deal. This took their total sponsorship of Huddersfield Town to six years and stretched into the new millennium. The new three-year package was worth over £350,000 and saw Panasonic on our Town shirts for all first and second team shirts until the end of the 2000-01 season. For the record Town had used 37 different players in this season, but our reserves certainly deserve a special mention given that they had used 62 players in just 27 league and cup games in this season and unlike our first team did not survive any great escape as they were relegated to Pontins League Two.

At the end of the season 1997-98 with a final league placing of 16th it was one of;

Played 46 games; won 14, lost 21, drew 11, goals for 50, goals against 72, Points 53

During the pre-season of 1998-1999 in readiness for Peter Jackson's first full season in charge of Town the terms of a possible transfer of Manchester United's Ben Thornley was not agreed by the United Board which resulted in the fee having to be decided by a tribunal. This was followed up with the news that Town's first game of the new season was Bury away. Given that their Board of Directors had announced that their new managerial signing was none other than Neil Warnock it certainly was going to be an opening day match in which to saviour at Gigg Lane.
The tribunal hearing had to be adjourned at the end of June due to Manchester United having to pull out of the hearing on Ben Thornley's transfer, with less than 24 hours' notice, citing that they had not had enough time to prepare their case. The second tribunal hearing to settle the fee for Ben was called off at short notice by United officials. Town became the first club in the country to resume pre-season training and embarked on ensuring that all Town players remained fitter than they had been for the start of last season to ensure any injuries to our squad wasn't a long-term contributory factor for any of this season's fixtures.
The League Cup had a new £23 million pound five-year sponsor deal with Worthington and from this season onwards was known as the Worthington Cup. It also coincided with a change to the format of the competition with the introduction of seeding in the First Round. This was so that it gave lower division clubs, and their supporters, an opportunity early in the season to play one of the country's leading clubs.

Town signed Nico Vaesen from Belgium club K.S.C Aalst and Ben Thornley from Manchester United after his initial transfer was set at a tribunal. One other transfer that took place at the same time as Ben's, that our Terry the Terrier was over the moon with, was that after Town had returned from the Isle of Man tournament Terry had a female Terrier, Tilly, to help with all the pre-match build up this season.

Our new North Stand, which was sponsored by Panasonic, was opened for the very first time this season against Port Vale on Saturday 15th August. The stand contained, amongst many other recreational facilities, the Herbert Chapman Suite named after our most famous Town Manager and was also home to our new 100 club. The North Stand was officially opened by Prince Andrew on 1st September 1998.

Nico-Jos Theodoor Vaesen – 'Nico' was a goalkeeper Jackson signed from Belgium club K.S.C Aalst in May 1998 for £80,000. He made 134 league appearances for Town before he signed for Birmingham City in 2001. His first ever Town appearance wearing our number one shirt was memorable for all the wrong reasons. Just nine minutes was on the clock of the opening match of the 1998-99 season, away to Bury, when Nico promptly got his marching orders and was sent off. He received his second sending off down at the Hawthorns against West Bromwich Albion, but thankfully made such a name for himself with some truly outstanding saves that he was voted Town Supporter's Player of the Year in his very first year.

Town started the new season with a 1-0 defeat to Bury before they beat Mansfield Town 3-2 in the Worthington Cup first round first leg at the McAlpine Stadium. The second leg having ended in a 1-1 draw at Mansfield's place meant that Town were through to the next round. The only defeat in the opening month of the new season was away to Grimsby Town. Watched by a crowd of 6,974 and with Steve Francis back in goal to replace the suspended Vaesen Town lost 1-0 at Blundell Park.
They reacted to this defeat by taking on 'Pompey' in front of a McAlpine Stadium crowd of 10,085 and after conceding an early goal at the start of both halves it left them with a mountain to climb. From looking like they were going to lose the game Town got back on level terms and after scoring a goal in the 90th minute looked like they were set to win the game. Somehow Portsmouth managed to score with the last attack of the game to make the final score 3-3.

By the start of September Town's clubcall issued a statement to say that "The Directors have been aware for some time of the need to secure additional funding for the club, so it can move forward from its present healthy position. With this in mind they have talked with several interested parties. For reasons of confidentiality they were not prepared to name the people at the time".
On the pitch meanwhile Town won their first three league games in September which gave them their highest league placing for 26 years as Town went top of the league for 24 hours after beating Tranmere Rovers 3-2 away. Faced with Everton at home in the Worthington Cup second round first leg in front of a crowd of 15,395 they all saw Wayne Allison score his fifth goal in four games as Town drew 1-1 with the men from Merseyside. The return leg at Goodison, along with 3,000 travelling Town fans, saw Stewart score the first goal after just 48 seconds of the game. It wasn't enough though as Town went down 2-1 and was knocked out of the cup. At the end of September against Stockport County they earned a 1-1 draw. The point saw them go second on goal difference in the Nationwide Football League Division One with 20 points from 11 games.

The month of October saw Town play Sunderland in a top of the table clash. Prior to the game Town topped the division on 26 points while Sunderland were second on 24 points. A record-breaking crowd of 20,971 at the McAlpine Stadium saw Marcus Stewart score Town's only goal of the game as Sunderland's Kevin Ball equalised just before half-time as the game finished in a 1-1 draw. By the end of the month, having lost 4-1 away to Norwich and drawn 1-1 down at Birmingham City, Town was replaced at the top of the division by Birmingham City. Mark Jackson had signed on loan from Leeds United and made his first team debut against Birmingham City wearing our number five shirt. He made five appearances before he went back to his parent club.

The following month saw Town win only one league match, and it also saw our heaviest defeat of many a season, having lost 7-1 to Barnsley at Oakwell, on Friday 27th November in front of the Sky cameras. Chris Beech had signed on loan from Hartlepool and made his first team debut in the Barnsley match as Delroy Facey scored his first ever senior goal, after coming on as a sub for Stewart, in the 7-1 hammering at Oakwell.

Delroy Michael Facey – was a striker who started his Town career in 1996. By 2002 he had signed for Bolton Wanderers on a two-year deal. Given that Delroy was under the age of 24 the Bosman ruling entitled Town to a compensation fee for him. After just ten games in the Premier League for Bolton Facey was sent out on loan and ended up playing for West Bromwich Albion by January 2004.

Malcolm Asquith our Town Chairman announced on November 28th that talks with an electronics millionaire, Barry Rubery, about a proposed takeover of our Club was continuing but was taking longer than anticipated. By the beginning of December Town was ninth in the Nationwide Football League Division One on 32 points. Immediately after the heavy Barnsley defeat Town reacted in a positive way by beating Crystal Palace 4-0 in front of a McAlpine Stadium crowd of 10,453. Tom Cowan back in our side after an injury-plagued 18 months got a standing ovation before kick-off against Palace and at the final whistle gave his famous salute to the Kilner Bank faithful. Steve Francis had been on the transfer list for the last 12 months but once again stepped in for the suspended Vaesen and had his own cause for celebration as he helped keep a clean sheet. Having lost 3-0 at home against West Bromwich Albion on 12th December Town finally lost their unbeaten home record for this season.

At the start of 1999 Town was faced with Q.P.R away in the third round of the FA Cup. Thanks to a goal from Wayne Allison Town won 1-0 and were through to the next round. Wayne came to the rescue once again down at Wrexham in the fourth round when after going 1-0 down, early on in the game, he scored to earn Town a replay.
Barry Rubery's takeover at Town was officially announced on 21st January in front of a packed news conference at the McAlpine Stadium. It was disclosed that he had acquired a controlling 70% of the shares to our Club. The current members of our Town Board remained, and David Asquith carried on as Chairman, while Trevor Cherry and Alan Sykes was immediately added to the new Town Board by Barry Rubery.
The FA Cup replay against Wrexham at the start of February was watched at the McAlpine Stadium by a crowd of 15,427. We were all treated to the biggest firework display ever seen in a football stadium to mark the start of a new era under Barry Rubery as goals from Stewart and Thornley, who was back from injury, helped Town win 2-1. 21,629 fans gathered at our McAlpine Stadium to witness Town draw 2-2 against Derby County in the fifth round of the FA Cup. The replay saw Derby County win 3-1 with our only goal scored by new Town signing Chris Beech.

Christopher Stephen Beech – was a midfielder signed by Jackson in 1998 from Hartlepool United. Chris was the first signing made by Town after the takeover from Barry Rubery and was signed for an initial £65,000 plus a further £30,000 on appearances after the fee was set by a tribunal. Chris made 63 league appearances, during which time he scored 12 league goals, before he signed for Rochdale in 2002.

Danny Schofield was an 18-year-old promising striker that was signed by Peter Jackson, for the remainder of this season and all the following season, from non-league Brodsworth Welfare after impressing in several Town reserve trials in the Pontin's League. Meanwhile, Des Hamilton a midfielder from Newcastle United was signed initially on loan for a month but then saw his loan extended until the end of the season.

Clifford Senior, having served as a Town Director between December 1977 and May 1990 and was a former Vice-President at Town having been awarded the honour in October 1990, sadly passed away in February this year aged 91. Meanwhile, Terry Fisher returned to Town as an Associate Director after resigning from the Town Board in November 1995. After a week of tough transfer negotiations Town signed Craig Armstrong for £750,000 from Nottingham Forest on 26th February 1999.

Steven Craig Armstrong – Craig was a former England U21 international that was able to play in central defence, at left-back or in midfield. Having been signed by Jackson he went on to make 101 league appearances and was voted Town's Player of the Year in 2001. By the following season he had signed for Sheffield Wednesday.

Having beaten Bolton Wanderers at the McAlpine Stadium on 2nd of March, it was Town's first league win of 1999, Paul Barnes then signed for Bury in a £50,000 transfer. Malcolm Asquith was honoured by Town and made 'Life Vice-President' after stepping down as our outgoing Chairman at the end of the season, he was replaced with Ian Ayre. Malcolm's fellow Directors Geoff Headey, David Taylor and Robert Whitely also stepped down at the end of the season.
Meanwhile, in the league Town sat five points outside the play-offs in ninth place on 54 points after 38 games. On transfer deadline day they exclusively announced on Huddersfield Town's clubcall that the Terriers had signed Bournemouth's highly rated left-back Jamie Vincent for £550,000 while Marcus Browning had left for Gillingham in a £200,000 transfer.

Jamie Vincent – was a defender Jackson signed from Bournemouth. He was voted Town Player of the Year in 2000. After 54 league games, during which time he scored two goals, he signed for Portsmouth for £800,000 in 2001.

Raymond Chappell, Town's groundsman, retired from working full-time at the McAlpine Stadium in April, but continued to work for Town on a part-time basis. Having known Raymond for many years, as author of this book, I am sure that he would not mind me saying that having started out as something of a hobby, and then by working for Town from the 1970s at our old ground and at our new home, Town fans certainly appreciated all his hard work and efforts.
In front of 11,719 fans at the McAlpine Stadium on Monday 5th April Town lost 2-1 to Swindon. The defeat signalled the end of any play-off hope any Town fan may have had. This was further compounded by Town losing 2-0 to the 'Champions' elect up at Sunderland on Saturday 10th April in front of a packed crowd of 41,074 at the Stadium of Light. It was the biggest crowd Town had played in front of, apart from Wembley, for 27 years. By the end of the season Town had achieved their highest league position for thirty years and the largest run in the FA Cup for 27 years. By far the biggest shock was the departure of Peter Jackson and Terry Yorath not long after the final ball of the season had been kicked. Steve Bruce was convinced by Town's owner Barry Rubery to take up the position of Manager.

At the end of the season 1998-99 with a final league placing of 10th it was one of;

Played 46 games; won 15, lost 15, drew 16, goals for 62, goals against 71, Points 61

With Managing Director Ian Ayre's support Steve Bruce wasted no time in making some serious investments by signing the likes of; Clyde Wijnhard, Chris Lucketti, Georgios Donis, Scott Sellars, Kenny Irons, Ken Monkou and Dean Gorre. Martyn Margetson also signed from Southend United as understudy to Nico Vaesen.

Steven Richard Baker – was a defender Bruce signed on loan from Middlesbrough just 24 hours prior to the Q.P.R match due to an injury to Steve Jenkins. He made three appearances wearing our number two shirt before he went back to his parent club.

Christopher James Lucketti – 'Chris' was a defender Bruce signed from Bury. Having been made captain at Town he made 75 league appearances before he signed for Preston North End for £750,000 in 2001.

Georgios Donis – was a midfielder Bruce signed from Sheffield United. Having played ten league games for Town he retired from professional football altogether by the end of the following season.

Kenneth Irons – 'Kenny' was a midfielder Bruce signed from Tranmere Rovers in a transfer deal worth approximately £500,000. Kenny added a touch of steel to our midfield and after a Town career in which he made 120 league appearances he then signed for Irish side Linfield in 2003.

Scott Sellars – was a midfielder Bruce signed from Bolton Wanderers. He made 29 league appearances for Town before he signed for Danish side AGF Aarhus in 2001.

Clyde Wijnhard – was a striker Bruce signed from Leeds United for £750,000. He made 51 league appearances for Town before he signed for Preston North End in 2002.

Kenneth John Monkou – 'Ken' was a defender Bruce signed initially on a three-month contract from Southampton. After his loan period had finished he signed permanently for Town, but after just 21 league appearances Ken ended his career at our Club in 2001.

Martyn Walter Margetson – was a goalkeeper Bruce signed on a free transfer from Southend United. He was forced to wait, until April 2001, to make his debut for Town. Following the sale of Nico Vaesen to Birmingham City Margetson took over as first-choice goalkeeper and played in every game as Town reached the Play-offs. Martyn was released by Town in 2002 and promptly signed for Cardiff City.

Town beat Scunthorpe United 2-0 in the Worthington Cup first round first leg tie at the McAlpine Stadium and drew the second leg 0-0 to go through to the next round. In front of 13,670 fans, and the Sky cameras, Town recorded their first league win of the season at the McAlpine Stadium on Friday 13th August. Thanks to two goals from Marcus Stewart and one from Rob Edwards Town ran out 3-2 winners against Blackburn Rovers. On Saturday 28th August Town played Crystal Palace in front of a McAlpine Stadium crowd of 10,656. They all bore witness as Town, having annihilated Palace 7-1, recorded their biggest league win for over 20 years. In the second round of the Worthington Cup having beaten Notts County 2-1 at home and won 1-0 away Town were through to the next round. Faced with having to travel down to Stamford Bridge on Wednesday 13th October to play Chelsea in the third round of the Worthington Cup, over 2,000 travelling Town fans saw a Wijnhard goal disallowed before Kenny Irons scored the only goal of the game in a 1-0 win. Having collected the ball from Gorre's pass in the 79th minute from over 25 yards out Kenny fired a spectacular shot into the top left-hand corner of the Chelsea goal, it was a goal to grace any Premier League ground never mind Stamford Bridge. At the final whistle both players and supporters alike celebrated like Town had won the cup never mind the round. The following league match at Bolton Wanderers saw Town not only lose 1-0 but had Chris Lucketti stretchered off with a fracture just above his left ankle. Ken Monkou finished the Bolton game injured and was out of action for quite a while. Towards the end of November Steve Bruce was welcomed onto the Town Board as a Director.

Town meanwhile unveiled their latest signing, against Premiership club Wimbledon, nicknamed 'Zico' 23-year-old Kiatisuk Senamuang was the biggest footballing name in Thailand. Without even making an appearance at first team level he had left Town by the year 2000.

Having lost 2-1 to Wimbledon in the fourth round Town was knocked out of the Worthington Cup. The FA Cup third round match against Liverpool ended in a 2-0 defeat for Town. Immediately after the match Steve Bruce travelled to Brazil to help the BBC with their coverage of the World Club Championship. Lou Macari meanwhile was appointed as European Scout by Town. By the time Town took to the field against Portsmouth on 5th February the shocking news of the sale of Marcus Stewart to Ipswich Town for £2.75 million pounds was still sinking in with every fan. The defeat to 'Pompey' was then followed by a defeat against Ipswich Town, which was further enhanced by the fact that Marcus Stewart had scored 'The Tractor Boys' winning goal. Having lost 2-0 at home to lowly Stockport and after losing 3-0 away at Fulham it left Town fans, with any play-off dream and promotion hope, in pieces.

At the end of the season 1999-2000 with a final league placing of 8th it was one of;

Played 46 games; won 21, lost 14, drew 11, goals for 62, goals against 49, Points 74

10 years of Huddersfield Town's history from 1990

1990-91 11th in Division 3   FA Cup second round
Football League Cup first round
Football League Trophy preliminary round

1991-92 3rd in Division 3 **(play-off semi-finalist)**   FA Cup fourth round
Football League Cup second round
Football League Trophy Area semi-finalist

1992-93 15th in Division 3   FA Cup fourth round
Football League Cup second round
Football League Trophy Area semi-finalist

1993-94 11th in Division 3   FA Cup second round
Coca-Cola Cup second round
Autoglass finalist runners-up

1994-95 5th in Division 3 **(play-off winners-promoted)**   FA Cup second round
Coca-Cola Cup second round
Yorkshire Electric Cup winners
Auto Windshield Area quarter-finalist

1995-96 8th in Division 1   FA Cup fifth round
Coca-Cola Cup second round

1996-97 20th in Division 1   FA Cup third round
Coca-Cola Cup third round

1997-98 16th in Division 1   FA Cup fourth round
Coca-Cola Cup second round

1998-99 10th in Division 1   FA Cup fifth round
Worthington Cup second round

1999-00 8th in Division 1   FA Cup third round
Worthington Cup fourth round

Town's 'Noughties Decade' - Chapter 12

This new decade brought many changes in the world it was also an era when social networking revolutionised how everyone communicated and received information. Phrases such as 'the war on terror' became familiar the world over. The idea of playing a cassette tape or watching a film on VHS became 'old school'. By the time the decade had ended such things as a TDK D-90 tape was looked upon fondly as if they were from a Victorian museum, given that no one owned a Walkman anymore and everyone had an iPod, as mobile phones just got smaller and smaller. Even the everyday reading book was under threat in this decade as television made celebrities out of nobodies. The greatest economic crisis since the Great Depression, or maybe ever, sank the world's economy as the world's Banks was cast as arch villains. The decade's defining moment took place on 11th September 2001 which brought a new perspective to the world on international terrorism.

On home soil an epidemic of foot-and-mouth disease broke out in February 2001 which lasted nine months and paralysed rural Britain. The country lost one of our iconic figures when the Queen Mother sadly passed away at the age of 101. Climate change became an important issue, and still is to this very day, as the world looks for a more environment friendly renewable energy.

In sport, supported by Lord Sebastian Coe and backed by David Beckham, The International Olympic Committee awarded London the 2012 games. Town meanwhile had its own financial crisis to deal with in this decade and Arsenal in 2004 became the very first team to go an entire football season unbeaten.

Sadly Chris Hamilton, a keen Town supporter for over 70 years and former Vice-President of our Huddersfield Town Supporters Club for many years, passed away on 17th June 2000 aged 83. Town's reserves was the first team in this new decade to celebrate any kind of football success having just missed out on the Pontin's League Championship Lou Macari's young reserves lifted the Pontin's League Cup. More than a thousand fans turned up to witness the occasion as Simon Baldry scored the only goal eleven minutes from the end of normal time. For Lou Macari it was a moment to savour given that the reserves had finished runners-up in the league and had been unbeaten since he had taken over from Terry Dolan mid-season last year.

Expectations were high for all Town fans, for the 2000-2001 season, having narrowly missed out on a Play-off place last season. Besides Euro 2000, The talk all summer was "Is this going to be Town's year". Martin Smith, Dean Gorre and Kenny Irons were back from injury and was ready for the start of the new season.

Martin Geoffrey Smith – was a striker that was signed by Bruce for £300,000 from Sheffield United towards the end of the 1999-2000 season. Smith suffered an injury that kept him out of the first team until the start of this season. After 72 league games, during which time he had scored 29 goals, Martin signed for Northampton Town in 2003.

Town gave trials to Kevin Gallen, Gregg Berhalter and Sebastian Sansoni in the pre-season friendly at Port Vale. Kevin Gallen was the only signing Town made from the three that were on trial.

Kevin Andrew Gallen – was a striker that was signed by Bruce on a free transfer from Q.P.R in August 2000. After 30 league games he signed for Barnsley in 2001.

Faced against Watford for the first league match of the season at the McAlpine Stadium in front of a crowd of 13,018 Town lost 1-0. The following week, at Hillsborough, against Sheffield Wednesday Town came away with a valuable 3-2 win.

The Worthington Cup first round first leg at Oldham Athletic ended in a 1-0 defeat for Town. The following league match at home against Crystal Palace end in a 2-1 defeat as Town rounded the month of August off with a 0-0 draw at Stockport County.

Tragically Clyde Wijnhard was involved in a serious car accident in the early hours of Sunday 3rd September 2000. Thankfully having survived the accident he was then treated for a series of injuries, the most serious of which was a compound fracture of his right arm which was broken in four places and required a four-hour operation. He later underwent a further operation in order to try to save his arm before he was able to resume his football career.

Having lost the second leg of the Worthington Cup 2-0 at home against Oldham Athletic Town was out of the cup for another season. Ian Ayre meanwhile announced to the football world that he was to step down as Chairman and Chief Executive at the end of September. Chris Holland having been signed from Birmingham City earlier in the year for £100,000 had hobbled off the pitch at half-time against Stockport County.

Christopher James Holland - was a midfielder signed by Bruce, from Birmingham City, in the spring of 2000. He made 113 league appearances for Town before he signed for Boston United in 2004.

Such was Town's injuries that after only six league and cup matches they only had three ever present players at this early stage of the season Nico Vaesen, Jamie Vincent and Chris Lucketti. In front of a crowd of 12,248 Bolton Wanderers secured a 3-2 win over Town at the McAlpine Stadium as Bruce played his two recent loan signings in the game Rob Kozlok from Sheffield United and Kevin Kyle from Sunderland.

By the end of September Town were third from bottom in the league with just five points on the board as Fulham topped the division with 21 points. By the middle of October, Town without a win in either the league or cup this season saw Steve Bruce relieved of his duties as Manager. Steve had been our sixth manager in the last 12 years alone as Lou Macari stepped up from Reserve Team Manager to that of First Team Manager. He was assisted by Joe Jordan, while John Deehan carried on as First Team Coach.

By the end of October Town sat rock bottom of the Nationwide Football League One on seven points as Watford now headed the division with 35 points. Saturday 2nd of December was a date to remember for all Town fans given that it was the day that they recorded their first league win of the season. 10,603 fans at the McAlpine Stadium saw Town beat Crewe Alexandra 3-1 and earn three very much needed league points. After the Crewe game local newspaper reports announced that a group of businessmen from Norway had been sat in the crowd and had an interest in Huddersfield Town. Barry Rubery made an announcement that any interest they had in Town was at a very early preliminary stage.

The publication of Town's annual accounts was very worrying given that they showed an operating loss of £4,227,797. The loss was in part due to not generating enough income, while maintaining financial disciplines. The large increase of player costs was also a factor, along with players wages increasing from £2.6 million in 1999 to £5.5 million in 2000, an increase of 116%. As author of this book in my own opinion the accounts generally told their own story 'players wages'.

The home game against Wolves on Saturday 9th December was when Town fans first saw a minor miracle occur with the loan signing made by Lou Macari of Zimbabwean international Peter Ndlovu. He single handily improved Town's fortunes as 11,506 fans saw Ndlovu score his first Town goal four minutes into the second half as he smashed the ball home into the roof of the net.

In the 86th minute Ndlovu turned provider as his cross was met by Delroy Facey who finished superbly with a first-time effort to score Town's second goal. Deep into injury time Ndlovu was alive to a bad back pass and pounced to score his second goal and Town's final goal of the game. With Ndlovu in our side Town won five out of seven games whilst drawing the other two in the month of December. This was enough for Macari to be awarded the Manager of the Month award for December 2000. Warnock pulled the rug from under Macari's feet by signing Ndlovu before Town had sorted out a permanent deal with Peter's parent club Birmingham City. Adie Moses meanwhile was recruited from Barnsley by Macari.

Adrian Moses – 'Adie' was a defender signed by Macari from near neighbour's Barnsley for a fee of £250,000. He made 63 league appearances for Town before he signed for Crewe Alexandra in 2003.

Town sat 19th in the league by the end of December, on 24 points, with many fans thinking that maybe a repeat of 'The Great Escape' of three seasons ago was possible once again. The start of 2001 saw Town take on Bristol City in the FA Cup third round at the McAlpine Stadium 9,192 fans saw them knocked out of the cup after losing the game 2-0 to 'The Robins'.

By the beginning of March Barry Rubery announced that since buying our club, regardless of the sum he paid, some £13 million pounds would have been put into our club by the end of this season. This was besides any funds that was received from the sale of Marcus Stewart and Jamie Vincent. The harsh reality for Town in this season was that our total revenue income was just £4.3 million pounds compared to the wage bill and overheads of £9.2 million pounds. Over £3 million pounds was spent on players, from the day Rubery took over until the point when he parted company from Town.
Lou Macari in the meantime tried to strengthen our squad before the transfer deadline and had agreed to take Jamie Lawrence from Bradford City, but he received an injury on international duty for Jamaica and was out injured. Lee Morris arrived at Town on loan from Derby County and played four league games wearing our number nine shirt and scored within the first ten minutes of his debut against Barnsley at Oakwell.
Town announced a new shirt deal with fashion designer 'Joe Bloggs' for the new season, and they also secured a three-year sponsorship deal with Prime Time Recruitment worth £500,000 as Town fans got a chance to choose the kit that they wanted from five different designs. By far the best news in this season was the capture of our former legend Andy Booth from Sheffield Wednesday for £200,000. In true legend style Boothy got his second spell with Town off to a flying start when he grabbed a goal on his home debut against Portsmouth on Saturday 31st March 2001, as Town ran out 4-1 winners. With just nine league games left until the end of the season Town's fate was very much still in our own hands. Two defeats in the month of April severely affected our chances of survival as they began the final month of the season having drawn 1-1 down at Wimbledon. The draw saw Town drop to 20th in the league with 48 points, just two points off a relegation place.
Q.P.R and Tranmere Rovers were already relegated before our final league game had been played against Birmingham City. It meant that only a defeat for Town at our McAlpine Stadium and wins for both Crystal Palace and Portsmouth could condemn Town to relegation. With a hotly disputed goal for Crystal Palace that secured their 1-0 win over Stockport and a 3-1 win for Portsmouth over Barnsley it meant that Town's 2-1 home defeat to Birmingham City saw them relegated back down to the Second Division. It would be a long time before they would be back in the second tier of English football once again.

At the end of the season 2000-2001 with a final league placing of 22nd **(relegated)** it was one of;

Played 46 games; won 11, lost 20, drew 15, goals for 48, goals against 57, Points 48

Lou Macari's first pre-season in charge for the 2001-02 season saw Town back in the Second Division as Nico Vaesen left for Birmingham City and Town signed Gareth Evans from Leeds United. Chris Lucketti also left our club for Preston North End whilst Macari promoted young Nathan Clarke from our reserves into the first team. Other Town reserves Danny Schofield, John Thorrington, Dwayne Mattis and Thomas Heary also featured in this season. Fraser Digby was signed by Macari as goalkeeping cover for Margetson and Jonathon Dyson was rewarded with a testimonial against Manchester City on July 31st. Meanwhile, Barry Rubery entered into negotiations with our former Vice-Chairman David Taylor to relinquish the majority of his shareholding of our club.

Nathan Clarke – was a defender that started his football career with Town in 2001 within three months of his league debut he was called up to the England U19 side. By the end of the 2005-06 season he was runner-up in the 'Player of the Year' award and was made vice-captain of our team at the age of just 21. The following year he won the title as well as winning the 'players player award'. In all Clarke played under eight different Town Managers and was in the starting line-up for each one. After failing to break into Lee Clark's team in January 2011 he joined Colchester United on loan until the end of the season. By June 2012 after a twenty-year association with our club he signed for Leyton Orient.

Town started the new football season with a 1-0 home win over Bournemouth but this was followed up with a 1-0 defeat down at Reading. Faced with Rochdale in the Worthington Cup first round Town lost 1-0 at the McAlpine Stadium and was knocked out of the cup for another season. Robin Wray retired as Youth Team Coach and was replaced with ex-player John Dungworth. Town finished the month of August with a 2-0 home win over Bury and a Bank Holiday 2-1 away win down at Peterborough United.

After beating Wycombe 2-1 at the McAlpine Stadium and having drawn 1-1 with Stoke City away Town found themselves, by goal average, third in the Second Division on 13 points the same points as Brentford who were the divisional leaders. On Friday 7th September 2001 a 21st Anniversary Re-Union Dinner for our Fourth Division Championship winning team of 1979-80 took place in the Banqueting Suite at the McAlpine Stadium and was very well attended by both fans and legendary ex-footballers. Meanwhile, in the league Town suffered two back-to-back league defeats with a 4-2 hammering by Blackpool at the McAlpine Stadium which was then followed in midweek with a 1-0 defeat at the hands of Wigan Athletic. Towards the middle of October Town started to slide down the league as they sat seventh on 20 points and was faced with Halifax in the LDV Vans Trophy first round at the McAlpine Stadium. The tie finished 0-0 and was settled by Town as they won 4-3 on penalties. The league match down at Northampton on Tuesday 23rd October saw Leon Knight wearing our number nine shirt. He had been signed on loan by Lou Macari from Chelsea and earned himself the nickname 'neon light' given that his performances were so electrifying brilliant at a time when Town needed a much-needed boost.

Leon Leroy Knight – was a forward Macari signed on loan from Chelsea in 2001. He made 31 league appearances for Town during which time he scored 16 league goals as he formed a deadly partnership with Boothy. Sadly, Leon was sent off just prior to the end of our season and was suspended for the play-off matches. By the end of the season he went back to his parent club and signed on loan for Sheffield Wednesday in 2002.

Meanwhile, Lou's son, young striker Paul Macari, after arriving last season at Town on non-contract forms started to appear on our first team sub bench. He made a total of 24 appearances on our bench this season.

Dr Leslie Ballon our former Club Doctor sadly passed away in October 2001 aged 86. Dr Ballon still regularly attended our McAlpine Stadium, until ill-health, even though it meant an 80-mile round trip from his family home in Wilmslow. He was our Club Doctor for over 10 years including the season when Town achieved promotion to the old First Division in 1970.

By the beginning of November David Taylor had all the draft agreements from Barry Rubery's Lawyer and the expectations were that they going to be signed off sometime very shortly so that David Taylor could officially take over.

In the FA Cup first round Town having beaten Gravesend and Northfleet 2-1 was then faced with Mansfield Town away in the next round. Then after winning 4-1 at the McAlpine Stadium against Scunthorpe United in the LDV Vans Trophy Quarter-Final Town was faced with playing Hull City away in the Semi-Final. Four days later Town took on Mansfield Town away in the FA Cup second round and in front of 6,836 fans was hammered out of the cup 4-0. After 21 league games Town sat seventh in the league on 32 points while Brighton and Hove Albion topped the division with 43 points.

Having taken over at Town David Taylor, a lifelong Town fan himself, considered in the New Year about switching the 'away end' to allow Town fans to sit behind the goal in our South Stand for certain games. For logistical reasons this sadly wasn't feasible for the full season until years later.

Town having won 1-0 against Hull City in the LDV Vans Trophy was faced with Blackpool away in the first leg Final. Having lost 3-1 to Blackpool at their place it was always going to be an uphill battle for Town for the return leg at the McAlpine Stadium. After 90 minutes Town was 2-0 up against Blackpool and was faced with extra-time. The prospect of another Iain Dunne golden goal winning the tie for Town sadly wasn't to be on this occasion as Blackpool managed to score the golden goal that earned them the LDV Vans Trophy.

David Taylor announced in March that Town had recorded a record club loss and steps had been taken to address the situation. This announcement in the coming years had huge ramifications for every Town fan far and wide. At this point in the season Town began a project with the spirit of co-operation that exists between our public and private sectors to bring about a football complex to our Leeds Road playing fields. Work was expected to start within a month or so of the season ending and completion was scheduled for Autumn. In later years after achieving our Premier League status this project was revisited, and further developments made, which affected every Town fan.

Town managed a 2-1 win over Port Vale at our McAlpine Stadium but lost 2-1 away to Notts County in our final match of the season. It was enough to leave Town sixth in the league and in the play-offs. With Leon Knight suspended, having been sent off against Oldham Athletic at the beginning of April, Town drew 0-0 in the first leg against Brentford at the McAlpine Stadium. The second leg down at their place saw Boothy score in the first five minutes of the game but by the time the final whistle had gone Town had lost 2-1 and were knocked out of the play-offs.

At the end of the season 2001-2002 with a final league placing of 6th (play-offs) it was one of;

Played 46 games; won 21, lost 10, drew 15, goals for 65, goals against 47, Points 78

Town had a new Manager for the start of pre-season training in 2002. Mick Wadsworth had taken over from Lou Macari as the new Town board carried on with the number one priority of trying to ensure the longer-term survival of our club. The loss of television revenue from the collapse of ITV Digital had a big impact on not just Huddersfield Town but also throughout football in general.

Scott Bevan and Scott MacDonald both joined Town on loan from Southampton. Bevan figured in most of our league matches in this season until March 2003 when Phil Senior took over in goal. Scott MacDonald went back to Southampton having played just over a dozen league games. Town fans meanwhile saw a new 4-3-3 formation for our first team as our Academy's talented youth was put to the test this season.

The first league game of this season ironically saw Town face last season's semi-final play-off opponents Brentford at the McAlpine Stadium. One promising young academy player by the name of Jon Stead made his first team debut for Town in the 2-0 defeat to Brentford. Paul Scott was another academy player who also made his first team debut against 'The Bees'. Jon Worthington having broken into our first team last season now started to figure more this season.

Jonathon Graham Stead – 'Jon' was a striker who started in our academy and made the breakthrough into Town's first team in the 2002-2003 season. He made 42 league appearances in this season and scored half a dozen league goals along the way. By January 2004 Jon had attracted the interests of the then Premier League side Blackburn Rovers. After signing a four-and-a-half-year contract with them for well over one million pounds Jon was back at Town to collect his Play-Off winners' medal at the end of our 2004 promotion winning season. He was given a large and rousing send off by everyone inside our Stadium as his parting words to all Town fans were "I've moved on, but I know I won't find a friendlier place than this club".

Paul Scott – was a right-back who having made his break through into the first team in 2002 went on to make 18 league appearances in a Town shirt, but by 2004 had signed for Bury.

Jonathan Alan Spencer Worthington – 'Jon' was a central midfielder that joined our Town Academy at the age of nine and progressed right through to our first team. By the end of the 2002-2003 season, he had established himself fully in our first eleven as the lynchpin to our midfield. By 2004 he had been made captain of our first team. After playing 153 league games for Town, he went on loan to Yeovil Town, before he signed permanently for Oldham Athletic in 2009.

The following match was a long haul down to Plymouth Argyle made worse for all fans travelling back after seeing Town concede a second goal in added time in a 2-1 defeat. If that wasn't bad enough the coach some Town fans were on broke down and set on fire, thankfully everyone on board got off safely. Town finally got off the mark and won our first league match of the season 1-0 against Peterborough United thanks to a goal from Dwayne Mattis at their place.

Dwayne Anthony Mattis – was a midfielder who began his football career with Town in our 1998-99 season. Having made 59 appearances he was released by Town and signed for Bury in 2004.

Another player who figured more in this season was *Danny Schofield* – having been signed in 1998 from Brodsworth Welfare for the princely sum of £2,000 pounds, he made his break through into the first team in the 2001-02 season. By 2008 after making over 250 appearances he scored his final ever league goal for Town in a 2-0 win over Walsall. By the start of the 2008-2009 season Danny had signed permanently for Yeovil Town. In December 2016 he joined Leeds United as coach working with the under 15's and under 16's. By August 2017 he was then promoted to the role of Professional Development Phase Coach working alongside none other than Carlos Corberan Town's new Team Coach as of 2020. Danny started back working at Town as the B Team coach and was soon promoted to Carlo's Assistant to the first team in 2020.

John Thorrington – was a midfielder who made his break through into the first team in the 2001-2002 season. John had been signed by Macari on a free transfer from Manchester United and made 48 league appearances before he signed for Grimsby Town in March 2004.

Already some Town fans saw that the 4-3-3 formation wasn't working nor was our team adapting to the change in the style of play for this season. Kevin Sharp a left-back was signed by Wadsworth from Wrexham in the summer of 2002 and played most of this season in a defence that regularly changed due to injuries and illnesses. The first six league games of the season had been played and Town sat fourth from bottom in Nationwide Division Two on five points, just three points off rock bottom Cheltenham. By the start of September Mick Wadsworth had signed forward Kevin Gallacher from Sheffield Wednesday.

Faced with Darlington in the first round of the Worthington Cup in front of a crowd of just 3,810 at the McAlpine Stadium Town won 2-0 and were faced with a home draw against Burnley. Meanwhile, back in the league Town finished the month of September having won none of their league matches after beating Darlington. In fact, the away game down at Q.P.R in the middle of September was more memorable for the loss of Eddie Youds from our defence through injury than the actual 3-0 defeat itself.

Edward Paul Youds – 'Eddie' was a no-nonsense defender who was signed from Charlton Athletic. He played 25 league games for Town before he left professional football altogether in 2003, having signed for non-league Grays Athletic.

Given the injuries, to both Jonathon Dyson and Adie Moses, Nat Brown was another player from our Town academy that made his first team debut in this season. Nat had an impressive debut at centre-half alongside Eddie Youds in the 0-0 draw away against Northampton Town.

Nathaniel Levi Brown – 'Nat' was a central defender who having come through our Town ranks made his first team debut in 2002. After 56 league games, during which time he had played in many different positions, he signed for Lincoln City in 2005.

5,887 fans at the McAlpine Stadium saw Burnley beat Town 1-0 in the second round of the Worthington Cup. This was then followed up with a 2-2 draw at home against Port Vale in the league. On 12th October having beaten Notts County 3-0 in front of a home crowd of 9,984 Town recorded only their third league win of the season. Even with the win over County, which was aided by Jon Stead having scored his first two league goals, Town still found themselves second from bottom in the league on ten points and already on a minus-ten goal difference.

Town Director Geoff Headey then went on record to say that Huddersfield Town was struggling for cash and had approached the PFA about re-opening talks on the playing contracts of our players. Given that their contracts had been agreed and signed well before the takeover of the Club in January this year the stance from the PFA was that it was not possible to do so. It was noted by our Town Board that our players were willing, sympathetic to the cause and were keen to help.

Faced with having to play Wrexham away in the LDV Vans Trophy first round 1,350 fans saw Town knocked out at the first time of asking, having lost 2-1 to the 'Red Dragons'. By November with Town's finances getting more precarious as the season went on an initiative was launched in order to raise £100,000 before Christmas. It was called the Huddersfield Town Grand Roll of Honour the first people to respond to the challenge was our Town players who immediately volunteered to put their cash in straight away. Many Town fans in the first couple of days also donated £100 each to help aid the cause. Simply put with cash flow difficulties, if Town didn't raise the necessary money, then the club would fall into the hands of administrators.

Bucket collections akin to our 1919-20 season was also undertaken at our McAlpine Stadium for fans to give as much as they could possibly afford to give to help preserve football at our McAlpine Stadium. The chances of raising much-needed revenue and the opportunity of a big pay-day in round two of the FA Cup took a severe dent when Town lost 1-0 away to Swindon Town and with it the winner's cheque of £20,000 went as well.

In order to try to improve Town's fortunes Mick Wadsworth unable to sign anyone permanently sought to sign forward Lee Ashcroft on loan from Wigan Athletic. The loan deal, the first of its kind, was actually paid for by John Smith a long-standing and loyal Town fan. Lee played four league games before he returned to his parent club at Wigan. Meanwhile, David Taylor welcomed Stuart Bragan, a new Director, to our Town Board.

By the end of the year David Taylor, along with our Board of Directors, had presided over Huddersfield Town for almost twelve months. They had a difficult job to start with, but the problems Town now faced was compounded with the collapse of ITV Digital, the stagnant transfer market, the failure to win promotion via the Play-offs last season and the subsequent reduction in attendance in Division Two. There were very few local derbies which resulted in low numbers of visiting supporters. Town celebrated Christmas third from bottom in the league and was just three points off rock bottom Mansfield Town.

With only the league to play for in 2003 Town started off the New Year with a 1-1 draw away at Blackpool. It wasn't enough to take Town out of the bottom three, in fact, the draw only served to send them to the very bottom of the league table as teams above them started to open up a points gap. Having lost 1-0 to Peterborough United at home Town was then faced with Crewe Alexandra away. If having lost in injury time wasn't bad enough, Town had to play with ten men for part of the game, having had Scott Bevan sent off as Phil Senior was handed his senior debut after taking over in goal.

More importantly though behind the scenes at Town was utter chaos as David Taylor met Mick Wadsworth in an amicable meeting to discuss and negotiate compensation. Even with the mutually agreed reduced amount, which Mick kindly agreed to accept, it still could not be funded by our Board. Town basically could not afford to sack Mick Wadsworth at any price. After those turn of events on 22nd January 2003 Geoff Headey resigned from our Board of Directors as Town sought desperately to seek new investors and an injection of cash. The thought of Town not being in business by the end of the season was as a Town fan unthinkable. It's hard to imagine while writing this book what those in power at our McAlpine Stadium was thinking of with a change of Manager and different style of play from Lou Macari's sixth place finish last season. With a woeful start and having been in the relegation zone for most of the season it hurt me as a Town fan to watch events unfold this season. From being the envy of the footballing world in the 1920s it seemed Town was now in financial ruin and in total meltdown.

Eddie Youds took over as captain in mid-February, given that Steve Jenkins had left for Cardiff City, as Town took on Cheltenham in a real six pointer down at the foot of the table. A 3-3 battle at our McAlpine Stadium did nothing for either team to be able to climb out of the bottom three. This was followed up by Town winning 1-0 away against Barnsley at Oakwell. Over 2,500 travelling Town fans signalled to the footballing world that our survival was more than just a pipe dream. Our massed choir banked high behind the Barnsley goal sang themselves hoarse that day as every man on the pitch performed heroics. None more so than Phil Senior who in the third minute of stoppage time made an outstanding save to ensure Andy Booth's 25th minute header was enough to earn Town three points. It's worth mentioning that on the field of play eight of our first eleven players who had beaten Barnsley was home-grown talent that had been developed by our Academy.

Victory at the McAlpine Stadium over Northampton at the beginning of March gave Town some much-needed relief from being sat in the bottom three in the division. Thanks to goals from Baldry and Smith 9,661 fans saw Town win 2-0. Q.P.R obviously hadn't read the script correctly because in the very next league game Town suffered a heavy 3-0 defeat at the McAlpine Stadium. The result was bad enough but compounded with the fact that the bottom eleven teams in the league were separated by just nine points it was to be another nail in Town's coffin.

David Taylor went on record as saying that he was unable to personally bankroll Huddersfield Town beyond Sunday 23rd March 2003. He had been involved in a long succession of meetings and a formal announcement was to be made on Monday 24th March at which point the Club may well be out of his control.

Town did not win another league game until April 5th when they beat Chesterfield 4-0 at our McAlpine Stadium. By that time, David Taylor and the Town Board had lost total control of our club, Huddersfield Town had sadly entered into administration and into the unknown. Town fans were happy to know that despite owing over £300,000 to the Stadium Company KDSL they were still able to play the remainder of the season at the McAlpine Stadium. The size of our total debt was rumoured to be in excess of £17 million pounds.

Our newly formed Supporter's Trust run by Robert Pepper was busy trying to raise capital to aid our financial plight, just like in our 1919-20 season, the good townsfolk of Huddersfield once again rallied to Town's cause. For the Chesterfield match, and for the rest of the season, in temporary charge of first team affairs was none other than Mel Machin given that Mick Wadsworth had been relieved of his duties as Team Manager.

By the time Town had taken to the field to line up against league leaders Wigan Athletic on 19th April 2003 former players and legends Denis Law, Steve Kindon and Keith Hanvey had given their full backing to our Huddersfield Town Survival Trust. Denis Law had accepted an invitation and became President of our Trust as Steve Kindon and Keith Hanvey both kindly agreed to become Vice-President's. David Acland as joint administrator placed on record his thanks to all Town players who had not been paid for the last four months but was still giving one hundred percent as a professional footballer. He also expressed his gratitude to every fan for supporting Huddersfield Town when they were in desperate need for an investor.

By Easter our Survival Trust had raised about £40,000 which by the end of the season had risen to somewhere in the region of £65,000. By the time they had left the field against Port Vale on April 26th, after a humiliating 5-1 away defeat, Huddersfield Town had been relegated to Division Three.

Our final league game of the season at the McAlpine Stadium saw Oldham Athletic manage a 1-1 draw to cement their place in the Play-offs. The football season may have finished but the fight to save Huddersfield Town over the summer was a real battle that our fans just dared not lose.

At the end of the season 2002-2003 with a final league placing of 22nd **(relegated)** it was one of;

Played 46 games; won 11, lost 23, drew 12, goals for 39, goals against 61, Points 45

The enormity and magnitude of Town's problems slowly became apparent over the summer months. A total of twenty million pounds was owed to our creditors as the club was declared 'clearly insolvent' in the High Court. Huddersfield Town needed administration, after the valiant efforts to keep them alive last season, to move forward. We had gone from being a 'top 30' English football club to bottom 30 in just three years. The Club had no accounting information, no shop or stock or kit contract, barely a lottery and just 110 of the clubs corporate database still spending with it.

Huddersfield Town was unable to put season tickets on sale because of administration. Our Academy had previously been under the threat of closure and had been given a rough ride in recent years with a distinct lack of investment.

In August 2003 Ken Davy having rescued our club from extinction, just eight days prior to our first match of the season, confirmed the appointment of Peter Jackson and Terry Yorath as Town's management set up. The first problems that Jackson and Yorath encountered was a distinct lack of players on Town's books with just eight professional players reporting back for pre-season training.

So, Jacko built a Town team from football's free transfers and youngsters from our Academy. Given the positive news that was coming out of the McAlpine Stadium In the first two weeks of August alone Town actually sold 6,700 season tickets and the Blue and White Foundation went from nothing four months previous to 1,200 members. On the financial front Town reduced the £1.4 million pound debt owed to our players from last season to just £600,000 by the end of the 2003-2004 season. Town's new Board consisted of Roger Armitage, Martin Byrne, Ralph Rimmer and Chief Executive Andrew Watson, a former player who had first joined Town in our 1983-84 season.

Town fans sadly found out that during the close season one of our most loyal and best known supporter's Henry Ward known simply as 'H' had passed away. Having spent almost all of his 47 years watching Town his devotion to our cause was unflinching, through thick and mostly thin, like the rest of us fans he had suffered many more lows than highs. His first ever football match, I believe, was our very first match under floodlights at our old home at Leeds Road in the FA Cup in 1961 against Wolves. By the mid-80's he commenced an amazing sequence of ten complete seasons without missing a match home or away. He was well-known, the length and breadth of the country, by Town fans from all areas. He was a committee member of our Supporters Club and organised coach travel to away matches from the old Town shop on Leeds Road which as author of this book is where I got to know him from as I also helped assist with coach travel during the late 80s. Not only that, but he was also a member of our Patrons Association from its launch date in 1986. The best way I could describe 'H' for me as a Town fan is to say he was always there with his brother John wherever Town played, home or away.

Our new football season could not have had a better start given that we had played nine pre-season friendlies, won six and drawn the other three games. Our captain for the season was none other than Rob Edwards our former player who had signed for Town from Chesterfield. He was joined by an array of newly signed players; Ian Grey, Martin Booty, Jon Newby, Ian Hughes, Tony Carss, Steve Yates, Efe Sodje, Lee Fowler and Tyrone Thompson. Joining them from our Academy at the start of the season was Adnan Ahmed, Andy Holdsworth and Anthony Lloyd.

10,319 fans gave Peter Jackson and Terry Yorath a fantastic welcome back to our Alfred McAlpine Stadium as chants of 'Jacko's coming home' could be heard before kick-off as Town took on Cambridge United in our first league match of the 2003-04 season. But for Cambridge United scoring with only a minute to go Town would have gone on to record a 2-1 win as it were, they had to settle for a 2-2 draw. Town was then faced with Derby County three days later in the first round of the Carling Cup. Thanks to goals from Jon Stead and John Thorrington 6,672 fans saw them win 2-1 and was through to the next round. By the end of August Town had recorded their first league win of the new season, a 2-1 home win over Bristol Rovers thanks to goals from both Rob Edwards and Jon Stead. Having scored his fourth goal in his first six games of the season Jon's goalscoring exploits had now started to attract scouts from other clubs.

The Blue and White Foundation was officially launched on Wednesday 3rd September 2003 to help our Town Academy financially. Since administration our costs for the Academy had increased to almost £500,000 a year. After grants from our Patrons and Yorkshire Building Society supporter accounts had been received the cost still stood at £300,000.

In Gerry Murphy's time in charge of our Academy up to 2003, 31 lads had made the first team with ten being sold on for £4 million pounds as ten lads currently on Town's books this season had made the first team.

Down at the Vetch Field both Ian Hughes and Paul Scott was sent off as Town lost 2-0 to Swansea City. This was then followed up three days later with a resounding 4-2 Carling Cup second round victory over Sunderland as Andy Holdsworth scored his first senior goal for Town in front of a 13,516 away crowd. Town were the only Division Three side left in the Carling Cup this season and was drawn away against Reading. By the end of September Jon Stead had been named as the Nationwide Division Player of the Month.

Having beaten Southend United 2-1 away Town was up to ninth in the league on 19 points whilst Hull City lead the division with 27 points. Then having beaten Torquay United 1-0 at home in the league Town was then faced with playing Lincoln City away. 1,704 Town fans made the short journey down to Lincoln only to see Town beaten 3-1. Thanks to a minority of fans that were arrested in the stands, for football related violence, football played second fiddle to the hooliganism that took place that day. My memory of this game was seeing young Town fans in tears shortly after the second half had started. Thankfully the stance on the matter from our club was to issue a life-ban for any convicted Town fan. By the end of the month Town had lost 1-0 to Reading and was knocked out of the Carling Cup for another season. A heavy 6-2 league defeat away at the hands of Scunthorpe United brought Town's Halloween season in with a frightening start. This was then followed up by a 2-0 defeat away at the hands of Carlisle United in the LDV Vans Trophy. Worse followed in the very next game when Town not only lost 1-0 away to Accrington Stanley in the FA Cup first round with their goal coming in injury time, but we also had Jon Worthington sent off. He was the seventh player this season to have received their marching orders.

Off the field of play Stadium Chief Executive Kevin Collinge sadly passed away while on holiday on Tuesday 11th November 2003. By the middle of November without a win in four games they took on Divisional Leaders Hull City. In front of a McAlpine Stadium crowd of 13,893 Town won 3-1. This was then followed by a 3-3 draw away against Mansfield as Town sat tenth in the league on 29 points while Oxford United now topped the division with 38 points.

Town started the New Year with a right bang winning all four league games in the month of January as speculation was now building over the assumed sale of Jon Stead. With Town going on record as stating that they were looking at a financial loss given that we had started the new season with a massive deficit. Town's only valuable source of income sadly, was the sale of players. So, by the time Town took to the field against Darlington, on Saturday 7th February 2004, Jon Stead had been sold to Premier League side Blackburn Rovers and Peter Jackson had just picked up his first ever Manager of the Month Award.

Striker Pawel Abbott was loaned from Preston North End to replace Jon Stead and marked his debut down at Bristol Rovers with a goal that earned Town a 1-1 draw. By the end of February, they faced Lincoln City at the McAlpine Stadium and keen to avenge our away defeat back in October Town and Pav ensured the game was best remembered for the football this time. Having gone behind to Lincoln City by half-time, Town within two minutes of the restart equalised thanks to a header from Efe Sodje. Then on 66 minutes Pawel collected the ball on the edge of the Lincoln penalty area and finished coolly after he had rounded their keeper. Huge controversy arose over whether Abbott was in an offside position when he collected the ball after a Lincoln defender flicked on Sodje's powerful header. Most of the Lincoln team had stopped play, but the ref ruled over his Assistant's off-side flag and gave the goal. With just five minutes of normal time left to play Phil Senior pulled off a brilliant one-handed save to deny Lincoln an equaliser and earned Town three valuable points in a 2-1 win. Our Alfred McAlpine Stadium up to this point had never seen a more controversial goal in its short football history.

As Town entered an important stage of the season, they signed Paul Rachubka a goalkeeper from Charlton Athletic on loan, just as John Thorrington signed for Grimsby Jacko also tried to sign Pawel Abbott on a permanent contract basis. By the middle of March, it was announced that Town had signed Abbott as Jon McAliskey made his first senior team appearance against Macclesfield and promptly scored in the 77th minute to help Town to a 4-0 home win. 19-year-old Gary Harkins signed on loan from Blackburn Rovers until the end of the season while Iffy Onoura signed on for the final nine games of the season. Town had two reasons to celebrate at the end of March given that Peter Jackson had received his second Manager of the Month Award and Efe Sodje won the Player of the Month Award.

By the beginning of April Town stood third in the league on 70 points just six points off an automatic promotion place while Doncaster Rovers topped the league with 79 points. Town slipped up on Easter Monday down at Kidderminster Harriers as they went down 2-1. Thankfully they recovered for their next league game as 12,108 fans watched Town beat Scunthorpe United 3-2 at our McAlpine Stadium. Having lost 3-1 to Mansfield Town at our McAlpine Stadium it was left to our final match of the season away against Cheltenham to ensure own automatic promotion place was assured.

Within the first twenty minutes of the match at Whaddon Road Town was 1-0 up thanks to a Boothy trademark goal, his 100th Town goal. Then with just 15 minutes left of the game Pawel Abbott, who to this day I cannot understand or reason why as author of this book, having received the ball just inside his own half ran backwards towards our goal and horrendously under hit a back pass that allowed the 'Robins' to equalise. This, together with Torquay's win at Southend United, condemned Town to a play-off spot, by virtue of our inferior goal difference.

Town came through the play-off semi-final games against Lincoln City 4-3 on aggregate and was faced with Mansfield Town for the play-off final down at Cardiff's Millennium Stadium. Just before the end of normal time with the scores still 0-0 the Stags actually scored, but the linesman controversially ruled that the cross had gone out over the by-line just before the ball hit the back of the net. After a goalless period of extra-time a penalty shoot-out then followed and thanks to Rob Edwards, Danny Schofield, Tony Carrs and Lee Fowler, who all scored from the spot, Town won 4–1.

Having won promotion at the first attempt Jacko and Yorath saw Town home and out of Division Three at the first attempt, securing our place in the newly named Football League One. By the end of the season there was an Antoni Memorial Trophy Draw. The trophy had been kindly donated by the Kaminski family in memory of Antoni who was a Huddersfield University studying sport-psychology when sadly his life came to an end at the young age of 22. The trophy was to be awarded each year for outstanding achievement of a Youth Academy Player. John McAliskey was awarded it for this season and next season saw Tom Clark earn the prestigious honour.

At the end of the season 2003-2004 with a final league placing of 4th **(promoted)** it was one of;

Played 46 games; won 23, lost 11, drew 12, goals for 68, goals against 52, Points 81

Promotion for Town was celebrated with an open-top parade and a civic reception at Huddersfield Town Hall which was enjoyed by almost 4,000 watching Town fans.

Saturday 31st July 2004 at precisely 8pm a new era in Huddersfield's magnificent stadium and conference centre formerly known as the McAlpine Stadium was born. A pop concert and party celebrated the first ten successful years as a regional, national and international sporting venue, while simultaneously embracing the new dawn. In true celebratory style the new name was announced by Girls Aloud and Darius as 'The Galpharm Stadium'. When the announcement was made 2000 Galpharm Stadium balloons was released as party-goers was showered by a series of mighty confetti cannons to mark the special occasion.

As well as a new stadium name, Town kicked off our 2004-2005 season in a new division at the same time as Coca-Cola announced their sponsorship of the Football League this meant Town was now playing in Coca-Cola League One. Pre-season wins over Rotherham United, and Macclesfield set Town up for the season ahead as Jacko brought in two new faces Chris Brandon and Junior Mendes.

Christopher William Brandon – 'Chris' was a midfielder Peter Jackson signed from Chesterfield in the summer of 2004. He made 95 league appearances during which time he scored ten goals. After a loan spell in 2007 at Blackpool he signed for Bradford City in 2008.

Albert Junior Hillyard Andrew Mendes – Junior was a striker that was signed by Jacko after he had played against Town on a number of occasions last season for Mansfield. He played for Town until 2006 when after loan spells with Northampton Town and then at Grimsby Town Junior signed permanently for Notts County.

The first league match of the new season saw Town make a perfect start. A 3-2 win at Edgeley Park against Stockport County was a real see-saw game. With Town trailing 2-1 Peter Jackson made two inspired substitutions when he sent on Brandon and Abbott fifteen minutes before the end. Chris Brandon set up Andy Booth for our equaliser with a trademark header before Boothy himself turned provider for Pawel Abbott to seal the three points in the final minute of injury time.
This was followed up with a 0-0 draw against Chesterfield at our newly named The Galpharm Stadium as 11,942 fans watched on as Town recorded the highest league attendance for Saturday 10th August. The following Monday on 16th August 2004 Town not only faced Hartlepool United at home but also had the added prospect of having the game televised live on Sky. In front of the cameras Town lost the game 2-0. Next up was two Yorkshire derbies first Sheffield Wednesday away at Hillsborough and in front of a crowd of 26,264 Town lost 1-0. Then faced with Leeds United away in the first round of the Carling Cup Town went down 1-0 to our local Yorkshire rivals.
After a 2-1 August Bank Holiday away defeat at the hands of Doncaster Rovers Town ended the month well below half-way in the league while Luton Town topped the division due to their unbeaten start to the season. A 4-0 home win over Hull City on 5th September, watched by a crowd of 13,542, was the perfect start to the month. This was then followed up by a 3-0 away win over Port Vale the week after as Town destroyed their impressive home record. Port Vale's 33-game scoring run came to an end as Ian Gray kept a second consecutive clean sheet while Pawel Abbott hit a thirteen minute hat-trick and became the second fastest after Brian Stanton's Club record of six minutes in 1983. Coincidentally, when Akpo Sodje joined his brother Efe Sodje for the final five minutes of the Port Vale game, it was only the second time since 1946 Town had brothers on the field of play when Albert and Willie Watson plied their trade in the top-flight. The only other siblings since then had been the Collins brothers, Sam and Simon, in 1996. Having lost 2-0 at home against Barnsley and drawn 3-3 away down at Bristol City Town finished the month of September by beating Morecambe 3-0 at home in the LDV Vans Trophy first round.

Our newly named Galpharm Stadium received recognition in October after hosting an England v Holland U20 international football match which attracted a crowd of over 5,000. For Town the month started with a 3-1 home win over Walsall. A 2-1 away defeat down at Torquay followed next and was then followed up with a 2-1 away win against league leaders Luton. By the end of the month, they had drawn 1-1 away at Blackpool in the league. Town had to play Blackpool away again just three days later, but this time it was in the second round of the LDV Vans Trophy. Having had our captain, Efe Sodje, sent off during the game Town was faced with playing with ten men just three minutes into the second half. With the scores at 2-2 on ninety minutes Town finally lost 6-3 after extra time. Peter Jackson stripped Efe of the captaincy after the Blackpool game and handed the armband over to Jon Worthington.

November began with Town drawing 1-1 with Brentford at the Galpharm Stadium. This was followed up by a FA Cup first round 3-1 defeat away at the hands of Stockport County who were bottom of Coca-Cola League One. Town rounded the month off by drawing 0-0 away at Colchester United and losing 2-1 at home to Wrexham. Paul Rachubka after having a loan spell with Town last season, due to a serious hand injury to Ian Gray, came back on loan in November and signed permanently just before Christmas as Ian Gray retired from professional football altogether.

The start of 2005 brought with it some good news for Town supporter Kieron Tordorff. Having previously won and shared Town's half-time lottery draw with another supporter, Kieron and his wife Adele used their winning share towards IVF treatment and were now the proud parents of Aimee and Charley. On the field of play Town started the New Year with a 2-1 away defeat at the hands of Hull City. The next two home games saw them draw 2-2 with Bristol City and 1-1 with Torquay United. Luke Beckett having signed on loan from Sheffield United made his first Town appearance in the 4-2 defeat against Barnsley at Oakwell.

Luke John Beckett – was a striker that was initially signed on loan who played seven league games and scored six goals before he went back to his parent club. Peter Jackson then signed him on a three year deal, for £85,000, in July 2006 and by November 2008 he had signed for Gainsborough Trinity.

After 30 league games Town began the month of February in Coca-Cola League One in 14th place on 38 points while Luton Town, our next opponents, sat at the top of the division on 59 points. Thanks to a Luke Beckett 90th minute goal they managed to secure a 1-1 draw in front of a 12,611 Galpharm Stadium crowd against the league leaders. News broke in this month that the 'Rocket man' was to appear at our Galpharm Stadium on June 3rd. This of course was Elton John not 'Rocket Ron' our ex-player. His concert was aptly named the 'Field of Dreams' Concert.
Faced with having to beat Colchester United at home in April in order to keep our season alive Town drew the match 2-2. This effectively put paid to any outside chance they may have had for the play-offs this season. With Town needing to win our last nine matches they won eight and having drawn against Colchester United missed out on the play-offs by just one point. With Rob Edwards coming on as a second-half sub to score the fourth goal against Swindon Town he signed off his football career by scoring the 3,000th league goal for Town on home soil.

At the end of the season 2004-2005 with a final league placing of 9th it was one of;

Played 46 games; won 20, lost 16, drew 10, goals for 74, goals against 65, Points 70

Town jetted off on a pre-season tour of Ibiza in July and was well-supported by our travelling fans. During the close season Peter Jackson brought in three new players to bolster our squad for the start of the 2005-2006 season Mark Hudson from Chesterfield, Martin McIntosh from Rotherham and Gary Taylor-Fletcher from Lincoln.

Mark Hudson – was a midfielder signed from Chesterfield. He made his first team debut in the 2-1 away defeat to Nottingham Forest and scored the first goal of his Town career on 10th October 2005 against Bradford City in a 2-1 away win. Having made 55 league appearances he then signed for Rotherham United in 2007.

Martin Wyllie McIntosh – was a defender signed from Rotherham United, who after sustaining a knee injury in August was out of action for four months. He went on to make 44 league appearances before he signed for Mansfield Town in 2007.

Gary Taylor-Fletcher – was a forward signed from Lincoln City. Having to compete against the likes of Abbott and Booth he often had to settle for a place on the subs bench. By early 2006 Gary was used mainly as a right-winger where he scored many vital goals. On 8th August 2006 Taylor-Fletcher scored the 500,000th goal in the Football League with a 25-yard drive into the top-left corner of Rotherham United's goal. By July 2007 he had signed permanently for Blackpool.

For the start of this season Town re-adopted the Huddersfield coat of arms adage, Juvat Impigros Deus, as the motto for our club. The motto 'God Helps The Diligent or 'God Helps He Who Helps Himself' was first adopted by Town for the 1920 FA Cup Final, when Arthur Fairclough was Manager, and lasted until it was replaced by the current crest in 1970. 24,042 fans saw Town lose their first game of the new season at Nottingham Forest. The following match against Bristol City at our Galpharm Stadium saw two legends, Boothy and Stewart, line up against each other. Thanks to an 89th minute winner from Pawel Abbott Town won the game 1-0.

By the end of August, former England international and Town legend, Harold Hassall pointed out that the plaque which had been fitted at our former home at Leeds Road had the pitch showing the wrong way round. On closer inspection he was right, the engraved plaque did indeed need turning 90 degrees to be more authentic, as the pitch faced East to West rather than North to South.

After back-to-back wins over the Bank Holiday Town were top of Coca-Cola League One after just six games. The game against Hartlepool United put Pawel Abbott into our Huddersfield Town history books as he became the first Town player ever to score a goal in the opening six games of a season.
Off the field of play Peter Jackson won the Manager of the Month award for August as Town finished off a perfect month by seeing off Chesterfield 4-2 in the first round of the Carling Cup. For Tom Clarke this was his first game of the season after having broken through into the first eleven last season.

Thomas Clarke – Tom was a player who had progressed through the junior ranks along with his brother Nathan. He was considered to be one of the best kept secrets in the lower leagues of English football. Just three months after his seventeenth birthday he broke through into the first team and became a first team regular in defence. Tom also made a big impression at international level and earned his second call-up to the England squad. He made the step-up to the Three Lions U19 squad two years above his age and went on to start the game against Belgium and duly scored his first goal for his country in a 3-2 win. He suffered with injuries during his time with Town and after an eight-year career signed for Preston North End in May 2013.

Town travelled to Premiership side Blackburn Rovers for their second round Carling Cup tie and was buoyed by 4,986 travelling fans. It was our biggest following since last season's Carling Cup clash at Leeds United and the biggest following to travel outside of Yorkshire since the Play-Off Final at Cardiff. Sadly they lost 3-1 and was knocked out of the cup. By the end of September Town were third in Coca-Cola League One just behind Southend United and Swansea City on goal difference. With them drawing 2-2 at home against Bournemouth at the beginning of October Town set a new Club record for scoring in successive games. It was the 22nd game in which they had scored, beating a 73-year record set in 1932. Sadly, it came to an end in their 30th game at home against Bradford City when Town drew 0-0. Boston United away was their first round LDV Vans Trophy destination in October. Even with David Mirfin scoring for Town they still lost 2-1 and was knocked out of the competition altogether. By the end of the year, having beaten Welling United 4-1 at home in the first round of the FA Cup, and having beaten Worchester City 1-0 in the following round Town was up against Premier League Champions Chelsea away in the third round of the FA Cup.

6,100 tickets was sold out in just seven hours as fans, had queued from 4.30 in the morning, were desperate to get hold of a cup ticket. Town faced Chelsea in our all-new white away football shirt. Having taken to the field against Chelsea at Stamford Bridge, who were regarded as the best in the world, Town held them for seven amazing second-half minutes. Gary Taylor-Fletcher in the 75th minute hit a first-time effort, from sub-Collins right wing cross, it gave Cudicini no chance in the Chelsea goal as Gary scored Town's equaliser. From then on they were equal to Chelsea for every ball and every tackle made on that pitch. Finally, Robben chased down the left wing and centred for Gudjohnsen to hit an unstoppable right-hand shot past Phil Senior, with just eight minutes left remaining on the clock, to make the final score 2-1 to Chelsea.

By the end of January Town had taken David Graham on loan from Sheffield Wednesday. He scored three goals in his first four games and went on to win the 'Player of the Month' award for February. After a total of fourteen appearances, during which time he scored a total of eight goals, he returned to his parent club.

Town once again was chosen to host an international football match at our Galpharm Stadium, an England v Italy U17 on Tuesday 28th March was the curtain raiser, for a series of crucial qualifying group matches for England. It gave Huddersfield Town the opportunity to showcase our stadium on the world stage.

Andy Booth cemented his legendary status having scored his fourth hat-trick of his Town career against Rotherham United in a 4-1 home win. He became the first player to achieve that feat in over half a century. The last player to score four or more was the great Jimmy Glazzard in 1954. (Jimmy topped it in 1955 when he scored his fifth Town hat-trick). At the end of the season having dropped down the league Town ended up in the play-offs. Faced with Barnsley away they took a 1-0 lead into the home leg. Unfortunately they suffered a 3-1 home defeat and was knocked out of the play-offs 3-2 on aggregate. Meanwhile, James Hand won the Antoni's Memorial Trophy taking the trophy from last year's winner Tom Clarke.

At the end of the season 2005-2006 with a final league placing of 4th (play-offs) it was one of;

Played 46 games; won 19, lost 11, drew 16, goals for 72, goals against 59, Points 73

Peter Jackson having signed a two-year extension to his own contract on 18th May 2006 then made his first summer signing by snapping up 27-year-old goalkeeper Matt Glennon from St Johnstone on a free transfer. Then on 27th June 2006, just two days later, Junior Mendes moved to Notts County, while Phil Senior went to Northwich Victoria the following day, both without a transfer fee. On 3rd July 2006 Town signed 29-year-old Sheffield United striker Luke Beckett for £85,000 on a three-year deal (after his loan last season). Whilst some of our youngsters also figured more in this season, namely, Adnan Ahmed (who had figured partly last season in midfield), Michael Collins, Joe Skarz, Aaron Hardy, Matthew Young, Danny Racchi, James Berrett, Simon Eastwood, James Hand, Lucas Akins and John McCombe.

Pre-season tests for Town was a show-piece testimonial for Andy Booth against Real Sociedad which ended in a 0-0 draw. Abroad, Town lost 2-1 against Spanish side the Ibiza XI in the first game of the Copa Ibiza. They then bounced back against League Two's Swindon Town beating them 1-0 to finish second in the competition in July. This was then followed up with a 3-0 win over AFC Emley, a 1-1 draw with Harrogate Town, a 1-0 win over Ossett Albion and a 0-0 draw with Chester City.

Matthew William Glennon – 'Matt' having signed in June 2006 quickly became our first-choice goalkeeper and achieved a rare goalkeeping feat when he saved three penalty kicks. Two penalties was awarded, but one had to be retaken, against Crewe Alexandra on 24 February 2007 (Coincidentally, Town lost the game 2–1).

Having been sent off in a 4–1 defeat against Southend United at Roots Hall on 5th December 2007 17-year-old Alex Smithies was then forced to come on to take over in goal. Matt had his contract at Town terminated in 2010 and soon after joined Bradford City. By January 2012 he had left professional football altogether.

Town having kicked off the new season down at Gillingham in front of a 6,075 crowd went 2-0 down before Gary Taylor-Fletcher pulled a goal back to make the final score 2-1. Two successive home games followed the Gillingham defeat the first against Rotherham United saw Town win 3-0 in front of a 10,161 crowd. The game was marked by a special occasion as Gareth Taylor-Fletcher scored the 500,000 goal in English football in what was already considered by many Town fans to be 'the goal of the season'. It was also a match in which Town took to the field wearing black armbands to mark the passing of former Chairman Keith Longbottom who was a member of Town's Board for almost twenty years and was Chairman during Mick Buxton's era.

Keith was a lifelong Town fan, born and bred in Netherton, and joined the Town Board in 1974. He took over in May 1975 when Town was at one of their lowest-ever ebbs having been relegated to the Football League's basement division for the first time. Keith's master-stroke was appointing Mick Buxton and providing the funds for Mick to sign Steve Kindon and later broke the Club's transfer record to show his determination to return to the higher echelons of the Football League. In June 1987 he stood down as Chairman but remained on the Board headed by Roger Fielding. Keith returned for a second spell as Chairman but by then Huddersfield Town was hurtling towards relegation. After 16 years as Chairman Keith Longbottom sadly passed away after a battle with cancer in 2006 aged 72.

The second home match in four days saw Town beat Bristol City 2-1 in front of a 10,402 crowd. The game also saw Peter Jackson sent to the stands after grabbing Bristol City's Lee Johnson around the throat in a touchline altercation 10 minutes from time. On 30th August 2006 the FA charged Jackson with improper conduct over the incident, and he was fined £300. Tuesday 22nd August saw Town take on Mansfield in the Carling Cup first round. In front of a Galpharm crowd of 5,111 'The Stags' won 2-0 and knocked Town out of the cup. By the end of August Huddersfield Town had appointed, former Oldham Athletic Director of Marketing, Sean Jarvis as Director of Business Development for the Sporting Pride Group and Chief Executive Andrew Watson had been appointed as Vice-Chairman.

Eight games into the new season, by the middle of September, Town Chairman Ken Davy addressed concerns amongst many Huddersfield Town fans in regard to the playing budget for this season. Unfortunately it did nothing to stop the protest by some fans outside the stadium after the 3-2 home defeat to Yeovil. Amongst many things addressed the financial side to Town was simply put that in 2003-04 season they made a loss of £139,125 (audited). In 2004-05 season they made a loss of £392,191 (audited). In 2005-06 they made a profit of £36,283 (Management Accounts). For this season alone it was projected that a loss of £454,275 would be made given that a 12,500 average attendance had to be achieved in order to make that loss, as it were the average attendance was well under that loss making figure.

By the end of September Town supporters who had travelled down on the Supporter's Club coach to Swansea wondered if Alfred Hitchcock's film 'The Birds' had been reprised given that a feathered friend had attacked the coach without a single swan in sight. A pheasant had smashed the windscreen which put the coach out of action meant that the supporters had to wait at Stafford for a replacement coach to take them the rest of the way. It must have been a lucky omen as Town returned with all three points from the Liberty Stadium.

Having faced Doncaster Rovers in the Johnstone's Paint Trophy first round in the middle of October a Galpharm crowd of just 3,629 saw Town lose 2-1. Blackpool were the guests at the Galpharm Stadium in November as Town faced them in the FA Cup first round. A 1-0 defeat saw Town dumped out of the cup in front of a home crowd of just 6,597. A week later and Blackpool were once again the visitors to the Galpharm Stadium, this time Town was defeated 3-1 in the league. By the end of the month after a 3-0 home defeat, at the hands of Oldham Athletic, Town fans demonstrated outside the front of the main reception area of the Galpharm Stadium to voice their concerns.

Having left the field with a 1-1 draw against Northampton Town in December, in the days thereafter, newspaper reports stated that the Huddersfield Town Board of Directors had called an extraordinary meeting to discuss Peter Jackson's future. It was not true and totally not what the meeting was about. By the end of December Terry Yorath had left the Club by mutual consent and had been replaced by John Dungworth as First Team Coach, while Graham Mitchell was appointed U18 Coach.

Off the field of play Jean Leeming who worked hard behind the scenes at our Stadium washing all the Town kits as well as a host of other duties celebrated her 70th birthday by having the opportunity of walking out onto the Galpharm pitch at half-time against Swansea City. It must have been a lucky omen as Town ran out 3-2 winners over 'The Swans'. By the beginning of 2007 Jackson tried to bring new players in, after Town had conceded six goals over the Christmas period, while both Pawel Abbott and Danny Adams left our club.

Pawel Tadeusz Howard Abbott – 'Pav' was a striker initially signed on loan from Preston North End. He scored on his debut after coming off the bench against Bristol Rovers and went on to score four goals in six games while on loan. Having signed in early 2004 he became the first striker in six years to hit more than 20 goals as he struck 27 times in all competitions the following season. In 2006 after choosing to try to fight for a first team place, after rejecting a move away, Pawel's role became a bit-part player from the bench following a loss of goalscoring form. On 30 December 2006 he scored two goals, including a last-minute winner, against the club he ironically joined just a few days later, Swansea City. After making 126 appearances for Town, during which time he scored 51 goals, in his final game Pav was sent off against Doncaster Rovers on 1st January 2007.

Daniel Benjamin Adams – was a defender signed from Stockport County in 2005. Affectionately nicknamed 'Uncle Fester' by fans he went on to make 77 appearances in our Town colours before his contract was cancelled by mutual agreement in 2007.

On 5th January 2007 Town took on Yeovil away in front of the Sky cameras and within three minutes of the game was 1-0 down. After thirty-five minutes Town were 3-0 down and didn't muster a single shot on their goal until the final minute of the first half. Four minutes into the second half Gary Taylor-Fletcher managed to pull a goal back to make the final score 3-1.

Left-back Andy Taylor was signed by Peter Jackson on loan from Blackburn Rovers just before the transfer deadline closed and made seven league appearances before he returned to his parent club. Several other transfer targets failed to come fruition so to help bolster the team loan signings became very much sought after. Frank Sinclair having signed for the rest of the season was the next loan player that arrived at the Galpharm Stadium from Burnley. Both Taylor and Sinclair made their first team debut down at Bristol City and helped Town to earn a 1-1 draw.

The Football League introduced a 'smoke-free' policy that was to take effect at the start of following season. The new policy anticipated and exceeded expected government legislation for this area. Consequently, smoking was not permitted throughout the Stadium confines from July 2007 onwards.

On 3rd March after a heavy 5-1 battering down at Nottingham Forest our Town Board, in the days thereafter, announced that Peter Jackson had left the Club as Manager with Gerry Murphy having stepped up in the interim to cover as Caretaker Manager. The remit for Jackson at the start of the season was to achieve a play-off position. Unfortunately due to our early season form and the inability to attract key players in the January transfer window it meant that his objective looked remote. Gerry Murphy's first task as Caretaker Manager was to oversee Town beat our local neighbours Bradford City 2-0 and then agreed to release Chris Brandon to start a loan spell at Blackpool.

Sadly lifelong Town fan, Tony Lum aged 72 died suddenly at his home on Sunday 11th March. He was a lifelong supporter and member of the Huddersfield Town Gentleman's Sporting Club. Tony had watched Town ever since he was a five-year-old lad having sat on the bank above our old Leeds Road ground. He graduated to our old East Terrace where he stood for over 50 years before he moved across to our new stadium in 1994.

On 4th April 2007 a press conference was called at our Galpharm Stadium where it was announced that Phil Parkinson was the new Manager of Huddersfield Town. At the eleventh hour they were gazumped by Charlton, where Phil was the Assistant Manager, which left our club still looking to fill the role. By the middle of April Andy Ritchie was unveiled as our new Manager, his remit for next season was simply promotion.
Andy's first game in charge saw Town beaten 2-0 away at Scunthorpe United. The final three games of the season saw them beat Millwall 4-2 at home, draw 1-1 away at Northampton and beat Leyton Orient 3-1 at our Galpharm Stadium. Meanwhile, Mitre was announced as our new kit suppliers, for the up-and-coming season, having taken over from Admiral.

At the end of the season 2006-2007 with a final league placing of 15th it was one of;

Played 46 games; won 14, lost 15, drew 17, goals for 60, goals against 69, Points 59

During the close season of 2007-08 Andy Ritchie as Manager, having secured the signature of Frank Sinclair on a one-year deal at the end of last season, then signed Danny Cadamarteri and Malvin Kamara. While the following players were allowed to leave Adnan Ahmed (Tranmere Rovers), Paul Rachubka (Blackpool), John McAliskey and Martin McIntosh (both Mansfield Town), Mark Hudson (Rotherham United), James Hand (Shamrock Rovers) John McCombe (Hereford), Gary Taylor-Fletcher (Blackpool) Adam Wilson (Bradford Park Avenue).

Town would have signed Barnsley's Robbie Williams in July had he not had a training ground accident when he sustained a hairline fracture to his shin, as it was his transfer took place a month later, and he made his first team debut away against Leeds United in December. To boost our first team squad Andy Ritchie promoted the following players from our reserves Lucas Akins, James Berrett, Mitchell Bailey, Luke Malcher, Daniel Broadbent and keeper Simon Eastwood (who made several appearances on the bench last season). Whilst Shane Killock earned his first professional contract with Town.

Pre-season friendlies saw Town beaten by Rochdale, then after taking on Premiership side Blackburn Rovers beat them 2-1, before hammering Mansfield Town 4-0.

Daniel Leon Cadamarteri – 'Danny' signed as a forward on a free transfer in June 2007 from Leicester City and suffered with injuries for most of his time at Town. Having left in May 2009 he signed for Dundee United then returned to our Club at the end of January 2011. He made his second Town debut in the 4-1 win against Exeter City at St James Park and scored two minutes after coming on as a substitute. By June 2012 he had left our club for a second time having signed for Carlisle United.

Malvin Ginah Kamara – was a midfielder signed from Port Vale on a free transfer. In his first season he was an ever-present player who scored five goals including two against Accrington Stanley in the FA Cup first round. By the following September Malvin had joined Grimsby on loan and was released by our club in May 2009.

The first game of the new season saw Town beat Yeovil 1-0 thanks to a 15th minute Luke Beckett goal. Away at Bloomfield Road just days later Town lost 1-0 against Blackpool in the Carling Cup first round and was knocked out of the competition. By the time Town had travelled down to the South Coast to take on AFC Bournemouth Andy Ritchie found that his first team squad had been further depleted by a training ground injury to David Mirfin, along with injuries to both Frank Sinclair and Danny Cadamarteri, it meant a first team debut for Aaron Hardy. Ex-Manchester United winger Jamie Mullen having had a trial at Town wasn't given a contract by Ritchie.

Having lost 2-0 to Carlisle United at the Galpharm Stadium Town then travelled down to South East London and beat Millwall 2-1. Three days later at Blundell Park they were beaten 4-1 by Grimsby in the Johnstone's Paint Trophy and was knocked out of the competition at the first time of asking. Town then lost the next three league games on the trot before they beat Luton 2-0 at the Galpharm stadium at the end of September. Ronnie Wallwork was the next player to walk through our Galpharm doors after Richard Keogh had signed on loan mid-September. Ronnie having signed initially on loan for a month from West Bromwich Albion played 18 games during which he scored three goals before he went back to his parent club.

At the start of October an approach to buy Huddersfield Town came out of the blue and the Chairman's view remained that they were not interested in selling. The unsolicited approach from former Hull City Chairman Adam Pearson, at the same time he was linked with approaches to Derby County and Sheffield Wednesday, ultimately came to nothing at Huddersfield Town. Having beaten Accrington Stanley 3-2 at their place in the FA Cup first round Town were then faced with Grimsby at home in the next round. Thanks to two goals from new signing Phil Jevons and one from Luke Beckett they won 3-0 and progressed through to the third round of the FA Cup.

Phil Jevons – was a striker Ritchie signed from Bristol City for an undisclosed fee, after his initial loan, in January 2008. By 2010 he had signed for League Two side Morecambe.

Beaten 4-1 down at Southend United Town not only suffered a heavy defeat but also had Matt Glennon sent off and Frank Sinclair dismissed in added time. Both of whom were sorely missed over the festive football period as Ken Davy, Town's Chairman, presented his report on the fourth trading year of the company. Income during the year was £3.97 million with the result that the loss for the year was £1,055,094. Given that Town had not progressed in any Cup competition this season nor had they achieved the minimum target of the play-offs it resulted in a loss of extra revenue and commercial opportunities that the matches brought. On a positive note debts owed to former players was cleared during the season, some three years ahead of schedule.

For the first time ever Huddersfield Town set up a satellite beam, back at our stadium, for the Leeds United match given that only 1,710 tickets had been issued from Leeds for Town's away allocation. 2,200 fans braved the inclement weather to see them heavily beaten 4-0 on a big screen at our Galpharm Stadium.

Town started their Centenary year with a defeat at Forest this was then followed up with a FA Cup third round 2-1 home win against Premiership side Birmingham City on 5th January 2008. Thanks to goals from Chris Brandon and Luke Beckett, in front of a 13,410 Galpharm crowd, Town progressed through to the next round.

As part of the Centenary celebrations a summer clash with Arsenal was arranged and publicised given the special affinity both clubs had shared with Herbert Chapman. A rare and unique chance to celebrate and commemorate Huddersfield Town's Centenary saw fans given the chance to buy a brick and have it displayed with any message on the walkway between the Riverside Stand and the Panasonic Stand. Faced with Oldham Athletic away in the FA Cup fourth round Luke Beckett scored in the tenth minute which earned Town a 1-0 win. Robert Page having signed from Coventry City made his first team debut against Oldham wearing our squad number 29 shirt. Town having won the next three league games then travelled up to Brunton Park. In front of a 6,196 away crowd Robert Page scored his first league goal in our colours as Town lost 2-1 against Carlisle United.

Robert John Page – 'Rob' was a defender that was signed from Coventry City. After 19 appearances, during which time he was made Town captain and had been sent off for a second bookable offence against Swansea City, our Club failed to secure his services on a new playing contract which saw him sign for Chesterfield by the end of the season.

John Robinson the Safety Officer for football at our Galpharm Stadium had reason to ask a small minority of Town fans to adjust their match day behaviour. Given that both KDSL and Huddersfield Town worked closely with all supporters to try to create a more attractive place for younger fans and families to enjoy. Town's Director of Business Development Sean Jarvis meanwhile thanked our fans for their patience while the Club issued tickets for the fifth round FA Cup match against Chelsea. Sean was also tasked with improving the match day atmosphere while maintaining the safety within our Stadium.

41,324 home and away fans filled Stamford Bridge on Saturday 16th February 2008 as Town took on Chelsea in the FA Cup fifth round. Only seven minutes were on the clock when Robbie Williams came to the rescue when he got back to clear a goal bound shot off the line. After twenty minutes they were 1-0 down due to a terrific shot hit by, England international, Frank Lampard. Town reacted with a shot from Nathan Clark that had to be cleared off Chelsea's goal-line by, England international, John Terry. Amazingly Town managed to get back to 1-1 in first-half stoppage time when James Berrett's delicate chip allowed Michael Collins to get behind Chelsea's defence and beat Carlo Cudicini at his near post. In the second half Frank Lampard scored his second goal of the game to make it 2-1 to Chelsea after his initial shot had been blocked by Matt Glennon. It was all over when Salomon Kalou fired Chelsea's third goal under Glennon's diving body.

Knocked out of the FA Cup Town's attention turned to their league game against Millwall. A crowd of 6,326 turned up at our Galpharm Stadium to see them win 1-0, thanks to a Luke Beckett goal. Meanwhile, Danny Schofield asked to leave our club, having joined in 1998 from non-league Brodsworth Welfare, his name was circulated with a view to a loan or a permanent move by the end of the season. From early season form that saw Town go second in the table to the end of March, when they languished below mid-table, a play-off placing now looked unlikely at this stage of the season.

On April 1st 2008 after a heavy and quite frankly embarrassing 4-1 defeat at Oldham Athletic, only two days before, it was no April's Fool joke that Andy Ritchie had been relieved of his duties as Manager and Gerry Murphy had once again taken over the helm as Caretaker Manager. In a business driven by results Town had eight thousand season ticket holders this season and as the crowds suggested quite a number had been staying away more recently. Given that it was also our Centenary year in the Football League it was vital that Town looked to progress forward to give us fans something to shout about.

Off the field Jean and Brian Leeming, who had worked at Town for the last 54 years, celebrated their golden wedding anniversary on the same day Town drew 2-2 with Doncaster Rovers on April 5th. Jean worked in the laundry room at the Galpharm Stadium and before Brian's retirement he had spent the bulk of his working life taking care of the electrics at our old home at Leeds Road and then at our Galpharm Stadium.

Having beaten our old Yorkshire adversaries Leeds United 1-0, thanks to an Andy Holdsworth goal, in front of a 16,413 crowd. Town fans were given the exciting news that successful Yorkshire businessman and long-term supporter, Dean Hoyle, had accepted an invitation to join the Board. Having made a very supportive and confidential approach to our club in January the agreement was concluded in the first week of April. Dean was immediately appointed Chairman-Elect of our club and then took over the Chairmanship at the end of our Centenary season. One of the first benefits of both Davy and Hoyle working together was the ground-breaking price of £100 for an adult season ticket. It was a Centenary tribute to everyone who had stood on the terraces of Leeds Road just as they celebrated our rich heritage on the field, they never forgot the hundreds of thousands of supporters who over the many years had supported Huddersfield Town. Having swapped his regular seat in the Antich Stand for the Directors Box and Boardroom Dean Hoyle's shared determination with Ken Davy was to give Town a real opportunity to achieve their key goal of promotion to the Championship.

At the end of the season 2007-2008 with a final league placing of 10th it was one of;

Played 46 games; won 20, lost 20, drew 6, goals for 50, goals against 62, Points 66

Having played Sheffield United in a pre-season friendly at our Galpharm Stadium on Saturday 2nd August 2008 Dean Hoyle's first involvement as Chairman-Elect was four days later in the Herbert Chapman Trophy Centenary game against Arsenal. Hoyle explained that one of his reasons for having got involved with Huddersfield Town was that there was no passion and as a result supporters were leaving in their droves by the end of last season. As testament to both Ken Davy's and Dean Hoyle's commitment to Town 16,123 season tickets were sold by the end of the campaign beating the previous record of 14,058 which was set in 1970 when Town was promoted to the First Division. Director of Business Development Sean Jarvis after two years combining his role between Town and the Huddersfield Giants as of August 2008 set about focusing solely on the commercial activities of Huddersfield Town.

Stan Ternent having officially taken over from Andy Ritchie as Manager on 28th April, alongside his Assistant, ex-Town player Ronnie Jepson, signed Keigan Parker from Blackpool on a free transfer on 27th May. He then signed Jim Goodwin on a three-year deal from Scunthorpe United. Andy Butler was the next player to sign on a three-year deal from Scunthorpe United. Chris Lucketti was brought back and immediately made Captain on a two-year deal from Sheffield United, seven years after he first left our Stadium. Michael Flynn was brought in from Blackpool whilst Gary Roberts joined in a £250,000 transfer from Ipswich Town. Just one day before the new season started David Unsworth was brought in from Burnley to take Ternent's pre-season signings to seven. By the time the transfer window had closed they had completed one of their busiest transfer periods for a long number of years having signed a total of ten new players, including a loan signing, and had just missed out on signing an eleventh player.

Nine players who was released by Ternent were Chris Brandon, Danny Schofield, Frank Sinclair, Matty Young, Aaron Hardy, Danny Racchi, Lucas Akins, Mitchell Bailey and Luke Malcher. Whilst David Mirfin transferred to Scunthorpe United for £150,000.

David Matthew Mirfin – better known as 'Mirf' started out as a striker in our U16's but switched to centre-back and progressed through our ranks. He made his debut in a 1-1 draw against Oldham on 3rd May 2003. By the end of the 2006-07 season he pretty much swept the board at the end of season awards ceremony, having been presented with the Players 'Player of the Year' Trophy, the Fans 'Player of the Year' award, the Away Supporters 'Top Player' accolade, the 'Young Terriers' award and the Huddersfield Examiner 'Man of the Match' Trophy. After a total of 179 appearances, during which time he scored twelve goals, Mirf signed for Scunthorpe United in 2008.

Thanks to a goal from Boothy Town kicked off the new season in front of a home crowd of 15,578 with a 1-1 draw against Stockport County. This was then followed up three days later with a 4-0 home win over Bradford City in the Carling Cup first round. By the middle of August Town had signed Tom Denton from Wakefield FC for £60,000 and three days later Ian Craney had signed for an undisclosed fee from Accrington Stanley. The following day Liam Dickinson was signed on loan from Derby County.
Then having lost 3-1 to Milton Keynes Dons at home Town dropped to next to bottom in the league. This was then followed up with a 2-1 home defeat to Sheffield United in the Carling Cup second round as Michael Flynn recorded his first ever goal in a Town shirt. The first home league win of the season came against Northampton Town when 12,414 fans at our Galpharm Stadium saw Town win 3-2 thanks to two goals from Michael Flynn and one from Boothy. The following week they travelled over to Oldham and held the league leaders to a 1-1 draw thanks to Ian Craney scoring his first goal in Town's colours.
The North East was Town's next destination as they took on Darlington in the Johnstone's Paint Trophy first round. Beaten 1-0 in front of a lowly crowd of 1,791 on a miserable Tuesday night it was compounded even further when Gary Roberts was dismissed which was later rescinded afterwards by the FA on appeal. Sadly, the day after on 8th October lifelong Town fan Keith Connolly passed away. It was announced shortly after that Andy Booth needed surgery on a back problem which had limited him to just three appearances and a further appearance from the subs bench this season. After his goal against Northampton Town Boothy didn't play another league game until the New Year after having had an operation to release a trapped nerve due to a protruding disc in his back.

On Tuesday 21st October Town travelled up North and was battered 5-3 against Hartlepool in the league. Four days later, down at Peterborough, they were heavily beaten 4-0. Towards the end of the month Town took on Yeovil in front of a crowd of 10,719 at our Galpharm Stadium. Even though the game finished 0-0 it still gave some fans reason to cheer as it was the first time since our Stadium had opened that 600 home fans had been given a chance to support our mighty Terriers from the Pink Link Stand (South Stand). None of which would have been possible if it wasn't for our Huddersfield Town Supporters Association liaising with the Club over the finer details of the match.

Before the FA Cup first round match, at home against Port Vale, Town sat well below mid-table in the league. Dean Hoyle having spoken to our Manager Stan Ternent on Monday 3rd November ended the meeting with a difference of opinion. The following day a Board meeting was called and the unanimous decision was made that Huddersfield Town and our Manager had to go their own separate ways. With that Stan Ternent, Ronnie Jepson and Mick Docherty left our club. This was closely followed by Vice-Chairman Andrew Watson offering his resignation, which was reluctantly accepted after his five-year tenure had come to an end.

Gerry Murphy was appointed Caretaker Manager for the third time following Ternent's departure after just over six months in the job (except for Caretaker Managers it was the shortest reign of any Manager in our entire Town history). Murphy's first job was to get to know the many new faces in the dressing room given the amount who had been brought into the Club since the summer.

Working alongside Graham Mitchell and John Vaughan they all set about turning Town's fortunes around starting against Port Vale. Just 6,942 fans at the Galpharm saw Town lose 4-3 and ultimately knocked out of the FA Cup by Port Vale. A week later on Joe Skarz's 50th appearance he scored Town's equaliser after Leeds had taken an early 1-0 lead. It was also Joe's very first goal in league football and thanks to a Michael Collins goal in the final minute of the game Town won 2-1 in front of a packed Elland Road crowd of 32,028. It was roughly at this point of the season when a new group of supporters called the 'Cowshed Loyal' was formed and would over the coming years be based in our South Stand.

Joseph Peter Skarz – 'Joe' was a left-back who was born locally in Netherton, Huddersfield, and started his football career with Town having progressed through our youth ranks. He made his first team debut in a 1-1 draw against Scunthorpe United in 2006 and by 2007 had received the Football League award for League One Apprentice. By March 2009 he had gone on loan to Hartlepool United and the following season was loaned to Shrewsbury Town before he finally signed for Bury in August 2010.

With the announcement of Lee Clark, as Town's new Manager on 12th December 2008, he brought with him Terry McDermott as his Assistant, as well as Derek Fitzackerley as First Team Coach and Steve Black as Performance Coach, all of whom had worked together previously at Newcastle United. It coincided with the announcement that Nigel Clibbens had joined Town as their new Chief Executive.
Ken Davy as Chairman announced his report just before Christmas, on the fifth year of Huddersfield Town Association Football Club Ltd, that Town's income during the year increased to £4.63million (2007 it was £3.97million) with a loss for the year of £1 million (2007 it was £1.05 million). The Capital of the Company was increased on 8th April 2008 when Dean Hoyle was welcomed onto the Board and subscribed to a holding of forty percent of the enlarged number of shares issued.

Lee Clark's first match in charge as Manager saw Town beat Hereford United 2-0 in front of a Galpharm crowd of 13,070 just before Christmas. On Boxing Day having travelled up to Cumbria Town lost 3-0 to Carlisle United but finished off 2008 by beating Scunthorpe United 2-0 in front of a Galpharm crowd of 15,228.
On 20th January, Lee Clark made his first signing as Manager by signing German left-back Dominik Werling on a free transfer. Three days later he made a double signing with the capture of winger Anthony Pilkington from Stockport County and striker Lionel Ainsworth from Watford. As the transfer deadline closed, Clark made three more signings. Striker Lee Novak from Gateshead who was then immediately sent back to Gateshead for the rest of the season. Forward Jonathan Tehoue who was signed on a free transfer from Turkish side Konyaspor. Then on 13th February, 11 days after the deal was originally agreed, Polish striker Lukas Jutkiewicz joined Town on loan from Premier League side Everton until the end of the season.
By this time Director of Football Development Gerry Murphy had formally announced his decision after 20 years of outstanding and dedicated service to leave our club. Paul Stephenson, having previously worked as First Team Coach under Glenn Roeder at Norwich City, was appointed as the new Development Coach. Lee Clark meanwhile brought young Liverpool defender Martin Kelly in on loan on 26th March, just as the loan window shut. With nothing left to play for but professional pride for the final five games of the season it saw Town end the season on a high as they went unbeaten.

At the end of the season 2008-2009 with a final league placing of 9th it was one of;

Played 46 games; won 18, lost 14, drew 14, goals for 62, goals against 65, Points 68

Over the summer months Lee Clark's first pre-season with Town saw him sign Anthony Kay, Peter Clarke, Robbie Simpson, Theo Robinson, Lee Peltier while Lee Novak returned from his loan spell at Gateshead. As well as the retirement of Andy Booth, Clark released Jon Worthington, Malvin Kamara, Dominik Werling, Daniel Broadbent, Dan Codman. Meanwhile, Danny Cadamarteri and Andy Holdsworth both rejected new deals and subsequently left our club as ex-captain Worthington joined fellow League One side Oldham Athletic. He was joined later by both Andy Holdsworth and Keigan Parker. Midfielder Ian Craney and striker Phil Jevons joined League Two side Morecambe on season-long loans. Speculation linking Town to Bristol Rover's Rickie Lambert was dismissed by Dean Hoyle.

Town's pre-season friendlies at our Galpharm Stadium saw them line-up against Lee Clark's former club Newcastle United on 21st July 2009. Four days later Town then played host to, Lee Clark's former Fulham teammate and captain, Chris Coleman and Coventry City. Prior to last season's Centenary showcase against Arsenal you had to go back to Steve Bruce's time as Manager to when Town last played a decent home friendly against Leeds United at our Galpharm Stadium.

Even with Ken Davy and Dean Hoyle at the helm Town was still feeling the effect of pre-administration deals nearly six years on. With a new owner and management team in place they had to deal with the legacy of two previous managers and a previous regime with different priorities which took 12-18 months of wide-scale change before Town was able to kick on again. Meanwhile, Sean Jarvis joined Town's Board as Commercial Director after Ralph Rimmer (Director) and Roger Armitage (Finance Director) had stepped down following Dean's takeover on 1st June while Ann Hough was appointed Operation Director.

Following a rule change at the League's Annual General Meeting Town was allowed to name seven substitutes in all Football League matches as of this season. The rule change was initially proposed by Derby County and was approved by club officials after a vote, this brought League One matches in line with both the FA Cup and League Cup in terms of number of substitutes. Clubs were still only permitted to make three changes during a game though.

Having kicked off our new season, down at Roots Hall against Southend United Town came back with a point, from a 2-2 draw, thanks to Jordan Rhodes's 79th minute goal. This was then followed up with another two goals from Jordan wearing our number 17 shirt, in our Carling Cup first round match, as Town beat Stockport County 3-1 in front of a Galpharm crowd of 5,120. England U19 international Danny Drinkwater was then signed on a season long loan from Manchester United by Lee Clark.

Jordan Luke Rhodes – was a forward who was signed by Clark from Ipswich Town on 31st July 2009. In his first six games for Town he scored six goals and within three months of signing had scored a hat-trick of headers in just eight minutes, against Exeter City as Town won 4-0, which beat the previous record set by Dixie Dean in the 1930s. He was also the first Town player to score back-to-back hat-tricks since the 1920s. Rhodes then equalled a record, set by Dave Mangnall in 1931 and Alf Lythgoe in 1935, by scoring five goals in a league match against Wycombe Wanderers, as Town went on to win 6-0.

On 11th March 2012, Rhodes was named League One Player of the Year at the Football League Awards. On 3 April 2012 in a match against Leyton Orient Jordan surpassed both Sammy Taylor and George Brown, who jointly held the goalscoring record for the Club, with his 36th league goal of the season. Having finished the 2011-12 season he then joined Blackburn Rovers for a record-breaking eight million pounds. Nine years later he returned to our club having signed a three-year contract in July 2021.

By the middle of August 2009 the investment Dean Hoyle had made in personally funding transfer fees for Town in the last year alone was close to two million pounds. Compounded with agents fees, signing on fees and not forgetting a player's salary it was already a considerable investment given that about 25 percent of Town's total income was spent on stadium rent and match day expenses. After taking into account our Club's other running costs that left about one million pounds for player wages. To break-even and assemble a squad capable of winning promotion with such a wage bill was a big challenge and took a brave manager to take it on.

Having taken on Brighton and Hove Albion in a midweek league match, in front of a 13,587 crowd at our Galpharm Stadium, Town ran riot as they annihilated the Seagulls 7-1. The following league game saw Town beaten 1-0 down at Bristol Rovers and then had to travel up to the North East to face Newcastle United in the Carling Cup second round. 3,920 travelling Town fans saw the 'Magpies' win 4-3 in front of a 23,815 St. James crowd to knock Town out of the cup.
The start of September saw Town beat Rotherham United 2-1 away in the Johnstone's Paint Trophy first round. Faced with Chesterfield away on Tuesday 6th October in the Johnstone's Paint Trophy second round 3,003 fans saw Town draw 3-3 and ultimately lose the penalty shoot-out 4-2 to 'The Spireites'.
In front of a Galpharm Stadium crowd of 5,858 Town beat Dagenham and Redbridge 6-1 in the FA Cup first round on Friday 6th November. This was then followed up with a resounding 6-0 home win over Wycombe Wanderers in the league which was televised live but still attracted a Galpharm Stadium Crowd of 14,869. By the end of November Town had beaten Port Vale 1-0 away in the FA Cup second round as Lee Clark was named Manager of the month.

New Year 2010 saw Town faced against West Bromwich Albion in the FA Cup third round at our Galpharm Stadium. 13,472 fans saw Town knocked out of the cup by 'The Baggies' after they had lost 2-0. While the transfer window was open Lee Clark signed four players Nathan Eccleston on loan from Liverpool, Neal Trotman on loan from Preston North End, Krystian Peace on loan from Birmingham City and Dean Heffernan from Australian side Central Coast Mariners.
Sadly Annie Thomas, thought to be Town's oldest current season-ticket holder at the age of 96 passed away in this year but not before she had chance to recollect her very first Town match. "It was Alexander 'Skinner' Jackson's home debut, the opening game of the 1925-26 season. My friends and I had heard of the signing of the 19-year-old Scottish international, so we decided to go along and see him. We arrived long before kick-off and sat on a stone wall on Leeds Road with many more supporters and waved to him as he arrived in an open-top sports car. I don't remember much about the game with West Bromwich Albion, but we drew 1-1".

Lee Clark became the first Town Manager to be named 'Manager of the Month' on two separate occasions in one season since the award's inception in August 2005. The curse of the 'Manager of the Month' award in February saw Town's eleven-match unbeaten league run come to an end down at the Dell at the hands of Southampton. Dean Hoyle meanwhile became 100% shareholder of Huddersfield Town Football Club in this month and by the end of March, exactly a year after he became Chairman of Town, made a personal 'Premiership Pledge'. If Town were able, one day, to be promoted to the Premiership and he was still Chairman, then every Town fan who had been a season ticket holder in either 2008-09 or 2009-10 season and then continued to renew each year from 2010-11 would be able to purchase a season ticket for the first season in the Premiership for £100.

An empathic 6-0 away win at Stockport County on Saturday 24th April was followed up with a 2-1 home win over Colchester United. A 2-1 defeat down at Exeter City in the final league game of the season didn't derail Town taking the final play-off place at the expense of Southampton.

The first leg play-off semi-final saw Town draw 0-0 against Millwall at the Galpharm Stadium. The second leg down at The Den saw Millwall win 2-0 which sadly knocked Town out of the play-offs.

At the end of the season 2009-2010 with a final league placing of 6th it was one of;

Played 46 games; won 23, lost 12, drew 11, goals for 82, goals against 56, Points 80

10 years of Huddersfield Town's history from 2000

2000-01 22nd in Division 1 **(relegated)** — FA Cup third round
Worthington Cup first round
Pontins Reserve League Cup winners

2001-02 6th in Division 2 **(play-off semi-finalist)** — FA Cup second round
Worthington Cup first round
LDV Vans Trophy **finalist**

2002-03 22nd in Division 2 **(relegated)** — FA Cup first round
Worthington Cup second round
LDV Vans Trophy first round

2003-04 4th in Division 3 **(play-off winners-promoted)** — FA Cup first round
Carling Cup third round
LDV Vans Trophy first round

2004-05 9th in Coco-Cola League 1 — FA Cup first round
Carling Cup first round
LDV Vans Trophy second round
East League Reserve Champions
White Rose Reserve Trophy winners

2005-06 4th in Coco-Cola League 1 **(play-off semi-finalist)** — FA Cup third round
Carling Cup second round
LDV Vans Trophy first round

2006-07 15th in Coca-Cola League 1 — FA Cup first round
Carling Cup first round
Johnstone's Paint Trophy first round

2007-08 10th in Coca-Cola League 1 — FA Cup fifth round
Carling Cup first round
Johnstone's Paint Trophy first round

2008-09 9th in Coca-Cola League 1 — FA Cup first round
Carling Cup second round
Johnstone's Paint Trophy second round

2009-10 6t in Coca-Cola League 1 **(play-off semi-finalist)** — FA Cup third round
Carling Cup second round
Johnstone's Paint Trophy second round

Town's 'Ten's Decade' - Chapter 13

As this new decade began the world's deadliest natural disaster struck when an earthquake, that had a magnitude of seven on the Richter scale, hit the West Indian Island of Hispaniola. It killed approximately 200,000 to 250,000 people and affected some three million people. The disaster drew a worldwide humanitarian response, but the impact of the earthquake was felt throughout the decade as Haiti, which had been hit the worst, continued along the difficult path to recovery.

Meanwhile, the UK had its first Conservative leader for 13 years, and its youngest Prime Minister since 1812, when David Cameron's party won the general election. After failing to win an overall majority, the Tories scrambled to form a coalition government with Nick Clegg's Liberal Democrats. It was Britain's first post-war coalition government which lasted five years.

The growing use of social media fuelled mass protest movements, that brought millions of people together around the globe in pursuit of common objectives. Britain saw a new generation of Royals emerge, whilst countries around the world passed laws legalising same-sex marriage.

In mid-2016 Britons voted roughly 52 to 48 percent in favour of the United Kingdom's withdrawal from the European Union. The deadline for withdrawal was extended several times, as Parliament's steadfast opposition to a proposed deal led to Prime Minister Theresa May's resignation in mid-2019. Though May's successor, Boris Johnson, initially planned to force an exit, with or without a deal, opposition to this plan forced him to seek yet another extension, pushing the contentious issue into the next decade.

During the second decade following 9/11 the scourge of terrorism continued around the world. There were major terror attacks at the Boston Marathon, various venues in Paris, on London Bridge, a crowded Barcelona street and various places throughout America. This new decade also started amid the chaotic wake of a global financial crisis and ended with the impeachment of a U.S. President.

Meanwhile, in football in 2010 Qatar became the first middle eastern country to host the World Cup when they won the right to hold the 2022 FIFA World Cup, after four rounds of voting. The 22nd edition of the FIFA World Cup is scheduled to take place from 21st November to 18th December 2022 when for the last time 32 teams will compete for the coveted trophy. The tournament that's due to take place in the United States, Mexico and Canada in 2026 will then see a total of 48 teams compete with each other and at every World Cup tournament thereafter.

Having just missed out on a possible chance of promotion last season Town set about the 2010-11 season having signed a raft of new players. The first player to sign was Scotland U21 midfielder Scott Arfield for an undisclosed fee from Falkirk. Next to sign were Gary Naysmith from Sheffield United, Jamie McCombe from Bristol City, Joey Gudjonsson from Burnley, Ian Bennett from Sheffield United and Alan Lee from Crystal Palace. While the following players were all signed on loan; Graham Carey from Celtic, Lee Croft from Derby County, Joe Garner from Nottingham Forest and Damien Johnson from Plymouth Argyle.

The players that left the Club during the summer were; Dean Heffernan, Robbie Williams, Lewis Nightingale, Taser Hassen, Phil Jevons, Simon Eastwood, Tom Denton, Joe Skarz, Krystian Peace, Lionel Ainsworth, James Berrett, Michael Collins and Robbie Simpson-who went out on loan to Brentford.

Town kicked off the new season in front of a 10,342 crowd away at Notts County and came back with a 3-0 win thanks to two goals from Anthony Pilkington and one from Jordan Rhodes. Three days later Rhodes was once again on the score sheet in a 1-0 Carling Cup first round away win at Carlisle United. Having taken a point at our Galpharm Stadium in a 0-0 draw against Tranmere Rovers the following week they took on Peterborough United at their place and was heavily beaten 4-2.

Five days later 5,313 travelling fans was amongst the 28,901 crowd at Everton as Town were hammered 5-1 in the Carling Cup second round with all six goals having been scored by the home side.

For the first time ever Town had three players called up to the Under-21 squads Alex Smithies for England (who had progressed through Town's Academy since the age of eight), Scott Arfield for Scotland and Graham Carey for Ireland. As a result of the international call-ups Town choose not to postpone the home game with AFC Bournemouth at the beginning of September and earned a 2-2 draw in front of a 12,426 Galpharm Stadium crowd.

The month of October saw Town beat Peterborough 3-2 at home in the Johnstone's Paint Trophy whilst First Team Coach Derek Fazackerley left to team up with Sven-Goran Eriksson at Championship side Leicester City. Lee Clark having moved Paul Stephenson up as First Team Coach then appointed Steve Watson as Town's new development coach. Clark then signed goalkeeper Nick Colgan on a month's loan from Grimsby Town due to Smithies been injured. Nick was initially signed to provide first team cover for Ian Bennett and wore the number 25 shirt on Town's bench for the league game against Southampton. By the start of the New Year he had signed permanently for Town.

By the end of October John Drake a Yorkshire Post match reporter for Town for over 30 years had sadly passed away. Having beaten Sheffield Wednesday 2-0 in front of a crowd of 20,540 at their place at the beginning of November Town were second in the league. This result was then followed up with a 0-0 draw down at Cambridge United in the FA Cup first round. Three days later Town made the short journey to South Yorkshire and beat Rotherham United 5-2 in the Johnstone's Paint Trophy. Benik Afobe having signed on loan from Arsenal at the start of the month scored twice against 'The Millers' as Town's third away match on the trot saw them beaten 1-0 in front of a crowd of 7,723 at Oldham Athletic. The FA Cup first round replay at home against Cambridge United saw Town score twice in the final minute to win 2-1. Then an emphatic 6-0 home win over Macclesfield Town in the FA Cup second round towards the end of November saw Town drawn against Dover Athletic in the next round.

Late November saw Andy Kiwomya step up from Fitness Coach to the role of First Team Performance Coach after Steve Black left. It was around this time that the Rec Club's Management Committee voted unanimously to recommend a proposal whereby Huddersfield Town took over the operation of the business at Leeds Road and in doing so, secured community sports at the facility for the foreseeable future. After 18 months of negotiations a deal between Huddersfield Town and the Rec Club gained member approval from both parties and paved the way for a major multi-million pound improvement and investment scheme to take place. A new operational company Huddersfield Canalside Limited was formed to run the premises and business. The facility was renamed 'Canalside' as Huddersfield Town was able to realise a long-standing ambition to create a single site Premier League standard training facility and grassed area. The investment in changing facilities, classrooms and pitches was funded primarily by Town's Chairman Dean Hoyle, the new landowner.

Sadly at the age of 60 Martin Benson passed away on Monday 13th December. He had been a programme seller at Town for many years and when on holiday in Goa he always distributed his old football shirts to the children he met there every year. The day after a 2-0 away win against Tranmere Rovers in the Johnstone's Paint Trophy Semi-Final was witnessed by 410 travelling Town fans in a 2,598 crowd.

Having signed Kevin Kilbane on loan from Hull City for the rest of the season the New Year got off to a great start for Town as they beat Sheffield Wednesday 1-0 in front of a Galpharm Stadium crowd of 17,024 that was also televised on Sky. Five days later Town beat Dover Athletic 2-0 at home in the FA Cup to go through to the next round. Lee Clark having signed Tamas Kadar on a month's loan from Newcastle United then saw Town beat Walsall 4-2 away in the league. After travelling up North to take on Carlisle United in the Johnstone's Paint Trophy Northern Final first leg Town came away with a mountain to climb for the second leg given that 'The Cumbrians' had just won 4-0.

The transfer window closed with Lee Clark having signed Danny Cadamarteri on a short-term contract following his release from Dundee United. By the end of January 5,188 travelling fans in a Highbury crowd of 59,375 had seen Arsenal beat Town 2-1 in the FA Cup fourth round.

The second leg of the Northern Final Johnstone's Paint Trophy at our Galpharm Stadium in February was watched by a crowd of 6,528, which sadly, even a 3-0 victory over Carlisle United wasn't enough to win the trophy for Town. On 26th February, Town signed left-back Stephen Jordan on an emergency one-month loan from Sheffield United, following injuries to Gary Naysmith and Liam Ridehalgh.

Town fans were allowed to occupy part of the Pink Link South Stand as 12,531 fans at our Galpharm Stadium saw Anthony Pilkington suffer a broken leg and ankle against Rochdale on 8th March and ultimately had to undergo an operation. Danny Ward was brought in on loan from Bolton Wanderers for the rest of the season as Pilkington's replacement and Town bolstered their defensive options by signing centre-back Sean Morrison on loan from Reading on 23rd March.

By the start of April Town had moved up to second place in the league and the thought amongst many fans was, is this going to be our year. A 2-0 away win over Tranmere Rovers was watched by 2,165 travelling Town fans, given that the total crowd over in the Wirral was only 6,438, it was a great show of support. This was then followed up with a hard fought 1-1 draw against Peterborough United at our Galpharm Stadium. A 16,431 crowd saw Jack Hunt score Town's equaliser in the 90th minute to salvage a precious point which ultimately saw them drop to third in the League.
A 1-0 away win over Charlton Athletic was then followed up with a 3-1 away win over Milton Keynes Dons, that result saw Town climb back up to second place in the league. Easter Monday saw them beat Dagenham and Redbridge 2-1 in front of a 14,072 Galpharm Stadium crowd thanks to two first half goals from Jordan Rhodes. Strangely enough the result saw Town drop to third in the league due to Southampton beating Hartlepool 2-0 to claim the second spot heading into the final stage of the season.
A 3-2 away win over league leaders Brighton and Hove Albion wasn't enough for Town to claim back that final automatic promotion place from Southampton as 'The Saints' had beaten Brentford 3-0 at 'The Bees' ground.
Town's final match of this season was at home against Brentford. Nearly 14,000 fans saw both teams battle out an amazing 4-4 draw with Town's goals coming from Novak, Afobe and two from Ward. The result meant that Town had finished the season with a 25-match unbeaten run. Their last league defeat was the 4-1 hammering down at none other than Southampton on 28th December 2010 which ironically was the start of a 27-match unbeaten run for 'The Saints' which ultimately saw them automatically promoted in second place.
Faced with Bournemouth away in the first leg of the play-off semi-final, thanks to a Kevin Kilbane first half goal, Town came away with a 1-1 draw. The second leg at the Galpharm Stadium was watched by a crowd of over 16,000 fans. Thanks to Antony Kay's goal in extra-time the game ended 3-3 and had to be decided on penalties. Novak, Ward, Kilbane and Kay scored Town's first four penalties with ease as Bournemouth's Symes and Cooper scored from the spot. 'The Cherries' having lost 4-2 on penalties saw Town march onto the final against none other than Peterborough United.
A play-off final crowd of over 48,000 at Old Trafford saw 'The Posh' score three goals in just seven minutes in the second half to leave all Town fans, myself included, devastated at the final whistle. Peterborough United having won 3-0 was promoted at Town's expense.

At the end of the season 2010-2011 with a final league placing of 3rd it was one of;

Played 46 games; won 25, lost 9, drew 12, goals for 77, goals against 48, Points 87

Despite having lost in the play-off final there wasn't a mass exodus of players that left Town for the 2011-12 season. The first player that left during pre-season was right-back Lee Peltier, who joined Championship side Leicester City, for an undisclosed fee. Following him out of our Galpharm Stadium was young defender Leigh Franks who joined Conference North side Alfreton Town. Next to go was winger Anthony Pilkington, who joined Premier League new boys Norwich City in July for an undisclosed fee. Meanwhile, young striker Jimmy Spencer joined Cheltenham Town on loan and 19-year-old midfielder Chris Atkinson joined Conference side Darlington on loan. In August Nathan Clarke joined fellow League One side Oldham Athletic on loan until the end of January. Just as the transfer window shut on 31st August young midfielder Aidan Chippendale joined Scottish Premier League side Inverness Caledonian Thistle on loan until January 2012.

Town's first signing of the close season was right-back Calum Woods from newly promoted Scottish Premier League side Dunfermline Athletic on a free transfer at the start of June. By the beginning of July, two more signings had been added to our team, firstly defensive midfielder Oscar Gobern had signed from Southampton with his transfer fee of £275,000 having to be settled by a tribunal. Then winger Donal McDermott signed from Manchester City with his fee also having to be settled by a tribunal. Experienced midfielder Tommy Miller was then snapped up on a one-year deal following his release from Sheffield Wednesday.

At the start of July Town had confirmed the signing of defender Liam Cooper on a season-long loan from Championship side Hull City. By the middle of the month, winger Danny Ward, who had a successful loan spell at the Terriers at the end of last season, signed a permanent three-year deal for an undisclosed fee from Bolton Wanderers while Plymouth Argyle's midfielder Damien Johnson signed for a second consecutive season-long loan. Town's midfield was further bolstered with the signing of Anton Robinson from Bournemouth, by the start of August, for an undisclosed fee. Lee Clark then signed Canadian goalkeeper Simon Thomas on a free transfer following a successful loan spell.

Out of nine pre-season friendlies Town won seven but lost 2-0 to Sheffield United and 2-1 to Emley in the other two games. The first three league games of the season saw Town draw them all whilst in the Carling Cup they travelled down to Stoke-on-Trent and beat Port Vale 4-2 in the first round. Faced with another Carling Cup away tie for the second round Town travelled down to Wales to line-up against Cardiff City. Thanks to a late equaliser for City in injury time the match at 3-3 went into extra time. Having conceded two further goals Town was ultimately knocked out of the cup having lost 5-3. Having previously beaten Northampton Town 2-1 at their Sixfields Stadium in the Johnstone's Paint Trophy first round Town drew 2-2 with Bradford City in the next round. Faced with penalties at the Galpharm Stadium a crowd of over 10,000 ultimately saw Town lose 4-3 to City.

Having taken to the field against Walsall on Saturday 5th November Town wore a Help For Heroes charity kit which was a white shirt with a red and black double-chevon and was worn with blue shorts and white socks. Thanks to a second half goal from Novak Town came from behind to draw 1-1 against 'The Saddlers'. Drawn away against Swindon in the FA Cup first round Town took an early lead at the County Ground. Unfortunately by half-time Town was 2-1 down and were dumped out of the cup 4-1 by the time the full-time whistle had gone.

Bournemouth having travelled up to our Galpharm Stadium in December went home with all three points having beaten Town 1-0. The defeat against 'The Cherries' compounded the fact that travelling Town fans had just seen our unbeaten league run of 43 league games, a then Football League record, come to an end down at the Valley against Charlton Athletic only the match before. With Town's defensive injuries starting to pile up, Jamie McCombe's loan at Preston North End was cut short but owing to administrative reasons the termination of his loan could not go ahead, and he stayed at Deepdale until the New Year.

Town started the New Year having drawn 2-2 away at Meadow Lane against Notts County which was then followed up with a resounding 6-0 battering of Wycombe Wanderers at their place. Jordan Rhodes ran riot as he scored 5 goals, in less than 15 minutes in the second half, after Gobern had opened the scoring in the first half. On 31st January as the transfer window shut Donal McDermott left the Club, just six months after joining, to go back to his former club Bournemouth for an undisclosed fee.

By the middle of February Town had lost their unbeaten home record and suffered only their second league defeat of the season against Sheffield United. A goal in the first ten minutes was enough to give 'The Blades' all three points as Town remained third in the league. After the defeat Lee Clark was relieved of his duties as Manager and shortly after Simon Grayson was installed into the hot-seat.

In March, Nathan Clarke joined Bury on loan for the remainder of the season while young midfielder Matt Crooks joined Conference North side F.C. Halifax Town on loan. As the loan window shut, Kallum Higginbotham had been sent out on loan to Barnsley but was recalled by the end of April. By the end of March, goalkeeper Lloyd Allinson had been loaned out to Ilkeston for the rest of the season as Town's recent unbeaten run came to an abrupt end when they lost 2-1 away to Carlisle United.

By the end of the season having finished in fourth place and having secured a play-off semi-final place Town were faced with Milton Keynes Dons away for the first leg. Thanks to goals from both Rhodes and Hunt they came away with a 2-0 advantage for the second leg.

A Galpharm Stadium crowd of just over 15,000 fans saw Town take a 1-0 lead over 'The Dons' in the first half before they pulled a goal back to make it 3-1 on aggregate. In the second half they managed to survive until the third minute of injury time when 'The Dons' pulled another goal back on the day to make the final aggregate score 3-2. Town had thankfully made it to the play-off final at Wembley.

Sheffield United having overcome Stevenage in their semi-final play-off game ensured that a Yorkshire Wembley Final was watched by over 52,000 fans in the stadium, while thousands more fans watched on television. After ninety minutes with the game still goal-less extra-time came and went with no team able to break the deadlock, so the match had to be decided on penalties.

First up to take a penalty was Town's Tommy Miller, it took four penalties before United's Neil Collins scored the game's first penalty. By the end of the first five penalties the game was still tied at 2-2. Another five Town penalty takers were chosen and from the resulting ten penalties every player scored sending the tie into sudden-death penalties. Town's sudden-death penalty was taken and excellently scored by our keeper Alex Smithies whilst United's keeper Steve Simonsen was left to take their penalty. The pressure at that moment, given the intensity of the game, and ultimately the rewards for promotion may have weighed on his mind as he ran up to take the kick. Every fan inside the stadium, and all those at home watching the match, held their breath as Alex Smithies looked on as the ball sailed over his head and cleared his crossbar. Simonsen collapsed in a heap of tears, with his head in his hands, as every fan and player alike went wild with delight as Town was promoted to the Championship.

At the end of the season 2011-2012 with a final league placing of 4th(promoted) it was one of;

Played 46 games; won 21, lost 7, drew 18, goals for 79, goals against 47, Points 81

Simon Grayson's first full season in charge as Manager saw him sign Sean Scannell from Crystal Palace. Defender Paul Dixon, a free transfer from Dundee United, was the next player through our stadium doors. Town then beat off the challenge of Barnsley to sign young midfielder Oliver Norwood on a three-year deal from Manchester United. Grayson then raided his old club at Leeds United to sign midfielder Adam Clayton, a player he had only just previously signed not two seasons before for his old club.

Town then embarked on signing the following players; defender Joel Lynch from Nottingham Forest on a free transfer, midfielder Keith Southern from Blackpool on a two-year deal, defender Anthony Gerrard from Cardiff City on a three-year deal. Meanwhile, James Vaughan signed on a season long loan from Norwich City. As the transfer window was closing Simon Grayson signed Adam Hammill on loan from Wolverhampton Wanderers until January 2013.

Four pre-season defeats against Guiseley, Emley, Crewe Alexandra and a Barcelona B team from ten friendlies set Town up for their first league match in the Championship, down at Cardiff City. A crowd of over 21,000 saw them lose 1-0 having conceded a goal deep into injury time against 'The bluebirds'. Having lost 2-0 away to Preston North End in the Football League Cup first round Anthony Kay became the first player to leave this season, when he signed a two-year-deal at Milton Keynes Dons. The following day, defender Jamie McCombe had his contract terminated, which paved the way for a move to Doncaster Rovers. Defender Liam Ridehalgh joined Chesterfield on a one-month loan with his teammate Chris Atkinson joining up with him in September. By the end of August Town fans were left distraught after Jordan Rhodes was sold to our Championship rivals Blackburn Rovers for eight million pounds. It was a record transfer fee for Town, as well as a record purchase for Blackburn, and it was also at the time the highest fee paid for a player between two non-Premier League clubs.

The start of September saw Town come away from Portman Road with a 2-2 draw against Ipswich Town. Then following a 1-0 home win over Derby County at our newly named John Smith's Stadium Town went up to eighth in the league, and by the end of the month sat second in the table. Jermaine Beckford, having turned down the chance to join our club at the start of the season, now signed on a three-month loan deal from Leicester City.

From the middle of November Town went 12 league games without a league win until well into the New Year. This run of poor form, included a humiliating 6-1 away defeat at the hands of Leicester City, saw Simon Grayson's short tenure as Manager come to an end by the end of January. As the transfer window closed on 31st January, midfielder Anton Robinson joined League Two leaders Gillingham on loan for the rest of the season. However, he returned to the Club in April after rupturing his anterior cruciate ligaments, which ruled him out of football for nine months.

Town having beaten Charlton Athletic 1-0 in the first round of the FA Cup was then drawn with Leicester City in the next round. Ex-player Mark Lillis having taken over as Caretaker Manager for the Leicester City cup match helped Town to earn a 1-1 draw and oversaw them play a further three league games.

With Mark Robins installed as Town's new Manager in time for the FA Cup fifth round against Wigan Athletic he could only look on as Town suffered a 4-1 cup defeat. His first league game in charge of Town saw them take on Nottingham Forest at the City Ground, by full-time Robins had seen Town get battered 6-1.

Town took to the field against Barnsley at our John Smith's Stadium for the final match of the season with fans and players alike knowing that both teams needed to avoid a defeat to avoid any possibility of relegation. Barnsley opened the scoring first, but Town equalised early in the second half as nearly 22,000 fans willed on both teams to attack as Barnsley went back in front. Town equalised for the second time in the match to earn a 2-2 draw, and at the final whistle both teams and fans celebrated in and around our stadium together. Given that the draw meant both clubs had managed to avoid relegation.

At the end of the season 2012-2013 with a final league placing of 19th it was one of;

Played 46 games; won 15, lost 18, drew 13, goals for 53, goals against 73, Points 58

Financial fair play rules introduced by UEFA for the start of the 2012-13 season meant clubs had to demonstrate that their expenditure including wages was in line with revenue, or they would be barred from UEFA competitions. For all clubs in Football League Two salary caps was already in place. League One was 'shadowing' the rules and the Championship was looking at both the Premier League model of 'Financial fair play rules' and the Football League model. In later years the rules for financial fair play would play an important part on our field of dreams and did so from the start of the 2013-14 season.

Mark Robins had already made his first Town signing when he signed Daniel Carr from Dulwich Hamlet towards the end of last season for £100,000. He then followed this up with the signing of defender Jake Carroll from Partick Thistle in the summer. Robins then saw Tom Clarke sign for Simon Grayson's Preston North End while Allan Lee signed for Ipswich Town and Scott Arfield signed for Burnley. Lee Novak meanwhile had turned down the offer of a new deal at Town and signed for his former Manager Lee Clark at Birmingham City.

Kallum Higginbotham having left Town on a free transfer signed for Partick Thistle on a two-year deal. This was closely followed by Robins signing midfielder Adam Hammill from Wolverhampton Wanderers while our former striker Jon Stead returned on a free transfer from Bristol City. Northern Ireland international Martin Paterson was then signed by Robins on a two-year deal following his release from Burnley. Norwich City striker James Vaughan, who had a successful loan spell with Town the previous season, then signed on a three-year deal. One of the best Town signings in more recent times was the signature of central midfielder Jonathan Hogg on a three-year deal from fellow Championship side Watford. His battling terrier spirit was something to be admired by all Town fans from this season onwards as he went on to become a true legend and even graced the Premiership whilst wearing our Town colours. Spanish striker Cristian Lopez from Atletico Baleares was the last summer signing Robins made for Town. He signed on a free transfer after a successful trial period and was given a one-year deal.

Pre-season saw Town win only three of the eleven friendlies played, and it wasn't until the third league game of the season that they won their first game having beaten Millwall 1-0 down at their place. Bradford City having made the short journey to our John Smith's Stadium for the Capital One Cup first round left empty-handed as Town won 2-1. Having gone on a goal rampage, with Vaughan hitting a hat-trick, Town ran out 5-1 winners over Bournemouth in the league towards the end of August. The Capital One Cup second round saw them take on Charlton Athletic, at our John Smith's Stadium, then having gone behind in the game Town fought back to win 3-2 and went through to the next round. Just as the transfer window was about to close at the end of August our talented right-back Jack Hunt after being linked with a move to then Premier League sides Sunderland and Swansea City, while constantly being watched by Reading, Wigan Athletic and Cardiff City, left in a two million pound transfer for Premier League side Crystal Palace. At the start of September Robins signed defender Jazz Richards on a short-term loan, from Swansea City, by Christmas he had returned to his parent club. Having gone through the entire month almost unbeaten Huddersfield Town travelled over to Kingston-upon-Hull to take on Hull City in the third round of the Capital One Cup. Over 7,000 fans saw Town knocked out of the cup after they had conceded a second half goal which earned City a 1-0 win.

Finally, after years of ongoing discussions between all parties our great Club got its shares back in September of this year. Ten core values that was set in stone with the change of ownership had also started a 'New Era' which remains at the heart of everything our Club does, even still today, they are honesty, integrity, trust, character, commitment, success, value, quality, pride, respect. Over the coming years those values shone through in every area of the Club and was matched by every fan on our terraces.

By the end of November Robins signed striker Harry Bunn on loan, from Manchester City, then in late January made his loan permanent. After a 3-2 away defeat at the hands of Burnley in the league at the start of 2014 Town travelled across to Blundell Park and took on Grimsby Town in the FA Cup third round. Thanks to goals from Norwood and Paterson and a last-minute own goal, from Grimsby's Aswad Thomas, Town won 3-2.

Shortly after that cup game Mark Robins signed striker Nahki Wells from Bradford City for £1.3 million pounds. This was then followed up with the signing of Joe Lolley from Kidderminster Harriers for an undisclosed fee while Town defender Liam Ridehalgh signed for Tranmere Rovers. Faced with Charlton Athletic in the fourth round of the FA Cup over 10,000 fans saw Town lose 1-0 as U21 academy defender Tommy Smith sat on our sub's bench for the first time. By the end of January Norwegian midfielder Sondre Tronstad had signed for Town on a free transfer from IK Start.

The start of February saw Town travel across the M62 to face our old adversaries Leeds United. Over 31,000 fans saw Town take a 1-0 half-time lead before taking a 5-1 hammering as United scored five second half goals that day. A resounding 5-0 battering of Barnsley at our John Smith's Stadium in early March was the only win Town fans saw this month as three draws and three defeats saw them slide down the Championship table by the end of the month. From the start of April until the end of the season only travelling fans saw Town win again in the league. A 2-1 win down at Yeovil was then followed up with a 4-1 win down at Watford in the final league match of the season. By the end of the season goalkeeper Ian Bennett had retired from football and midfielder Anton Robinson had been released by Huddersfield Town.

At the end of the season 2013-2014 with a final league placing of 17th it was one of;

Played 46 games; won 14, lost 21, drew 11, goals for 58, goals against 65, Points 53

Mark Robins having surveyed last season's showing released the following players on a free transfer Callum Woods to Preston North End, Keith Southern to Fleetwood Town, Chris Atkinson to Crewe Alexandra, Cristian Lopez to Burgos, Peter Clarke to Blackpool and Paul Mullin to Morecombe. Robin's first summer signing was Coventry City goalkeeper Joe Murphy who signed on a free transfer. This was shortly followed up with the free transfer signing of Town's former player Lee Peltier from Leeds United.

Town's eleven pre-season friendlies saw them only lose two games against league opposition Scunthorpe United and Oldham Athletic. At the start of August Robins signed midfielder Conor Cody from Liverpool for £375,000 and then followed it up with the signing of midfielder Jacob Butterfield from Middlesbrough in exchange for Adam Clayton and an undisclosed fee. On the same day, as Butterfield signed, centre-forward Liam Coogans signed for Town from newly formed Airdrieonians (following the liquidation of Airdrie United Football Club in 2002). With midfielder Oliver Norwood having signed for Reading for an undisclosed fee midfielder Radoslaw Majewski was then brought in on a season long loan from Nottingham Forest.

Over 12,000 fans at our John Smith's Stadium watched the opening league match of the new season against Bournemouth. Town fans could only watch on in dismay as they conceded a goal in the opening minutes of the match. By the time the ref had blown his whistle for full-time they had slumped to a shocking 4-0 defeat. If Alex Smithies had not made as many saves and saved a penalty during the match the result could have been a lot worse as it was after just one game Town was rock bottom of the Championship. Immediately after the game Mark Robins met with the Board of Directors, and it was mutually agreed that he would leave our club.

Former player Mark Lillis once more stepped into the breach as Caretaker Manager. His first game back in charge saw them travel down to the Proact Stadium to take on Chesterfield in the Capital One Cup first round. Thanks to a hat-trick from Nahki Wells, two goals from Stead and a goal from Lolley Town won 5-3 after extra time.

Four days later having travelled down to Wales to take on Cardiff City in the league Town suffered a 3-1 defeat. The Madejski Stadium was the next destination as over 15,000 fans saw them record their first league win of the season with a 2-1 win over Reading. Given that Murray Wallace was shown a straight red card at our John Smith's Stadium against Charlton Athletic ten-man Town did well to hold off the South Londoners until deep into injury time to earn a 1-1 draw. A 2-0 defeat in the second round of the Capital One Cup away at Nottingham Forest was then followed up with a 4-2 away defeat at the hands of Watford. Towards the end of August defender Jack Robinson was brought to the Club on a season long loan from Queens Park Rangers while central defender Mark Hudson signed on a two-year deal from Cardiff City. It wasn't long before Hudson was handed the captain's armband at Town.

At the beginning of September former Charlton Athletic Manager Chris Powell was unveiled as Town's new Manager. Powell's first game in charge at the John Smith's Stadium, against Middlesbrough, was watched by a crowd of nearly 18,000 fans. Having lost 2-1 Town were third from bottom in the Championship. A goalless draw at home against Wigan Athletic was their savouring grace before a 3-0 defeat away at our old adversaries Leeds United. Straight after the Elland Road defeat Town went on a run of seven matches unbeaten before they lost 3-2 against Derby County at their Baseball ground. Powell's first loan signing as Manager was centre forward Grant Holt who was signed on a three-month loan from Wigan Athletic. Chris followed this up with the signing of his former Charlton Athletic midfielder Diego Poyet, who signed on loan from his new club West Ham United. Murray Wallace in the middle of December received his second red card of the season in the first half at Carrow Road. A crowd of well over 25,000 fans then witnessed ten-man Town go on to suffer a humiliating 5-0 away defeat against Norwich City.

Town started the New Year getting knocked out of the FA Cup third round, having lost 1-0 against Reading at the John Smith's Stadium. To make matters worse Jonathon Hogg was sent off in the dying minutes of the match. Birmingham City defender David Edgar was brought in on loan by Powell in January while Danny Ward signed on loan for Rotherham United, with a view to a permanent transfer. Lee Peltier was the next player to leave Town when he signed for Cardiff City for an undisclosed fee as Jon Stead for the second time this season went on loan to Bradford City. Adam Hammill also went out on loan to Rotherham United and Martin Paterson having previously been out on loan at Fleetwood Town went on loan again, but this time crossed the Atlantic Ocean and ended up at Orlando City Soccer Club. The month of January ended badly with our right-back Tommy Smith having to be airlifted to hospital with a head injury after a collision with our keeper Joe Murphy during the 2-1 defeat against Leeds United. Thankfully, Smith was discharged from hospital the following day which brought some relief to the 20,000 plus-crowd that witnessed the terrible accident. Centre forward Ismael Miller was signed for an undisclosed fee from Blackpool at the start of February. The month of March came and went without a league win for Town as Chris Powell signed Manchester United defender Reece James until the end of the season. Having gone eight games without a league win until the start of April when Town beat Ipswich 2-1 at the John Smith's Stadium it was also the last win of the season, as Town drew their last four league games of the season.

At the end of the season 2014-2015 with a final league placing of 16th it was one of;

Played 46 games; won 13, lost 17, drew 16, goals for 58, goals against 75, Points 55

Chris Powell's first pre-season at Town saw him bring in Callum Charlton on a free transfer from Brighouse Town. He also signed on free transfer left- back Jason Davidson from West Bromwich Albion and Middlesbrough's central midfielder Dean Whitehead. Shortly after that he signed midfielder Kyle Dempsey from Carlisle United for a fee reported to be approximately £300,000. Manchester City's young striker Jordy Hiwula was the next player through our doors closely followed by the free transfer signing of Martin Cranie from Barnsley. Meanwhile, young midfielder Jack Boyle was promoted through Town's youth system by Powell.

Having signed half a dozen new players Powell set about releasing the following players off Town's books. Centre forward Daniel Carr having previously been signed by Robins for £100,000 was now allowed to leave the Club on a free transfer and promptly signed for Cambridge United. Jake Carroll signed for Hartlepool United on a free transfer while Jon Stead signed for Notts County. Powell then released Anthony Gerrard who signed for Shrewsbury Town, Oscar Gobern who signed for Q.P.R and Martin Paterson who signed for Blackpool. Then at the start of July Town agreed on a two million pound deal and sold Conor Cody to Wolverhampton Wanderers.

Town's pre-season friendlies saw them unbeaten in the first two games and by the third game had travelled over to Spain to take on Leyton Orient in the La Cala Resort. Having travelled back from Spain they then set off for sunny Cleethorpes to take on Grimsby Town. A 3-1 defeat against 'The Mariners' was the first of three pre-season defeats for Town.

The first league fixture of the new season saw them take the relatively short journey over to Kingston upon Hull. Over 19,000 fans watched as Town went down 2-0 against Hull City. The first game of the season at the John Smith's Stadium saw them take on Notts County in the first round of the Capital One Cup. A lowly crowd of just over 4,000 fans saw Town knocked out of the cup as County having played the last twenty minutes with just ten men won 2-1. Just over 11,000 fans showed up at our John Smith's Stadium to see the first home league match of the season against Blackburn Rovers. After taking a first half lead Town drew 1-1 against 'The Blue and Whites'.

By the end of the month Powell had signed two players on loan, winger Mustapha Carayol from Middlesbrough and central midfielder Emyr Huws from Wigan, while selling our goalkeeper Alex Smithies to Q.P.R for £1.5 million pounds. Forward Jamie Paterson was the third player to be signed by Powell on a season long loan from Nottingham Forest at the start of September while midfielder Jacob Butterfield signed for Derby County for an undisclosed fee. Adam Hamill was then given consent by Town to go ahead and sign for Barnsley. The following week a 2-0 away defeat at the hands of Cardiff City, in front of a crowd of nearly 14,000 fans, saw Town sit next to bottom in the Championship. Defender Elliott Ward having recently signed on loan from Bournemouth played just five league games before he suffered a knee injury and didn't play another game until he returned to his parent club. Powell having initially signed Aston Villa keeper Jed Steer on a short-term loan, when the winter transfer window opened in January, then signed Jed on loan for the rest of the season.

A 4-1 home win over Bolton Wanderers in the middle of September and a 2-0 home win over Milton Keynes Dons were the only games that Town fans saw them win in the league until November. Then having travelled down to the Madejski Stadium to take on Reading a crowd of nearly 14,500 fans saw Town come away with a 2-2 draw. Despite taking the lead in the opening minutes they were unable to keep it. Then having got in front again at 2-1 within the first 30 minutes they somehow managed to lose control of the game in the second half and conceded a second goal. After the draw at Reading Chris Powell was relieved of his duties as Town's Chief Executive Nigel Clibbens issued the following statement. "We have decided to make this change after very careful deliberation. It is made with the long-term interests of the Club in mind. It signals a change of direction by the Club and a new approach".

At the John Smith's Stadium Nigel Clibbens announced to the waiting press that Town had appointed new Head Coach David Wagner and Assistant Head Coach Christoph Buhler as of the 5th of November. Wagner was Town's first ever overseas Head Coach and marked the beginning of a new era at the Club given that we no longer had a traditional football manager at the helm. David's answer as Head Coach, as to what his football philosophy was given our previous manager's style and way of playing, was quite simply refreshing at the time. His philosophy was to have Town play football with a real passion at high speed while trying to score goals. (something not too dissimilar from that of, Town's legendary Manager, Herbert Chapman's thinking)

Wagner's first game in charge, having had eight days in which to go through training and bring his style of play to Town, was against Sheffield Wednesday away on 21st November. Over 21,000 fans at Hillsborough saw Town take the lead before they went down 3-1 against 'The Owls'. On 19th November Wagner made his first signing when he and Head of Football Operations Stuart Webber brought Leicester City left-back Ben Chilwell to the Club on a three-month loan. Given that our only left-back Jason Davidson was away with international commitments it was an inspired signing given that 18-year-old Ben had just recently been called up to the England U21 squad.

Along with various Town players going out on loan James Vaughan also went out on loan to Birmingham City and signed for a further loan with 'The Blues' in the New Year for the rest of the season. A John Smith's Stadium crowd of nearly 15,500 fans saw Wagner's first home game end in a 2-0 defeat against Middlesbrough. Wagner's first league win as Head Coach came on 15th December against Rotherham United. Nearly 13,000 fans at our John Smith's Stadium saw them win 2-0 against 'The Miller's.

2016 started with a 2-0 away win against Bolton Wanderers, this was then followed up with a 2-2 home draw against Reading in the FA Cup third round, next Town ran riot as they thumped five goals past Charlton in a 5-0 home win. Town then signed Middlesbrough left-back James Husband on loan for a month. A 1-1 draw down at Fulham came next before Town was knocked out of the FA Cup third round after a 5-2 battering at the hands of Reading away.

The start of February saw Town sign Brighton and Hove Albion's forward Elvis Manu on a three-month loan. Next through the doors at Town was the loan signing of Wolves winger Rajiv van La Parra. By the end of March and with Wagner's footballing ideals firmly in place Town took on our old adversaries at Elland Road and after conceding an early goal battered Leeds United 4-1. A 2-0 away win over at Blackburn Rovers place in the middle of April was Town's next league win and was also our last for this season.

The season ended with a heavy 5-1 home defeat for Town at the hands of Brentford. A John Smith's Stadium crowd of just under 14,000 fans saw them go down to their heaviest defeat of the season. Many Town fans, including myself, struggled to see any positives from this game and wondered what next season would bring as mutterings from our stands was that relegation was looking more likely than any sign of promotion.

At the end of the season 2015-2016 with a final league placing of 19th it was one of;

Played 46 games; won 13, lost 21, drew 12, goals for 59, goals against 70, Points 51

On 1st July Town signed two goalkeepers on free transfer, Luke Coddington from Middlesbrough and George Dorrington from Manchester United. Oldham Athletic's Joel Coleman was the third keeper Town signed, for an undisclosed fee.

The next players through our John Smith's doors was free German transfers central defender Michael Hefele from Dynamo Dresden and left back Chris Lowe from 1. FC Kaiserslautern. Croatian defender Ivan Paurevic was the next player Town signed for an undisclosed fee whilst Southend United's central midfielder Jack Payne was subject to a compensation order given his age when Town signed him. By far the best signing Town made for many a season was with the capture of central defender Christopher Schindler's signature for a club record fee of £1.8 million pounds from 1860 Munich. Schindler went on to repay his value many times over with his 'Captain Fantastic' defensive displays. In the coming months the true strength of the man would be seen in front of millions of watching football fans at home and everyone that was inside Wembley Stadium that fateful day. By the end of his time at Town he had cemented his name into our football history and will always be remembered as a true legend by every Town fan that ever saw him play.

Rajiv van La Parra having previously signed on loan from Wolverhampton Wanderers saw his transfer to the Club made permanent. Slovenian central defender Jon Goren Stankovic from Borussia Dortmund II was the last player Town signed for an undisclosed fee during the summer months. Four other signings made over the summer came on loan for the season. Forward Elias Kachunga from FC Ingolstadt 04, midfielder Aaron Mooy from Manchester City, goalkeeper Danny Ward from Liverpool and midfielder Kasey Palmer from Chelsea.

With all the signings and loans Town undertook it was inevitable that players were released or sold on. A total of eleven players was released on a free transfer while Town's Joel Lynch having signed for Queens Park Rangers for an undisclosed fee made it twelve players that had left the Club during the summer.

The first pre-season of Wagner's reign as Head Coach saw our new signings settle in before they all headed off to a survival camp in Sweden. For four days the only cover Town players had for shelter, from the elements, was under a tent and had to make their own food as a group to survive. Having to stay with different people they didn't know each night in a tent in the middle of nowhere certainly helped with the bonding exercise Wagner had set out for his players.

Having returned from camp Town set off on their round of pre-season friendlies. Six games in, and they had won every one while conceding only a single goal. On 20th July Huddersfield Town faced Liverpool in a 'Shankly Trophy' match at our John Smith's Stadium. For the first time ever Liverpool's Manager, Jurgen Klopp, came face to face with his best friend, and our Head Coach, David Wagner. Over 21,000 fans, a pre-season friendly record-breaking crowd, saw them far from disgraced as they lost 2-0 against 'The Reds'. Town's only other pre-season defeat came against West Bromwich Albion at their training ground.

With the prospect of the new season ahead Town fans had come out in support of Huddersfield Town with over 15,000 season tickets having been sold. They were not to be disappointed this season nor were the near 18,500 fans who had taken their seat to watch Town play Brentford in the opening league fixture at our John Smith's Stadium. Every Town fan in our stadium, including our 'North Stand Loyal' that was now located in the South Stand, all saw tactically just how much Town had changed from having previously lost to 'The Bees' last season. This time round thanks to goals from Kachunga and Palmer they helped Town to an opening day 2-1 win. Three days later having travelled down to Shropshire to take on Shrewsbury Town in the League Cup first round Huddersfield Town went behind in the very first minute and was dumped out of the cup having lost 2-1 by the end of the match.

Having travelled up to St James' Park to take on Newcastle United in the second league match of the season, our captain, Mark Hudson had every reason to celebrate given that it was his 450th career appearance. The occasion was watched by a crowd of 52,079 who all saw Town win 2-1 thanks to goals from Nahki Wells who scored in first half stoppage time and Jack Payne who scored his first league goal, in only his second Town appearance, in the second half. The result saw Town go top of the Championship on six points with Villa Park their next destination.

Having taken to the field against Aston Villa 34,924 fans watched as Town went behind in the first 30 minutes from a headed goal. Kachunga's attempt from an overhead kick should have given Town an equaliser as it was Hefele's persistence, after coming on as a sub and with some hesitant Villa defending, saw him level the scores at 1-1 in unusual circumstances. The draw saw Town go third in the Championship on goal difference behind Brighton and Norwich City. By the end of August Tareiq Holmes-Dennis had signed for Town from Charlton Athletic for an undisclosed fee.

At the beginning of September Town made the short journey over to Elland Road to take on our local adversaries Leeds United in a league match. A crowd of 28,514 saw on-loan Aaron Mooy's second half spectacular long-range strike earn Town a 1-0 win and gave our fans cause for a double celebration as we sat top of the Championship on 16 points after six games. Three days later down at Brighton they suffered their first league defeat of the season when they lost 1-0 to 'The Seagulls'. Having lost 2-1, towards the end of September, the second league defeat of the season for Town came at the hands of Reading away.

The first league match after the second international break saw Town line-up against Sheffield Wednesday at the John Smith's Stadium. A sell-out crowd of 22,368, with the added bonus of live television cameras, saw a second half penalty for 'The Owls' give Wednesday a 1-0 win and condemn Town to their first home league defeat of the season. Craven Cottage boosted with 2,700 travelling Town fans at the end of October was the scene for the biggest league defeat of the season as Fulham put on a dazzling display to claim only their second league win in ten games. 'The Cottagers' having won 5-0 meant that Town dropped to third in the Championship.

Town's home game against Birmingham City on 5th November was the perfect time to hold its annual 'Remembrance Game' to honour and pay tribute to those connected to Town and beyond who served in the armed forces and, in many cases, made the ultimate sacrifice.

'We will always remember'

It was also a noteworthy date in the recent history of Huddersfield Town as on this day one year ago David Wagner was officially appointed as the first man from outside the UK or Ireland to lead our team as Head Coach. With our home attendances having gone up by 58 percent on this time last year Town fans had certainly made our John Smith's Stadium a place where the noise levels had shot through the roof. Given the high intensity of Wagner's style of football it was an exciting time to be a Town fan. A 1-0 win at the DW Stadium against Wigan Athletic was the perfect start to the New Year for Town while at our John Smith's Stadium a thumping 4-0 win over Port Vale in the FA Cup third round saw them go through to the next round. Having signed Chelsea forward Izzy Brown on loan for the rest of the season Town was then faced with Rochdale away in the FA Cup fourth round. Having cruised to another 4-0 FA Cup win they were then drawn against Premier League side Manchester City at home in the next round. Sadly, long-time Town supporter Anthony Hobson passed away on 11th February. Tony had first started watching the Terriers when they were in the old First Division and had seen the Club through many ups and downs across the country. He was a key organiser for coach trips for Town fans across the North Yorkshire area to home games.

With no home fans allowed in the Chadwick Lawrence Stand a record football crowd of 24,129 saw Town hold off Premier League side Manchester City thanks partly to the efforts of our keeper Joel Coleman. The result was something of an achievement for Town given that they were only the sixth team to have stopped City scoring this season after Barcelona, Man United, Everton, Tottenham and Liverpool. It was also the first clean sheet Town had kept against top-flight opposition in the FA Cup since 1971.

The fifth round replay at Manchester City's Etihad Stadium on 1st March in front of 42,425 fans saw Town take the lead in the seventh minute. Sadly, by the time the full-time whistle had sounded City had moved into the Quarter finals of the FA Cup having beaten Town 5-1.

The visit of Championship leaders Newcastle United to our John Smith's Stadium, three days after the City cup defeat, saw 'The Magpies' gain revenge as they ran out 3-1 winners in front of our highest league crowd of 23,213 fans. Thankfully the defeat for Town saw them still stay third in the Championship. On a brighter note after the Newcastle match of the top 20 football gates of 20,000 plus ever seen at our 23-year-old John Smith's Stadium an incredible 12 had been recorded in this season alone. After previously being placed on gardening leave, our Head of Football Operations, Stuart Webber on 30th March left Huddersfield Town to take up a new role at Norwich City.

Town's first league match after the international break on April Fool's Day was no joke given that Town had just lost 1-0 against Burton Albion in front of a John Smith's Stadium crowd of 20,154.

Aaron Mooy was named Hargreaves Memorial Trophy Player of the Year at Town's 2017 Annual Awards ceremony with Jonathon Hogg named as 'Club's Players Player of the Season'. Phillip Billing was awarded the 'Players Young Player of the Year award' and also picked up the 'Goal of the Season award' for his strike against Cardiff City. Young Terrier Lewis O'Brien was named as the 'Antoni's Memorial Academy Player of the Year' for the second season in a row. Meanwhile, Michael Hefele was named the 'Media Player of the Year' for very good reason. The final match of the season saw our old manager Neil Warnock return with Cardiff City and promptly left with all three points as ten-men Town went down 3-0 after having our on-loan keeper Danny Ward sent off in the 20th minute.

Our 600th competitive first team game at the John Smith's Stadium saw Town in the play-off semi-final against our South Yorkshire rivals Sheffield Wednesday. The first leg having ended goalless saw the second leg finish 1-1 after extra time. Then thanks to Lowe, Hefele, Wells and Mooy taking and scoring Town's first four penalties, while Jack Payne had missed his, and Danny Ward having already saved Hutchinson's first penalty it was down to Fernando Forestieri to score to keep 'The Owls' in the play-offs. Danny Ward dived to his right and pulled off a marvellous save from Forestieri while all the Wednesday fans looked on in sheer disbelief as Town went through 4-3 to the final.

The play-off final against Reading was watched by a crowd of well over 76,000 fans with thousands more watching live on television. With the scores still 0-0 after extra-time it was down to penalties to decide on one of the richest prizes in football. First up was Reading who scored as Lowe made no mistake for Town, then having seen Reading score their second penalty Hefele stepped up to take his and failed. Reading having scored their third penalty saw Wells score Town's third to make it 3-2. Reading completely missed their fourth penalty as Mooy made no mistake with his. All Reading fans could do was watch on as they saw their last penalty saved by our keeper Danny Ward. Our captain, Christopher Schindler, stepped up to take the final penalty knowing that if he scored Town would win and be promoted. Every Town fan in the stadium, and all those watching at home, held their breath as the ball hit the back of the net. The realisation for me as a Town fan and author of this book, after a 38-year wait, was too much and overwhelming. Everyone celebrated promotion to the Premier League that day as one big happy family.

At the end of the season 2016-2017 with a final league placing of 5th (**promoted**) it was one of;

Played 46 games; won 25, lost 15, drew 6, goals for 56, goals against 58, Points 81

After a 45-year wait, since Town had last played in the old First Division at Leeds Road, they were finally back in the top flight of English Football. Only this time around our John Smith's Stadium got to see them compete in the Premier League.

With the realisation of Town having to compete against football's elite clubs, it was a whirlwind of summer transfer activity, which involved spending in the region of £43.5 million pounds, the likes of which had never been seen before at Huddersfield Town. The first thing that had to be changed at our John Smith's Stadium was the floodlighting while huge investments was made on our squad, the stadium and our training ground.

The first transfer for Town was when they took up the option of signing Elias Kachunga for £1.27 million pounds on 1st July. This was quickly followed up with the signature of Laurent Depoitre from Porto for an undisclosed record transfer fee. However, his transfer fee record was quickly broken when Town signed Aaron Mooy from Manchester City for eight million pounds. Midfielder Tom Ince was the next to sign on a three-year deal for an undisclosed fee while Danny Williams signed on a free transfer from Reading. A week after signing Mooy, Town broke all transfer records when they signed Montpellier forward Steve Mounie for an initial eye-watering £11.5 million pounds. Next through the John Smith's doors was Fulham defender Scott Malone who signed for an undisclosed fee as Copenhagen defender Mathias Jorgenson signed for three years in a £3.5 million pound deal. Not content to stop there, Town then signed Mainz 05 goalkeeper Jonas Lossl on a season long loan, this was then followed up with the six-month loan signing of Chelsea midfielder Kasey Palmer.

Given the amount of money they had spent already and with the need to have additional strength in numbers Town released the following players; Flo Bojaj who signed for Welling United, Ronan Coughlan who signed for Bray Wanderers, Frank Mulhern who signed for Guiseley, Joe Murphy who signed for Bury, Jamie Spencer who signed for Bradford Park Avenue, Sam Warde who signed for Colchester United, while Kyle Dempsey signed for Fleetwood Town for £725,000. Numerous players on the books at Town was then sent out on various loans; Tareiq Holmes-Dennis to Portsmouth, Jordy Hiwula to Fleetwood Town, Fraser Horsfall to Gateshead, Rekeil Pyke to Port Vale and Jack Payne to Oxford United. Harry Bunn at the start of August signed for Bury for an undisclosed fee while Mark Hudson finally retired from professional football altogether and moved into coaching at Town. Out of the nine pre-season games played only two ended in defeat SV Sandhausen in Germany and at our John Smith's Stadium against Italian side Udinese.

On 12th August 2,805 travelling Town fans made the trip down to South London for the first Premier League game of the new season. Crystal Palace had never seen anything like it as our fans in a 25,448 crowd literally all sang their hearts out as Tommy Smith, newly installed as captain, led out our mighty blue and white team. Our 'twelfth man' on the terraces willed and wanted Town with every kick of the ball and at the final whistle went crazy as they left the field having won 3-0. The first weekend of the new football season saw Town second on goal difference in the Premier League. Town keeper Luke Coddington in the days thereafter signed for Northampton Town on a free transfer. Shortly after that winger Sean Scannell signed for Burton Albion on a six-month loan.

Newcastle United was the visitors for the first ever Premier League game played at our John Smith's Stadium. A record-breaking 24,128 crowd on 20th August saw Arron Mooy score in the second half to earn Town a 1-0 win. Three days later Rotherham United visited our John Smith's Stadium and with 8,290 fans watching Town recorded a 2-1 win in the third round of the Carabao Cup. By this time FC Ingolstadt right-back Florent Hadergjonaj had signed on loan for the rest of the season and 1. FC Nurnberg midfielder Abdelhamid Sabiri had signed for an undisclosed fee. The day after Town had drawn 0-0 with Southampton in the Premier League goalkeeper Robert Green had signed from our old adversaries Leeds United on a free transfer. By the end of August Town defender Jason Davidson had signed for Australian side Rijeka, while striker Nahki Wells had signed for Burnley for an undisclosed fee and David Wagner had been voted Premier League Manager of the Month.

On 19th September Town took on Crystal Palace at Selhurst Park in the Carabao Cup third round. Watched by a crowd of 6,607 Town went down 1-0 to give new Palace Manager Roy Hodgson his first win since taking charge. The 'Eagles' was a vastly different team, under Hodgson, to the one Town beat on the opening day of the season. Having had to wait over 46 years since Manchester United had last visited our old home at Leeds Road in the First Division and dished out a real footballing lesson to Town as they lost 3-0, thanks to goals from George Best, Denis Law and Bobby Charlton. A crowd of 24,169 fans filled our John Smith's Stadium on 21st October eager to see them take on United in the Premier League in the hope of seeing the 'Red Devils' defeated this time around. Thanks to Mooy they took a 28-minute 1-0 lead and just five minutes later Depoitre made it 2-0. Not until the 78th minute did United break our defence when Marcus Rashford, having come on as a second half sub, scored to make the final score a famous 2-1 home win for Town as they ended United's unbeaten start to the season. Prior to the Premier League match against West Bromwich Albion it was disclosed that Phillip Billing was side-lined with an ankle injury, which he sustained against Swansea City and was subsequently stretchered off with, that kept him out of the Town team for the next few months. He joined Stankovic, Hefele and Palmer who were already on Town's injury list.

The Remembrance match against the 'Baggies' saw Town win 1-0 in front of a packed John Smith's Stadium crowd of 24,121. By November, they were getting a real lesson in the Premier League as first Bournemouth beat them 4-0 away, and then after losing 2-1 at home to Manchester City, Town then travelled down to London to take on Arsenal. Already 1-0 down after the first five minutes Town found themselves on the end of a 5-0 battering by the time the final whistle had sounded at the Emirates Stadium. The month of December saw them beaten just once in the Premier League. A 3-1 defeat against the reigning Premier League Champions Chelsea in front of a 24,169 crowd at our John Smith's Stadium saw Town end the year twelfth in the Premier League. A 3-0 New Year's Day away defeat at the hands of Leicester City started off 2018 with a whimper for Town. Thankfully, five days later, in the FA Cup they beat Bolton Wanderers 2-1 at their place to earn a fourth round home draw against Birmingham City. Lining up in defence wearing our number five shirt against West Ham United was our new defensive loan signing Terence Kongolo from AS Monaco. Midfielder Alex Pritchard, just recently signed from Norwich City, witnessed the 4-1 home defeat against 'The Hammers' sat alongside Wagner in Town's dug-out. Town then lost 2-0 away to Stoke City before they took on Birmingham City in the FA Cup fourth round. A 1-0 first half lead at the John Smith's Stadium against the team from the Midlands finished up as a 1-1 draw. By the end of January, with the visit of Liverpool to the John Smith's Stadium, the old pals act between David Wagner and Jurgen Klopp was put aside for 90 minutes as 'The Reds' ran out 3-0 winners. Next up was the visit to Old Trafford, and the highest crowd of our Premier League season, 74,742, saw Town go down 2-0 to the 'Red Devils'. 3,121 travelling Town fans let their voices be heard at Old Trafford as they sang their way through the entire 90 minutes. Never before had Old Trafford witnessed anything like it as Town fans left their mark as our 'twelfth man' at Premier League grounds up and down the country. The fourth round FA Cup replay down at St. Andrews, after extra time, saw Town beat Birmingham City 4-1. To help celebrate the year of the dog Town beat Bournemouth 4-1 at home in the league and then lost 2-0 to Manchester United at home in the FA Cup fifth round. By the beginning of April our position in the Premier League was giving Town fans real cause for concern. A 0-0 draw at Manchester City was followed up with a memorable night down at Stamford Bridge as Town drew 1-1 with Chelsea to ensure our Premiership survival. Arsene Wenger's final match as Arsenal Manager after 22 years was a cause of celebration for the Arsenal fans, but for all Town fans it was time for a Premiership party at our John Smith's Stadium for the final match of the season.

At the end of the season 2017-2018 with a final league placing of 16th it was one of;

Played 38 games; won 9, lost 19, drew 10, goals for 28, goals against 58, Points 37

Our second season in the Premier League was to be one of shock, horror and surprise. Given our sad demise the last time they were in the old First Division in 1971-72 season this year beat that hands down. Right-back Florent Hadergjonaj was the first Town player to put pen to paper on a permanent deal during pre-season. Goalkeeper Jonas Lossl soon joined him for an undisclosed fee from Mainz 05 whilst keeper Ben Hamer signed on a free transfer from Leicester City. Perhaps the biggest shock for Town fans this year was the rumoured record-breaking £18.5 million pounds paid for the permanent signing of Terence Kongolo from AS Monaco. This was then followed up with the £5.7 million pound signing of midfielder Ramadan Sobhi whilst Groningen midfielder Juninho Bacuna signed for Town for an undisclosed fee.

After coming on as a late sub in the Arsenal match last season midfielder Dean Whitehead, after a Town career which saw him play well over 50 league games, retired from professional football altogether. His new career saw him begin coaching in Town's U17 Academy. Goalkeeper Robert Green meanwhile was given a free transfer and was promptly signed as third-choice keeper at fellow Premier League side Chelsea. A flutter of undisclosed transfer activity began during the middle of July when Town signed defender Erik Durm from Borussia Dortmund and Adama Diakhaby from AS Monaco. It also triggered the undisclosed transfer release of midfielder Sean Scannell to Bradford City, defender Tareiq Holmes-Dennis to Bristol Rovers, midfielder Tom Ince to Stoke City, forward Jordy Hiwula to Coventry City, defender Jordan Williams to Barnsley, defender Scott Malone to Derby County and defender Michael Hefele to Nottingham Forest.

Town meanwhile sent out the following players on loan; midfielder Regan Booty to Aldershot Town, forward Rekeil Pyke to Wrexham, midfielder Jack Payne to Bradford City and goalkeeper Joel Coleman to Shrewsbury Town.

Pre-season friendlies saw Town travel to Bury and to Accrington Stanley before they set off to Germany where they played two matches against Dynamo Dresden and Darmstadt 98. Back home at our John Smith's Stadium they took on French side Lyon before they jetted off to Austria where they took on French side Bologna and German side RB Leipzig.

Prior to the start of the season young Montpellier forward Isaac Mbenza signed on loan as 2,090 travelling fans watched Town kick off our new Premier League season with a 3-0 defeat down at Stamford Bridge against Chelsea. This was followed up a week later with a 6-1 battering at the Etihad Stadium against Manchester City. 2,735 travelling Town fans tried to lift our team to the level we were at last season but to no avail. The only good news was that Kongolo had scored his first goal in our Town colours even though it was an own goal in the 84th minute. The first Premier League home game of the season saw them take on Cardiff City in front of a John Smith's crowd of 23,787. Jonathon Hogg after a second-half clash, with Cardiff's Harry Arter, got a straight red card as ten-man Town fought to earn a 0-0 draw. Three days later they travelled down to the Bet365 Stadium to take on Stoke City in the Carabao Cup second round. 692 travelling fans saw Town knocked out of the cup 2-0. Around this time our young midfielder Lewis O'Brien was sent out on loan to Bradford City while young Manchester City defender Demeaco Duhaney signed on with Town.

Bonfire night went off with a blast for Town as they recorded their first Premier League win of the season having beaten Fulham 1-0 at the John Smith's Stadium in front of a crowd of 21,855. By the end of November they had recorded their second Premier League win of the season having beaten Wolves 2-0 at their Molineux Stadium. The win saw Town move up to 14th place in the Premier League. Sadly, this was the highest league placing all Town fans saw this season as things went from bad to worse. By the time the New Year celebrations had finished Huddersfield Town were rock bottom of the Premier League. Surprisingly young Tottenham defender Jaden Brown signed for Town and was immediately loaned out to Exeter City for the rest of the season. Three days later Huddersfield Town signed Crystal Palace midfielder Jason Puncheon on loan.

Ramadan Sobhi meanwhile was loaned out to Egyptian side Al Ahly SC for £800,000 and midfielder Rajiv van La Parra was sent to Middlesbrough for the rest of the season.

A 1-0 defeat at the hands of Championship side Bristol City in the FA Cup third round saw our cup run come to an end for another season. More importantly it was now a run of nine games without a win as our statistics gave a truly grim reading. Having won only twice in 21 league games they were nine points from safety when they took on Cardiff City at their Stadium.

Match ref Lee Mason had initially awarded a 76th minute penalty to Town for a foul on Hadergjonaj by Cardiff's Joe Bennett but assistant referee Stuart Burt intervened to tell Mason that the foul was on Bennett. The ref reversed his decision and sparked off a huge reaction from our dug out as the game finished in a 0-0 draw.

Less than two weeks after the Cardiff City game Head Coach David Wagner had left our Club after both sides had mutually agreed to terminate his contract. Mark Hudson, having taken over temporarily, oversaw the 3-0 Premier League defeat to Manchester City just six days later. Having been previously linked to our Club in January Borussia Dortmund II Manager Jan Siewert accepted the position of Head Coach on 21st January 2019. Jan had previously played as a defensive midfielder for German side TuS Mayen but had retired at the age of 22 due to injury.

Jan's first Premier League match as Head Coach saw the visit of Everton to our John Smith's Stadium. 23,699 fans watched as Town went 1-0 down in the first five minutes. Even with Everton down to ten men for the final 24 minutes Town could not find a way through the 'Toffees' defence and equalled an unenviable record for the fewest top-flight goals of five, which was level with Arsenal in their 1912-13 season, after 13 home games. Town was on record as having failed to score in 50% of all our home Premier League games which was the highest percentage in the competition's history. For the record, at this point in the season, Town had only scored 13 goals in 24 Premier League games.

Charlton forward Karlan Grant having signed on 30th January 2019 was a second half sub when our run of poor form continued with a 5-0 battering down at Stamford Bridge against Chelsea on 2nd February. A week later Grant scored his first Premier League goal for Town in a 2-1 home defeat at the hands of Arsenal. Even with Jan Siewert in the 'hot-seat' our dismal results did not change until the visit of Wolverhampton Wanderers when thanks to an injury time winner from Mounie Huddersfield Town won 1-0 at our John Smith's Stadium. It was the last Premier League win Town fans saw all season.

By the time they had left the Selhurst Park pitch having lost 2-0 to Crystal Palace at the end of March another unenviable record had been set by Town. They had suffered the joint earliest relegation to the Championship since Derby County in 2008. Thankfully they avoided the record for the least amount of points in a season.

The month of April saw Town concede 15 goals in just four Premier League games while they only managed to score two goals in reply. A 5-0 battering at the hands of Liverpool at Anfield was bad enough, but Town created another truly unenviable record. They gave the men from Merseyside their fastest ever Premier League goal after just 15 seconds when Naby Keita swept the ball home from Mohamed Salah's pass. Town signed off our Premier League days at the John Smith's Stadium against Manchester United. Needing all three points to maintain their push for a top four finish United took an eighth minute lead only for Town to deny them their much-needed win to earn a respectable 1-1 draw. The last Premier League match of this miserable season was down at St. Mary's Stadium. A crowd of 30,367 saw Town midfielder Alex Prichard pounce on an error by the Saint's keeper in the 55th minute to make the final score 1-1.

At the end of the season 2018-2019 with a final league placing of 20th (**Relegated**) it was one of;

Played 38 games; won 3, lost 28, drew 7, goals for 22, goals against 76, Points 16

Having suffered the humiliation of relegation last season many Town fans were hoping that the similarities of Town's last relegation in 1972 from the old First Division wasn't going to mirror our sad demise any further. Chris Lowe having signed for Dynamo Dresden at the end of May for an undisclosed fee signalled the start of what many Town fans knew was coming. Over the summer months Town made the decision to release the following U23 and Academy players; Jake Barrett, Regan Booty who signed for Notts County, George Danaher, Jordon Eli, Sam Gibson and Ben Mills who both signed for Emley, Mason O'Malley who signed for Scunthorpe United, Dahomey Raymond, Gabriel Roserio and Harry Spratt who signed for York City. The first team players who left the Club prior to pre-season was Laurent Depoitre who signed for Gent, Erik Durm who signed for Eintracht Frankfurt, Jonas Lossl who signed for Everton, Jack Payne who signed for Lincoln City and Danny Williams who signed for Pafos. First through our John Smith's Stadium doors came midfielder Reece Brown who had been signed from Forest Green Rovers for an undisclosed fee. Next up was the free transfer signing of Aston Villa central defender Tommy Elphick. Josh Koroma from Leyton Orient was the next player Town signed for an undisclosed fee who was shortly followed by central defender Herbert Bockhorn from Borussia Dortmund II. Meanwhile, the loan signing of Montpellier's Isaac Mbenza was made permanent for an undisclosed fee. By the middle of July Liverpool's third-choice keeper Kamil Grabara had been taken on a season long loan by Town and club captain Tommy Smith had signed for Stoke City on a three-year contract for an undisclosed fee. Midfielder Phillip Billing was the next player to leave Town having signed for Premier League side Bournemouth for £15 million pounds.

Pre-season fixtures saw Town play half a dozen friendlies without defeat and gave some hope to watching fans that perhaps things were improving on the footballing side. Derby County was the visitors to our John Smith's Stadium for the opening Championship match at the beginning of August. Within three minutes of the opening half an hour they were 2-0 down and looking tactically worse than last season. Thanks to a 30th minute penalty, taken and scored by Karlan Grant, it gave Town a slight chance to get back into the game. By the time the full-time whistle had gone the 22,596 crowd had seen Town systematically beaten 2-1 by Derby County. The biggest shock of the season for all Town fans was the season long loan signing by Brighton and Hove Albion of our midfield general Aaron Mooy while goalkeeper Ben Hamer signed on loan for Derby County. Town then surprisingly signed Chelsea defender and midfielder Trevoh Chalobah on a season long loan and promptly sold Mathias Jorgenson to Fenerbahce for an undisclosed fee. Five days later they travelled down to Shepherd's Bush to take on Q.P.R in the league. A crowd of 14,377 saw them surrender a 1-0 lead in the 83rd minute which allowed Rangers to earn a 1-1 draw. Shortly after that Hull City forward Frazier Campbell was signed by Town on a free transfer. Having returned to our John Smith's Stadium for the Carabao Cup first round Town having made ten changes and had seven debutants on the pitch was outplayed and outclassed by League One Lincoln City. Thanks to keeper Ryan Schofield pulling off four fabulous saves before half-time Town managed to keep the score at 0-0.

Ten minutes into the second half Lincoln City scored to make the final score 1-0 and sent Town out of the cup at the first time of asking. After the humiliation and the manner of the cup defeat had started to sink in with everyone present that night an urgent meeting was called after the Fulham match by our new Chairman Phil Hodgkinson. Jan Siewert was relieved of his duties late on 16th August as ex-player Danny Schofield stepped in as Caretaker Manager in the interim.

By mutual consent midfielder Abdelhamid Sabiri left the Club to sign for German side Paderborn while Rajiv van La Parra signed for Serbian side Red Star Belgrade for an undisclosed fee. With Danny Schofield as Caretaker Manager Town played three league matches under his watch and all of them ended in defeat.

Lincoln City's management duo Danny and Nicky Cowley was unveiled as our new double act at the beginning of September. Danny Cowley was named as Manager while his brother Nicky was named as his Assistant. The first match under their watch ended with a 2-0 home defeat against Sheffield Wednesday which was witnessed by a John Smith's Stadium crowd of 22,754 fans. The first Championship win for the new management duo came at the beginning of October at the bet365 Stadium when Town beat Stoke City 1-0 thanks to a goal by Bacuna in the 82nd minute. It signalled a run of six unbeaten league matches that took Town up the Championship table. They surprisingly then went on a run of five games without a win with the worst defeat coming down at Bristol City. 4-1 down already at half-time at Ashton Gate, by the time the final whistle had gone Town had lost the match 5-2. New Year celebrations for all Town fans fell flat rather quickly when relegation battlers Stoke City visited our John Smith's Stadium. 21,933 fans watched as they went 1-0 down inside the first 15 minutes. Having managed to take a 2-1 lead inside the first five minutes of the second half they somehow conceded four goals in the second half to give Stoke City a 5-2 victory which moved them to within four points of Town. A 2-0 FA Cup third round defeat at the hands of Southampton down at St Mary's Stadium put paid to any FA cup run this season.

With the winter transfer window now open Town signed Sheffield United central defender Richard Stearman on a free transfer. This was then followed up with the loan signing of Arsenal midfielder Emile Smith Rowe. After the 2-1 defeat against Barnsley Town went back into the transfer market and signed Leicester City midfielder Andy King on loan and then swiftly signed Lincoln City left-back Harry Toffolo for an undisclosed fee while record signing Terence Kongolo went on loan to Fulham for the rest of the season. Having picked up a foot injury against Blackburn Rovers after coming on as a sub Kongolo returned to our John Smith's Stadium after playing less than 45 minutes for Fulham. Days later midfielder Adama Diakhaby joined Nottingham Forest on loan. By the end of January Town had sold midfielder Arron Mooy to Brighton and loaned keeper Jonas Lossl from Everton and winger Chris Willock from Benfica. Leaving the Club on loan was right-back Florent Hadergjonaj who had signed for Turkish side Kasimpasa and forward Josh Koroma who signed for Rotherham United. Two days after Town had lost 3-2 to Fulham at their place Isaac Mbenza went out on loan to French side Amiens. By the end of February they were just five points off a relegation place with many Town fans thinking that they were seeing a re-run of the 1970s all over again. Right after the 2-0 league defeat against Leeds United at Elland Road all outdoor activity in this country was suspended due to the COVID-19 Pandemic. Unlike previous measures these new restrictions were enforceable by police though fines and dispersal of gatherings. In early April the English FA decided to postpone all football. By late April 2020 over 300 million people were under lockdown in European nations, while around 200 million people were under lockdown in Latin America. Nearly 300 million people were under some form of lockdown in the United States, around 100 million people in the Philippines and about 59 million people in South Africa. Whilst over 1.3 billion people were under lockdown in India.

With strict measures in place football was able to resume and Town's first match behind our now closed John Smith's Stadium doors saw them take on relegation threatened Wigan Athletic on 28th June. A 2-0 defeat paled into insignificance as thousands was given the terrible news about the loss of a loved one during this pandemic. The remnants of this horrible season saw Town win two, draw three and lose three league games which saw them finish three points above the last relegation place. Having managed to steady the ship this season Town could now look at trying to rebuild our team, while most fans attempted to come to terms with the grief they were now carrying.

At the end of the season 2019-2020 with a final league placing of 18th it was one of;

Played 46 games; won 13, lost 21, drew 12, goals for 52, goals against 70, Points 51

One of Town's best-known fans Father-of-three David Scholefield aged 57, better known as 'Scoffa', was given the tribute he truly deserved when over 300 people turned out for his funeral service. Having sadly passed away in early June following a short illness he left his many friends stunned by his death. There was no shortage of them when they gathered at our John Smith's Stadium below a huge sign saying appropriately enough 'Pride of Yorkshire'. After around 150 fans sang Town favourite melodies such as 'Those were the Days' by Mary Hopkins and 'Smile A While' the cortege wound its way round to St Mary's Parish Church in Mirfield where a further 150 mourners, many of them wearing Town shirts, crowded into it.

Alan 'Booby' Boothroyd a close friend of David's for many years, and also a good friend and work colleague of mine for a long number of years now, gave a fitting eulogy. Booby recapped on how he met Scoffa when they were both teenagers in our old 'Cowshed' at Leeds Road. Having spent most of my youth there, as author of this book, I have to say there was no better place to be on a match day. More recently Scoffa was a part of the group in the old 'North Stand Loyal' days and played a part in the formation of the fans group 'Cowshed Loyal' in 2014 and is sorely missed by everyone at our John Smith's Stadium.

Having allowed Jon Gorenc Stankovic to sign for Austrian side Sturm Graz on a free transfer Town then released right-back Danny Simpson who signed for Bristol City. Kieran Phillips, who co-incidentally was born in Huddersfield and previously played for our academy side, was signed on a free transfer from Everton.

By far the biggest news to come out of our John Smith's Stadium over the summer was when Town announced that the Cowley brothers had been relieved of their duties with immediate effect and replaced with Spanish Head Coach Carlos Corberan Vallet. A former goalkeeper himself, and having retired from Spanish Football, he decided to pursue his passion in coaching. By June 2017 Carlos was announced as the new Leeds United U23 Manager and after the appointment of Marcelo Bielsa as Head Coach Corberan was promoted to first team coach in June 2018.

Having met Carlos personally at our John Smith's Stadium, when Town faced Leeds United, I have to say as author of this book he is very articulate in the way he presents himself and is fluent in Italian, Spanish and English. His passion for football is quite clear to see and made time to speak with everyone he met whilst translating for Bielsa. Carlos showed a great level of patience and understanding to everyone around both Bielsa and himself long after the United game had finished.

Settling into Town's hot-seat Corberan saw them release the following players; goalkeeper Joel Coleman who signed for Fleetwood Town, Elias Kachunga who signed for Sheffield Wednesday, Rekeil Pyke who signed for Shrewsbury Town and Herbert Bockhorn who signed for German side VfL Bochum. Young forward Kit Elliott meanwhile went out on a six-month loan to Irish side Cork City.

Town having signed winger Conor Falls from Glentoran, midfielder Brodie Spencer from Cliftonville and fellow midfielder Sonny Whittingham from Bradford City allowed Scott High to go out on a six-month loan to Shrewsbury Town and allowed Reece Brown to go to Peterborough United on a season long loan. By the middle of August Town had signed former player Danny Ward, from Cardiff City, on a free transfer.

Given that the end of last season had finished late due to the Covid-19 pandemic this season's pre-season friendlies was scheduled for the end of August and was limited to just two, behind closed doors, at our John Smith's Stadium. A 2-1 win over Bradford City was followed up with a 3-3 draw against Manchester United's U23 side. By the end of August Manchester United's young goalkeeper Joel Dinis Castro Pereira had signed on a season long loan at Town.

A flurry of transfer activity in the first week of September saw the following players sign for Town. Espanyol right-back Gonzalo Avila Gordon, aka Pipa, signed a three-year contract for an undisclosed fee. This was then followed up with the free transfer signing of Mouhamadou-Naby Sarr. Leaving the Club was winger Ramadan Sobhi who signed for Egyptian side Pyramids for an undisclosed fee and Steve Mounie who signed for French side Stade Brest 29.

Unusually, Town started the season of 2020-21 with a Carabao Cup first round tie at home against Rochdale Having lost 1-0 at our John Smith's Stadium thankfully no fan was there to see them knocked out of the cup at the first time of asking. This season was like no other before, with all football fans now banned from attending any football match due to the Covid-19 Pandemic.

A week later Town entertained Norwich at the now empty John Smith's Stadium for the opening Championship match. An 81st minute goal for the 'Canaries' condemned Town to an opening day 1-0 defeat. The first away match of the season saw Town travel down to London to take on Brentford. The 'Bees' marked their opening league match at their shiny new, now empty, 17,250-capacity Brentford Community Stadium with an easy 3-0 win. Ajax midfielder Carel Eiting was signed by Town on a season long loan and by the end of September Florent Hadergjonaj's loan move to Turkish side Kasimpasa had been made permanent with the signing of a three-year contract. October saw striker Karlan Grant transfer to West Bromwich Albion for an undisclosed amount. This was immediately followed by Terence Kongolo signing for Fulham on transfer deadline day for an undisclosed fee. Then having travelled down to Kings Park, to take on Bournemouth in the middle of December, 1,200 home fans were all treated to a goal fest as Town went down 5-0 against 'The Cherries'. Having released striker Colin Quaner on a free transfer he duly signed for Scottish side St. Mirren. The following day Plymouth Argyle was the visitors to our John Smith's Stadium for a third round FA Cup match. Having twice gone ahead in the first half Town was pegged back to 2-2 by half time. In the second half following a foul by Kieran Phillips 'The Pilgrims' scored in the 70th minute to send Plymouth through to the next round.

With the winter transfer window now open Town signed the following players Newcastle winger Rolando Aarons on a free transfer, Boreham Wood winger Sorba Thomas for an undisclosed fee, Milton Keynes Dons central defender Richard Keogh for an undisclosed amount and ex-Town midfielder Duane Holmes returned for an undisclosed fee. Goalkeeper Ben Hamer was the next Town player to leave the Club when he signed for Swansea City for an undisclosed fee. This was shortly followed by the transfer of Adama Diakhaby to French side Amiens for an undisclosed fee also. With the signing of goalkeeper Jayson Leutwiler and Yaya Sanogo and Oumar Niasse Town set off for Carrow Road to take on Championship leaders Norwich City. Town was battered by a rampant free scoring 'Canaries' side to the point that it was embarrassing to see a 5-0 half-time score line. All Town had to show for their efforts after ninety minutes was a yellow card for Mbenza in the 60th minute as Norwich recorded their highest league win of the season, and Town's heaviest defeat, with a 7-0 win. By the end of April having travelled over to Ewood Park Town returned with a heavy 5-2 defeat to show for their time and effort against Blackburn Rovers.

The last two league games of this unprecedented season saw Town remain undefeated, having drawn 1-1 with Coventry City at our John Smith's Stadium, they then drew 2-2 down at Reading.

At the end of the season 2020-2021 with a final league placing of 20th it was one of;

Played 46 games; won 12, lost 21, drew 13, goals for 50, goals against 71, Points 49

After five memorable years with Town the legend that is Christopher Schindler left our club on a free transfer and signed for German side FC Nurnberg at the end of May 2021.

So now as all Town fans look forward to our 113th year in our long and proud football history, having started from simple humble roots at our old home at Leeds Road, to be where we are today in our John Smith's Stadium. I truly hope that the journey you have all been on as a Terrier is one of immense pride and pleasure. My own time began at a point when Town was on their knees in the old Fourth Division so to have come from where we started from, even from 1979-80, to where we are now it's been one hell of a ride for me. I know there are many more Town fans reading this and thinking that they can go back even further on their own journey, but I am sure they will all sing the same song as me. In that no-one is born to be a Town fan it is just something either you become, or it becomes you. That's why we are all One Town, One Team, One Family.

10 years of Huddersfield Town's history from 2010

2010-11 3rd in League 1 **(play-off finalist)**   FA Cup fourth round
Carling Cup second round
Johnstone's Paint Trophy **Area Final**

2011-12 4th in League 1 **(play-off winners-promoted)**   FA Cup first round
Carling Cup second round
Johnstone's Paint Trophy second round

2012-13 19th in Championship   FA Cup fifth round
Capital One Cup second round

2013-14 17th in Championship   FA Cup fourth round
Capital One Cup third round

2014-15 16th in Championship   FA Cup third round
Capital One Cup second round

2015-16 19th in Championship   FA Cup third round
Capital One Cup first round

2016-17 5th in Championship**(play-off winners-promoted)**   FA Cup fifth round
EFL Cup first round

2017-18 16th in Premier League   FA Cup fifth round
Carabao Cup third round

2018-19 20th in Premier League **(relegated)**   FA Cup third round
Carabao Cup second round

2019-20 18th in Championship   FA Cup third round
Carabao Cup first round

10 years of Huddersfield Town's history from 2020

2020-21 20th in Championship   FA Cup third round
Carabao Cup first round

The Final Word – Chapter 14

Having finally reached the end of this book, I am now sat here, reflecting on the many years I have spent as a Town fan. I couldn't begin to imagine my life being any other way nor would I want to. I was born in Huddersfield and started out in life at 49 Spring Street, which is situated on one of the very few cobbled streets left in our Town, where the houses are all actually now deemed historically important enough to be grade II listed. My earlier life was like that of children in many families in and around Huddersfield at that time in the 1960s. However, sadly, by the time I had reached the age of nine my world was changed forever with the death of my father from a terminal illness. Losing him left a huge gap in my life. He was a proud, honest and hard-working Irishman who had bestowed upon me his good grace and values. He had also taught me to have respect for everything and everyone and was the moral compass to my journey in life.

Losing him was the worst time ever in my life.

One Saturday afternoon in the spring of 1979, bored with no money to go anywhere or do anything, along with a few of my newfound friends from our new family home in Newsome I walked along the old Carr Pit Road and onto the banking below Dalton. After a fruitless search of the old tip for any antique glass bottles, in the hope of selling any we found to a second-hand shop in Aspley, we all walked further along the banking to Bradley Mills. It was from that vantage point that I slowly began to see my very first professional football ground. From where we were standing we could see most of the football pitch, the footballers that were playing and some people that were stood watching the match inside the ground. One of my friends asked, "Anyone fancy watching the football inside the ground". We all agreed we would and quickly ran off down the hillside excited to discover more about what we had just seen. Little did I know then, that in years to come, as I grew from a child into a man this would become my 'new home', now sadly our old home at Leeds Road. From that day on I saved every penny I could find to get into our old home on match days (40p entry money and 20p for a programme was a lot of money to find on a weekly basis for a 12-year-old, especially when we didn't have much, wore free Yorkshire Purchasing Organisation clothing, and had free school meals).

Outside the ground leaning against the car park wall was an old man shouting "programmes, get your programmes here" I reached into my pocket and pulled out mostly coppers (two-pence's, pennies and half-pennies) I asked him "how much".

"Twenty pence" was his answer.

Taking my time to make sure I had enough money to get in as well as enough money to buy a programme I paid him the money. He just looked at it all tutted then chucked it into a big pocket inside his coat. My mates were first in the queue, waiting at the unopened turnstile door to get in, and as I joined them they joked with me saying "What did I want to buy one of those for"

"Because I wanted to have something to remind me of this very day" was my answer.

I have continued to buy a Town programme as part of my match day ritual ever since and still have my first ever programme. It's my pride and joy, Huddersfield Town v Aldershot Saturday 18th August 1979, from our Fourth Division days.

Standing at the unopened turnstile door we could all hear a strange noise from behind the blue slatted door. Over the years I would come to love the same noise and sound of that of hundreds and thousands of Huddersfield Town fans who had previously flocked through our turnstiles. The original Deluce's Rush Preventive Turnstiles was made by Ellison and Co. at Irlams O'Th'Height in Manchester (Some of them dating back to 1910, from our Main Stand at Leeds Road, are still in use at our John Smith's Stadium). Finally, after the turnstile doors opened and after paying my entry money, with a click of the turnstile and a big push from me, I was finally there, inside the ground.

Together with my friends we walked up past what appeared to be toilets on the left-hand side and reached a set of concrete steps to our right. We decided to walk up them to see what was there and arrived at the 'top step' to see this vast wide-open ground for the very first time. With its huge East Terrace to the left of me and the exposed open end at the other side I stood there amazed and simply gasped 'Wow' it felt like I had finally found a home, a place where I felt like I truly belonged.

Over the years it felt more and more like my home with every match I watched there. All of the faces and different people I saw became familiar, some by sight, some by names and others by the way they sang their hearts out in our old 'Cowshed'. They were all there to see our football team play, week in, week out. Our crowds were made up from fans from near and far, various professions, different parents or grandparents. Everyone paid their entrance fee, some were lucky to have bought season tickets, but we were all the same, Huddersfield Town fans. We made up a family and Leeds Road was 'our home'.

By April 1994, sadly, from the very same top step that I had first seen in 1979 it was for the final heart-breaking time. Looking around I could see other Town fans like me sadden, lost in thought, reliving moments in time while glancing momentarily skywards. The final whistle had been blown on our home and nobody seemed to know what to say or do. Leaving the ground that day, I stopped momentarily, then looked backwards from our 'Cowshed' gates to give a last look and nod to a dearly departed friend that I could still visualise in my mind on that very top step with me. Tragically he had passed away due to a terrible disease only a few years before, walking away from our home that day, it felt like I was leaving a big part of me behind as well as all the happy memories we had shared as friends with everyone else in our home.

Now after all these years as a Terrier and having two sons myself, I sometimes imagine what it would have felt like to have been there in our old home, at Leeds Road, with my dad. I have shared many happy times with my sons watching Town. One in particular was one of the greatest days of our lives, as Terriers, the day Town won promotion to the Premier League. No matter where they go, whatever they do in life and no matter where Huddersfield Town may be, they will always have the memories and times we shared together as a family, with the rest of our football family, in our new home. I hope that they will one day look back and tell their own children and good friends 'I remember that day with our dad, we were there', because without a shadow of a doubt 'Those were the days my friend'.

Printed in Great Britain
by Amazon